KOREA   JAPAN

.E.ASIA

THE COMPLETE
ORIENTAL
COOK BOOK

Marshall Cavendish

CONTENTS

CHINA

INDIA

JAPAN

S.E.ASIA

Picture Credits

Rex Bamber	21, 36, 76, 109
Pat Brindley	108
Patrick Cocklin	106
Patrick Cochrane	170
Desjardins/Top	233(T)
Alan Duns	19, 51, 56, 64(T), 88, 92, 99, 105, 122/3, 175, 211, 215/6, 219, 240, 314/5, 335, 357, 385, 395, 404, 416
Mark Edwards	121
Garner/AAA Photos	330
Gascoigne/Robert Harding Assoc.	120
Burt Glinn/Magnum	234, 327
Tom Hanley	118
Robert Harding Assoc.	8/9
Jerry Harpur	155
Denis Hughes-Gilbey	184/5
Paul Kemp	11, 34, 41, 111, 128/9, 149, 181, 193, 269, 319, 342
Peter Larsen	230(T)
Don Last	140
David Levin	114, 389
David Meldrum	102
Roland Michaud/J. Hillelson	230(B)
E. Miyazawa/Black Star	233(B)
Roger Phillips	10, 13, 14, 26/7, 31, 32/3, 43, 44/5, 49, 53, 58, 63, 64(B), 67, 70, 72, 74, 81, 82/3, 87, 91, 101, 112, 125, 143, 147, 153, 156, 157, 159, 165, 168/9, 172, 177, 186, 189, 190, 237, 247, 252, 256, 259, 277, 284, 288, 290, 295, 300/1, 305, 309, 322, 338, 348, 354(B), 363, 368, 371, 378, 383, 392, 399, 409, 413, 418
Iain Reid	23, 60, 97, 134/5, 136/7, 162/3, 199, 354(T)
Red Saunders	144
Raghubir Singh/J. Hillelson	326, 329
David Smith	39, 272, 281, 398
Sunday Times	7
George Wright	358

Edited by Isabel Moore and Jonnie Godfrey

Published by Marshall Cavendish Books Limited
58 old Compton Street
London W1V 5PA

© Marshall Cavendish Limited 1978 – 84

First printing 1978
Second printing 1979
Third printing 1982
This printing 1984

Printed and bound in Hong Kong by Dai Nippon Printing Co.

ISBN 0 85685 476 X

INTRODUCTION TO CHINA

Sharmini Tiruchelvam

Good cooking has been an integral part of the brilliant and ancient Chinese culture from the beginning, but it is only comparatively recently that it has been acknowledged outside China as one of the three great 'original' cuisines of the world.

Perhaps that is because it has only been in our own century that most ordinary people in the West have been able to sample even a fraction of the glory of Chinese cooking – although for most of us the 'sampling' could go on for most of our lives for there is a positively bewildering range of dishes, ranging from the almost universally accepted to the downright esoteric!

There are few people today, for instance, who have not tasted or at least heard of Sweet and Sour Pork, Fried Rice, Barbecued Spareribs, Crispy Spring Rolls, Won Tons . . . There are quite a few, too, who know how to make these delicacies at home, for a lot of Chinese cooking is, once one knows how it should look and taste, not at all difficult. Once one has mastered the basic discipline of preparing the food for cooking, it is simplicity itself to do. But of course, there are the rarer gourmet items which could possibly prove more expensive and more difficult to assemble – shark's fin, fish lips, turtle's skirt, bear's paw, sea slugs . . . not to mention the very acquired taste one would need to eat some of them!

Ironically this great heritage originated prior to the days of the sumptuous Courts of Peking and the cosmopolitan elegance of Shanghai in regions of Old China where for one reason or another there was an almost chronic paucity of food. But never was necessity more triumphantly the mother of invention; nothing, absolutely nothing, was wasted. Everything edible (whether from land, fresh water or ocean, or from any part of any animal conventionally despised or ignored) was eaten and combined in several computations with a myriad of other ingredients. Many 'flavours' and textures were created by inventing many different techniques of cooking; the cuisine boasts some 80-odd different ways in all. A few shreds of meat, some diced fresh or dried prawns or shrimps, a handful of cheap chopped vegetables, a touch of garlic, soy or black bean sauce and several minor masterpieces well within the reach of even a poor man were born.

Flavour, texture, quality . . . the Chinese savours each mouthful and is a great connoisseur of his own food. Indeed it is the only way to approach this cuisine oneself: to become swiftly aware of how a dish should look and taste at its best. It is a vitally alive art: adapting, changing sometimes even from its classic origins, to give way to some marvellous new version. Very few taboos operate here, but there are, of course, some basic guidelines; knowledge of the intrinsic qualities of the ingredients being used and of what would best combine with what is still essential.

Cantonese cooking, especially, has stayed close to the Taoist principle that food should be eaten as near to its natural state as possible, with as little cooking and seasoning as possible. Chemical tenderizers such as *vetsin* (monosodium glutamate) are avoided, and cutting and scoring the meats, vegetables and fish in such a way as to achieve the required tenderness preferred. This relies, of course, not only on a knowledge of the 'grain' of the raw materials but also on a knowledge of 'cooking time' and the correct methods of application of heat. A lot of this becomes instinctive after a little practise and one discovers how very little cooking time Chinese food can take. Often a mere dunking in boiling broth or swirling stir-frying in a very little oil will suffice to achieve the required doneness. In today's health-conscious age, this cuisine is among the most enlightened in the world in that easily destroyed precious vitamins are retained intact in the cooked dish.

It is generally held that there are five major schools of Chinese cooking: Canton, Shantung, Schezuan, Fukien and Honan, and two minor ones: Yang Chow and Temple Vegetarian.

Canton

Canton is in southern China, on the coast. A mild climate and access to the sea gave the province a vast variety of foodstuffs and ingredients and it is credited with the invention of the greatest number of dishes – some say around 400,000, with 250 different ways of cooking pork alone!

Cantonese is, however, a no-holds-barred school: practically everything which may be eaten with impunity, from pig's testicles, to snails, frog's legs, fish and chicken heads, ducks' tongues and webbed feet, snakes and sea-urchins, is cooked and eaten. And it is here that the now universally popular *Dim Sum* originated.

Literally translated, *Dim Sum* means 'something to dot the heart with.' Traditionally a tea-house repast, many Chinese restaurants today will keep the *Dim Sum* trays – tiers of steaming bamboo baskets piled high over boiling water or bouillon, with those items needing the least cooking at the very top – coming from morning until evening. Mouth-sized morsels of delicious, steamed spare-ribs in sauce, called *Thai Kuat*; red-cooked sweet-savoury pork in cloud-light white buns called *Char Siew Pau*; and a magically successful combination of diced pork and crisp, sliced water-chestnuts wrapped in the merest skin of egg-dough topped with crab's eggs, called *Siew Mai*, are among the classic array of low-calorie, steamed, high-protein snacks suitable for eating from morning until cocktail time.

Cantonese cooking also specializes in soups, especially turtle soup, steamed, roasted and grilled (broiled) pork and poultry dishes; 'double-pan' and large earthenware casserole-type cooking. A great deal of clear chicken broth is used as a stock or base for light gravies and is preferred to the sugar used by other schools to achieve 'sweetness'. And, of course, in keeping with the Taoist principle, underdone is well done, literally, in Canton! This is particularly true of their low-oil, quick, stir-fried 'chow' dishes, a technique which originated in Yang Chow; hence the name.

Shantung
Shantung is the northernmost of all the different schools with Peking perhaps the best known city which follows this style of cooking. It has nothing like the range or variety of Canton but is famous for a handful of wondrous dishes like Fragrant and Crispy Peking Duck and Duck Soup.

This area is specially noted for its 'drunken' dishes – i.e. dishes marinated or cooked in wines, such as swan's liver. Although the cooking is not heavy, on the whole the sauces are richer than those of Canton. Flavouring is heavier, with light and dark soy, with the accent on the latter, crushed garlic, black and red bean pastes and sauces. Plum sauce is another favourite accompaniment. Wheat, not rice, is the staple of the north and dumplings and noodles made from it are cooked in every conceivable way, and combined with pork, seafood, poultry, offal (variety meat) and vegetables.

History plays a great part; for the Mongols came and ruled here, and brought with them their techniques of marinating and barbecueing meats. The Mongolian Hot Pot is obviously the ancestor of the modern Firepot: a dish where each diner can cook his own food in a central hot-pot, dipping into a variety of sauces and ladling a little of the soup into his own individual bowl. And the Mongols also left their taste for dairy produce and mutton, much disliked by the rest of China. The five-spice mixture of anise, cinnamon, cloves, fennel and star anise is used as a seasoning.

Szechuan
In the western part of the central province is a vast basin of luxuriant vegetation, bounded by mountain ranges and densely populated: Szechuan.

Szechuan is famous for its spicy, piquant dishes; for its fungi, particularly truffles, and for the subtlety of its 'hot', multi-flavoured cuisine. It is also known as the site of the Chinese equivalent of Camelot!

The preponderance of hot spicy food has its roots in history. Only one great crop was produced each year, and in order to ensure an adequate supply of food the year round, they took to preserving their produce. The humidity precluded sun-drying or salting (both popular on the coast) and so spicing was used instead. They made chilli and peppercorn pastes, fermented rice, made wine vinegar and added a fair bit of brown sugar. All of which resulted in a series of fascinating savoury-hot, hot-sour-spiced, sweet-sour and sweet-hot-sharp dishes.

One of those dishes is *Yu Hsiang Jou si*, succulent pork strips stir-fried with what are called 'spicy' fish ingredients and fungi. Another is beef, carrots and peppers cut into strips and fried crisp, with chillis. This school also specializes in paper-wrapped cooking of poultry and various meats.

The fungi which grow in Szechuan are particularly delicious. And like nearby Yunan – which is famous rather like Parma in Italy for just one thing: ham – it also specializes in preserving meats by curing and smoking them. Its dishes tend to be more oily than those of the other schools.

Fukien
Fukien is very much a specialist school. It has none of the variety of Canton or Szechuan, but it is noted for the quality and lightness of its cooking, specializing in clear and tasty soups. Indeed, there are those who would fault it on this basis, saying that most Fukien dishes are perhaps too soupy. Fukien is famous for the quality of its soy sauce and for red-cooked dishes – meat or vegetables cooked or braised in a soy sauce-based liquid. The province has a long sea coast and seafood is therefore very popular, and what cannot be used in any one season is salted and sun dried for the next. Dried scallops form the basis of some of the best soups of the region, and have a unique and unforgettably delicate flavour.

During a short break from work, Chinese workers drink tea on the historic Great Wall of China.

Honan

Like Shantung, Honan was once the capital, the seat of a great court. Like Szechuan it grows the most wondrous fungi.

It was the cooks of Honan who first produced one of China's best-known flavours: the sweet-sour sauce. And it is they who devised a dip-fry method using boiling oil to cook ingredients like kidneys which shrink greatly on cooking through loss of moisture. The Honan method of dip-frying consists of intermittently dipping then removing the food from boiling oil, and results in a delicate balance between a crisp sealed outside and a tender-textured inside all at once.

Yang Chow

The Yangtze river bisects China, running from west to east. At its easternmost end, where it empties its great self into the magical-sounding China Sea, stands the luminous city of Shanghai. Claimed to be the most cosmopolitan of the great centres of cooking, it has its roots in the classic cooking of the school of Yang Chow.

Yang Chow was formerly a salt-rich mining city full of wealthy merchants and together the two cities stood at the easternmost end of the Yangtze. Yang Chow had all the advantages of wealth, of access to the sea and its produce, and to the fruits of the fertile valley of the river. The cooks of Yang Chow specialized in a wide range of cooking from long slow-cooking casseroles to light, airy, swiftly prepared snacks.

Access to the salt-trading post of Ningpo, also close by, which specialized in lightly spiced and steamed foods, and the availability of fresh sea-foods, greatly added to its own repertoire. They too, turned into a great art, sun-drying, salting, smoking and curing, and specialized in spicing and preserving seafoods such as squid and prawns (shrimp). They were among the first to combine both the fresh and the dried variety of the same ingredient in the same dish – an idea now copied by much of the rest of South East Asia.

Two dishes from Yang Chow have been adopted by all the schools of cooking and are now regarded as national dishes: *Chow Mein* and *Chow Fan*. In short they originated Fried Noodles and Fried Rice . . . and the all-important technique of 'Chow' cooking. Chow cooking – that is low-oil, quick stir-frying came originally from Yang Chow. (Ironically, however, it was Canton which went on to exploit it best.) But in time Shanghai grew and surpassed and eclipsed Yang Chow in power, fame and sophistication; so much so that, apart from a few who know how much Chinese cooking owes to the school of Yang Chow, it has faded from memory, and is today regarded as only a minor school, with Canton and Shanghai receiving the credit for many Yang Chow masterpieces.

The Vegetarian School

The Buddhist temples of China adhered very strictly to a vegetarian diet. Today the West is discovering with interest this particular school of cooking.

The Chinese on the whole dislike dairy products, but obviously if both dairy products and meat are removed from the diet a substitute is necessary for properly balanced nutrition. In all of China, and emanating from this style of cooking, that substitute is the soy bean. It reigns supreme, taking not only the place of dairy products but indeed of every meat and fish under the sun. For such is the consummate knowledge of cooking it that almost every conceivable type of dish has been made out of every part of the soy plant – milk, curd, 'cheese', cake and sprouts, in marvellous imitation of the texture, flavour and shape of meat and fish so as to be (almost) indistinguishable from them. Sautéed soy bean curd is produced to taste and look in turn like delicate calves' brains or the fluffiest omelette.

Water buffaloes are traditionally used in agriculture to plough rice-paddies.

Preparation

There is no doubt that the bulk of the 'work' of Chinese cooking lies in assembly and preparation. A basic part of this preparation is the cutting up of food, and, to get the best results, some knowledge of the 'grain' of the meats and vegetables are required. There are five main types of cutting: dicing, slicing, chopping, oblique-cutting and shredding. To watch a Chinese cook deftly wielding a Chinese chopper at speed is to watch the performance of an artist. But they do say that, although it does look unwieldy and far more difficult to use than a sharp knife, once one gets the hang of it, it is far easier to use!

Techniques of Cooking

The Chinese claim to have evolved some 80-odd techniques of cooking and combining foods. Some of these, of course, are the ordinary ones known to every Western cook and housewife, such as steaming and boiling, and some are refinements and variations of those methods. Some of them are, however, unique to Chinese cooking. 'Stir-frying' for instance is a form of swift, light sautéeing where the food is kept constantly in motion so that every morsel is evenly and swiftly cooked. The ubiquitous *wok*, a sort of frying-pan with gently sloping sides, is best for this type of cooking, especially when used with wooden cooking chopsticks (which are longer than eating ones). Red-cooking is also uniquely Chinese and is not a slang expression denoting political leanings, but rather a method of cooking a whole range of meat, poultry, game and fish dishes, in soy sauce, resulting in a lovely, rich red glaze to the food. Meats cooked like this, especially, will keep well and combine well later – hot or cold – with other ingredients.

(Left) The Chinese chopper and shredder are essential tools in the preparation of Chinese food.

(Below) The wok is the traditional cooking utensil in China and is ideal for stir-frying.

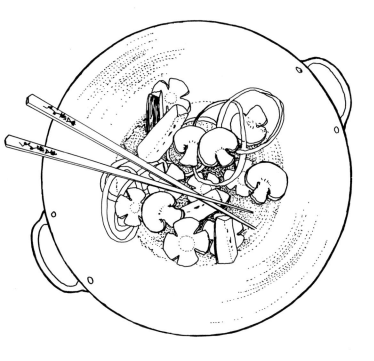

Eating Chinese

Without doubt part of the fun of cooking Chinese is to serve and eat Chinese.

Setting: The classic Chinese table is usually round because dishes are traditionally brought in one at a time, diners helping themselves from a common central dish, and it is important that each guest be an equal distance from the central dish.

Each place setting has bowls, a china spoon, chopsticks, saucers. Condiments are set out: usually vinegar and soy sauce in pourers and chilli sauce, chilli oil and mustard sauce in saucers.

Etiquette: Etiquette decrees that each diner reaches for food from the central dish, serving himself with his own chopsticks from that part of the dish facing him. Perfect politeness also decrees that he should endeavour not to let the chopsticks touch his mouth and that he picks up every piece of food that his chopsticks touch from the main dish. When laying down one's chopsticks never cross them. That is taken by many Chinese to be the height of bad manners and even of enmity, for they believe crossed chopsticks to be a sign of ill-luck for the host.

Tea: Hot tea without milk or sugar is the usual accompaniment to a Chinese meal unless wine or spirits are being drunk.

Tea is usually drunk between dishes to cleanse the palate. It also has a social and ceremonial function and is said to be 'healthy', dissolving the grease in the food and washing it through the system and away. Curiously, in hot weather the tea induces a gentle pleasant sweating and thereby cools the body. In the winter it warms it. Certain herbal teas also have a medicinal value and are meant to be very good for the liver and the kidneys – quite apart from the delicate aroma and delicious flavours. Vanity too is served here, for some of them are supposed to be good for the complexion and for the brightness of the whites of the eyes. So they say.

Wine: Warmed sake with hot weak tea as a chaser makes a good winter accompaniment, but for those purists who would like to stay with Chinese wines here is the briefest resumé:

Gao Liang, from northern China, is a rice wine somewhat stronger than vodka or gin. More suitable for winter than summer. *Shao Hsing*, from central China, is a rather milder, sweeter, yellowish wine also made from rice. This is by far the most popular wine to drink while eating. *Liao Pan* – whose literal translation means 'half-strength' – is an orange blossom or green plum wine from south China. It is usually very mild and pleasant, although there are more potent forms of it: you will only discover the strength by tasting each jar or bottle as it comes!

Some Final Thoughts

The garnishing and presentation of food is as much an art with the Chinese as the cooking of it. The 'look of it' is important from a point of view of colour, form and imagination. The 'placing' of the dish within the order of the menu is another grace note, for unlike an Indian meal where everything is served at once these dishes, to be appreciated fully, should be served one at a time and each should act as an appetizer to the next.

The naming of dishes, too, makes the imagination soar back into the mists of the romantic past: Gold Coin; Eight-Jewel Duck; Splashed Shrimps; Red-Cooked Lion's Head. There is always a story. Like the one about the Emperor Chien-lung wandering incognito into an inn in search of a meal. The innkeeper, clean out of food but unwilling to disappoint anyone at all, remembers that he has a piece of crusty, near-burned rice at the bottom of his empty pot of cooked rice. He fishes it out and ingeniously uses part of it to make a rice broth and uses part of the toasty rice as a biscuit to serve with the broth! The Emperor was so taken with this unique dish that he ordered his own chefs to discover how this was made. Through experiments they produced its equivalent, the dish which is today known as *Gaw Bar* and is a classic part of the Chinese repertoire.

So now read on, sample and delight in the wonders of an ancient, yet very modern cuisine.

SOUPS & DIM SUM

Birds' Nest Soup

Metric/Imperial	American
4 birds' nests	4 birds' nests
1.5 l./2½ pints chicken stock	6¼ cups chicken stock
salt and pepper to taste	salt and pepper to taste
125g./4oz. cooked chicken, finely shredded	½ cup finely shredded cooked chicken
4 slices of ham, finely chopped	4 slices of ham, finely chopped
¼ tsp. monosodium glutamate (optional)	¼ tsp. M.S.G. (optional)

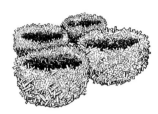

Soak the nests for 12 hours in warm water, changing the water once or twice during the period. Remove any protruding feathers with tweezers.

Pour the stock into a large saucepan and bring to the boil. Season to taste and drop in the birds' nests. Cover the pan, reduce the heat to low and simmer for 20 minutes. Stir in the remaining ingredients and simmer for a further 1 minute.

Pour into a warmed tureen and serve.

Serves 4
Preparation and cooking time: 12½ hours

Wonton Soup

Metric/Imperial	American
½kg./1lb. lean pork or beef, minced	1lb. lean pork or beef, ground
2 Tbs. soya sauce	2 Tbs. soy sauce
2.5cm/1in. piece of fresh root ginger, peeled and finely chopped	1in. piece of fresh green ginger, peeled and finely chopped
1 tsp. salt	1 tsp. salt
1 tsp. grated nutmeg	1 tsp. grated nutmeg
275g./10oz. chopped spinach	1½ cups chopped spinach
225g./8oz. wonton dough (see page 39) thinly rolled and cut into 36 squares, or 36 bought wonton wrappers	8oz. wonton dough (see page 39) thinly rolled and cut into 36 squares, or 36 bought wonton wrappers
1.75l./3 pints chicken stock	2 quarts chicken stock
1 bunch of watercress, chopped	1 bunch of watercress, chopped

Put the pork or beef, soy sauce, ginger, salt, nutmeg and spinach in a bowl and mix thoroughly.

Lay the wonton squares or wrappers on a flat surface. Put a little filling just below the centre and wet the edges of the dough. Fold one corner of the dough over the filling to make a triangle and pinch the edges together to seal. Pull the corners at the base together and pinch to seal.

Half-fill a large saucepan with water and bring to the boil. Drop in the wontons and return to the boil. Cook for 5 minutes, or until the wontons are tender but still firm.

Remove from the heat and pour off the water. Return the wontons to the pan and pour in the stock. Bring to the boil, then add the watercress. Return to the boil and transfer to a warmed tureen before serving.

Serves 6
Preparation and cooking time: 20 minutes

Hot and Sour Soup

Metric/Imperial	American
2 Tbs. sesame oil	2 Tbs. sesame oil
2 medium onions, finely chopped	2 medium onion, finely chopped
2 Tbs. flour	2 Tbs. flour
1.2 l./2 pints chicken stock	5 cups chicken stock
1 Tbs. lemon juice	1 Tbs. lemon juice
2 Tbs. soya sauce	2 Tbs. soy sauce
salt and pepper to taste	salt and pepper to taste
275g./10oz. bean sprouts	1¼ cups bean sprouts
2 dried mushrooms, soaked in cold water for 30 minutes, drained and chopped	2 dried mushrooms, soaked in cold water for 30 minutes, drained and chopped
125g./4oz. tin water chestnuts drained and chopped	4oz. can water chestnuts, drained and chopped
125g./4oz. crabmeat, diced	½ cup diced crabmeat

Heat the oil in a heavy saucepan. When it is hot, add the onions and cook, stirring occasionally, until they are soft. Remove the pan from the heat and stir in the flour to make a smooth paste. Gradually add the stock, then stir in the lemon juice, soy sauce, salt, pepper, bean sprouts, mushrooms, water chestnuts and crabmeat. Return the pan to moderate heat and bring to the boil, stirring constantly. Cover then simmer for 1 hour. Transfer to a warmed tureen and serve.
Serves 6
Preparation and cooking time: 1½ hours.

Wonton Soup contains delicious wonton triangles stuffed with pork or beef and spinach.

13

Tsingshih Ham and Cucumber Soup

Metric/Imperial	American
2 large cucumbers, peeled and cubed	2 large cucumbers, peeled and cubed
2 dried mushrooms, soaked in cold water for 30 minutes, drained and chopped	2 dried mushrooms, soaked in cold water for 30 minutes, drained and chopped
900ml./1½ pints chicken stock	3¾ cups chicken stock
salt and pepper to taste	salt and pepper to taste
225g./8oz. smoked ham, finely chopped	1 cup finely chopped smoked ham

Put the cucumbers and mushrooms into a large saucepan and add the stock and seasoning. Bring to the boil. Cover the pan, reduce the heat to low and simmer the soup for 20 minutes. Stir in the ham and simmer for a further 5 minutes.

Transfer to a warmed tureen and serve.

Serves 4
Preparation and cooking time: 1 hour

Yu-chi Tang

(Shark's Fin Soup)

This dish is one of the great delicacies of China, and is often served on special occasions. It is traditionally accompanied by a small bowl of cooked bamboo shoots.

Metric/Imperial	American
2 Tbs. sesame oil	2 Tbs. sesame oil
1 spring onion, finely chopped	1 scallion, finely chopped
2.5cm./1in. piece of fresh root ginger, peeled and finely chopped	1in. piece of fresh green ginger, peeled and finely chopped
4 dried mushrooms, soaked in cold water for 30 minutes, drained and thinly sliced	4 dried mushrooms, soaked in cold water for 30 minutes, drained and thinly sliced
2 Tbs. rice wine or dry sherry	2 Tbs. rice wine or dry sherry
2l./3½ pints chicken stock	2¼ quarts chicken stock
125g./4oz. ready-prepared shark's fin, soaked for 1 hour in cold water and drained	½ cup ready-prepared shark's fin, soaked for 1 hour in cold water and drained
225g./8oz. boned chicken breast, shredded	1 cup boned shredded chicken breast
225g./8oz. shelled small shrimps	1⅓ cups peeled small shrimp
1½ Tbs. soya sauce	1½ Tbs. soy sauce
1½ Tbs. cornflour, mixed to a paste with 1 Tbs. chicken stock	1½ Tbs. cornstarch, mixed to a paste with 1 Tbs. chicken stock

Heat the oil in a saucepan. When it is hot, add the spring onion (scallion), ginger, mushrooms and rice wine or sherry and fry, stirring occasionally, for 5 minutes. Add half the stock and the shark's fin and bring to the boil. Simmer for 10 minutes, then add the chicken, shrimps and soy sauce. Pour in the remaining stock and cornflour (cornstarch) mixture and bring to the boil, stirring. Simmer for 10 minutes, stirring occasionally.

Pour into a warmed tureen and serve.

Serves 8-10
Preparation and cooking time: 1½ hours

No important feast or dinner can pass without serving Yu-Chi-Tang (Shark's Fin Soup), one of China's most famous delicacies.

Egg Drop Soup

Metric/Imperial	American
1 Tbs. vegetable oil	1 Tbs. vegetable oil
1 medium onion, thinly sliced	1 medium onion, thinly sliced
1 small cucumber, finely diced	1 small cucumber, finely diced
1.75l./3 pints chicken stock	2 quarts chicken stock
4 medium tomatoes, quartered	4 medium tomatoes, quartered
1 egg, lightly beaten	1 egg, lightly beaten

Heat the oil in a large saucepan. When it is hot, add the onion and fry for 1 minute, stirring constantly. Add the cucumber and fry for 1 minute. Stir in the stock and bring it to the boil. Reduce the heat to low and simmer for 10 minutes, stirring occasionally. Stir in the tomato quarters and simmer very gently for a further 5 minutes.

Remove the pan from the heat and using a whisk or fork, carefully whisk the egg into the soup.

Serve at once.

Serves 6
Preparation and cooking time: 25 minutes

Watercress and Pork Soup

Metric/Imperial	American
6 dried mushrooms, soaked in cold water for 30 minutes and drained	6 dried mushrooms, soaked in cold water for 30 minutes and drained
½kg./1lb. pork fillets, cut into thin strips	1lb. pork tenderloin, cut into thin strips
2 bunches of watercress, chopped	2 bunches of watercress, chopped
1.75l./3 pints chicken stock	2 quarts chicken stock
2 celery stalks, cut into strips	2 celery stalks, cut into strips
2 carrots, cut into thin strips	2 carrots, cut into thin strips
6 spring onions, chopped	6 scallions, chopped
1 tsp. salt	1 tsp. salt
1 tsp. sugar	1 tsp. sugar
½ tsp. white pepper	½ tsp. white pepper
1 Tbs. soya sauce	1 Tbs. soy sauce

Remove the stalks from the mushrooms then cut the mushroom caps into thin strips and set aside.

Put the pork and watercress into a large saucepan and pour over the stock. Bring to the boil. Reduce the heat to low and simmer the soup for 20 minutes. Stir in all the remaining ingredients and bring to the boil. Simmer the soup for a further 5 minutes.

Pour into a warmed tureen and serve at once.

Serves 6-8
Preparation and cooking time: 1 hour

Chicken and Sweetcorn Soup

Metric/Imperial	American
3 Tbs. vegetable oil	3 Tbs. vegetable oil
4cm./1½in. piece of fresh root ginger, peeled and chopped	1½in. piece of fresh green ginger, peeled and chopped
125g./4oz. cooked chicken meat, finely chopped	⅔ cup finely chopped cooked chicken meat
4 dried mushrooms, soaked in cold water for 30 minutes, drained and stalks removed	4 dried mushrooms, soaked in cold water for 30 minutes, drained and stalks removed
400g./14oz. tin sweetcorn, drained	14oz. can sweetcorn, drained
600ml./1 pint chicken stock	2½ cups chicken stock
1 tsp. salt	1 tsp. sugar
2 tsp. cornflour, mixed to a paste with 1 Tbs. water	2 tsp. cornstarch, mixed to a paste with 1 Tbs. water

Heat the oil in a large saucepan. When it is hot, add the ginger and stir-fry for 2 minutes. Add the chicken meat and stir-fry for 2 minutes. Chop the mushrooms if they are large, then stir them into the pan with the sweetcorn. Pour over the stock and sugar. Bring to the boil, reduce the heat to low and simmer the soup for 10 minutes.

Stir in the cornflour (cornstarch) mixture until the liquid thickens slightly and becomes translucent. Serve at once.

Serves 4
Preparation and cooking time: 30 minutes

Wontons with Pork

Metric/Imperial	American
225g./8oz. lean pork, minced	8oz. lean pork, ground
2 tsp. rice wine or dry sherry	2 tsp. rice wine or dry sherry
2 tsp. soya sauce	2 tsp. soy sauce
1 tsp. salt	1 tsp. salt
1 tsp. sugar	1 tsp. sugar
2 tsp. cornflour	2 tsp. cornstarch
1 Chinese or savoy cabbage leaf, chopped	1 Chinese or savoy cabbage leaf, chopped
3 water chestnuts, finely chopped	3 water chestnuts, finely chopped
1 spring onion, finely chopped	1 scallion, finely chopped
225g./8oz. wonton dough (see page 39), thinly rolled and cut into 36 squares, or 36 bought wonton wrappers	8oz. wonton dough (see page 39) thinly rolled and cut into 36 squares, or 36 bought wonton wrappers

Put the pork, wine or sherry, soy sauce, salt, sugar and cornflour (cornstarch) into a bowl and knead gently to blend. Beat in the cabbage, water chestnuts and spring onion (scallion).

Lay the wonton squares or wrappers on a flat surface. Put a little filling just below the centre and wet the edges of the dough. Fold one corner of the dough over the filling to make a triangle and pinch the edges together to seal. Pull the corners at the base together and pinch to seal. Repeat this process until all the wonton wrappers are filled and sealed.

Half-fill a large saucepan or the bottom of a steamer with water and bring to the boil. Place the wontons in a heatproof bowl on the top half of the steamer and wontons should be arranged in one layer). Steam the wontons for 30 minutes.

Transfer to a warmed serving dish and serve piping hot.

Serves 6-8
Preparation and cooking time: 1½ hours (if cooking in two batches)

Wontons with Pork and Prawn or Shrimps

Metric/Imperial	American
2 Tbs. vegetable oil	2 Tbs. vegetable oil
225g./8oz. lean pork, minced	8oz. lean pork, ground
225g./8oz. peeled prawns, finely chopped	1⅓ cups finely chopped peeled shrimps
2 Tbs. soya sauce	2 Tbs. soy sauce
1 Tbs. rice wine or dry sherry	1 Tbs. rice wine or dry sherry
½ tsp. salt	½ tsp. salt
5 bamboo shoots, finely chopped	5 bamboo shoots, finely chopped
2 dried mushrooms, soaked in cold water for 30 minutes, drained and chopped	2 dried mushrooms, soaked in cold water for 30 minutes, drained and chopped
2 spring onions, finely chopped	2 scallions, finely chopped
1 tsp. cornflour, mixed to a paste with 1 Tbs. water	1 tsp. cornstarch, mixed to a paste with 1 Tbs. water
225g./8oz. wonton dough (see page 39), thinly rolled and cut into 36 squares, or 36 bought wonton wrappers	8oz. wonton dough (see page 39), thinly rolled and cut into 36 squares, or 36 bought wonton wrappers
vegetable oil for deep-frying	vegetable oil for deep-frying

Heat the oil in a frying-pan. When it is hot, add the pork and fry until it loses its pinkness. Stir in the prawns or shrimp, rice wine or sherry, soy sauce, salt, bamboo shoots, mushrooms and spring onions (scallions) and fry for 1 minute, stirring constantly. Stir in the cornflour (cornstarch) mixture until the pan mixture thickens. Remove from the heat and transfer the mixture to a bowl. Set aside to cool.

Lay the wonton squares or wrappers on a flat surface. Put a little filling just below the centre and wet the edges of the dough. Fold one corner of the dough over the filling to make a triangle and pinch the edges together to seal. Pull the corners at the base together and pinch to seal. Repeat this process until all the wonton wrappers are filled and sealed.

Fill a large saucepan one-third full with oil and heat until it is hot. Carefully lower the wontons into the oil, a few at a time, and fry for 2 to 3 minutes, or until they are golden brown. Remove from the oil and drain on kitchen towels.

Transfer the wontons to a warmed serving dish and serve hot.

Serves 6-8
Preparation and cooking time: 1 hour

Hsia Jen Tu Ssu

(Shrimp Toast)

Metric/Imperial	American
225g./8oz. peeled shrimps	1⅓ cups peeled shrimp
25g./1oz. lean salt pork, blanched in boiling water for 5 minutes to remove excess salt	1oz. lean salt pork, blanched in boiling water for 5 minutes to remove excess salt
2 Tbs. rice wine or dry sherry	2 Tbs. rice wine or dry sherry
salt and white pepper to taste	salt and white pepper to taste
2 egg whites, beaten until frothy	2 egg whites, beaten until frothy
2 Tbs. cornflour	2 Tbs. cornstarch
1 tsp. very finely chopped parsley	1 tsp. very finely chopped parsley
1 egg, lightly beaten	1 egg, lightly beaten
10-12 thin slices of white bread, cut into rounds, squares or triangles	10-12 thin slices of white bread, cut into rounds, squares or triangles
vegetable oil for deep-frying	vegetable oil for deep-frying

Wontons have a marvellous variety of fillings and can be served as an hors d'oeuvre, as part of a main meal or as a sweet.

Put the shrimps and salt pork in a dish and chop and pound them together until they are pulpy. Beat in the wine or sherry, seasoning, egg whites, half the cornflour (cornstarch) and parsley until the mixture forms a thick paste. Alternatively, put all the above ingredients in a blender and purée until smooth.

Beat the remaining cornflour (cornstarch) and egg together, then lightly brush the mixture over the bread shapes. Spread the shrimp paste over the bread shapes.

Fill a large saucepan one-third full with oil and heat until very hot. Carefully lower the shrimp toasts into the oil, a few at a time, and fry for about 3 minutes, shrimp side up. (You may have to use a slotted spoon to keep the toasts this side up.) Turn over and fry for a further 3 minutes on the other side, or until they are deep golden brown and crisp. Remove from the oil and drain thoroughly on kitchen towels. Serve piping hot.

Serves 6-8
Preparation and cooking time: 40 minutes

Chinese Spareribs

Metric/Imperial	American
1kg./2lb. American-style spareribs, cut into individual ribs	2lb. spareribs, cut into individual ribs
1 tsp. salt	1 tsp. salt
4 Tbs. peanut oil	4 Tbs. peanut oil
2 garlic cloves, crushed	2 garlic cloves, crushed
½ small onion, finely chopped	1 small onion, finely chopped
4cm./1½in. piece of fresh root ginger, peeled and finely chopped	1½in. piece of fresh green ginger, peeled and finely chopped
4 Tbs. soya sauce	4 Tbs. soy sauce
3 Tbs. dry sherry	3 Tbs. dry sherry
1 Tbs. castor sugar	1 Tbs. superfine sugar
black pepper to taste	black pepper to taste
150ml./5fl.oz. chicken stock	⅔ cup chicken stock

Rub the spareribs all over with salt. Heat the oil in a large frying pan. When the oil is very hot, add the garlic, onion and ginger. Stir-fry for 1 minute. Add the ribs, reduce the heat slightly and stir-fry for a further 5 minutes. Remove the ribs from the pan. Stir the soy sauce, sherry, sugar and pepper into the pan and stir-fry for 2 minutes. Return the ribs to the pan.

Pour in the stock and turn the ribs so that they are well coated. Reduce the heat to low and simmer for 5 minutes. Cover and leave to simmer gently for 20 minutes. Remove the lid. Turn the ribs, re-cover and continue to simmer for 10 minutes.

Preheat the oven to fairly hot 190°C (Gas Mark 5, 375°F). Arrange the ribs in a roasting pan and spoon over any remaining sauce. Put into the oven for 5-10 minutes, or until the surface of the ribs is dry and crisp. Serve at once.
Serves 4
Preparation and cooking time: 1 hour

Dumplings with Crab Meat

Metric/Imperial	American
6 dried mushrooms, soaked in cold water for 30 minutes and drained	6 dried mushrooms, soaked in cold water for 30 minutes and drained
2 Tbs. sesame oil	2 Tbs. sesame oil
1 Tbs. chopped spring onion	1 Tbs. chopped scallion
1 tsp. finely chopped fresh root ginger	1 tsp. finely chopped fresh green ginger
225g./8oz. crabmeat, shell and cartilage removed and flaked	8oz. crabmeat, shell and cartilage removed and flaked
salt and pepper to taste	salt and pepper to taste
¼ tsp. sugar	¼ tsp. sugar
1 tsp. soya sauce	1 tsp. soy sauce
1 Tbs. sherry	1 Tbs. sherry
DUMPLINGS	DUMPLINGS
225g./8oz. flour	2 cups flour
125ml./4.floz. boiling water	½ cup boiling water

Cut off the mushroom stalks and chop the caps finely.

Heat the oil in a frying-pan. When the oil is very hot, add the spring onion (scallion), ginger, mushrooms and crabmeat and stir-fry for 3 minutes over moderately high heat.

Stir in the salt, pepper, sugar, soy sauce and sherry and stir-fry for a further 1 minute. Remove from the heat and set aside.

Sift the flour into a bowl, then gradually pour in the water, mixing until all the flour is incorporated and the dough comes away from the sides of the bowl. Cover with a cloth and set aside for 30 minutes.

Roll out the dough into a sausage about 2.5cm./1in. in diameter, then cut into slices about 2.5cm./1in. wide. Flatten the slices until they are about 7.5cm./3in. in diameter.

Put a teaspoonful of the crabmeat mixture on one side of each circle, then fold over to make a semi-circle. Seal the edges by pinching them together.

Half-fill a large saucepan with water and bring to the boil.

Put the dumplings in a heatproof bowl or the top half of a steamer and place over the boiling water. (If the dumplings will not fit in the bowl in one layer, steam them in two batches.)

Cover and steam the dumplings for 10 minutes. Serve hot.

Serves 4
Preparation and cooking time: 1½ hours

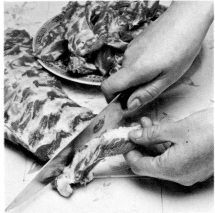

Chinese Spareribs are made with individual American style ribs stir-fried in a delicious mixture of sherry, soy sauce, sugar and pepper.

NOODLES, RICE & FOO YUNG

Lo Mein

(Beef and Vegetables with Noodles)

Metric/Imperial	American
225g./8oz. rump steak, cut across the grain into thin strips	8oz. rump steak, cut across the grain into thin strips
4 Tbs. oyster sauce	4 Tbs. oyster sauce
125ml./4fl.oz. sesame oil	$\frac{1}{2}$ cup sesame oil
350g./12oz. egg noodles or spaghetti	12oz. egg noodles or spaghetti
4 dried mushrooms, soaked in cold water for 30 minutes, drained and sliced	4 dried mushrooms, soaked in cold water for 30 minutes, drained and sliced
125g./4oz. bamboo shoots, finely chopped	$\frac{1}{2}$ cup finely chopped bamboo shoots
225g./8oz. Chinese cabbage, shredded	$1\frac{1}{3}$ cups shredded Chinese cabbage
225g./8oz. bean sprouts	1 cup bean sprouts
1 tsp. soft brown sugar	1 tsp. soft brown sugar
2 Tbs. soya sauce	2 Tbs. soy sauce
2 spring onions, chopped	2 scallions, chopped
125ml./4fl.oz. beef stock	$\frac{1}{2}$ cup beef stock

Put the meat strips into a shallow bowl. Pour over 3 tablespoons of the oyster sauce and 1 tablespoon of sesame oil and toss to coat them thoroughly. Set aside to marinate at room temperature for 30 minutes.

Meanwhile, cook the noodles or spaghetti in boiling, salted water until they are just tender. Drain and keep hot.

Heat the remaining oil in a large, deep frying-pan. When it is warm but not hot, add the beef strips and stir-fry for 2 minutes, taking care to keep the strips separate. Push the strips to the side of the pan and add the vegetables. Fry for 1 minute, stirring constantly. Add the sugar, soy sauce and remaining oyster sauce and fry for a further 30 seconds, stirring constantly. Stir the beef strips back into the vegetables the spring onions (scallions) and noodles or spaghetti. Pour over the stock and bring to the boil, stirring constantly. Stir-fry for 2 minutes.

Transfer the mixture to a warmed serving bowl and serve at once.
Serves 4
Preparation and cooking time: $1\frac{1}{4}$ hours

Egg Noodles with Pork Sauce

Metric/Imperial	American
1 large cucumber	1 large cucumber
3 spring onions, finely chopped	3 scallions, finely chopped
4 garlic cloves, crushed	4 garlic cloves, crushed
3 Tbs. vegetable oil	3 Tbs. vegetable oil
$\frac{1}{2}$kg./1lb. lean pork, minced	1lb. lean pork, ground
2 Tbs. rice wine or dry sherry	2 Tbs. rice wine or dry sherry

2 Tbs. Worcestershire sauce	2 Tbs. Worcestershire sauce	*Another recipe with an*
1 Tbs. soya sauce	1 Tbs. soy sauce	*unusual sweet-sour flavour*
1 large onion, finely chopped	1 large onion, finely chopped	*is Egg Noodles with Pork*
2 tsp. brown sugar	2 tsp. brown sugar	*Sauce, strongly flavoured*
75ml./3fl.oz. chicken stock	$\frac{1}{3}$ cup chicken stock	*with garlic.*
350g./12oz. egg noodles	12oz. egg noodles	

Peel the cucumber, then cut in half lengthways. Scoop out the seeds. Cut lengthways into $\frac{1}{2}$cm./$\frac{1}{4}$in. slices, then cut each slice into strips about 5cm./2in. long. Arrange the cucumber and spring onions (scallions) on a serving plate and sprinkle with the garlic. Set aside.

Heat 2 tablespoons of oil in a large frying-pan. When it is hot, add the pork and fry until it loses its pinkness. Stir in the wine or sherry, Worcestershire sauce, soy sauce, onion, sugar and chicken stock, and bring to the boil. Cook for 10 to 15 minutes, or until the liquid has evaporated. Cover the pan and remove from the heat. Keep hot while you cook the noodles.

Cook the noodles in boiling, salted water for 6 to 8 minutes, or until they are just tender. Drain and toss in the remaining oil. Arrange the noodles in a warmed serving dish and cover with the pork sauce. Sprinkle over some of the garnish and serve at once, accompanied by the remaining garnish.

Serves 4-6
Preparation and cooking time: 40 minutes

Transparent Noodles with Beef

Metric/Imperial	American
½kg./1lb. rump of beef, cut across the grain into thin strips	1lb. rump of beef, cut across the grain into thin strips
3 Tbs. soya sauce	3 Tbs. soy sauce
1 Tbs. rice wine or dry sherry	1 Tbs. rice wine or dry sherry
75ml./3fl.oz. peanut oil	⅓ cup peanut oil
2 Tbs. cornflour	2 Tbs. cornstarch
225g./8oz. transparent noodles	8oz. transparent noodles
1½ tsp. sugar	1½ tsp. sugar
1 tsp. salt	1 tsp. salt
175g./6oz. bean sprouts	¾ cup bean sprouts
3 spring onions, finely chopped	3 scallions, finely chopped
50ml./2fl.oz. beef stock	¼ cup beef stock

Put the beef strips into a shallow bowl. Combine 2 tablespoons of soy sauce, the wine or sherry, 1 tablespoon of oil and the cornflour (cornstarch) until they are well blended. Pour the mixture over the beef strips and toss gently to coat them. Set aside to marinate at room temperature for 1 hour.

Meanwhile, put the noodles into a bowl and pour over boiling water. Set aside to soak for 30 minutes. Drain.

Heat the remaining oil in a large frying-pan. When it is hot, add the beef and stir-fry over high heat for 2 minutes. Push the strips to the side of the pan and add the noodles and remaining ingredients. Fry for 1 minute, then stir the beef strips into the noodles. Add the remaining soy sauce and fry for a further 2 minutes, stirring frequently.

Transfer the mixture to a warmed serving dish and serve at once.

Serves 4
Preparation and cooking time: 1¼ hours

Chow Mein

(Fried Noodles)

Metric/Imperial	American
½kg./1lb. egg noodles or spaghetti	1lb. egg noodles or spaghetti
225g./8oz. French beans, chopped	1⅓ cups chopped green beans
50ml./2fl.oz. vegetable oil	¼ cup vegetable oil
1 medium onion, thinly sliced	1 medium onion, thinly sliced
1 garlic clove, crushed	1 garlic clove, crushed
125g./4oz. chicken meat, finely shredded	½ cup finely shredded chicken meat
2 Tbs. soya sauce	2 Tbs. soy sauce
1 tsp. sugar	1 tsp. sugar
1 Tbs. rice wine or dry sherry	1 Tbs. rice wine or dry sherry
20g./¾oz. butter	1½ Tbs. butter
3 Tbs. chicken stock	3 Tbs. chicken stock
½ chicken stock cube, crumbled	½ chicken bouillon cube, crumbled

Cook the noodles or spaghetti in boiling, salted water until they are just tender. Drain the noodles or spaghetti and keep hot. Cook the beans in boiling, salted water for 5 minutes. Drain and keep hot.

Heat the oil in a large frying-pan. When it is hot, add the onion and garlic. Fry for 2 minutes, stirring constantly. Add the chicken and stir-fry for 1 minute. Add the beans, soy sauce, sugar and rice wine or sherry and stir-fry for a further 1½ minutes. Using a slotted spoon, transfer the chicken and bean mixture to a bowl. Keep hot.

Add the butter, stock and stock (bouillon) cube to the oil remaining in the frying-pan. Stir in the noodles or spaghetti and fry for 2 minutes, stirring frequently. Stir in half the bean and chicken mixture, then transfer the whole mixture to a warmed serving dish. Keep hot.

Return the remaining bean and chicken mixture to the pan and increase the heat to high. Stir-fry for 1 minute, adding more oil or soy sauce if necessary. Spoon over the spaghetti mixture and serve at once.

Serves 6
Preparation and cooking time: 40 minutes

Hui Mein

(Noodles in Sauce or Gravy)

Metric/Imperial	American
½kg./1lb. egg noodles or spaghetti	1lb. egg noodles or spaghetti
225g./8oz. French beans, chopped	1⅓ cups chopped green beans
3½ Tbs. vegetable oil	3½ Tbs. vegetable oil
1 large onion, thinly sliced	1 large onion, thinly sliced
1 garlic clove, crushed	1 garlic clove, crushed
2.5cm./1in. piece of fresh root ginger, peeled and chopped	1in. piece of fresh green ginger, peeled and chopped
125g./4oz. chicken meat, finely shredded	½ cup finely shredded chicken meat
3 Tbs. soya sauce	3 Tbs. soy sauce
1 tsp. sugar	1 tsp. sugar
1 Tbs. rice wine or dry sherry	1 Tbs. rice wine or dry sherry
450ml./15fl.oz. chicken stock	2 cups chicken stock
2 tsp. butter	2 tsp. butter
½ chicken stock cube, crumbled	½ chicken bouillon cube, crumbled
1 Tbs. cornflour, mixed to a paste with 4 Tbs. chicken stock	1 Tbs. cornstarch, mixed to a paste with 4 Tbs. chicken stock

Cook the noodles or spaghetti in boiling, salted water until they are just tender. Drain and keep hot. Cook the beans in boiling, salted water for 5 minutes. Drain and keep hot.

Heat the oil in a large frying-pan. When it is hot, add the onion, garlic and ginger. Fry for 1½ minutes, stirring constantly. Add the chicken, beans, 2 tablespoons of soy sauce, the sugar and wine or sherry. Increase the heat to high and stir-fry for 2 minutes. Remove from the heat and keep hot.

Put the stock into a saucepan and bring to the boil. Add the butter, stock (bouillon) cube and the remaining soy sauce and stir well. Add the cornflour (cornstarch) mixture and cook, stirring constantly, until the sauce thickens and becomes translucent. Add the noodles or spaghetti to the saucepan and cook for 2 to 3 minutes, or until they are heated through.

Divide the noodle mixture between four serving bowls. Keep hot.

Return the frying-pan to moderate heat and stir-fry for 1 minute to reheat the bean and chicken mixture. Spoon the mixture over the noodle mixture and serve at once.

Serves 4
Preparation and cooking time: 40 minutes

Two recipes for a sustaining meal with noodles are Tan Mein (on the left) and Cha Chiang Mein (on the right). The former can be eaten not only as a soup but also as a main dish or as a snack, and the latter makes a meal in itself, complete with accompaniments.

Tan Mein

(Soup Noodles)

Metric/Imperial	American
350g./12oz. egg noodles or spaghetti	12oz. egg noodles or spaghetti
1½ Tbs. vegetable oil	1½ Tbs. vegetable oil
1 small onion, thinly sliced	1 small onion, thinly sliced
4cm./1½in. piece of fresh root ginger, peeled and chopped	1½in. piece of fresh green ginger, peeled and chopped
225g./8oz. lean pork, finely shredded	8oz. lean pork, finely shredded
15g./½oz. butter	1 Tbs. butter
125g./4oz. mushrooms	1 cup mushrooms
125g./4oz. cabbage, blanched for 1 minute and drained	⅔ cup cabbage, blanched for 1 minute and drained
125g./4oz. bean sprouts, blanched for 1 minute and drained	½ cup bean sprouts, blanched for 1 minute and drained
125g./4oz. shrimps, shelled	⅔ cup peeled shrimp
1½ Tbs. soya sauce	1½ Tbs. soy sauce
1 tsp. sugar	1 tsp. sugar
300ml./10fl.oz. water	1¼ cups water
1 chicken stock cube, crumbled	1 chicken bouillon cube, crumbled
600ml./1 pint chicken or beef stock	2½ cups chicken or beef stock

Cook the noodles or spaghetti in boiling, salted water until they are just tender. Drain and keep hot.

Heat the oil in a large frying-pan. When it is hot, add the onion, ginger and pork and fry for 2 minutes, stirring constantly. Add the butter, and, when it has melted, stir in the mushrooms, cabbage, bean sprouts and shrimps. Stir-fry for 1½ minutes. Stir in the soy sauce and sugar and stir-fry for 1½ minutes. Remove from the heat and keep warm.

Bring the water to the boil in a large saucepan. Reduce the heat to moderate and add the stock (bouillon) cube, stirring until it has dissolved. Add half the pork mixture to the stock and bring the mixture to the boil. Stir in the noodles or spaghetti and simmer for 3 minutes.

Meanwhile, return the frying-pan to high heat and stir-fry the remaining pork mixture for 1 minute to reheat it.

Divide the noodle mixture between four or six serving bowls. Spoon over the pork mixture and serve at once.
Serves 4-6
Preparation and cooking time: 30 minutes

Cha Chiang Mein

(Noodles in Meat Sauce with Shredded Vegetables)

Traditionally, in this dish, each diner is given a bowl of noodles to which he is expected to add as much meat sauce and shredded vegetables as he likes.

Metric/Imperial	American
½kg./1lb. egg noodles or spaghetti	1lb. egg noodles or spaghetti
3 Tbs. vegetable oil	3 Tbs. vegetable oil
1 medium onion, thinly sliced	1 medium onion, thinly sliced

Metric/Imperial	American
2 garlic cloves, crushed	2 garlic cloves, crushed
4cm./1½in. piece of fresh root ginger, peeled and chopped or ½ tsp. ground ginger	1½in. piece of fresh green ginger, peeled and chopped or ½ tsp. ground ginger
350g./12oz. lean pork or beef, minced	12oz. lean pork or beef, ground
1 Tbs. sesame oil	1 Tbs. sesame oil
5 Tbs. soya sauce	5 Tbs. soy sauce
2 Tbs. rice wine or dry sherry	2 Tbs. rice wine or dry sherry
1 Tbs. sugar	1 Tbs. sugar
1 Tbs. cornflour, mixed to a paste with 4 Tbs. chicken stock	1 Tbs. cornstarch, mixed to a paste with 4 Tbs. chicken stock
SHREDDED VEGETABLES	SHREDDED VEGETABLES
75-125g./3-4oz. (or a heaped side-dishful) shredded cabbage, blanched for 4 minutes and drained	½-⅔ cup (or a heaped side-dishful) shredded cabbage, blanched for 4 minutes and drained
75-125g./3-4oz. (or a heaped side-dishful) shredded carrots, blanched for 4 minutes and drained	½-⅔ cup (or a heaped side-dishful) shredded carrots, blanched for 4 minutes and drained
75-125g./3-4oz. (or a heaped side-dishful) bean sprouts, blanched for 1 minute and drained	⅓-½ cup (or a heaped side-dishful) bean sprouts, blanched for 1 minute and drained
75-125g./3-4oz. (or a heaped side-dishful) shredded cucumber	½-⅔ cup (or a heaped side-dishful) shredded cucumber
50-75g./2-3oz. (or a saucerful) shredded radishes	¼-⅓ cup (or a saucerful) shredded radishes
25-50g./1-2oz. (or a saucerful) mixed pickle	2 Tbs.-¼ cup (or a saucerful) mixed pickle
25-50g./1-2oz. (or a saucerful) chutney	2 Tbs.-¼ cup (or a saucerful) chutney

Arrange the shredded vegetables, pickle and chutney on individual serving dishes and set aside.

Cook the noodles or spaghetti in boiling, salted water until they are just tender. Drain and keep hot.

Heat the oil in a large frying-pan. When it is hot add the onion, garlic and ginger and fry for 1½ minutes, stirring constantly. Add the pork or beef and stir-fry until it loses its pinkness. Stir in the sesame oil, soy sauce, wine or sherry and sugar and stir-fry for a further 3 minutes. Add the cornflour (cornstarch) mixture and cook, stirring constantly, until the sauce thickens and becomes translucent. Remove from the heat and transfer the sauce to a warmed serving bowl.

Divide the noodles or spaghetti between four serving bowls. Serve at once, with the meat sauce and accompaniments.

Serves 4
Preparation and cooking time: 45 minutes

Shrimp Chow Mein

Metric/Imperial	American
vegetable oil for deep-frying	vegetable oil for deep-frying
225g./8oz. thin egg noodles, cooked and drained	8oz. thin egg noodles, cooked and drained
8 dried mushrooms, soaked in cold water for 30 minutes, drained and sliced	8 dried mushrooms, soaked in cold water for 30 minutes, drained and sliced
2 Tbs. peanut oil	2 Tbs. peanut oil
2 carrots, thinly sliced on the diagonal	2 carrots, thinly sliced on the diagonal

An unusual, exotic recipe, Prawn (Shrimp) Chow Mein is usually served on a crisp layer of deep-fried noodles.

Metric/Imperial	American
225g./8oz. bean sprouts	1 cup bean sprouts
225g./8oz. water chestnuts, sliced	1 cup water chestnuts, sliced
125ml./4fl.oz. chicken stock	½ cup chicken stock
1 Tbs. rice wine or dry sherry	1 Tbs. rice wine or dry sherry
1 Tbs. soya sauce	1 Tbs. soy sauce
350g./12oz. shrimps, shelled	12oz. shrimp, peeled

Fill a large saucepan one-third full with oil and heat until it is very hot. Carefully lower the noodles into the oil and fry for 3 to 4 minutes, or until they are golden brown. Remove from the oil and drain on kitchen towels. Arrange the noodles in a serving dish and keep hot while you prepare the shrimp mixture.

Heat the oil in a large frying-pan. When it is hot, add the mushrooms, carrots, bean sprouts and water chestnuts and fry for 5 minutes, stirring frequently. Pour in the stock and wine or sherry and bring to the boil. Reduce the heat to low and stir in the soy sauce and shrimps. Cover and simmer for 3 to 5 minutes, or until the shrimps are heated through.

Remove from the heat. Make a well in the centre of the noodles and spoon in the shrimp mixture. Serve at once.
Serves 3-4
Preparation and cooking time: 1 hour

Mee Feng Yu Pien

(Sliced Fish in Ground Rice)

Metric/Imperial	American
700g./1½lb. sole fillets, skinned	1½ lb. sole fillets, skinned
4cm./1½in. piece of fresh root ginger, peeled and chopped	1½in. piece of fresh green ginger, peeled and chopped
2 Tbs. soya sauce	2 Tbs. soy sauce
1½ tsp. chilli sauce	1½ tsp. chilli sauce
150g./5oz. coarsely ground rice	1¼ cups coarsely ground rice
SAUCE	SAUCE
2½ Tbs. soya sauce	2½ Tbs. soy sauce
1½ Tbs. tomato purée	1½ Tbs. tomato paste
1 tsp. chilli sauce	1 tsp. chilli sauce
1 Tbs. rice wine or dry sherry	1 Tbs. rice wine or dry sherry
½ Tbs. hoisin sauce	½ Tbs. hoisin sauce
1 Tbs. wine vinegar	1 Tbs. wine vinegar

Cut the sole fillets into thin pieces about 5cm./2in. by 4cm./1½in. Combine the ginger, soy sauce and chilli sauce together and rub the mixture into the sole pieces so that they are evenly coated on both sides. Set aside to marinate for 1 hour.

Heat a large dry frying-pan over moderate heat. Add the rice to the pan and fry, stirring constantly, until it begins to turn brown. Arrange the sole pieces in the pan so that they become thickly coated with the rice. Remove from the heat.

Transfer the sole pieces to a heatproof dish and put the dish into a steamer. Cover and steam over moderate heat for 10 to 12 minutes, or until the fish is cooked through and flakes easily. Remove the dish from the steamer and keep hot.

To make the sauce, combine all the ingredients in a saucepan and cook over moderate heat for 2 minutes, or until it is heated through.

Serve the fish at once, accompanied by the sauce.
Serves 4-6
Preparation and cooking time: 1½ hours

Brown Rice has only the husk removed and, as a result, retains most of its goodness. As it is so nutritious, it is ideal for many vegetarian dishes.

Avorio Rice, a thick, short-grain, absorbent Italian rice, requires slow cooking and is especially suitable for risottos.

Basmati Rice, a long-grain rice, is very popular in Indian cooking. Use as an accompaniment to curries or in rice dishes such as pilaff or biryani.

Rice Paper can be deep-fried and is often used in Chinese cooking as a wrapping for savoury parcels. It is edible.

Wild Rice is technically not a rice, but a water grass grown only in North America. It is expensive but makes an exotic delicacy for special occasions.

Round-Grain Rice is useful in Oriental cooking as it is similar in texture to the rice used in Japanese *gohan* dishes. It is also suitable for puddings.

Rice Flour, very finely ground rice, is used as an ingredient in baking, such as cakes and biscuits (cookies). It is also an effective thickener.

Ground Rice can be made at home by putting long-grain rice through a grinder. It is a basic ingredient in many sweet and savoury recipes.

Natural Rice is unrefined and is commonly used in wholefood cooking as, through not being milled, it keeps its protein, minerals and vitamins.

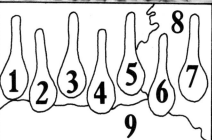

1 Brown Rice 2 Avorio Rice 3 Basmati Rice 4 Wild Rice 5 Round-Grain Rice 6 Ground Rice 7 Rice Flour 8 Natural Rice 9 Rice Paper, similar in name only, comes from an Asiatic tree.

Pork Fried Rice

Metric/Imperial	American
3 Tbs. vegetable oil	3 Tbs. vegetable oil
1 small onion, thinly sliced	1 small onion, thinly sliced
4cm./1½in. piece of fresh root ginger, peeled and chopped	1½in. piece of fresh green ginger, peeled and chopped
2 celery stalks, thinly sliced on the diagonal	2 celery stalks, thinly sliced on the diagonal
2 small carrots, thinly sliced on the diagonal	2 small carrots, thinly sliced on the diagonal
½ small Chinese or savoy cabbage, shredded	½ small Chinese or savoy cabbage, shredded
225g./8oz. cooked roast pork, cut into strips	1 cup cooked roast pork strips
½ tsp. black pepper	½ tsp. black pepper
2 Tbs. soya sauce	2 Tbs. soy sauce
225g./8oz. cooked long-grain rice	3 cups cooked long-grain rice
2 eggs, lightly beaten	2 eggs, lightly beaten
½ tsp. salt	½ tsp. salt

Heat 2 tablespoons of oil in a large frying-pan. When it is hot, add the onion and ginger. Stir-fry for 2 minutes. Add the celery and carrots and fry for 5 minutes, stirring constantly. Stir in the cabbage, pork, pepper, soy sauce and rice and cook, stirring constantly, for a further 2 to 3 minutes, or until the mixture has heated through. Remove from the heat and keep hot while you make the garnish.

Heat the remaining oil in a small frying-pan. When it is hot, add the beaten eggs and salt and cook for 2 minutes. When the bottom has set, turn the omelet over and cook for a further 2 to 3 minutes, or until it is completely set. Remove from the pan and cut the omelet into strips about 2.5cm /1in. by ½cm./¼in.

Transfer the rice mixture to a warmed serving dish. Garnish with the omelet strips and serve at once.

Serves 4

Preparation and cooking time: 35 minutes

An assortment of vegetables and long-grain rice combine to make Pork Fried Rice a popular and colourful dish.

Chinese Fried Rice

Metric/Imperial	American
225g./8oz. long-grain rice, washed, soaked in cold water for 30 minutes and drained	1⅓ cups long-grain rice, washed, soaked in cold water for 30 minutes and drained
salt	salt
1 Tbs. peanut oil	1 Tbs. peanut oil
2 tsp. soya sauce	2 tsp. soy sauce

Cook the rice in boiling, salted water for 11 minutes, then remove from the heat and drain. Set aside to cool.

Heat the oil in a large frying-pan. When it is hot, add the rice and cook for 1 minute, stirring constantly to coat the rice with the oil. Stir in half the soy sauce and fry, stirring frequently, until the rice is lightly browned. Remove from the heat and stir in the remaining soy sauce. Transfer to a warmed serving dish and serve at once.

Serves 4
Preparation and cooking time: 1½ hours

Chow Fan

(Fried Rice)

Metric/Imperial	American
225g./8oz. long-grain rice, soaked in cold water for 30 minutes and drained	1⅓ cups long-grain rice, soaked in cold water for 30 minutes and drained
450ml./15fl.oz. water	2 cups water
1½ tsp. salt	1½ tsp. salt
2 Tbs. vegetable oil	2 Tbs. vegetable oil
2 medium onions, chopped	2 medium onions, chopped
225g./8oz. cooked ham, finely chopped	1⅔ cups finely chopped cooked ham
2 Tbs. petits pois	2 Tbs. petits pois
2 medium tomatoes, blanched, peeled and quartered	2 medium tomatoes, blanched, peeled and quartered
225g./8oz. frozen shrimps, shelled	1⅓ cups frozen peeled shrimp
1 Tbs. soya sauce	1 Tbs. soy sauce
1 egg, lightly beaten	1 egg, lightly beaten

Put the rice into a saucepan and pour over the water and 1 teaspoon of salt. Bring to the boil, reduce the heat to low and cover the pan. Simmer for 15 to 20 minutes, or until the rice is cooked and tender, and the liquid has been absorbed. Remove from the heat.

Heat the oil in a large saucepan. When it is hot, add the onions and fry, stirring occasionally, until they are soft. Stir in the ham, petits pois, tomatoes, shrimps and remaining salt and cook for 1 minute. Stir in the cooked rice and cook for 2 minutes, stirring constantly. Add the remaining ingredients and stir-fry for 2 minutes.

Transfer the mixture to a warmed serving bowl and serve at once.

Serves 4-6
Preparation and cooking time: 1¼ hours

Chinese omelet, Foo Yung, is often used as a garnish and here it is used as a decoration for Special Fried Rice with Foo Yung.

Special Fried Rice with Foo Yung

Metric/Imperial	American
225g./8oz. long-grain rice, soaked in cold water for 30 minutes and drained	1⅓ cups long-grain rice, soaked in cold water for 30 minutes and drained
600ml./1 pint cold water	2½ cups cold water
1 tsp. salt	1 tsp. salt
5 Tbs. peanut oil	5 Tbs. peanut oil
2 medium onions, finely chopped	2 medium onions, finely chopped
75g./3oz. button mushrooms, sliced	¾ cup sliced button mushrooms

4 Tbs. cooked peas	4 Tbs. cooked peas
250g./8oz. peeled shrimps	1⅓ cups peeled shrimp
50g./2oz. cooked ham, shredded	¼ cup shredded cooked ham
FOO YUNG	FOO YUNG
2 large eggs	2 large eggs
1 Tbs. soya sauce	1 Tbs. soy sauce
salt and pepper to taste	salt and pepper to taste
15g./½oz. butter	1 Tbs. butter

Put the rice into a saucepan and pour over the water and salt. Bring to the boil, reduce the heat to low and cover the pan. Simmer for 15 to 20 minutes, or until the rice is cooked and tender and the liquid has been absorbed. Remove from the heat and set aside until cold.

Heat the oil in a large frying-pan. When it is very hot, add the onions, mushrooms, peas and shrimps and stir-fry for 1 minute. Add the ham and stir-fry for 30 seconds. Stir in the cold rice and cook for a further 2 minutes.

Transfer the rice to a warmed ovenproof serving dish and keep warm in the oven while you cook the foo yung.

Beat the eggs, soy sauce and seasoning together until they are frothy. Heat the butter in a 25cm./10in. omelet pan until it stops foaming. Add the egg mixture and stir twice. Leave to set. Preheat the grill (broiler) to moderate.

When the bottom of the foo yung has set, transfer the pan to the grill (broiler) and leave for 1 minute, or until the top is set and browned.

Tip the foo yung on to a plate and cut into strips. Use to decorate the rice mixture and serve at once.

Serves 4-6
Preparation and cooking time: 2 hours

Crab and Ginger Foo Yung

Metric/Imperial	American
6 eggs	6 eggs
3 Tbs. sesame oil	3 Tbs. sesame oil
125g./4oz. crabmeat, shell and cartilage removed and flaked	4 oz. crabmeat, shell and cartilage removed and flaked
4cm./1½in. piece of fresh root ginger, peeled and finely chopped	1½in. piece of fresh green ginger, peeled and finely chopped
2 spring onions, finely chopped	2 scallions, finely chopped
1 Tbs. soya sauce	1 Tbs. soy sauce
1 Tbs. dry sherry	1 Tbs. dry sherry

Beat the eggs until they are frothy. Heat 1 tablespoon of the oil in a small, heavy-based frying-pan. When it is very hot, add the crabmeat, ginger, spring onions (scallions), soy sauce and sherry and stir-fry for 1 minute. Remove the pan from the heat and add the mixture to the eggs. Beat gently to mix.

Put the remaining oil in the frying-pan and return to the heat. When the oil is hot, pour in about a quarter of the egg mixture. Stir with a fork to distribute the mixture and cook for 1 minute. Place a plate over the pan and invert quickly so that the foo yung falls on to the plate. Slide the foo yung back into the pan and cook for a further 1 minute. Turn out in the same way as before and keep warm while you cook the remaining mixture in the same way.

Serves 4
Preparation and cooking time: 20 minutes

Egg Foo Yung

Metric/Imperial	American
4 eggs	4 eggs
1 Tbs. soya sauce	1 Tbs. soy sauce
salt and pepper to taste	salt and pepper to taste
25g./1oz. butter	2 Tbs. butter
1 spring onion, very finely chopped	1 scallion, very finely chopped
125g./4oz. bean sprouts	½ cup bean sprouts

Beat the eggs, soy sauce and seasoning together until the mixture is light and fluffy.

Melt the butter in a frying-pan. Add the spring onion (scallion) and bean sprouts and fry for 4 to 5 minutes, stirring occasionally. Pour in the egg mixture, stir with a fork and leave to set.

Preheat the grill (broiler) to high.

When the bottom of the foo yung has set, transfer the pan to the grill (broiler) and leave for 1 minute or until the top is set and lightly browned.

Serve at once, cut into wedges.

Serves 2-3

Preparation and cooking time: 15 minutes

Shrimp and Egg Foo Yung

Metric/Imperial	American
3 Tbs. vegetable oil	3 Tbs. vegetable oil
225g./8oz. shrimps, chopped	8oz. shelled shrimps, chopped
125g./4oz. mushrooms, sliced	⅔ cup mushrooms, sliced
125g./4oz. bean sprouts	½ cup bean sprouts
4 eggs, lightly beaten	4 eggs, lightly beaten
SAUCE	SAUCE
250ml./8fl.oz. chicken stock	1 cup chicken stock
2 tsp. soy sauce	2 tsp. soy sauce
¼ tsp. salt	¼ tsp. salt
1 Tbs. cornflour, mixed to a paste with 1 Tbs. water	1 Tbs. cornstarch, mixed to a paste with 1 Tbs. water

Heat 1 tablespoon of oil in a frying-pan. When it is hot, add the shrimps and stir-fry for 3 minutes. Remove from the heat and keep hot.

To make the sauce, combine all the ingredients in a small saucepan and bring to the boil, stirring constantly. Cook for 1 minute, stirring constantly, or until the sauce becomes translucent. Set aside.

Combine the mushrooms, bean sprouts, eggs and shrimps and beat together.

Return the frying-pan to the heat and add the remaining oil. When it is hot, add a quarter of the egg mixture and cook for 1 minute, or until the bottom is set and golden brown. Turn the omelet over and cook for a further 1 minute, or until it is just set. Cook the remaining egg mixture in the same way, to make three more omelets.

Return the saucepan to the heat and bring to the boil, stirring constantly. Remove from the heat and pour a little over the omelets. Serve at once, with the sauce.

Serves 4

Preparation and cooking time: 30 minutes

Wonton Dough

Wonton wrappers can be bought from oriental delicatessens, but it isn't very difficult to make your own, using this recipe. Roll out the dough very thinly, to not more than ⅛cm./ 1/16 in. thick, and cut into shapes as you require.

Metric/Imperial	American
450g./1lb. plain flour	4 cups all-purpose flour
2 tsp. salt	2 tsp. salt
2 eggs, lightly beaten with 75ml./3fl.oz. water	2 eggs, lightly beaten with ⅓ cup water

Sift the flour and salt into a bowl. Make a well in the centre and pour in the egg mixture. Using your fingers or a spatula, draw the flour into the liquid until it has all been incorporated and the dough comes away from the sides of the bowl.

Turn the dough out on to a lightly floured surface and knead for 10 minutes, or until it is smooth and elastic.

It is now ready to use.

Makes 450g/1 pound (4 cups)
Preparation time: 15 minutes

Shrimp Egg Foo Yung, a more exotic form of the basic Egg Foo Yung, makes an appetizing light meal.

MEAT

Hao Yiu Ngiu Jou Pien

(Quick-fried Beef with Oyster Sauce)

Metric/Imperial	American
700g./1½lb. lean fillet steak, cut into thin strips	1½lb. lean fillet steak, cut into thin strips
1½ tsp. salt	1½ tsp. salt
¼ tsp. white pepper	¼ tsp. white pepper
¼ tsp. ground ginger	¼ tsp. ground ginger
1 Tbs. cornflour	1 Tbs. cornstarch
1 Tbs. soya sauce	1 Tbs. soy sauce
2½ Tbs. oyster sauce	2½ Tbs. oyster sauce
1 tsp. sugar	1 tsp. sugar
2 Tbs. rice wine or dry sherry	2 Tbs. rice wine or dry sherry
75ml./3fl.oz. vegetable oil	⅓ cup vegetable oil
1 medium onion, thinly sliced	1 medium onion, thinly sliced
1 garlic clove, crushed	1 garlic clove, crushed

Rub the beef strips with salt, pepper, ginger and cornflour (cornstarch).

Combine the soy sauce, oyster sauce, sugar and rice wine or sherry in a bowl and set aside.

Heat the oil in a large frying-pan. When it is hot, add the onion and garlic and fry for 30 seconds, stirring constantly. Add the beef to the pan and fry for 2 minutes, stirring constantly. Pour off all but a thin film of oil from the pan.

Pour the reserved oyster sauce mixture over the beef and cook for a further 1½ minutes, stirring constantly. Remove from the heat and transfer the beef slices to a warmed serving dish. Pour over the sauce and serve at once.
Serves 4
Preparation and cooking time: 30 minutes

K'Ou Tse Ngiu Lan

(Leg of Beef in Fruit Sauce)

Metric/Imperial	American
2 Tbs. vegetable oil	2 Tbs. vegetable oil
1 medium onion, thinly sliced	1 medium onion, thinly sliced
2 garlic cloves, crushed	2 garlic cloves, crushed
2.5cm./1in. piece of fresh root ginger, peeled and chopped	1in. piece of fresh green ginger, peeled and chopped
1 x 1½kg./3lb. boned leg of beef, cubed	1 x 3lb. boned leg or shin of beef, cubed
juice of 1 lemon	juice of 1 lemon
juice of 2 oranges	juice of 2 oranges
4 Tbs. soya sauce	4 Tbs. soy sauce
300ml./10fl.oz. red wine	1¼ cups red wine
600ml./1 pint water	2½ cups water
1 tsp. black pepper	1 tsp. black pepper
1 tsp. salt	1 tsp. salt

Preheat the oven to cool 150°C (Gas Mark 2, 300°F).

Heat the oil in a large flameproof casserole. When it is hot, add the onion, garlic and ginger and stir-fry for 1 minute. Add the beef to the casserole and fry for 3 minutes, stirring and turning occasionally. Stir in all the remaining ingredients and bring to the boil, stirring occasionally.

Transfer the casserole to the oven and bake for 4 hours, stirring two or three times during the cooking period. Remove from the oven and serve at once.

Serves 8

Preparation and cooking time: 4½ hours

A side dish of crunchy bean sprouts complements K'Ou Tse Ngiu, a rich, fruity beef stew.

Stir-Fried Beef with Broccoli

Metric/Imperial	American
½kg./1lb. fillet of beef, thinly sliced across the grain into 7.5cm./3in. x 5cm./2in. pieces	1lb. fillet of beef, thinly sliced across the grain into 3in. x 2in. pieces
3 Tbs. soya sauce	3 Tbs. soy sauce
1 Tbs. rice wine or dry sherry	1 Tbs. rice wine or dry sherry
2.5cm./1in. piece of fresh root ginger, peeled and chopped	1in. piece of fresh green ginger, peeled and chopped
50ml./2fl.oz. vegetable oil	¼ cup vegetable oil
½kg./1lb. broccoli, broken into flowerets	1lb. broccoli, broken into flowerets
75ml./3fl.oz. beef stock	⅓ cup beef stock
15g./½oz. vegetable fat	1 Tbs. vegetable fat
2 tsp. cornflour, mixed to a paste with 4 Tbs. water	2 tsp. cornstarch, mixed to a paste with 4 Tbs. water

Put the beef strips in a shallow bowl. Combine the soy sauce, wine or sherry, ginger and 1 tablespoon of oil together, then pour over the strips, basting to coat them thoroughly. Set aside to marinate at room temperature for 10 minutes, stirring occasionally. Meanwhile, cut the broccoli into bite-sized pieces.

Heat the remaining oil in a large frying-pan. When it is hot, add the beef mixture and stir-fry for 1½ minutes. Using a slotted spoon, transfer the beef strips to a plate. Add the beef stock to the pan and bring to the boil, stirring constantly. Add the broccoli and fry for 1 minute, stirring constantly. Reduce the heat to very low, cover and simmer the mixture for 4 minutes. Using the slotted spoon, transfer the broccoli to a warmed serving dish. Keep hot while you finish off the meat.

Add the vegetable fat to the pan and melt it. Return the beef strips to the pan and stir-fry for 30 seconds. Add the cornflour (cornstarch) and stir-fry for 1 minute, or until the sauce becomes translucent. Remove from the heat.

Using the slotted spoon, transfer the beef strips over the broccoli, then pour over the sauce. Serve at once.

Serves 4
Preparation and cooking time: 35 minutes

Gingered Beef

Metric/Imperial	American
2 tsp. ground ginger	2 tsp. ground ginger
5 Tbs. soya sauce	5 Tbs. soy sauce
2 tsp. cornflour	2 tsp. cornstarch
½ tsp. sugar	½ tsp. sugar
700g./1½lb. rump steak, thinly sliced across the grain	1½lb. rump steak, thinly sliced across the grain
50ml./2fl.oz. vegetable oil	¼ cup vegetable oil
5cm./2in. piece of fresh root ginger, peeled and chopped	2in. piece of fresh green ginger, peeled and chopped
125g./4oz. bamboo shoots, cubed	½ cup cubed bamboo shoots
4 dried mushrooms, soaked in cold water for 30 minutes, drained and sliced	4 dried mushrooms, soaked in cold water for 30 minutes, drained and sliced

Combine the ground ginger, soy sauce, cornflour (cornstarch) and sugar together until they are well blended. Stir in the meat slices and baste them thoroughly. Set aside to marinate at room temperature for 1 hour, basting occasionally. Remove the meat from the marinade and pat dry with kitchen towels. Discard the marinade.

Heat the oil in a large frying-pan. When it is hot, add the ginger and fry for 3 minutes, stirring constantly. Stir in the meat, bamboo shoots and mushrooms and fry, stirring and turning occasionally, for 6 to 8 minutes, or until the meat is cooked through.

Transfer the mixture to a warmed serving dish and serve at once.

Serves 4-6
Preparation and cooking time: 1¾ hours

A quick and easy dish to make, Stir-Fried Beef with Broccoli, served with Fried Rice, is filling and tasty.

Quick Fried Beef with 'Triple Shreds'

Quick Fried Beef with 'Triple Shreds' is ideal for practising the Chinese method of eating with chopsticks.

Metric/Imperial	American
½kg./1lb. fillet of beef, sliced across the grain, then cut into strips	1lb. fillet of beef, sliced across the grain, then cut into strips
3 Tbs. soya sauce	3 Tbs. soy sauce
1 Tbs. dry sherry	1 Tbs. dry sherry
1 tsp. sugar	1 tsp. sugar
salt and pepper to taste	salt and pepper to taste
3 Tbs. vegetable oil	3 Tbs. vegetable oil
2.5cm./1in. piece of fresh root ginger, peeled and thinly sliced	1in. piece of fresh green ginger, peeled and thinly sliced
1 large leek, white part only, sliced	1 large leek, white part only, sliced

| 1 onion, thinly sliced | 1 onion, thinly sliced |
| 25g./1oz. butter | 2 Tbs. butter |

Put the beef strips in a shallow bowl. Combine the soy sauce, sherry, sugar and salt and pepper and pour over the strips, rubbing the mixture into the meat with your fingers. Set aside for 10 minutes.

Heat the oil in a frying-pan. When the oil is very hot, add the ginger, leek and onion and stir-fry for 1 minute over moderately high heat.

Transfer to a warmed plate and set aside.

Add the butter to the pan and melt it over moderately high heat. Add the beef strips and stir-fry for 1 minute. Return the vegetables to the pan and stir-fry for a further 1 minute.

Transfer the mixture to a warmed dish and serve.

Serves 4

Preparation and cooking time: 20 minutes

Braised Beef in Soy Sauce

Metric/Imperial	American
300ml./10fl.oz. water	1¼ cups water
3 Tbs. soya sauce	3 Tbs. soy sauce
5 Tbs. rice wine or dry sherry	5 Tbs. rice wine or dry sherry
1 Tbs. sugar	1 Tbs. sugar
1 Tbs. salt	1 Tbs. salt
3 Tbs. vegetable oil	3 Tbs. vegetable oil
1kg./2lb. braising steak, cubed	2lb. chuck steak, cubed

Combine the water, soy sauce, wine or sherry, sugar and salt and set aside.

Heat half the oil in a large frying-pan for 30 seconds. Add half the meat to the pan and fry for 2 minutes, stirring and turning constantly. Transfer the cubes to a plate. Add the remaining oil and remaining beef cubes to the pan and fry until they are lightly browned. Return the first batch of cubes to the pan and stir in the soy sauce mixture. Bring to the boil. Cover, reduce the heat to low and simmer for 1½ to 2 hours, stirring occasionally, or until the beef is cooked through and tender.

Transfer the mixture to a warmed serving dish and serve at once.

Serves 6
Preparation and cooking time: 2¼ hours

Hung Shao Ngiu Jou

(Red-Cooked Beef with Star Anise)

Metric/Imperial	American
75ml./3fl.oz. vegetable oil	⅓ cup vegetable oil
1 x 1½-2kg./3-4lb. leg or shin of beef, cubed	1 x 3-4lb. leg or shin of beef, cubed
3 pieces star anise	3 pieces star anise
150ml./5fl.oz. water	⅔ cup water
½ beef stock cube, crumbled	½ beef bouillon cube, crumbled
7 Tbs. soya sauce	7 Tbs. soy sauce
2.5cm./1in. piece of fresh root ginger, peeled and finely chopped	1in. piece of fresh green ginger, peeled and finely chopped
2 tsp. sugar	2 tsp. sugar
150ml./5fl.oz. red wine	⅔ cup red wine

Preheat the oven to cool 150°C (Gas Mark 2, 300°F).

Heat the oil in a flameproof casserole. When it is hot, add the beef cubes and fry until they are evenly browned. Remove from the heat and pour off all the excess oil.

Stir in the star anise, water, stock (bouillon) cube and 4 tablespoons of soy sauce. Return the casserole to the heat and bring to the boil, stirring constantly. Transfer to the oven and cook for 1 hour, turning the meat once.

Remove from the oven and stir in the remaining ingredients. Return to the oven and cook for a further 2 hours, turning the meat every 30 minutes.

Remove from the oven and serve at once.

Serves 8-10
Preparation and cooking time: 3½ hours

Stir-Fried Beef with Mixed Vegetables and Peanuts

Metric/Imperial	American
½kg./1lb. rump steak, thinly sliced across the grain, then cut into strips	1lb. rump steak, thinly sliced across the grain, then cut into strips
salt and pepper to taste	salt and pepper to taste
1 tsp. ground ginger	1 tsp. ground ginger
1 Tbs. cornflour	1 Tbs. cornstarch
50ml./2fl.oz. peanut oil	¼ cup peanut oil
5cm./2in. piece of fresh root ginger, peeled and chopped	2in. piece of fresh green ginger, peeled and chopped
175g./6oz. bean sprouts	¾ cup bean sprouts
2 spring onions, chopped	2 scallions, chopped
3 Tbs. unsalted peanuts	3 Tbs. unsalted peanuts
2 Tbs. soya sauce	2 Tbs. soy sauce
1 tsp. wine vinegar	1 tsp. wine vinegar
1 tsp. brown sugar	1 tsp. brown sugar

Rub the beef strips with the salt, pepper, ginger and cornflour (cornstarch).

Heat the oil in a large, deep frying-pan. When it is hot, add the root (green) ginger and fry for 1 minute, stirring constantly.

Add the beef and stir-fry for 2 minutes. Stir in the vegetables and peanuts and fry for 2 minutes, stirring constantly. Add the remaining ingredients and stir-fry for a further 1½ minutes.

Transfer the mixture to a warmed serving dish and serve at once.

Serves 4
Preparation and cooking time: 30 minutes

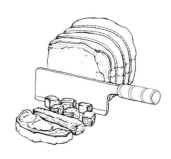

Sweet and Sour Beef

Metric/Imperial	American
2 Tbs. cornflour	2 Tbs. cornstarch
1 Tbs. soya sauce	1 Tbs. soy sauce
300ml./10fl.oz. beef stock	1¼ cups beef stock
2 Tbs. tomato purée	2 Tbs. tomato paste
2 Tbs. red wine vinegar	2 Tbs. red wine vinegar
2 tsp. clear honey	2 tsp. clear honey
4 Tbs. peanut oil	4 Tbs. peanut oil
2 large red peppers, pith and seeds removed and cut into small pieces	2 large red peppers, pith and seeds removed and cut into small pieces
1 large onion, finely chopped	1 large onion, finely chopped
1 garlic clove, crushed	1 garlic clove, crushed
4cm./1½in. piece of fresh root ginger, peeled and finely chopped	1½in. piece of fresh green ginger, peeled and finely chopped
700g./1½lb. rump of beef, cut into 5cm./2in. slivers	1½lb. rump of beef, cut into 2in. slivers

Accompanied by Chinese
Fried Rice and Chinese
Roast Pork, Ching-chiao-
ch'ao niu jou is a delicious
mixture of rump steak and
beansprouts, tomatoes and
green peppers.

Combine the cornflour (cornstarch), soy sauce, beef stock, tomato purée (paste), vinegar and honey in a small bowl, beating until they are well blended. Set aside.

Heat half the oil in a large frying-pan. When it is very hot, add the red peppers, onion, garlic and ginger and stir-fry for 2 minutes. Using a slotted spoon, transfer the vegetable mixture to a plate.

Add the remaining oil to the frying-pan. When it is very hot, add the beef strips and stir-fry for 3 minutes, or until they are evenly browned.

Stir in the reserved peppers, onion, ginger and garlic mixture until it is thoroughly blended.

Pour the cornflour (cornstarch) and stock mixture into the pan and bring to the boil, stirring constantly. Cook the mixture over moderate heat until the sauce thickens and becomes translucent.

Transfer the mixture to a warmed serving dish and serve at once.

Serves 4-6
Preparation and cooking time: 25 minutes

Ching-Chiao-Chao Niu Jou

(Steak with Pepper)

Metric/Imperial	American
½kg./1lb. rump steak, cut 2.5cm./1in. thick	1lb. rump steak, cut 1in. thick
4 Tbs. peanut oil	4 Tbs. peanut oil
2 garlic cloves, crushed	2 garlic cloves, crushed
salt and pepper	salt and pepper
4 Tbs. soya sauce	4 Tbs. soy sauce
2 tsp. sugar	2 tsp. sugar
225g./8oz. bean sprouts	1 cup bean sprouts
2 tomatoes, blanched, peeled and quartered	2 tomatoes, blanched, peeled and quartered
2 green peppers, pith and seeds removed, and coarsely diced	2 green peppers, pith and seeds removed, and coarsely diced
½ Tbs. cornflour, mixed to a paste with 2 Tbs. cold water	½ Tbs. cornstarch mixed to a paste with 2 Tbs. cold water
4 spring onions, sliced	4 scallions, sliced

Cut the beef diagonally into short, thin strips.

Heat the oil in a heavy frying-pan. When it is hot, mix in the garlic and salt and pepper to taste. Add the beef and stir-fry for 3 to 4 minutes or until it is golden brown.

Increase the heat to high. Stir in the soy sauce and sugar, cover and cook for 5 minutes.

Uncover and stir in the bean sprouts, tomatoes and peppers. Re-cover and cook for 5 minutes.

Stir in the cornflour (cornstarch) mixture until the mixture thickens and becomes translucent.

Transfer to a warmed serving dish and sprinkle over the spring onions (scallions).

Serves 4
Preparation and cooking time: 25 minutes

Sweet and Sour Liver

Metric/Imperial	American
700g./1½lb. lambs' liver, cut into 7.5cm./3in. by 5cm./2in. pieces	1½lb. lambs' liver, cut into 3in. by 2in. pieces
vegetable oil for deep-frying	vegetable oil for deep-frying
MARINADE	MARINADE
5 Tbs. soya sauce	5 Tbs. soy sauce
2 Tbs. rice wine or dry sherry	2 Tbs. rice wine or dry sherry
2 tsp. sugar	2 tsp. sugar
SAUCE	SAUCE
4 Tbs. wine vinegar	4 Tbs. wine vinegar
3 Tbs. sugar	3 Tbs. sugar
3 Tbs. orange juice	3 Tbs. orange juice
1 Tbs. tomato purée	1 Tbs. tomato paste
1½ Tbs. soya sauce	1½ Tbs. soy sauce
1½ Tbs. rice wine or dry sherry	1½ Tbs. rice wine or dry sherry
1 Tbs. cornflour, mixed to a paste with 5 Tbs. water	1 Tbs. cornstarch, mixed to a paste with 5 Tbs. water

Combine all the marinade ingredients in a large bowl and add the liver pieces. Baste well, then set aside at room temperature for 3 hours, basting occasionally. Remove the liver from the marinade and pat dry with kitchen towels. Discard the marinade.

Fill a large saucepan one-third full with oil and heat until it is very hot. Carefully lower the liver strips into the oil, a few at a time, and fry for 1 minute, or until they are browned and crisp. Remove the liver from the oil and drain on kitchen towels.

Combine all the sauce ingredients in a saucepan and bring to the boil, stirring constantly. Add the liver pieces to the sauce and cook, stirring constantly, until the sauce thickens and becomes translucent. Remove from the heat and transfer the mixture to a warmed serving dish. Serve at once.

Serves 4
Preparation and cooking time: 3½ hours

Run Tsa Chin Kan

(Plain Deep-Fried Liver and Kidneys)

Metric/Imperial	American
350g./12oz. lambs' liver	12oz. lambs' liver
350g./12oz. lambs' kidneys, trimmed	12oz. lambs' kidneys, trimmed
5 Tbs. soya sauce	5 Tbs. soy sauce
2 Tbs. rice wine or dry sherry	2 Tbs. rice wine or dry sherry
2 tsp. sugar	2 tsp. sugar
vegetable oil for deep-frying	vegetable oil for deep-frying
DIP	DIP
1 Tbs. black pepper	1 Tbs. black pepper
1 Tbs. salt	1 Tbs. salt

Slice the liver and kidneys thinly then cut the slices into uniform strips, about 4cm./1½in. by 2.5cm./1in. Put the liver strips in one bowl and the kidney strips in another.

Combine the soy sauce, wine or sherry and sugar until they are well blended. Pour equal amounts over the liver and kidneys and toss gently until the strips are thoroughly coated. Set aside to marinate at room temperature for 3 hours, basting occasionally.

Fill a large saucepan one-third full with oil and heat until it is hot. Carefully lower the liver strips into the oil and fry for 1 minute, or until they are browned and crisp. Remove from the oil and drain on kitchen towels. Keep hot while you fry the kidney strips in the same way.

To make the dip, fry the salt and pepper in a small frying-pan over moderately low heat for 4 minutes, stirring constantly. Remove from the heat and transfer the mixture to a small bowl. Serve the liver and kidney strips at once, with the dip.

Serves 4
Preparation and cooking time: 3½ hours

Marinated and deep-fried, Run Tsa Chin Kan is an unusual recipe for succulent liver and kidneys.

Shao k'o Yang Jou

(Steamed Lamb)

Metric/Imperial	American
1 x 1½kg./3lb. leg of lamb	1 x 3lb. leg of lamb
1 tsp. crushed black peppercorns	1 tsp. crushed black peppercorns
5cm./2in. piece of fresh root ginger, peeled and finely chopped or grated	2in. piece of fresh green ginger, peeled and finely chopped or grated
125g./4oz. mixed sweet pickle	½ cup mixed sweet pickle
75ml./3fl.oz. soya sauce	⅓ cup soy sauce
150ml./5fl.oz. dry sherry	⅔ cup dry sherry
2 onions, thinly sliced	2 onions, thinly sliced
1 tsp. butter	1 tsp. butter

Half-fill a saucepan with water and bring to the boil. Add the lamb, cover and boil for 4 minutes over moderately high heat.

Remove the pan from the heat and drain the lamb. Put the lamb on a chopping board and cut it, including the skin, into cubes. Arrange the cubes, skin side down, on the bottom of a heatproof basin. Sprinkle over the peppercorns and ginger and spoon over the pickle.

Combine the soy sauce and sherry and pour over the lamb. Arrange the onions on top. Cover tightly with a greased circle of greaseproof or waxed paper and foil about 10cm./4in. wider than the rim of the basin and tie with string.

Put the basin in a large saucepan and pour in enough boiling water to come about two-thirds of the way up the basin. Cover and place over low heat. Steam for 2½ hours, adding more boiling water if necessary.

When the lamb has finished steaming, lift the basin out of the water and remove the paper and foil circles. Transfer the mixture to a warmed dish and serve.
Serves 6
Preparation and cooking time: 2¾ hours

Crispy Roast Pork

Metric/Imperial	American
1 x 1½kg./3lb. belly of pork	1 x 3lb. belly or bacon of pork
1½ Tbs. salt	1½ Tbs. salt
1 tsp. 5-spice powder	1 tsp. 5-spice powder
1½ Tbs. cornflour, mixed to a paste with 1 egg white	1½ Tbs. cornstarch, mixed to a paste with 1 egg white
SAUCE	SAUCE
4 Tbs. soya sauce	4 Tbs. soy sauce
4 Tbs. tomato ketchup	4 Tbs. tomato ketchup

Rub the pork all over with the salt and spice powder. Set aside at room temperature for 8 hours or overnight.

Preheat the oven to fairly hot 190°C (Gas Mark 5, 375°F).

Quickly dip the pork in a saucepan half-filled with boiling water—the meat should be in the water for only a second or two. Dry with kitchen towels, then rub all over with the cornflour (cornstarch) mixture.

Place the pork on a rack in a roasting pan and put in the oven. Roast for 1¼ hours, or until it is completely cooked through.

Transfer the pork to a carving board and cut, through the skin, into ½cm./¼in. thick slices (each one should have a little skin attached to it).

Combine the soy sauce and ketchup, then serve with the pork.

Serves 4
Preparation and cooking time: 9½ hours

Crispy Roast Pork (left) has a crunchy outer layer and juicy tender centre. Steamed Lamb (right) is succulent and spicy.

Jou Si Chow Ching Ts'Ai

(Shredded Pork Stir-fried with Spring Greens)

Metric/Imperial	American
350g./12oz. lean pork, cut into strips	12oz. lean pork, cut into thin strips
½ tsp. salt	½ tsp. salt
¼ tsp. black pepper	¼ tsp. black pepper
2 tsp. cornflour	2 tsp. cornstarch
3 Tbs. vegetable oil	3 Tbs. vegetable oil
½kg./1lb. spring greens or cabbage, shredded	2½ cups shredded collards or cabbage
15g./½oz. vegetable fat	1 Tbs. vegetable fat
50ml./2fl.oz. beef stock	¼ cup beef stock
2 Tbs. soya sauce	2 Tbs. soy sauce
1 tsp. sugar	1 tsp. sugar
2 Tbs. dry sherry	2 Tbs. dry sherry

Put the pork strips on a plate and sprinkle them with the salt, pepper and cornflour (cornstarch), rubbing them into the flesh with your fingers.

Heat the oil in a large frying-pan. When it is hot, add the pork and fry for 3 minutes, stirring constantly. Push the pork strips to the side of the pan and add the greens (collards) or cabbage with the vegetable fat. Stir and mix the greens (collards) or cabbage with the remainder of the oil and the vegetable fat. Reduce the heat to moderate and stir in the stock, soy sauce and sugar. Fry the greens (collards) or cabbage for 3 minutes, turning constantly.

Stir the pork strips into the vegetables. Pour over the wine or sherry and fry for a further 1 minute, stirring constantly. Remove from the heat and transfer to a warmed serving dish. Serve at once.

Serves 4
Preparation and cooking time: 30 minutes

Cantonese Roast Pork

Metric/Imperial	American
1 x 1½kg./3lb. loin of pork, trimmed	1 x 3lb. loin of pork, trimmed
50ml./2fl.oz. soya sauce	¼ cup soy sauce
4 Tbs. soft brown sugar	4 Tbs. soft brown sugar
½ tsp. 5-spice powder	½ tsp. 5-spice powder
2 Tbs. dry sherry	2 Tbs. dry sherry
4cm./1½in. piece of fresh root ginger, peeled and sliced	1½in. piece of fresh green ginger, peeled and sliced

Cut the meat in half. Mix the soy sauce, sugar, five-spice powder, sherry and ginger together in a large shallow dish. Put in the pork and set aside to marinate at room temperature for 4 hours, basting frequently.

Preheat the oven to fairly hot 190°C (Gas Mark 5, 375°F). Put the pork and marinade in a roasting pan and roast for 10 minutes. Turn the meat over and increase the temperature to very hot 230°C (Gas Mark 8, 450°F). Continue to roast for about 40 minutes, turning and basting frequently during cooking. Test the meat for doneness with a skewer; the juice should run out clear.

Preheat the grill (broiler) to high.

Put the meat under the grill (broiler), and grill (broil) for 4 to 6 minutes, or until it is evenly browned.

Transfer to a serving dish, discarding the marinade, and slice before serving.
Serves 6
Preparation and cooking time: 5¼ hours

Yu Hsiang Jou si

(Quick-Fried Shredded Pork with 'Fish' Ingredients)

This dish comes from the province of Szechuan in Western China, where there is a tradition of cooking spicy dishes.

Metric/Imperial	American
½kg./1lb. pork fillet, thinly sliced and shredded	1lb. pork tenderloin, thinly sliced and shredded
4 Tbs. soya sauce	4 Tbs. soy sauce
2 tsp. cornflour, mixed to a paste with 2 Tbs. water	2 tsp. cornstarch, mixed to a paste with 2 Tbs. water
5 Tbs. vegetable oil	5 Tbs. vegetable oil
2 Tbs. fried salted black beans, soaked in cold water for 15 minutes, drained and chopped	2 Tbs. fried salted black beans, soaked in cold water for 15 minutes, drained and chopped
2 small dried chillis, finely chopped	2 small dried chillis, finely chopped
2 garlic cloves, crushed	2 garlic cloves, crushed
4 dried mushrooms, soaked in cold water for 30 minutes, drained and finely chopped	4 dried mushrooms, soaked in cold water for 30 minutes, drained and finely chopped
1 leek, white part only, finely chopped	1 leek, white part only, finely chopped
1 Tbs. 'wood ear' fungi	1 Tbs. 'wood ear' fungi
2.5cm./1in. piece of fresh root ginger, peeled and finely chopped	1in. piece of fresh green ginger, peeled and finely chopped
75g./3oz. bamboo shoots, finely chopped	⅓ cup finely chopped bamboo shoots
2 tsp. sesame oil	2 tsp. sesame oil
1½ Tbs. wine vinegar	1½ Tbs. wine vinegar
2 Tbs. dry sherry	2 Tbs. dry sherry
1½ tsp. sugar	1½ tsp. sugar

Combine the pork and 2 tablespoons of soy sauce. Work the sauce into the meat with your fingers. Add the cornflour (cornstarch) mixture and stir to blend. Set aside for 10 minutes.

Heat 3 tablespoons of oil in a deep frying-pan. When it is hot, add the pork mixture, spreading it out over the bottom of the pan. Stir-fry for 1 minute. Transfer the pork to a plate.

Add the remaining oil to the pan. When it is hot, add the black beans and chillis and stir-fry for 10 seconds. Increase the heat to moderately high and add the garlic, mushrooms, leek, 'wood ear' fungi, ginger and bamboo shoots. Stir-fry for 3 minutes. Return the pork to the pan and stir in the sesame oil, remaining soy sauce, vinegar, sherry and sugar. Stir-fry for 1½ minutes, or until the mixture is heated through.

Transfer to a warmed dish and serve.
Serves 4
Preparation and cooking time: 30 minutes

Lou Jou

(Pork Simmered in Master Sauce)

Metric/Imperial	American
1 x 1½kg./3lb. leg of pork, boned and trimmed of excess fat	1 x 3lb. leg of pork, boned and trimmed of excess fat
SAUCE	SAUCE
600ml./1 pint soya sauce	2½ cups soy sauce
300ml./10fl.oz. rice wine or dry sherry	1¼ cups rice wine or dry sherry
150ml./5fl.oz. chicken stock	⅔ cup chicken stock
4 Tbs. soft brown sugar	4 Tbs. soft brown sugar
2 garlic cloves, crushed	2 garlic cloves, crushed
2.5cm./1in. piece of fresh root ginger, peeled and chopped	1in. piece of fresh green ginger, peeled and chopped
2 bouquets garnis	2 bouquets garnis

Put the pork in a large saucepan and just cover with water. Bring to the boil, reduce the heat to moderate and cook for 6 minutes. Remove from the heat, drain the pork and set aside. Discard the cooking liquid.

To prepare the sauce, combine all the ingredients together until they are thoroughly blended. Bring to the boil, stirring frequently. Reduce the heat to low and carefully arrange the pork in the sauce, immersing it completely. Simmer for 1½ hours, turning the pork every 30 minutes.

Remove from the heat and transfer the pork to a carving board. Cut the meat into thin slices and arrange the slices decoratively on a warmed serving dish. Strain the sauce into a sauceboat and pour a little over and around the meat. Serve at once, accompanied by the remaining sauce.

Serves 6
Preparation and cooking time: 2 hours

All the main ingredients must be shredded into very fine strips so essential to the texture of this well-flavoured dish of Pork with Bamboo Shoots.

Pork with Bamboo Shoots

Metric/Imperial	American
700g./1½lb. pork fillet, cut across the grain into thin strips	1½lb. pork tenderloin, cut across the grain into thin strips
75ml./3fl.oz. soya sauce	⅓ cup soy sauce
1 Tbs. rice wine or dry sherry	1 Tbs. rice wine or dry sherry
2 tsp. cornflour	2 tsp. cornstarch
150ml./5fl.oz. groundnut or peanut oil	⅔ cup groundnut or peanut oil
1 leek, thinly sliced crosswise on the diagonal	1 leek, thinly sliced crosswise on the diagonal
450g./1lb. bamboo shoots, thinly sliced on the diagonal	1lb. bamboo shoots, thinly sliced on the diagonal
2 tsp. sugar	2 tsp. sugar

Put the pork strips in a bowl. Combine 2 tablespoons of soy sauce, the rice wine or sherry and cornflour (cornstarch) until they are well blended, and pour over the pork. Toss the strips gently to coat them thoroughly. Set aside to marinate for 10 minutes, basting occasionally.

Heat a large frying-pan over high heat for 30 seconds. Add the oil and swirl it around the pan. Add the pork and leek and fry for 5 minutes, stirring constantly. Stir in the bamboo shoots. Stir in the remaining soy sauce and sugar, reduce the heat to low and simmer the mixture for 10 minutes, stirring frequently.

Transfer the mixture to a warmed serving bowl and serve at once.
Serves 4
Preparation and cooking time: 45 minutes

Hung Shao Chu Jo

(Red-Cooked Pork in Soy Sauce)

Metric/Imperial	American
1 x 2kg./4lb. belly of pork	1 x 4lb. belly or bacon of pork
75ml./3fl.oz. vegetable oil	⅓ cup vegetable oil
7 Tbs. soya sauce	7 Tbs. soy sauce
1 Tbs. sugar	1 Tbs. sugar
150ml./5fl.oz. chicken or beef stock	⅔ cup chicken or beef stock
150ml./5fl.oz. red wine	⅔ cup red wine

Preheat the oven to warm 170°C (Gas Mark 3, 325°F).

Cut the pork through the skin into 12 pieces. Heat the oil in a flameproof casserole. When it is hot, add the pork slices and fry until they are evenly browned. Remove from the heat and pour off excess oil. Add 4 tablespoons of the soy sauce, half the sugar and 75ml./3fl.oz. (⅓ cup) each of the stock and wine. Turn the meat in this sauce several times. Return to the heat and bring to the boil.

Transfer the casserole to the oven and roast for 1 hour, turning the meat once. Remove from the oven and add the remaining soy sauce, sugar, stock and wine. Turn the meat over several times. Return the casserole to the oven and reduce the oven temperature to cool 150°C (Gas Mark 2, 300°F). Roast for a further 1 hour, turning the meat once.

Remove from the oven and serve at once.
Serves 4-6
Preparation and cooking time: 2½ hours

Colourful Pork Balls with Ginger is served here with refreshing jasmine tea.

Shao Jou I

(Cantonese Roast Pork)

Metric/Imperial	American
1½kg./3lb. pork fillets, cut into strips about 15cm./6in. long by 4cm./1½in. thick	3lb. pork tenderloin, cut into strips about 6in. long by 1½in. thick
2 Tbs. vegetable oil	2 Tbs. vegetable oil
MARINADE	MARINADE
1 onion, very finely chopped	1 onion, very finely chopped
5 Tbs. soya sauce	5 Tbs. soy sauce
1 Tbs. sugar	1 Tbs. sugar
1 Tbs. dry sherry	1 Tbs. dry sherry
1½ tsp. ground ginger	1½ tsp. ground ginger
1 Tbs. hoisin sauce (optional)	1 Tbs. hoisin sauce (optional)

To make the marinade, combine all the ingredients and beat well. Add the pork strips and baste to coat. Set aside at room temperature for 2 hours, basting occasionally.

Preheat the oven to moderate 180°C (Gas Mark 4, 350°F).

Remove the pork from the marinade and reserve the marinade. Put the strips in a roasting pan, large enough to take them in one layer, then baste with half the marinade and 1 tablespoon of oil. Put the pan into the oven and roast for 15 minutes. Remove from the oven and turn over the strips. Baste again with the marinade and remaining oil and return the pan to the oven. Roast the pork for a further 15 minutes.

Transfer the pork to a chopping board and cut the strips into thin slices before serving.

Serves 6-8

Preparation and cooking time: $2\frac{3}{4}$ hours

Pork Balls with Ginger

Metric/Imperial	American
700g./1½lb. minced pork	1½lb. ground pork
2.5cm./1in. piece of fresh root ginger, peeled and finely chopped	1in. piece of fresh green ginger, peeled and finely chopped
4 water chestnuts, drained and finely chopped	4 water chestnuts, drained and finely chopped
1 egg	1 egg
1 tsp. salt	1 tsp. salt
1 Tbs. soya sauce	1 Tbs. soy sauce
5 Tbs. cornflour	5 Tbs. cornstarch
1 tsp. sugar	1 tsp. sugar
8 dried mushrooms, soaked in cold water for 30 minutes	8 dried mushrooms, soaked in cold water for 30 minutes
1 bamboo shoot	1 bamboo shoot
1 red pepper, pith and seeds removed	1 red pepper, pith and seeds removed
1 green pepper, pith and seeds removed	1 green pepper, pith and seeds removed
8 Tbs. vegetable oil	8 Tbs. vegetable oil
SAUCE	SAUCE
5 Tbs. wine vinegar	5 Tbs. wine vinegar
5 Tbs. dry sherry	5 Tbs. dry sherry
2 Tbs. sugar	2 Tbs. sugar
2 Tbs. tomato purée	2 Tbs. tomato paste
salt and pepper to taste	salt and pepper to taste
1 tsp. cornflour, mixed to a paste with 2 Tbs. water	1 tsp. cornstarch, mixed to a paste with 2 Tbs. water

Combine the pork, ginger, water chestnuts, egg, salt, soy sauce, 2 tablespoons of cornflour (cornstarch) and sugar thoroughly. Shape into walnut-sized balls. Put the remaining cornflour (cornstarch) on a plate and roll the balls in it to coat them.

Remove the mushrooms from the water and squeeze dry. Remove and discard the stalks. Cut them, and the other vegetables, into equal-sized dice.

Heat 6 tablespoons of the oil in a frying-pan. When it is hot, reduce the heat to moderately low and add the pork balls. Fry, turning frequently, for 15 minutes or until they are cooked through and crisp. Transfer to a warmed dish. Cover and keep hot.

Combine all the sauce ingredients together, except the cornflour (cornstarch).

Pour off and discard the oil in the pan. Rinse and wipe the pan dry, and return it to high heat for 30 seconds. Add the remaining oil and reduce the heat to moderate. Heat for a further 30 seconds. Add the vegetables and stir-fry for 3 minutes. Pour over the sauce and stir-fry for a further 3 minutes. Stir in the cornflour (cornstarch) mixture and stir-fry until the sauce becomes translucent and thickens. Pour over the pork balls and serve.

Serves 4

Preparation and cooking time: 50 minutes

Shih-Tzu-Tou, pork balls served on a layer of Chinese cabbage, is a traditional dish.

Shih-Tzu-Tou

(Pork and Cabbage Casserole)

Metric/Imperial	American
½kg./1lb. lean pork, minced	1lb. lean pork, ground
1 shallot, finely chopped	1 shallot, finely chopped
4 water chestnuts, chopped	4 water chestnuts, chopped
2.5cm./1in. piece of fresh root ginger, peeled and chopped	1in. piece of fresh green ginger, peeled and chopped
1 Tbs. cornflour	1 Tbs. cornstarch
3 Tbs. light soya sauce	3 Tbs. light soy sauce
1 egg yolk	1 egg yolk
1 tsp. salt	1 tsp. salt
2 Tbs. vegetable oil	2 Tbs. vegetable oil
250ml./8fl.oz. chicken stock	1 cup chicken stock
1 Tbs. rice wine or dry sherry	1 Tbs. rice wine or dry sherry
½kg./1lb. Chinese cabbage, shredded	2½ cups shredded Chinese cabbage

Preheat the oven to moderate 180°C (Gas Mark 4, 350°F).

Put the pork, shallot, water chestnuts, ginger, cornflour (cornstarch), half the soy sauce, egg yolk and salt in a bowl. Mix and knead the mixture until it is well blended, then divide into four pieces. Roll each piece into a ball and set aside.

Heat the oil in a large flameproof casserole. When it is hot, add the pork balls and fry until they are evenly browned. Pour in the remaining soy sauce, stock and wine or sherry and bring to the boil. Cover and transfer the casserole to the oven. Bake for 40 minutes.

Remove from the oven and, using a slotted spoon, remove the pork balls from the casserole. Arrange the cabbage in the casserole and arrange the pork balls on top. Return to the oven and bake for a further 10 to 15 minutes, or until the cabbage is slightly crisp but cooked.

Remove from the oven and serve at once.

Serves 4

Preparation and cooking time: 1¼ hours

Lui Jou-Pien

(Sliced Pork in Wine Sauce)

Metric/Imperial	American
700g./1½lb. pork fillet, cut into 5cm./2in. by 2.5cm./1in. pieces	1½lb. pork tenderloin, cut into 2in. by 1in. pieces
1 tsp. salt	1 tsp. salt
½ tsp. black pepper	½ tsp. black pepper
1 Tbs. soya sauce	1 Tbs. soy sauce
1 Tbs. rice wine or dry sherry	1 Tbs. rice wine or dry sherry
1 Tbs. soya paste	1 Tbs. soy paste
1 Tbs. cornflour	1 Tbs. cornstarch
75ml./3fl.oz. vegetable oil	⅓ cup vegetable oil
SAUCE	SAUCE
15g./½oz. vegetable fat	1 Tbs. vegetable fat
1½ Tbs. spring onion	1½ Tbs. chopped scallion
75ml./3fl.oz. dry white wine	⅓ cup dry white wine
50ml./2fl.oz. chicken stock	¼ cup chicken stock
1 Tbs. soya sauce	1 Tbs. soy sauce
1 tsp. sugar	1 tsp. sugar
¼ tsp. salt	¼ tsp. salt
2 tsp. cornflour, mixed to a paste with 3 Tbs. water	2 tsp. cornstarch, mixed to a paste with 3 Tbs. water

Put the pork slices on a chopping board and sprinkle with the salt, pepper, soy sauce and wine or sherry, rubbing them in gently with your fingers. Add the soy paste and mix evenly with the pork. Dust with the cornflour (cornstarch) and set aside.

Heat the oil in a large frying-pan. When it is hot, add the pork pieces and stir-fry for 2 minutes. Reduce the heat to low and cook the pork for a further 4 minutes, stirring and turning the meat from time to time. Remove from the heat.

To make the sauce, melt the fat in a small saucepan. Add the spring onion (scallion) and cook for 30 seconds, stirring constantly. Add the remaining sauce ingredients except the cornflour (cornstarch) mixture and bring to the boil, stirring frequently. Pour in the cornflour (cornstarch) mixture and cook for 1 minute, stirring frequently, or until the sauce becomes translucent. Remove the pan from the heat and pour the sauce over the pork pieces.

Return the frying-pan containing the pork to high heat and cook for 30 seconds, stirring constantly. Remove from the heat and transfer the mixture to a warmed serving dish. Serve at once.

Serves 4

Preparation and cooking time: 30 minutes

Quick-Fried Spinach with Shredded Pork

Metric/Imperial	American
3 Tbs. vegetable oil	3 Tbs. vegetable oil
225g./8oz. pork fillet, cut across the grain into thin strips	8oz. pork tenderloin, cut across the grain into thin strips
2 Tbs. soya sauce	2 Tbs. soy sauce
1 Tbs. rice wine or dry sherry	1 Tbs. rice wine or dry sherry
1 tsp. sugar	1 tsp. sugar
½ tsp. black pepper	½ tsp. black pepper
40g./1½oz. vegetable fat	3 Tbs. vegetable fat
½kg./1lb. spinach, chopped	2 cups chopped spinach
1 tsp. salt	1 tsp. salt

Heat the oil in a large saucepan. When it is hot, add the pork strips and stir-fry for 2 minutes. Add the soy sauce, wine or sherry, sugar and pepper and stir-fry for a further 2 minutes. Transfer the pork to a plate and set aside.

Add 25g./1oz. (2 tablespoons) of the vegetable fat to the pan and melt it over moderate heat. Add the spinach and salt and stir-fry for 3 minutes. Add the remaining fat to the pan and stir-fry for a further 30 seconds. Using a slotted spoon, transfer the spinach to a warmed serving dish. Increase the heat to moderately high and return the pork strips to the pan. Stir-fry for 1 minute, to reheat them thoroughly.

Remove from the heat and pour the pork strips and juices over the spinach. Serve at once.

Serves 2
Preparation and cooking time: 25 minutes

Sweet and Sour Pork

Metric/Imperial	American
1 Tbs. soya sauce	1 Tbs. soy sauce
1½ Tbs. rice wine or sherry	1½ Tbs. rice wine or sherry
2 Tbs. water	2 Tbs. water
1 egg white, beaten until frothy	1 egg white, beaten until frothy
2 Tbs. cornflour	2 Tbs. cornstarch
½kg./1lb. pork fillet, cut into small cubes or large strips	1lb. pork tenderloin, cut into small cubes or large strips
vegetable oil for deep-frying	vegetable oil for deep-frying
SAUCE	SAUCE
50ml./2fl.oz. peanut oil	¼ cup peanut oil
5cm./2in. piece of fresh root ginger, peeled and chopped	2in. piece of fresh green ginger, peeled and chopped
1 red or green pepper, pith and seeds removed and cut into strips	1 red or green pepper, pith and seeds removed and cut into strips
125g./4oz. tin pineapple chunks	125g./4oz. can pineapple chunks
1 carrot, sliced	1 carrot, sliced
2 Tbs. sugar	2 Tbs. sugar
3 Tbs. wine vinegar	3 Tbs. wine vinegar
2 Tbs. soya sauce	2 Tbs. soy sauce
2 Tbs. tomato purée	2 Tbs. tomato paste

2 tsp. lemon or orange juice	2 tsp. lemon or orange juice
2 Tbs. water	2 Tbs. water
1 Tbs. cornflour	1 Tbs. cornstarch

Combine the soy sauce, wine or sherry, water, egg white and cornflour (cornstarch) to a batter in a large bowl. Stir in the pork pieces until they are well coated, then set aside for 1 hour.

Fill a large saucepan one-third full with oil and heat until it is very hot. Carefully lower the pork pieces into the oil and fry for 3 to 4 minutes, or until they are brown and crisp. Remove from the oil and drain on kitchen towels.

To make the sauce, heat the oil in a large frying-pan. When it is hot, add the ginger and pepper and stir-fry for 2 minutes. Add the pork and all the remaining ingredients except the cornflour (cornstarch) and stir-fry for 2 minutes. Stir in the cornflour (cornstarch) and heat until the sauce has thickened and is translucent. Serve at once.

Serves 4
Preparation and cooking time: 1½ hours

Sweet and Sour Pork, a variation of one of the most famous recipes to come out of China, has a rich, tangy sauce which adds an attractive, translucent sheen.

Run Tsa Li Chi

(Plain Deep-Fried Sliced Pork)

Metric/Imperial	American
700g./1½lb. pork fillet	1½lb. pork tenderloin
2 egg whites	2 egg whites
1½ Tbs. cornflour	1½ Tbs. cornstarch
vegetable oil for deep-frying	vegetable oil for deep-frying
DIP	DIP
1 Tbs. black pepper	1 Tbs. black pepper
1 Tbs. salt	1 Tbs. salt

Slice the pork against the grain into thin slices. Using a mallet, beat the slices until they are very thin, then cut into uniform strips, about 7.5cm./3in. by 5cm./2in. Put the strips into a bowl and set aside.

Beat the egg whites until they are frothy. Gradually beat in the cornflour (cornstarch) until the mixture forms a smooth batter. Pour the batter into the bowl and toss the pork strips until they are thoroughly coated. Set aside for 10 minutes.

Fill a large saucepan one-third full with oil and heat until it is hot. Carefully lower the meat strips, a few at a time, into the oil and fry for 1 minute until they are browned and crisp. Remove from the oil and drain on kitchen towels.

To make the dip, fry the salt and pepper in a small frying-pan over moderately low heat for 4 minutes, stirring constantly. Remove from the heat and transfer the mixture to a small bowl. Serve the pork at once, with the dip.
Serves 4
Preparation and cooking time: 30 minutes

Two simple recipes for pork, Run Tsa Li Chi (above) and Kuo Pa Jou Tin (below), offer a contrast of tastes, the former coated in crisp batter, the latter covered in a delicious sauce.

Kuo Pa Jou Tin

(Diced Pork on Crackling Rice)

Metric/Imperial	American
½kg./1lb. pork fillet, cubed	1lb. pork tenderloin, cubed
salt and pepper to taste	salt and pepper to taste
1½ Tbs. cornflour	1½ Tbs. cornstarch
½kg./1lb. cooked rice	5 cups cooked rice
vegetable oil for deep-frying	vegetable oil for deep-frying
SAUCE	SAUCE
150ml./5fl.oz. chicken stock	⅔ cup chicken stock
3 Tbs. soya sauce	3 Tbs. soy sauce
1 Tbs. sugar	1 Tbs. sugar
2 Tbs. dry sherry	2 Tbs. dry sherry
2 Tbs. corn oil	2 Tbs. corn oil
1 onion, thinly sliced	1 onion, thinly sliced
1 garlic clove, crushed	1 garlic clove, crushed
1½ Tbs. cornflour, mixed to a paste with 4 Tbs. water	1½ Tbs. cornstarch, mixed to a paste with 4 Tbs. water

Preheat the oven to very cool 140°C (Gas Mark 1, 275°F).

Sprinkle the pork with salt, pepper and cornflour (cornstarch), rubbing them into the meat with your fingers. Set aside.

Place the rice in an ovenproof dish and put into the oven. Dry out the rice for 15 to 20 minutes, or until it is crisp.

Heat the oil until is is hot. Carefully lower the pork cubes, a few at a time, into the oil and fry for 3 to 4 minutes or until they are golden. Remove the cubes from the oil and drain on kitchen towels.

To make the sauce, combine the stock, soy sauce, sugar and sherry and set aside.

Heat the oil in a frying-pan. When it is hot, add the onion and garlic and stir-fry for 1 minute. Pour in the stock mixture and bring to the boil. Add the pork, basting well, and reduce the heat to low. Simmer for 2 minutes. Stir in the corn-flour (cornstarch) mixture and stir-fry for 2 minutes, or until the sauce has thickened.

Remove the rice from the oven. Return the saucepan with the oil to moderate heat and reheat the oil until it registers 180°C (350°F) on a deep-fat thermometer, or until a small cube of stale bread dropped into the oil turns golden in 55 seconds. Put the rice into a narrow-meshed deep-frying basket and carefully lower it into the oil. Fry for $1\frac{1}{2}$ minutes, then drain on kitchen towels.

Transfer the rice to a warmed serving dish and pour over the pork and sauce.

Serves 4
Preparation and cooking time: 45 minutes

Mi Tse Ho Tui, a leg of gammon (ham), is delicately flavoured with a honey syrup sauce.

Mi Tse Ho Tui

(Ham in Honey Syrup)

Metric/Imperial	American
1 x 1½kg./3lb. middle leg of gammon, washed, soaked in cold water overnight and drained	1 x 3lb. ham, washed, soaked in cold water overnight and drained
SAUCE	SAUCE
2 Tbs. sugar mixed with 4 Tbs. water	2 Tbs. sugar mixed with 4 Tbs. water
2 Tbs. clear honey	2 Tbs. clear honey
2 Tbs. rice wine or sherry	2 Tbs. rice wine or sherry
2 tsp. cherry brandy	2 tsp. cherry brandy
2 tsp. cornflour, mixed to a paste with 3 Tbs. water	2 tsp. cornstarch, mixed to a paste with 3 Tbs. water

Half-fill the lower part of a large steamer with boiling water. Put the gammon (ham) in the upper part and place the steamer over moderate heat. Steam the gammon (ham) for $2\frac{1}{4}$ hours. Remove from the heat and remove the gammon (ham) from the steamer. Set aside until it is cool enough to handle.

When the gammon (ham) is cool, cut it into ½cm./¼in. slices. Arrange the slices on a heatproof serving dish.

To make the sauce, combine all the ingredients in a saucepan and bring to the boil, stirring constantly. Remove from the heat and pour the sauce evenly over the gammon (ham) slices.

Put the serving dish in the top part of the steamer and return the steamer to moderate heat. Steam the meat and sauce for 3 minutes.

Remove the steamer from the heat and remove the serving dish. Serve at once—the dish should be brought to the table still wreathed in steam.

Serves 6-8
Preparation and cooking time: $14\frac{1}{2}$ hours

Double Cooked Pork

Metric/Imperial	American
1 x 2kg./2lb. lean belly of pork	1 x 2lb. lean belly or bacon of pork
50ml./2fl.oz. vegetable oil	¼ cup vegetable oil
1 large green pepper, pith and seeds removed and cut into thin strips	1 large green pepper, pith and seeds removed and cut into thin strips
1 red pepper, pith and seeds removed and cut into thin strips	1 red pepper, pith and seeds removed and cut into thin strips
3 garlic cloves, crushed	3 garlic cloves, crushed
3 spring onions, chopped	3 scallions, chopped
1 chilli, chopped	1 chilli, chopped
1½ Tbs. bean paste	1½ Tbs. bean paste
2 tsp. sugar	2 tsp. sugar
2 Tbs. rice wine or sherry	2 Tbs. rice wine or sherry

Put the pork into a large saucepan and cover with water. Bring to the boil, cover and simmer for 1 hour, or until the pork is cooked through. Drain and rinse in cold water. When it is cool enough to handle, chop or cut through the lean and fat into thin strips.

Heat half the oil in a frying-pan. When it is very hot, add the pork pieces and stir-fry for 5 minutes. Remove the pan from the heat, transfer the pork to a dish and drain off the oil.

Add the remaining oil to the pan. When it is very hot, add the peppers, garlic and spring onions (scallions) and stir-fry for 2 minutes. Add the pork, chilli and bean paste and stir-fry for 1 minute. Stir in the remaining ingredients and stir-fry until they are heated through. Serve at once.

Serves 4
Preparation and cooking time: 1½ hours

Jou Ping Hui Por-Ts'Ai

(Fried and Baked Pork Cakes with Spinach)

Metric/Imperial	American
½kg./1lb. lean pork, minced	1lb. lean pork, ground
2 medium onions, chopped	2 medium onions, chopped
1 egg	1 egg
2 Tbs. cornflour	2 Tbs. cornstarch
2 tsp. sugar	2 tsp. sugar
2½ Tbs. soya sauce	2½ Tbs. soy sauce
1 Tbs. tomato purée	1 Tbs. tomato paste
1 tsp. salt	1 tsp. salt
¼ tsp. black pepper	¼ tsp. black pepper
vegetable oil for deep-frying	vegetable oil for deep-frying
25g./1oz. vegetable fat	2 Tbs. vegetable fat
25g./1oz. butter	2 Tbs. butter
½kg./1lb. spinach, chopped	2½ cups chopped spinach

Combine the pork, onions, egg, cornflour (cornstarch), 1 teaspoon of sugar, 1½ tablespoons of soy sauce, the tomato purée (paste), half the salt and the pepper until they are well blended. Shape the mixture into four or six balls, then press the balls down to form patties about 7.5cm./3in. in diameter.

Fill a large saucepan one-third full with oil and heat until it is hot. Put two or three of the patties into a deep-frying basket and carefully lower them into the the oil. Fry for 3 to 4 minutes, or until they are lightly and evenly browned. Remove from the oil and drain on kitchen towels.

Preheat the oven to hot 220°C (Gas Mark 7, 425°F).

Melt the vegetable fat with half the butter in a large frying-pan. Add the spinach and fry for 1 minute, stirring constantly. Add the remaining salt, the remaining sugar and the remaining soy sauce and fry for a further 3 minutes, stirring constantly. Remove from the heat.

Spread the spinach over the bottom of a casserole dish and arrange the meat cakes on top. Cut the remaining butter into small pieces and dot over the tops of the cakes. Cover the casserole and put it into the oven. Bake for 8 minutes.

Remove from the oven and serve at once.

Serves 4-6
Preparation and cooking time: 40 minutes

Jou Yuantsa Hui

(Meatball Chop Suey)

Metric/Imperial	American
350g./12oz. lean pork, minced	12oz. lean pork, ground
50g./2oz. water chestnuts, finely chopped	⅓ cup finely chopped water chestnuts
1 small egg	1 small egg
½ tsp. sugar	½ tsp. sugar
½ tsp. salt	½ tsp. salt
¼ tsp. white pepper	¼ tsp. white pepper
1 Tbs. soya sauce	1 Tbs. soy sauce
1 Tbs. cornflour	1 Tbs. cornstarch
vegetable oil for deep-frying	vegetable oil for deep-frying
2 Tbs. vegetable oil	2 Tbs. vegetable oil
2 medium onions, thinly sliced	2 medium onions, thinly sliced
225g./8oz. cabbage, shredded	1⅓ cups shredded cabbage
300ml./10fl.oz. chicken stock	1¼ cups chicken stock
225g./8oz. bean sprouts	1 cup bean sprouts
¼ small cucumber, shredded	¼ small cucumber, shredded

Combine the pork, water chestnuts, egg, sugar, salt, pepper, soy sauce and cornflour (cornstarch) until they are well blended. Form the mixture into 10 or 12 small balls.

Fill a large saucepan one-third full with vegetable oil and heat until it is hot. Carefully arrange a few of the meatballs in a deep-frying basket and lower them into the oil. Fry for 3 to 4 minutes, or until they are lightly browned. Remove from the oil and drain. Keep hot while you cook the remaining meatballs.

Heat the vegetable oil in a flameproof casserole. When it is hot, add the onions and cabbage and cook, stirring occasionally, until the vegetables are soft. Pour in the stock and bring to the boil. Reduce the heat to low and simmer the mixture, stirring occasionally, for 5 minutes. Spread the bean sprouts evenly over the vegetable mixture, then top with the shredded cucumber. Arrange the meatballs on top of the vegetables. Simmer the mixture for 5 to 8 minutes, or until the meatballs have been heated through.

Remove from the heat and serve at once.

Serves 4
Preparation and cooking time: 1 hour

POULTRY

Chicken with Broccoli and Walnuts

Metric/Imperial	American
2 large chicken breasts, boned and cut into small cubes	2 large chicken breasts, boned and cut into small cubes
1 tsp. salt	1 tsp. salt
1 tsp. ground ginger	1 tsp. ground ginger
2 Tbs. cornflour	2 Tbs. cornstarch
1 large egg white, lightly beaten	1 large egg white, lightly beaten
75ml./3fl.oz. peanut oil	$\frac{1}{3}$ cup peanut oil
4 large broccoli spears, cut into small pieces	4 large broccoli spears, cut into small pieces
225g./8oz. shelled walnuts, halved	2 cups shelled halved walnuts
1 tsp. soft brown sugar	1 tsp. soft brown sugar
2 Tbs. soya sauce	2 Tbs. soy sauce
3 Tbs. rice wine or dry sherry	3 Tbs. rice wine or dry sherry

Rub the chicken cubes first with the salt, then the ginger and finally with the cornflour (cornstarch). Transfer them to a bowl and pour over the beaten egg white. Stir around gently so that all the cubes are coated.

Heat the oil in a large frying-pan. When it is very hot, add the chicken cubes and stir-fry over moderately high heat for 3 minutes. Using a slotted spoon, transfer the cubes to a plate and keep hot.

Add the broccoli pieces and walnuts to the pan and stir-fry for 3 minutes. Return the chicken cubes to the pan and stir-fry for 1 minute, or until they are well blended.

Stir in the sugar, soy sauce and wine or sherry and cook for 1½ minutes. Transfer the mixture to a warmed serving bowl and serve at once.

Serves 4
Preparation and cooking time: 30 minutes

Kuo Tieh Chi (Egg-Braised Sliced Chicken) is exquisitely flavoured with a blend of parsley, sherry, soy sauce and lemon juice.

Kuo Tieh Chi

(Egg-Braised Sliced Chicken)

Metric/Imperial	American
350g./12oz. boned chicken breasts, cut into thin strips	1½ cups boned chicken breasts, cut into thin strips
salt and pepper	salt and pepper
2 tsp. sugar	2 tsp. sugar
1 tsp. chilli sauce	1 tsp. chilli sauce
2 Tbs. dry white wine	2 Tbs. dry white wine
1 Tbs. cornflour	1 Tbs. cornstarch
vegetable oil for deep-frying	vegetable oil for deep-frying
3 eggs, lightly beaten	3 eggs, lightly beaten
75ml./3fl.oz. sesame oil	⅓ cup sesame oil
1 Tbs. chopped parsley	1 Tbs. chopped parsley
1½ Tbs. dry sherry	1½ Tbs. dry sherry
1½ Tbs. soya sauce	1½ Tbs. soy sauce
1½ Tbs. lemon juice	1½ Tbs. lemon juice

Rub the chicken strips with the salt, pepper, sugar, chilli sauce, wine and corn-flour (cornstarch). Set aside at room temperature for 1½ hours.

Fill a large saucepan about one-third full with oil and heat until it is hot. Carefully lower the chicken strips, a few at a time, into the oil and fry for 1 to 2 minutes, or until they are golden. Drain on kitchen towels.

Put the eggs in a shallow bowl. Dip the cooked chicken strips in the eggs and coat thickly.

Heat the sesame oil in a large frying-pan. When it is hot, add the strips to the pan, in one layer if possible. Shake and tilt to distribute the oil evenly and, turning occasionally, fry for 2 minutes or until the strips are golden brown.

Transfer to a large, warmed serving dish and sprinkle over the parsley, sherry, soy sauce and lemon juice.

Serves 4
Preparation and cooking time: 2 hours

Lemon Chicken

Metric/Imperial	American
1 x 2kg./4lb. chicken, skinned	1 x 4lb. chicken, skinned
1½ tsp. salt	1½ tsp. salt
2.5cm./1in. piece of fresh root ginger, peeled and grated	1in. piece of fresh green ginger, peeled and grated
1 egg, lightly beaten	1 egg, lightly beaten
125g./4oz. ground rice	1 cup ground rice
vegetable oil for deep-frying	vegetable oil for deep-frying
juice of 1 lemon	juice of 1 lemon
1 spring onion, chopped	1 scallion, chopped
1 lemon, cut into thin slices	1 lemon, cut into thin slices
SAUCE	SAUCE
75ml./3fl.oz. chicken stock	⅓ cup chicken stock
2 Tbs. rice wine or dry sherry	2 Tbs. rice wine or dry sherry
¼ tsp. salt	¼ tsp. salt
1½ tsp. sugar	1½ tsp. sugar

Cut the chicken, using a cleaver, through the bone, into 20 or 24 pieces. Sprinkle the pieces with salt and ginger, rubbing them into the flesh.

Dip the chicken pieces in the beaten egg one by one, then roll in the ground rice until they are thoroughly coated, shaking off any excess.

Fill a large saucepan one-third full with oil and heat until it is very hot. Carefully lower a few of the chicken pieces into the oil and fry for 3 to 5 minutes, or until they are golden brown and crisp. Remove from the oil and drain on kitchen towels.

To make the sauce, put all the ingredients in a small saucepan and bring to the boil. Remove from the heat and pour over the chicken pieces.

Sprinkle the lemon juice and spring onion (scallion) over the chicken. Arrange the lemon slices around the chicken and serve at once.

Serves 4-6
Preparation and cooking time: 40 minutes

Yu-lang-chi

(Chicken and Ham)

Metric/Imperial	American
1¾l./3 pints chicken stock	7½ cups chicken stock
4cm./1½in. piece of fresh root ginger, peeled and chopped	1½in. piece of fresh green ginger, peeled and chopped
3 spring onions, chopped	3 scallions, chopped
1 x 2kg./4lb. chicken	1 x 4lb. chicken
4 slices prosciutto	4 slices prosciutto
700g./1½lb. broccoli spears	1½lb. broccoli spears
1 Tbs. soya sauce	1 Tbs. soy sauce
1 tsp. cornflour, blended to a paste with 1 Tbs. water	1 tsp. cornstarch, blended to a paste with 1 Tbs. water

Put the stock, ginger and spring onions (scallions) into a large saucepan. Bring to the boil, then add the chicken and enough boiling water to cover the chicken. Return to the boil. Reduce the heat to low, cover the pan and simmer the chicken for 40 minutes.

Remove from the heat and set aside, covered, for 2 hours. (The chicken will cook through during this time.)

Remove the chicken from the stock, reserving about 450ml./15fl.oz. (2 cups) of it. Put the chicken on a chopping board, remove the flesh from the bones, discarding the skin, and cut into serving pieces. Arrange the chicken pieces and ham strips on a warmed serving dish.

Strain the reserved stock and return it to the saucepan. Bring to the boil, then add the broccoli spears. Return to the boil.

Remove the pan from the heat and set aside for 5 minutes. Drain the broccoli, reserving 125ml./4fl.oz. (½ cup) of stock. Arrange the broccoli around the chicken and ham mixture.

Combine the reserved stock and soy sauce, then pour into a small saucepan. Bring to the boil. Add the cornflour (cornstarch) mixture and cook, stirring constantly, until the sauce thickens a little and becomes translucent.

Pour the sauce over the chicken and ham and serve at once.

Serves 6
Preparation and cooking time: 3 hours

Pai chou chi

(White Cooked Chicken)

Metric/Imperial	American
2.5l./4 pints water	2½ quarts water
1 x 2kg./4lb. chicken, cleaned	1 x 4lb. chicken, cleaned
6 spring onions, finely chopped	6 scallions, finely chopped
SAUCE A	SAUCE A
5cm./2in. piece of fresh root ginger, peeled and chopped	2in. piece of fresh green ginger, peeled and chopped
4 Tbs. boiling water	4 Tbs. boiling water
1 Tbs. hot oil	1 Tbs. hot oil
½ tsp. salt	½ tsp. salt
SAUCE B	SAUCE B
2 garlic cloves, crushed	2 garlic cloves, crushed
3 Tbs. soya sauce	3 Tbs. soy sauce
2 Tbs. vinegar	2 Tbs. vinegar

Yu Lang Chi is tender chicken and ham on a bed of fresh, green broccoli. Serve with steamed rice for a satisfying meal.

Pour the water into a saucepan and bring to the boil. Add the chicken and return the water to the boil. Reduce the heat to low and simmer the chicken for 1¼ hours. Remove from the heat, cover and allow to cool for 3 hours.

73

Drain the chicken, discarding the cooking liquid, and transfer it to a chopping board. Chop the chicken, through the bone, into about 20 large-bite pieces. Transfer the pieces to a serving plate and set aside.

To make sauce A, put the chopped ginger into a small serving bowl. Add all the remaining ingredients and stir to blend.

To make sauce B, put the garlic into a small serving bowl. Add the remaining ingredients and stir to blend.

Sprinkle the chopped spring onions (scallions) over the chicken pieces and serve at once, with sauces.

Serves 4
Preparation and cooking time: 4½ hours

Hung Shao Chi (Red-Cook-ed Chicken) adds colour and a delicate quality to chicken.

Hung Shao Chi

(Red-Cooked Chicken)

You can either use a roasting chicken for this dish, or a cheaper boiling chicken. If you use the latter, increase the cooking time by about 30 minutes.

Metric/Imperial	American
2 spring onions, cut into 5cm./2in. lengths	2 scallions, cut into 2in. lengths
4cm./1½in. piece of fresh root ginger, peeled and sliced	1½in. piece of fresh green ginger, peeled and sliced
1 x 1½kg./3lb. chicken	1 x 3lb. chicken
75ml./3fl.oz. vegetable oil	⅓ cup vegetable oil
75ml./3fl.oz. soya sauce	⅓ cup soy sauce
300ml./10fl.oz. water	1¼ cups water

½ chicken stock cube, crumbled	½ chicken bouillon cube, crumbled
2 tsp. sugar	2 tsp. sugar
3 Tbs. sherry	3 Tbs. sherry

Stuff the spring onions (scallions) and ginger into the cavity of the chicken and secure it with a skewer or trussing needle and thread.

Heat the oil in a large saucepan. When it is hot, arrange the chicken in the pan and fry it, turning frequently, until it is evenly browned. Remove from the heat and pour off the excess oil.

Add the soy sauce, water, stock (bouillon) cube, sugar and sherry and stir to blend. Return the pan to the heat and bring the mixture to the boil. Cover the pan, reduce the heat to low and simmer for 30 minutes. Turn the chicken over, re-cover the pan and simmer for a further 45 minutes, or until the chicken is cooked through and tender.

Transfer the chicken to a carving board. Untruss and carve into serving pieces. Transfer the pieces to a warmed serving dish and pour over the cooking liquid. Serve at once.

Serves 4

Preparation and cooking time: 1½ hours

Pai Chiu Tung Chi

(Long-Simmered Chicken in White Wine)

The cooking liquid from this dish is sometimes served separately as a soup course.

Metric/Imperial	American
1 x 2kg./4lb. chicken, cleaned	1 x 4lb. chicken, cleaned
600ml./1 pint water	2½ cups water
300ml./10fl.oz. dry white wine	1¼ cups dry white wine
3 Tbs. soya sauce	3 Tbs. soy sauce
1½ Tbs. sesame oil	1½ Tbs. sesame oil
½kg./1lb. Chinese cabbage, shredded	2½ cups shredded Chinese cabbage
STUFFING	STUFFING
75g./3oz. long-grain rice, soaked in cold water for 30 minutes and drained	⅓ cup long-grain rice, soaked in cold water for 30 minutes and drained
4 spring onions, chopped	4 scallions, chopped
4 lean bacon slices, chopped	4 Canadian bacon slices, chopped
5cm./2in. piece of fresh root ginger, peeled and chopped	2in. piece of fresh green ginger, peeled and chopped
1 chicken stock cube, crumbled	1 chicken bouillon cube, crumbled
salt and white pepper to taste	salt and white pepper to taste

Preheat the oven to cool 150°C (Gas Mark 2, 300°F).

To make the stuffing, combine all the ingredients in a bowl, then stuff into the cavity of the chicken. Close with a skewer or trussing needle and thread.

Put the chicken in a flameproof casserole and pour over the water. Bring to the boil, and transfer the casserole to the oven. Bake the chicken for 1 hour. Add the wine and cook the chicken for a further 45 minutes, or until it is cooked through and tender. Remove from the oven and transfer the chicken to a warmed serving dish. Keep hot.

Combine the soy sauce and sesame oil and pour the mixture over the chicken. Serve at once. To serve the cooking liquid as a soup course, stir in the cabbage and bring to the boil, stirring occasionally. Cook for 5 minutes, then serve at once.

Serves 4-6

Preparation and cooking time: 2¾ hours

Sweet and Sour Chicken

Metric/Imperial	American
½ tsp. salt	½ tsp. salt
1 tsp. cornflour	1 tsp. cornstarch
2 chicken breasts, boned and cut into thin strips	2 chicken breasts, boned and cut into thin strips
4 Tbs. corn oil	4 Tbs. corn oil
25g./1oz. bamboo shoots, chopped	3 Tbs. chopped bamboo shoots
1 green pepper, pith and seeds removed and finely chopped	1 green pepper, pith and seeds removed and finely chopped
1 small onion, chopped	1 small onion, chopped
4cm./1½in. piece of fresh root ginger, peeled and finely chopped	1½in. piece of fresh green ginger, peeled and finely chopped
1 garlic clove, chopped	1 garlic clove, chopped
SAUCE	SAUCE
1 Tbs. soya sauce	1 Tbs. soy sauce
1 Tbs. red wine vinegar	1 Tbs. red wine vinegar
1 Tbs. soft brown sugar	1 Tbs. soft brown sugar
1 Tbs. tomato purée	1 Tbs. tomato paste
4 Tbs. chicken stock	4 Tbs. chicken stock

Thinly sliced chicken breasts combine with a tasty assortment of vegetables and a piquant sweet-sour sauce to make this mouthwatering dish of Sweet and Sour Chicken.

Mix the salt and cornflour (cornstarch) together and gently rub into the chicken strips with your fingertips.

Heat the oil in a large frying-pan. When it is very hot, add the chicken, in one layer if possible, and stir-fry for 4 minutes. Remove the strips from the pan and drain on kitchen towels. Set aside and keep warm.

Add the bamboo shoots, pepper, onion, ginger and garlic and stir-fry for 1 minute. Mix all the sauce ingredients together in a small bowl.

Return the chicken strips to the pan, with the sauce. Cook for 1 minute, or until all the strips and vegetables are well coated with the sauce.

Transfer to a warmed tureen and serve.

Serves 4
Preparation and cooking time: 20 minutes

Quick-Fried Chicken cubes in White Sauce

Metric/Imperial	American
4 chicken breasts, boned	4 chicken breasts, boned
1 tsp. ground ginger	1 tsp. ground ginger
1½ tsp. salt	1½ tsp. salt
1 tsp. black pepper	1 tsp. black pepper
1 Tbs. cornflour	1 Tbs. cornstarch
15g./½oz. butter	1 Tbs. butter
2 Tbs. vegetable oil	2 Tbs. vegetable oil
125g./4oz. shelled shrimps	⅔ cup peeled shrimp
1 small red pepper, pith and seeds removed and cut into 1cm./½in. lengths	1 small red pepper, pith and seeds removed and cut into ½in. lengths
½ cucumber, halved and cut into 1cm./½in. lengths	½ cucumber, halved and cut into ½in. lengths
SAUCE	SAUCE
75ml./3fl.oz. chicken stock	⅓ cup chicken stock
15g./½oz. butter	1 Tbs. butter
50ml./2fl.oz. dry white wine	¼ cup dry white wine
1 Tbs. cornflour, mixed to a paste with 4 Tbs. water	1 Tbs. cornstarch, mixed to a paste with 4 Tbs. water
125ml./4fl.oz. single cream	½ cup light cream

Cut the chicken flesh into small cubes, then rub them with ginger, salt, pepper and cornflour (cornstarch). Set aside.

Melt the butter with the oil in a large frying-pan. Add the chicken cubes and stir-fry for 30 seconds. Add the shrimps, pepper and cucumber and stir-fry for 2 minutes. Remove from the heat and set aside.

To make the sauce, bring the stock to the boil in a small saucepan. Stir in the butter and wine and boil until the butter has melted. Reduce the heat to low and stir in the cornflour (cornstarch) mixture. Simmer for 2 minutes, stirring constantly, until the sauce has thickened. Stir in the cream.

Remove from the heat and pour the sauce over the chicken cubes. Return the frying-pan to moderate heat and cook the mixture, turning the meat and vegetables in the sauce, for 2 minutes.

Transfer the mixture to a warmed serving dish and serve at once.
Serves 4
Preparation and cooking time: 30 minutes

White Cut Chicken

Metric/Imperial	American
1.2l./2 pints chicken stock	5 cups chicken stock
1 Tbs. rice wine or dry sherry	1 Tbs. rice wine or dry sherry
50ml./2fl.oz. soya sauce	¼ cup soy sauce
4 spring onions, cut into 2.5cm./1in. lengths	4 scallions, cut into 1in. lengths
2.5cm./1in. piece of fresh root ginger, peeled and sliced	1½in. piece of fresh green peeled and sliced
1 tsp. sugar	1 tsp. sugar
1 tsp. salt	1 tsp. salt
1 x 2kg./4lb. chicken, oven-ready	1 x 4lb. chicken, oven-ready

Put the stock, wine or sherry, 1 tablespoon of soy sauce, the spring onions (scallions), ginger, sugar and salt in a large saucepan and bring to the boil. Reduce the heat to low and add the chicken. Cover and simmer for 30 minutes.

Remove from the heat and set aside for 2 hours, or until the chicken has cooled completely. Remove from the pan and discard the cooking liquid. Remove and discard the skin from the chicken and cut the flesh into 5cm./2in. pieces. Transfer the pieces to a serving dish.

Pour the remaining soy sauce into a bowl. Serve the chicken immediately, accompanied by the soy sauce.

Serves 6

Preparation and cooking time: 3 hours

Steamed Drumsticks

Metric/Imperial	American
12 chicken drumsticks	12 chicken drumsticks
5cm./2in. piece of fresh root ginger, peeled and chopped	2in. piece of fresh green ginger, peeled and chopped
6 spring onions, cut into 5cm./2in. lengths	6 scallions, cut into 2in. lengths
1 tsp. salt	1 tsp. salt
1 tsp. butter	1 tsp. butter
25g./1oz. vegetable fat	2 Tbs. vegetable fat
1 medium onion, chopped	1 medium onion, chopped
2 tsp. sugar	2 tsp. sugar
$\frac{1}{4}$ tsp. cayenne pepper	$\frac{1}{4}$ tsp. cayenne pepper
$\frac{1}{2}$ tsp. 5-spice powder	$\frac{1}{2}$ tsp. 5-spice powder
1 Tbs. soya sauce	1 Tbs. soy sauce
1 tsp. chilli sauce	1 tsp. chilli sauce
2 Tbs. tomato purée	2 Tbs. tomato paste
125ml./4fl.oz. chicken stock	$\frac{1}{2}$ cup chicken stock
2 tsp. cornflour, mixed to a paste with 1 Tbs. stock	2 tsp. cornstarch, mixed to a paste with 1 Tbs. stock

Half-fill a large saucepan with water and bring to the boil. Add the drumsticks and boil for 2 minutes. Remove the pan from the heat and drain the drumsticks on kitchen towels. Transfer to a large basin. Add the ginger and spring onions (scallions) and sprinkle over half the salt. Cut out circles of greaseproof or waxed paper and foil and grease with the butter. Make a pleat across the centre and put the paper circle, greased side down, over the basin; tie securely with string. Put the basin into a large saucepan and pour in enough boiling water to come halfway up the sides. Cover the pan and set over low heat. Steam the chicken for 45 minutes to 1 hour, depending on the size of the drumsticks.

Meanwhile, melt the fat in a large frying-pan. When it is hot, add the onion and stir-fry for 2 minutes. Add the sugar, cayenne, 5-spice powder, soy sauce, chilli sauce, tomato purée (paste), stock and remaining salt and bring to the boil, stirring constantly. Add the cornflour (cornstarch) mixture and cook, stirring constantly, until the sauce thickens and becomes translucent. Remove from the heat and keep hot.

Remove the saucepan from the heat and lift the basin out of the pan. Remove and discard the paper circles. Transfer the mixture to a warmed serving dish.

Pour the chicken cooking liquids into the sauce and stir well to blend. Pour the sauce over the chicken mixture and serve at once.

Serves 6

Preparation and cooking time: 1$\frac{1}{2}$ hours

Chicken Congee

Metric/Imperial	American
1 x 1½kg./3lb. chicken	1 x 3lb. chicken
1.75l./3 pints water	7½ cups water
1 onion, quartered	1 onion, quartered
12 peppercorns	12 peppercorns
2 bay leaves	2 bay leaves
125g./4oz. long-grain rice, soaked in cold water for 30 minutes and drained	⅔ cup long-grain rice, soaked in cold water for 30 minutes and drained
GARNISH	GARNISH
½ small Chinese cabbage, shredded	½ small Chinese cabbage, shredded
4 spring onions, chopped	4 scallions, chopped
125ml./4fl.oz. soya sauce	½ cup soy sauce

Put the chicken into a large saucepan and pour over the water. Add the onion and flavourings and bring to the boil. Reduce the heat to low, cover the pan and simmer for 1 to 1½ hours, or until the chicken is cooked through. Transfer the chicken to a chopping board, strain the cooking liquid and reserve it.

Put the rice into a saucepan and pour over the stock. Bring to the boil, cover and simmer the mixture for 1 hour.

Meanwhile, when the chicken is cool enough to handle, skin and chop the meat into bite-sized pieces. Divide the meat into light or dark and put half of both into the saucepan with the rice. Simmer for a further 15 minutes.

Meanwhile, arrange the remaining chicken pieces in separate bowls, for light and dark meat, and arrange the garnishes in appropriate serving bowls.

Remove the pan from the heat and pour the mixture into a warmed tureen. Serve at once, with the meat and garnishes.
Serves 6
Preparation and cooking time: 3½ hours

Stir-Fry Duck with Ginger and Pineapple

Metric/Imperial	American
1 x 2kg./4lb. duck	1 x 4lb. duck
pepper to taste	pepper to taste
1 tsp. ground ginger	1 tsp. ground ginger
5 Tbs. soya sauce	5 Tbs. soy sauce
50ml./2fl.oz. vegetable oil	¼ cup vegetable oil
12.5cm./5in. piece of fresh root ginger, peeled and chopped	5in. piece of fresh green ginger, peeled and chopped
2 spring onions, chopped	2 scallions, chopped
1 Tbs. soft brown sugar	1 Tbs. soft brown sugar
2 Tbs. wine vinegar	2 Tbs. wine vinegar
225g./8oz. can pineapple chunks with the can juice reserved	8oz. pineapple chunks, with the can juice reserved
1 Tbs. cornflour, mixed to a paste with 2 Tbs. water	1 Tbs. cornstarch, mixed to a paste with 2 Tbs. water

Preheat the oven to warm 170°C (Gas Mark 3, 325°F).

Put the duck on the rack of a roasting pan. Mix the pepper, ground ginger and half of the soy sauce together and brush over the duck. Put into the oven and roast for 2 to 2½ hours, basting frequently with the pan juices, or until the duck is cooked through and tender, and the skin is crisp. Remove from the oven and set aside until it is cool enough to handle. Using a cleaver, chop the duck, through the skin, into bite-sized pieces.

Heat the oil in a large, deep frying-pan. When it is hot, add the chopped ginger and stir-fry for 1 minute. Add the duck pieces and spring onions (scallions), and stir-fry for 1 minute. Add the soy sauce, sugar, vinegar and pineapple chunks and can juice. Bring to the boil and cook for 2 minutes, stirring occasionally.

Stir in the cornflour (cornstarch) mixture and cook, stirring constantly, until the sauce thickens and becomes translucent. Transfer the mixture to a warmed serving dish and serve at once.

Serves 6
Preparation and cooking time: 3 hours

Yun Yook

(Roasted Wood Pigeons)

Metric/Imperial	American
2 Tbs. chilli oil	2 Tbs. chilli oil
4 slices streaky bacon	4 slices fatty bacon
4 young wood pigeons, oven-ready	4 young wood pigeons, oven-ready
12 vine leaves	12 vine leaves
125g./4oz. sultanas	$\frac{2}{3}$ cup seedless raisins
8 mint leaves	8 mint leaves
10 pickling onions, boiled for 5 minutes and drained	10 pearl onions, boiled for 5 minutes and drained
225g./8oz. button mushrooms	2 cups button mushrooms
2 Tbs. olive oil	2 Tbs. olive oil
salt and pepper to taste	salt and pepper to taste
2 Tbs. chopped parsley or coriander	2 Tbs. chopped parsley or coriander

Preheat the oven to moderate 180°C (Gas Mark 4, 350°F).

Heat the oil in a frying-pan. When it is hot, add the bacon and fry until it is crisp. Remove the pan from the heat and set aside.

Put the pigeons on a flat surface. Lay one bacon slice over the breast of each one and cover each pigeon with three vine leaves, so that they overlap or enclose the pigeons. Secure with cocktail sticks or trussing thread. Arrange the pigeons in a casserole large enough to hold them in one layer. Add the sultanas (seedless raisins), mint leaves, onions and mushrooms, olive oil and salt and pepper to taste. Cover and put into the oven. Cook for 25 to 30 minutes or until the pigeons are cooked through and tender.

Remove the casserole from the oven, remove the sticks or trussing thread and sprinkle over the parsley or coriander. Serve at once.

Serves 4
Preparation and cooking time: 1 hour

Mongolian Steamboat

Metric/Imperial	American
1 x 2kg./4lb. roasting chicken	1 x 4lb. roasting chicken
1 medium onion, chopped	1 medium onion, chopped

1 bouquet garni
10 peppercorns
2 bay leaves
1 tsp. salt
1.2l./2 pints water
175g./6oz. crabmeat
175g./6oz. large prawns, shelled
VEGETABLES
125g./4oz. mushrooms, sliced
1 red pepper, pith and seeds removed and
   sliced
1 green pepper, pith and seeds removed
   and sliced
175g./6oz. Chinese cabbage, shredded
125g./4oz. canned lotus root, drained and
   sliced
GARNISHES
275g./10oz. cooked rice
4 Tbs. chopped spring onion
10cm./4in. piece of fresh root ginger,
   peeled and finely chopped

1 bouquet garni
10 peppercorns
2 bay leaves
1 tsp. salt
5 cups water
6oz. crabmeat
1 cup large peeled shrimp
VEGETABLES
1 cup sliced mushrooms
1 red pepper, pith and seeds removed
   and sliced
1 green pepper, pith and seeds removed
   and sliced
1 cup shredded Chinese cabbage
4oz. canned lotus root, drained and
   sliced
GARNISHES
4 cups cooked rice
4 Tbs. chopped scallion
4in. piece of fresh green ginger, peeled
   and finely chopped

(See over) The cooking liquid of wine and stock used to steam Pai Chiu Tung Li Yu can be made into a savoury soup.

Remove the skin, bones and flesh from the chicken. Set the flesh aside and put the skin, bones and giblets into a saucepan with the onion, bouquet garni, peppercorns, bay leaves, salt and water. Bring to the boil, skimming off any scum from the surface. Reduce the heat to low, cover and simmer the stock for 1 to 1½ hours. Remove from the heat and strain the stock. Set aside.

Meanwhile, prepare the meat and fish. Cut the chicken flesh into bite-sized pieces and arrange decoratively on a large serving platter. Cut the crabmeat and prawns (shrimp) into bite-sized pieces and arrange with the chicken.

To prepare the vegetables, arrange them attractively on a large serving platter and set them aside with the meat and fish.

Put all the garnishes into separate bowls and arrange with the other dishes.

Put the firepot or fondue pot in the centre of the table and arrange the various platters around it. Bring the stock to the boil in a saucepan and pour into the fondue pot. Light the spirit burner. The food is now ready to be cooked, in the same way as fondue.

Serves 6
Preparation and cooking time: 2½ hours

Derived from an ancient Cantonese recipe, succulent young wood pigeons wrapped in vine leaves result in Yun Yook, a dish for special occasions.

FISH

Pai Chiu Tung Li Yu

(Carp Steamed in White Wine)

Metric/Imperial	American
1 x 1½kg./3lb. carp, cleaned and gutted	1 x 3lb. carp, cleaned and gutted
150ml./5fl.oz. water	⅔ cup water
150ml./5fl.oz. beef stock	⅔ cup beef stock
300ml./10fl.oz. dry white wine	1¼ cups dry white wine
3 Tbs. soya sauce	3 Tbs. soy sauce
1½ Tbs. sesame oil	1½ Tbs. sesame oil
1 bunch of watercress, shredded	1 bunch of watercress, shredded
STUFFING	STUFFING
4 Tbs. rice, soaked in cold water and drained	4 Tbs. rice, soaked in cold water and drained
4 slices lean bacon, chopped	4 slices Canadian bacon, chopped
4 spring onions, finely chopped	4 scallions, finely chopped
1 chicken stock cube, crumbled	1 chicken bouillon cube, crumbled
7.5cm./3in. piece of fresh root ginger, peeled and finely chopped	3in. piece of fresh green ginger, peeled and finely chopped
salt and pepper to taste	salt and pepper to taste

To make the stuffing, combine all the ingredients and stuff the mixture into the fish. Close the cavity with a skewer or trussing needle and thread.

Put the carp into an oval-shaped heatproof casserole and pour over the water. Fill the bottom part of a double boiler or steamer to a depth of 5cm./2in. with boiling water. Put the casserole in the top part and cover. Place the boiler or steamer over moderate heat and steam for 45 minutes.

Pour the stock and wine into the casserole and steam for a further 45 minutes or until the fish flesh flakes easily. Transfer the fish to a warmed dish and reserve the cooking liquid.

Combine the soy sauce and sesame oil and pour over the fish before serving.

To serve the cooking liquid as a soup, stir in the watercress and bring to the boil. Boil for 2 minutes before serving.

Serves 4-6

Preparation and cooking time: 1¾ hours

Liu Yu-pien

(Sliced Fish in Wine Sauce)

Metric/Imperial	American
575g./1¼lb. sole fillets, cut into 5cm./2in. by 2.5cm./1in. pieces	1¼lb. sole fillets, cut into 2in. by 1in. pieces
1 tsp. salt	1 tsp. salt
½ tsp. black pepper	½ tsp. black pepper
½ tsp. ground ginger	½ tsp. ground ginger
2 tsp. cornflour	2 tsp. cornstarch
1 egg white, lightly beaten	1 egg white, lightly beaten
75ml./3fl.oz. vegetable oil	⅓ cup vegetable oil
SAUCE	SAUCE
2 tsp. vegetable fat	2 tsp. vegetable fat
50g./2oz. dried mushrooms, soaked in	½ cup dried mushrooms, soaked in cold

cold water for 30 minutes, drained and sliced	water for 30 minutes, drained and sliced
75ml./3fl.oz. dry white wine	⅓ cup dry white wine
50ml./2fl.oz. chicken stock	¼ cup chicken stock
1 tsp. sugar	1 tsp. sugar
½ tsp. salt	½ tsp. salt
2 tsp. cornflour, mixed to a paste with 3 Tbs. water	2 tsp. cornstarch, mixed to a paste with 3 Tbs. water

Put the fish pieces on a chopping board and sprinkle with the salt, pepper, ginger and cornflour (cornstarch), rubbing them into the flesh with your fingers. Pour over the egg white and gently toss to coat thoroughly. Set aside.

Heat the oil in a large frying-pan. When it is hot, add the fish pieces, in one layer if possible. Cook for 30 seconds, tilting the pan so that the oil flows around the fish. Turn and cook for a further 1 minute. Remove the pan from the heat and pour off the excess oil. Set aside.

To prepare the sauce, melt the fat in a small saucepan. Add the mushrooms and cook for 1 minute, stirring constantly. Add the wine, stock, sugar and salt and bring to the boil. Stir in the cornflour (cornstarch) mixture and cook, stirring constantly, until the sauce thickens and becomes translucent. Remove from the heat and pour the sauce over the fish. Stir carefully around the fish and return the frying-pan to moderate heat. Cook, turning the pieces occasionally, for 2 minutes.

Transfer the mixture to a warmed serving dish and serve at once.

Serves 4
Preparation and cooking time: 30 minutes

Kuo Tieh Yu Pien

(Egg-Braised Sliced Fish)

Whiting or plaice (flounder) fillets can be used instead of sole, if you wish to economize in this recipe.

Metric/Imperial	American
½kg./1lb. sole fillets, cut into small strips about 5cm./2in. x 2.5cm./1in.	1lb. sole fillets, cut into small strips about 2in. x 1in.
2½ tsp. salt	2½ tsp. salt
2.5cm./1in. piece of fresh root ginger, peeled and grated	1in. piece of fresh green ginger, peeled and grated
1½ Tbs. cornflour	1½ Tbs. cornstarch
1 Tbs. corn oil	1 Tbs. corn oil
3 eggs, lightly beaten	3 eggs, lightly beaten
vegetable oil for deep-frying	vegetable oil for deep-frying
75ml./3fl.oz. sesame oil	⅓ cup sesame oil
50ml./2fl.oz. chicken stock	¼ cup chicken stock
2 Tbs. rice wine or dry sherry	2 Tbs. rice wine or dry sherry
1 Tbs. chopped parsley	1 Tbs. chopped parsley
1½ Tbs. soya sauce	1½ Tbs. soy sauce
1½ Tbs. lemon juice	1½ Tbs. lemon juice

Sprinkle the fish strips with 1½ teaspoons of salt, the ginger, cornflour (cornstarch) and corn oil, rubbing them into the flesh with your fingers. Set aside for 1 hour. Beat the eggs and remaining salt together, and set aside.

Fill a large saucepan one-third full with oil and heat until it is very hot. Carefully lower the fish strips into the oil, a few at a time, and fry for 1½ minutes, or until they are lightly browned and crisp. Remove from the oil and drain on kitchen towels.

Heat the sesame oil in a large frying-pan. When it is hot, add the fish strips, in one layer if possible, and fry for 1 minute. Pour in the beaten egg, tilting the pan so that the oil flows freely and the fish strips move and slide in the pan. When the egg is half-set, remove the pan from the heat and turn the fish strips over. Return the pan to the heat. When the egg has completely set, sprinkle over the stock and wine or sherry. Turn the fish strips over once more and cook for a further 30 seconds.

Transfer the strips to a warmed served dish, arranging them in one layer. Sprinkle over the remaining ingredients, and serve at once.

Serves 4-6
Preparation and cooking time: 1½ hours

Hwang chi yu Pien

(Sliced Fish in Tomato Sauce)

Metric/Imperial	American
½kg./1lb. lemon sole fillets, skinned	1lb. lemon sole fillets, skinned
1 tsp. salt	1 tsp. salt
¼ tsp. ground ginger	¼ tsp. ground ginger
1 Tbs. cornflour	1 Tbs. cornstarch
1 egg white, lightly beaten	1 egg white, lightly beaten
75ml./3fl.oz. vegetable oil	⅓ cup vegetable oil
SAUCE	SAUCE
20g./¾oz. butter	1½ Tbs. butter
4 medium tomatoes, blanched, peeled and quartered	4 medium tomatoes, blanched, peeled and quartered
2½ Tbs. soya sauce	2½ Tbs. soy sauce
2 Tbs. tomato purée	2 Tbs. tomato paste
2 tsp. cornflour	2 tsp. cornstarch
75ml./3fl.oz. chicken stock	⅓ cup chicken stock
2 Tbs. sherry	2 Tbs. sherry

Cut the sole fillets into 5cm./2in. by 2.5cm./1in. slices. Mix the salt, ginger and cornflour (cornstarch) together in a shallow dish. Add the fish pieces and coat them thoroughly. Mix in the egg white, and toss gently until the pieces are coated.

Heat the oil in a large frying-pan. When it is hot, remove the pan from the heat and carefully slide the fish pieces, well spaced, into the pan. Return to the heat and cook the fish for 1 minute, tilting the pan from side to side so that the oil flows around. Turn over and cook for 30 seconds. Remove from the heat and transfer the fish to a plate. Cover and keep hot.

Pour off the oil from the pan and return to the heat. Add the butter and melt it. Add the tomato quarters to the pan and cook for 2 minutes, stirring constantly. Stir in the soy sauce and tomato purée (paste) and cook for 30 seconds.

Combine the cornflour (cornstarch), stock, wine or sherry and sugar and pour into the pan. Cook, stirring constantly, until the sauce thickens and becomes translucent. Return the fish to the pan and coat them gently in the sauce. Reduce the heat to low and simmer for 2 minutes.

Transfer the mixture to a warmed serving dish and serve at once.

Serves 4
Preparation and cooking time: 25 minutes

Chinese Steamed Fish

Metric/Imperial	American
2 firm white fish fillets or small steaks	2 firm white fish fillets or small steaks
125g./4oz. button mushrooms, thinly sliced	1 cup thinly sliced button mushrooms
1 tsp. cornflour	1 tsp. cornstarch
2 Tbs. soya sauce	2 Tbs. soy sauce
2 spring onions, finely chopped	2 scallions, finely chopped
1 garlic clove, crushed	1 garlic clove, crushed
4 Tbs. sesame oil	4 Tbs. sesame oil
1 Tbs. white wine vinegar	1 Tbs. white wine vinegar
$\frac{1}{4}$ tsp. sugar	$\frac{1}{4}$ tsp. sugar
salt and pepper	salt and pepper

Bamboo steamers, universally popular in China, are filled with fish and placed on a steamer shelf over a wok – this is a very successful method of cooking as it retains the flavour ¤d goodness of the fish.

Arrange the fish pieces on a large lightly greased heatproof plate. Scatter over the mushrooms and set aside.

Combine the cornflour (cornstarch) and soy sauce until they are well blended, then gradually stir in all of the remaining ingredients. Pour the mixture over the fish. Cover with foil or a second heatproof plate, and arrange in the top half of a steamer. Half-fill the bottom half of the steamer with boiling water, set the pan over moderately low heat and steam the fish for 10 to 15 minutes, or until the flesh flakes easily.

Remove from the heat and transfer the fish and sauce mixture to a warmed serving dish. Serve at once.

Serves 2
Preparation and cooking time: 25 minutes

Pao Yu Ts'Ai Hsin

(Stir-Fried Abalone and Chinese Cabbage)

Metric/Imperial	American
3 Tbs. peanut oil	3 Tbs. peanut oil
2.5cm./1in. piece of fresh root ginger, peeled and chopped	1in. piece of fresh green ginger, peeled and chopped
1 small leek, white part only, thinly sliced into rings	1 small leek, white part only, thinly sliced into rings
1 small Chinese cabbage, shredded	1 small Chinese cabbage, shredded
¼ tsp. monosodium glutamate (optional)	¼ tsp. MSG (optional)
salt and white pepper to taste	salt and white pepper to taste
2 tsp. soya sauce	2 tsp. soy sauce
1½ Tbs. fresh lemon juice	1½ Tbs. fresh lemon juice
450g./1lb. tinned abalone, drained and sliced	1lb. canned abalone, drained and sliced

Pao Tu Ts'Ai Hsin contains Chinese cabbage and abalone, a shellfish famous for its yield of high-grade mother-of-pearl.

Heat the oil in a large frying-pan. When it is hot, add the ginger and leek and stir-fry for 2 minutes. Add the cabbage and stir-fry for 4 minutes, or until the cabbage is cooked but still crisp. Sprinkle over the monosodium glutamate (MSG), if you are using it, salt, pepper, soy sauce and lemon juice. Stir in the abalone and cook for 5 minutes, stirring constantly.

Transfer the mixture to a warmed serving dish and serve at once.

Serves 4-6

Preparation and cooking time: 25 minutes

Steamed Bass with Black Bean Sauce

Fermented black beans can be purchased from Chinese or oriental delicatessens.

Metric/Imperial	American
1 x 1kg./2lb. sea bass, gutted (the head and tail can be left on or removed, as you wish)	1 x 2lb. sea bass, gutted (the head and tail can be left on or removed, as you wish)
125ml./4fl.oz. rice wine or dry sherry	½ cup rice wine or dry sherry
5cm./2in. piece of fresh root ginger, peeled and chopped	2in. piece of fresh green ginger, peeled and chopped
SAUCE	SAUCE
3 Tbs. vegetable oil	3 Tbs. vegetable oil
5cm./2in. piece of fresh root ginger, peeled and chopped	2in. piece of fresh green ginger, peeled and chopped
2 spring onions, chopped	2 scallions, chopped
2 garlic cloves, crushed	2 garlic cloves, crushed
2 tsp. sugar	2 tsp. sugar
2 Tbs. fermented black beans	2 Tbs. fermented black beans
2 Tbs. soya sauce	2 Tbs. soy sauce
2 Tbs. rice wine or dry sherry	2 Tbs. rice wine or dry sherry

Arrange the fish on a heatproof dish and pour over the wine or sherry. Scatter over the chopped ginger. Half-fill the bottom half of a double boiler or steamer with water and bring to the boil. Put the dish into the top half and arrange over the boiling water. Cover and steam over moderate heat for 20 to 25 minutes, or until the fish flakes easily.

Meanwhile, to make the sauce, heat the oil in a frying-pan. When it is hot, add the ginger, spring onions (scallions), and garlic and stir-fry for 2 minutes. Add all the remaining ingredients and bring to the boil, stirring constantly. Cook for 1 minute.

Remove the fish from the steamer and transfer to a warmed serving dish. Pour over the sauce and serve at once.
Serves 4-6
Preparation and cooking time: 35 minutes

Abalone with Mushrooms in Oyster Sauce

Metric/Imperial	American
3 Tbs. vegetable oil	3 Tbs. vegetable oil
8 dried mushrooms, soaked in cold water for 30 minutes, drained and sliced	8 dried mushrooms, soaked in cold water for 30 minutes, drained and sliced
2 spring onions, chopped	2 scallions, chopped
4 Tbs. rice wine or dry sherry	4 Tbs. rice wine or dry sherry
125ml./4fl.oz. oyster sauce	½ cup oyster sauce
½ tsp. soft brown sugar	½ tsp. soft brown sugar
2 tsp. cornflour, mixed to a paste with 2 Tbs. water	2 tsp. cornstarch, mixed to a paste with 2 Tbs. water
450g./1lb. tinned abalone, drained and sliced	1lb. canned abalone, drained and sliced

Heat the oil in a large frying-pan. When it is hot, add the mushrooms and spring onions (scallions) and stir-fry for 2 minutes. Stir in the wine or sherry, oyster sauce and sugar and bring to the boil. Add the abalone slices and baste well. Cook for 5 minutes, turning occasionally, or until the abalone is heated through.

Transfer the abalone slices to a warmed serving dish and keep hot. Stir the cornflour (cornstarch) mixture into the pan and cook, stirring constantly, until the sauce thickens and becomes translucent. Pour over the abalone slices and serve at once.

Serves 4-6
Preparation and cooking time: 30 minutes

Velvet Crab

Metric/Imperial	American
300ml./10fl.oz. single cream	1¼ cups light cream
250ml./8fl.oz. water	1 cup water
1 tsp. sugar	1 tsp. sugar
½ tsp. salt	½ tsp. salt
½ tsp. white pepper	½ tsp. white pepper
3 eggs, lightly beaten	3 eggs, lightly beaten
1 Tbs. cornflour, mixed to a paste with 2 Tbs. water	1 Tbs. cornstarch, mixed to a paste with 2 Tbs. water
1 tsp. paprika	1 tsp. paprika
350g./12oz. crabmeat, shell and cartilage removed and flaked	12oz. crabmeat, shell and cartilage removed and flaked
225g./8oz. vermicelli, deep-fried until crisp, drained and kept hot	8oz. vermicelli, deep-fried until crisp, drained and kept hot

Put the cream, water, sugar, salt and pepper into a large saucepan and bring to the boil. Reduce the heat to low and, using a wire whisk or beater, beat in the eggs. Stir in the cornflour (cornstarch) mixture and paprika and beat until smooth and thick. Stir in the crabmeat and cook for 2 minutes, or until the crabmeat is heated through. Remove from the heat.

Arrange the vermicelli on a warmed serving dish and spoon over the crabmeat mixture. Serve at once.

Serves 4
Preparation and cooking time: 25 minutes

Shrimps Stir-Fried with Ginger

Metric/Imperial	American
2 Tbs. vegetable oil	2 Tbs. vegetable oil
3 garlic cloves, crushed	3 garlic cloves, crushed
2 spring onions, chopped	2 scallions, chopped
1 leek, white part only, cut into thin strips	1 leek, white part only, cut into thin strips
7.5cm./3in. piece of fresh root ginger, peeled and finely chopped	3in. piece of fresh green ginger, peeled and finely chopped
2 Tbs. soya sauce	2 Tbs. soy sauce
1 tsp. sugar	1 tsp. sugar

$\frac{1}{4}$ tsp. salt

700g./1$\frac{1}{2}$lb. frozen peeled shrimps,
    thawed and drained

225g./8oz. bean sprouts

125g./4oz. petits pois

$\frac{1}{4}$ tsp. salt

1$\frac{1}{2}$lb. frozen peeled shrimp, thawed and
    drained

1 cup bean sprouts

$\frac{1}{2}$ cup petits pois

Heat the oil in a frying-pan. When it is hot, add the garlic, spring onions (scallions), leek and ginger and stir-fry for 3 minutes. Add the soy sauce, sugar and salt and stir-fry for 1 minute.

    Stir in the shrimps, bean sprouts and petits pois and stir-fry for 5 minutes. Transfer to a warmed serving dish and serve.

Serves 4

Preparation and cooking time: 20 minutes

Velvet Crab, as its name suggests, is an elegant dish of crabmeat and cream, served on a crisp layer of vermicelli.

This recipe for crispy Prawn or Shrimp Fritters served with a savoury dip is delicious as an hors d'oeuvre or as a light meal.

Prawn or Shrimp Fritters

Metric/Imperial	American
700g./1½lb. prawns, shelled, with the tails left on and deveined	1½lb. shrimp, peeled, with the tails left on and deveined
6 Tbs. cornflour	6 Tbs. cornstarch
1 tsp. salt	1 tsp. salt
¼ tsp. cayenne pepper	¼ tsp. cayenne pepper
2 eggs, separated	2 eggs, separated
3 Tbs. water	3 Tbs. water
vegetable oil for deep-frying	vegetable oil for deep-frying
SAUCE	SAUCE
1 Tbs. wine vinegar	1 Tbs. wine vinegar
1 Tbs. soft brown sugar	1 Tbs. soft brown sugar
1 Tbs. tomato purée	1 Tbs. tomato paste
1 Tbs. soya sauce	1 Tbs. soy sauce
1 Tbs. vegetable oil	1 Tbs. vegetable oil
¼ tsp. salt	¼ tsp. salt
50ml./2fl.oz. rice wine or dry sherry	¼ cup rice wine or dry sherry
1 Tbs. cornflour, mixed to a paste with 125ml./4fl.oz. water	1 Tbs. cornstarch, mixed to a paste with ½ cup water
2 lemons, cut into wedges	2 lemons, cut into wedges

Wash the prawns (shrimp) in cold water and drain on kitchen towels.

Combine the cornflour (cornstarch), salt and cayenne. Make a well in the centre and add the egg yolks and water. Slowly incorporate the dry ingredients into the liquids until the mixture forms a smooth batter. Set aside for 20 minutes.

Meanwhile, make the sauce. Put the ingredients, except the cornflour (cornstarch) mixture, into a saucepan and bring to the boil, stirring constantly. Reduce the heat to low and stir in the cornflour (cornstarch) mixture. Cook, stirring constantly, until the sauce thickens and becomes translucent. Remove from the heat and set aside.

Beat the egg whites until they form stiff peaks, fold into the egg yolk batter.

Fill a large saucepan one-third full with oil and heat until it is hot. Holding the prawns (shrimp) by the tails, dip each one in the batter then drop them carefully into the oil, a few at a time. Fry for 3 to 4 minutes, or until they are golden brown. Remove from the oil and drain on kitchen towels.

Arrange the fritters on a warmed serving dish and garnish with the lemon wedges. Reheat the sauce, then pour into small individual bowls. Serve at once, with the fritters.

Serves 6-8
Preparation and cooking time: 1 hour

Cantonese Lobster

Metric/Imperial	American
1 x 1kg./2lb. lobster, claws cracked and sac removed	1 x 2lb. lobster, claws cracked and sac removed
75ml./3fl.oz. peanut oil	$\frac{1}{3}$ cup peanut oil
1 garlic clove, crushed	1 garlic clove, crushed
5cm./2in. piece of fresh root ginger, peeled and chopped	2in. piece of fresh green ginger, peeled and chopped
125g./4oz. lean pork, minced	4oz. lean pork, ground
250ml./8fl.oz. chicken stock	1 cup chicken stock
1 Tbs. rice wine or dry sherry	1 Tbs. rice wine or dry sherry
1 Tbs. soya sauce	1 Tbs. soy sauce
1 tsp. sugar	1 tsp. sugar
1 Tbs. cornflour, mixed to a paste with 2 Tbs. water	1 Tbs. cornstarch, mixed to a paste with 2 Tbs. water
3 spring onions, chopped	3 scallions, chopped
2 eggs	2 eggs

Cut the lobster into bite-sized pieces and set aside.

Heat half the oil in a large, deep frying-pan. When it is hot, add the garlic and stir-fry for 1 minute. Add the lobster pieces and stir-fry for 3 to 5 minutes, or until they are heated through. Transfer to a warmed serving dish and keep hot while you cook the sauce.

Heat the remaining oil in the same frying-pan. When it is hot, add the ginger and pork and fry, stirring constantly, until the pork loses its pinkness. Pour over the stock and bring to the boil, stirring constantly. Combine the wine or sherry, soy sauce and sugar, then stir the mixture into the pan. Stir-fry for 1 minute. Stir in the cornflour (cornstarch) mixture and cook, stirring constantly, until the sauce thickens and becomes translucent. Stir in the spring onions (scallions) and stir-fry for 1 minute.

Turn off the heat and beat the eggs once or twice until they are just combined. Gently pour them over the pan mixture, lifting the sides of the mixture to allow the egg to run over and under. When the eggs become creamy and slightly 'set', spoon the sauce over the lobster and serve at once.

Serves 2-4
Preparation and cooking time: 40 minutes

Shrimps with Eggs and Petits-pois

Metric/Imperial	American
5 eggs	5 eggs
1 tsp. salt	1 tsp. salt
25g./1oz. butter	2 Tbs. butter
2.5cm./1in. piece of fresh root ginger, peeled and chopped	1in. piece of fresh green ginger, peeled and chopped
1 small onion, sliced	1 small onion, sliced
125g./4oz. small shelled shrimps	4oz. small peeled shrimp
225g./8oz. petits pois	1 cup petits pois
1 Tbs. soya sauce	1 Tbs. soy sauce
½ tsp. sugar	½ tsp. sugar
2 Tbs. vegetable oil	2 Tbs. vegetable oil

Beat the eggs and salt together until they are blended. Set aside.

Melt the butter in a saucepan. Add the ginger and onion and stir-fry for 30 seconds. Add the shrimps, petits pois, soy sauce and sugar and stir-fry for a further 1½ minutes. Remove from the heat and set aside.

Heat the oil in a large frying-pan. When it is hot, pour in the egg mixture. Stir, then leave for a few seconds until the bottom sets. Remove from the heat and add the shrimps and petits pois. Turn, mix and toss the mixture a few times. Return to the heat and cook for 1 minute, stirring occasionally.

Transfer the mixture to a warmed serving dish and serve at once.

Serves 2-3
Preparation and cooking time: 20 minutes

Quick Fried Shrimps with Cashews

Metric/Imperial	American
½kg./1lb. small shelled shrimps	1lb. small peeled shrimp
1 Tbs. rice wine or sherry	1 Tbs. rice wine or sherry
1 egg white, lightly beaten	1 egg white, lightly beaten
1½ Tbs. cornflour	1½ Tbs. cornstarch
salt and pepper	salt and pepper
1 tsp. ground ginger	1 tsp. ground ginger
50ml./2fl.oz. vegetable oil	¼ cup vegetable oil
125g./4oz. unsalted cashews	1 cup unsalted cashews
5cm./2in. piece of fresh root ginger, peeled and chopped	2in. piece of fresh root ginger, peeled and chopped
3 spring onions, chopped	3 scallions, chopped

Put the shrimps into a shallow dish. Beat half the wine or sherry, the egg white, 1 tablespoon of cornflour (cornstarch), seasoning and ground ginger together until the mixture forms a smooth batter. Pour over the shrimps and toss gently to coat them. Set aside for 30 minutes.

Heat the oil in a large, deep-frying-pan. When it is hot, add the cashews and fry, turning occasionally, for 5 minutes. Push them to the side of the pan and stir in the shrimps. Stir-fry for 3 minutes, or until they are heated through. Stir in the remaining ingredients, except the wine or sherry and cornflour (cornstarch) and stir-fry for a further 2 minutes. Stir in the remaining wine or sherry and cornflour (cornstarch) and mix the cashews into the other ingredients. Cook, stirring constantly, until the sauce thickens and becomes translucent.

Transfer the mixture to a warmed serving dish and serve at once.
Serves 6
Preparation and cooking time: 25 minutes

Stir-Fry Shrimps with Mange-tout

Metric/Imperial	American
3 Tbs. vegetable oil	3 Tbs. vegetable oil
350g./12oz. shelled shrimps	2 cups peeled shrimp
225g./8oz. mange-tout, cut into 5cm./2in. lengths	1⅓ cups snow peas, cut into 2in. lengths
125g./4oz. bean sprouts	½ cup bean sprouts
2 Tbs. rice wine or dry sherry	2 Tbs. rice wine or dry sherry
1 Tbs. soya sauce	1 Tbs. soy sauce
½ tsp. soft brown sugar	½ tsp. soft brown sugar
1 Tbs. cornflour, mixed to a paste with 2 Tbs. water	1 Tbs. cornstarch, mixed to a paste with 2 Tbs. water

Heat the oil in a large frying-pan. When it is hot, add the shrimps and stir-fry for 2 minutes. Add the mange-tout (snow peas) and bean sprouts and stir-fry for a further 2 minutes. Add all the remaining ingredients and bring to the boil, stirring constantly. Cook, stirring constantly, until the sauce thickens and becomes translucent.

Transfer the mixture to a warmed serving dish and serve at once.
Serves 4
Preparation and cooking time: 20 minutes

Hwang Chi Hsia Ren

(Shrimps in Tomato Sauce)

Metric/Imperial	American
½kg./1lb. shrimps, shelled	1lb. shrimp, peeled
1 tsp. salt	1 tsp. salt
½ tsp. ground ginger	½ tsp. ground ginger
1½ tsp. cornflour	1½ tsp. cornstarch
75ml./3fl.oz. vegetable oil	⅓ cup vegetable oil
SAUCE	SAUCE
20g./¾oz. butter	1½ Tbs. butter
3 medium tomatoes, blanched, peeled and quartered	3 medium tomatoes, blanched, peeled and quartered
2½ Tbs. soya sauce	2½ Tbs. soy sauce
2 Tbs. tomato purée	2 Tbs. tomato paste
2 tsp. cornflour	2 tsp. cornstarch
75ml./3fl.oz. chicken stock	⅓ cup chicken stock
2 Tbs. rice wine or sherry	2 Tbs. rice wine or sherry
1 tsp. sugar	1 tsp. sugar

Put the shrimps in a shallow dish. Sprinkle over the salt, ginger and cornflour (cornstarch) and rub them in to the flesh with your fingers.

Heat the oil in a large frying-pan. When it is hot, add the shrimps and fry for 2 minutes, stirring constantly. Remove from the heat and, using a slotted spoon, transfer the shrimps to a plate. Cover and keep hot.

Pour off the oil from the pan and return to the heat. Add the butter and melt it. When it has melted, add the tomato quarters and fry for 2 minutes, stirring constantly. Stir in the soy sauce and tomato purée (paste) and cook for a further 30 seconds.

Combine the cornflour (cornstarch), stock, wine or sherry and sugar. Pour the mixture into the pan and cook, stirring constantly, until the sauce thickens and becomes translucent. Return the shrimps to the sauce and baste well. Cook for a further 1½ minutes, stirring constantly.

Transfer the mixture to a warmed serving dish and serve at once.

Serves 4
Preparation and cooking time: 25 minutes

Shrimps with Bean Curd

Metric/Imperial	American
½kg./1lb. shelled shrimps	1lb. peeled shrimp
1 tsp. salt	1 tsp. salt
½ tsp. ground ginger	½ tsp. ground ginger
2 Tbs. cornflour	2 Tbs. cornstarch
50ml./2fl.oz. vegetable oil	4 Tbs. vegetable oil
10cm./4in. piece of fresh root ginger, peeled and chopped	4in. piece of fresh green ginger, peeled and chopped
1 garlic clove, crushed	1 garlic clove, crushed
1 dried red chilli, chopped	1 dried red chilli, chopped
3 bean curd cakes, sliced then chopped	3 bean curd cakes, sliced then chopped
50ml./2fl.oz. chicken stock	¼ cup chicken stock
2 Tbs. water	2 Tbs. water

Put the shrimps into a shallow dish. Sprinkle over the salt, ground ginger and half the cornflour (cornstarch) and gently rub them into the flesh with your fingers. Set aside for 10 minutes.

Heat the oil in a large, deep frying-pan. When it is hot, add the ginger and garlic and stir-fry for 1 minute. Add the chilli and stir-fry for 30 seconds. Stir in the bean curd and stock, reduce the heat to low and simmer for 3 minutes, stirring occasionally.

Mix the remaining cornflour (cornstarch) with the water, then stir into the pan mixture. Cook, stirring constantly, until the sauce thickens.

Transfer the mixture to a warmed serving dish and serve at once.

Serves 4-6
Preparation and cooking time: 25 minutes

Winter Prawns or Shrimps

Metric/Imperial	American
10 egg whites	10 egg whites
2 tsp. cornflour	2 tsp. cornstarch
½ tsp. salt	½ tsp. salt

175g./6oz. prawns	1 cup peeled shrimp
vegetable oil for deep-frying	vegetable oil for deep-frying
¼ tsp. monosodium glutamate (optional)	¼ tsp. MSG (optional)
50g./2oz. cooked chicken, minced	¼ cup ground cooked chicken
2 Tbs. chopped chives	2 Tbs. chopped chives

Winter Prawns will form a fairy-light and exquisite part of any Chinese dinner.

Beat 1 egg white, the cornflour (cornstarch) and salt together until they form a smooth batter. Put the prawns (shrimp) in the batter and gently toss to coat thoroughly.

Fill a large saucepan one-third full with oil and heat until it is very hot. Arrange the prawns (shrimp) in a deep-frying basket and carefully lower into the oil. Fry for 1 minute. Remove from the oil and drain on kitchen towels. Set aside.

Beat the remaining egg whites with the monosodium glutamate (MSG). Pile half the egg whites on to a dish. Lay the prawns (shrimp) on top and, using a spatula, gently spread the remaining egg whites over the top. Carefully tilt the pan over the saucepan containing the oil and gently slide it into the oil. Fry for 3 minutes basting the top with oil if it is not fully covered. Remove the pan from the heat and, using a fish slice or spatula, remove from the oil and drain on kitchen towels.

Transfer the mixture to a warmed serving dish and sprinkle over the chicken and chives. Serve at once.

Serves 4-6
Preparation and cooking time: 30 minutes

Prawn Balls with Green Peas

Metric/Imperial	American
50g./2oz. cornflour	½ cup cornstarch
vegetable oil for deep-frying	vegetable oil for deep-frying
2 Tbs. peanut oil	2 Tbs. peanut oil

Metric/Imperial	American
4cm./1½in. piece of fresh root ginger, peeled and finely chopped	1½in. piece of fresh green ginger, peeled and finely chopped
1 Tbs. wine vinegar	1 Tbs. wine vinegar
1 Tbs. soya sauce	1 Tbs. soy sauce
1 Tbs. tomato purée	1 Tbs. tomato paste
2 tsp. soft brown sugar	2 tsp. soft brown sugar
125ml./4fl.oz. chicken stock	½ cup chicken stock
125g./4oz. frozen green peas, thawed	½ cup frozen green peas, thawed
1 Tbs. cornflour, blended to a paste with 1½ Tbs. water	1 Tbs. cornstarch mixed to a paste with 1½ Tbs. water
PRAWN BALLS	PRAWN BALLS
½kg./1lb. shelled prawns, finely chopped	1lb. peeled shrimp, finely chopped
1 tsp. ground ginger	1 tsp. ground ginger
2 Tbs. fresh white breadcrumbs	2 Tbs. fresh white breadcrumbs
1 tsp. cornflour	1 tsp. cornstarch
1 egg yolk	1 egg yolk

First make the prawn (shrimp) balls. Combine all the ingredients in a mixing bowl. Using your hands, shape the mixture into small, walnut-sized balls. Toss gently in the cornflour (cornstarch).

Fill a large saucepan about one-third full with vegetable oil and heat it until it is very hot. Carefully lower the prawn (shrimp) balls, a few at a time, into the hot oil and fry until they are golden brown and crisp. Remove from the oil and drain on kitchen towels. Set aside.

Heat the peanut oil in a large frying-pan. When it is hot, add the ginger and stir-fry for 1 minute. Add the vinegar, soy sauce, tomato purée (paste), sugar and stock and stir until they are well blended. Stir in the peas and bring to the boil. Return the prawn (shrimp) balls to the pan and stir-fry for 2 minutes.

Stir in the cornflour (cornstarch) mixture and cook until the sauce thickens and becomes translucent. Transfer the mixture to a warmed serving dish and serve at once.

Serves 4-6
Preparation and cooking time: 30 minutes

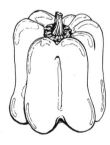

Prawns or Shrimps in Sweet and Sour Sauce

Metric/Imperial	American
3 Tbs. vegetable oil	3 Tbs. vegetable oil
700g./1½lb. Dublin Bay prawns, shelled	1½ lb. large Gulf shrimp, peeled
¼ tsp. cayenne pepper	¼ tsp. cayenne pepper
SAUCE	SAUCE
2 tsp. soya sauce	2 tsp. soy sauce
2 Tbs. soft brown sugar	2 Tbs. soft brown sugar
2 Tbs. vegetable oil	2 Tbs. vegetable oil
2 Tbs. wine vinegar	2 Tbs. wine vinegar
½ tsp. ground ginger	½ tsp. ground ginger
salt and pepper to taste	salt and pepper to taste
300ml./10fl.oz. pineapple juice	1¼ cups pineapple juice
1 large green pepper, pith and seeds removed and cut into 1cm./½in. lengths	1 large green pepper, pith and seeds removed and cut into ½in. lengths
2 Tbs. cornflour, mixed to a paste with 6 Tbs. water	2 Tbs. cornstarch, mixed to a paste with 6 Tbs. water

Heat the oil in a large frying-pan. When it is hot, add the prawns (shrimp) and sprinkle over the cayenne. Cook for 5 minutes, stirring frequently.

Meanwhile, to make the sauce put the ingredients, except the pepper and cornflour (cornstarch) mixture, into a saucepan and bring to the boil, stirring constantly. Add the pepper, reduce the heat to low and cover the pan. Simmer for 3 minutes. Stir in the cornflour (cornstarch) mixture. Cook, stirring constantly, until the sauce thickens and becomes translucent. Remove from the heat.

Arrange the prawns (shrimp) on a warmed serving dish and pour over the sauce. Serve at once.

Serves 6
Preparation and cooking time: 20 minutes

A splash of colour on a bed of fried rice, Prawns or Shrimps in Sweet and Sour Sauce make a tempting main dish.

VEGETABLES

Chow Barg Choy

(Fried Cabbage)

Metric/Imperial	American
2 Tbs. vegetable oil	2 Tbs. vegetable oil
1 garlic clove, crushed	1 garlic clove, crushed
700g./1½lb. Chinese cabbage, shredded	3½ cups shredded Chinese cabbage
½ tsp. salt	½ tsp. salt
75ml./3fl.oz. water	⅓ cup water
2 tsp. soya sauce	2 tsp. soy sauce
1 tsp. flour	1 tsp. flour
½ tsp. sugar	½ tsp. sugar

Heat the oil in a large, deep frying-pan. When it is hot, add the garlic and stir-fry for 1 minute. Add the cabbage and salt and cook for 6 minutes, stirring occasionally.

Combine the water, soy sauce and flour together until they form a smooth paste. Stir in the sugar, then pour the mixture into the pan. Stir-fry for 2 minutes.

Remove the pan from the heat and transfer the mixture to a warmed serving bowl. Serve at once.

Serves 4-6
Preparation and cooking time: 25 minutes

Nai-Yu-Ts'Ai Hsin

(Cabbage in Cream Sauce)

Metric/Imperial	American
15g./½oz. butter	1 Tbs. butter
1 Tbs. sesame oil	1 Tbs. sesame oil
3 spring onions, sliced	3 scallions, sliced
2 small Chinese cabbages, shredded	2 small Chinese cabbages, shredded
salt and pepper	salt and pepper
1 Tbs. white wine vinegar	1 Tbs. white wine vinegar
125ml./4fl.oz. single cream	½ cup light cream
2 tsp. soya sauce	2 tsp. soy sauce

Melt the butter with the oil in a large frying-pan. When it is hot, add the spring onions (scallions) and cabbage and stir-fry for 3 minutes. Sprinkle over the salt, pepper and vinegar and stir-fry for a further 3 minutes, or until the cabbage is cooked but still crisp.

Stir in the remaining ingredients and cook, stirring frequently, for 4 minutes, or until the sauce comes to the boil. Transfer the mixture to a warmed serving dish and serve at once.

Serves 6-8
Preparation and cooking time: 25 minutes

A savoury recipe for cabbage, Hung Shao Pai Ts'Ai, through being cooked only for a very short time, remains delectably crunchy.

Hung Shao Pai Ts'Ai

(Red-Cooked Cabbage)

Metric/Imperial	American
40g./1½oz. butter	3 Tbs. butter
3 Tbs. vegetable oil	3 Tbs. vegetable oil
1 Chinese cabbage, shredded	1 Chinese cabbage, shredded
3½ tsp. sugar	3½ tsp. sugar
5 Tbs. soya sauce	5 Tbs. soy sauce
3 Tbs. water	3 Tbs. water
½ chicken stock cube, crumbled	½ chicken bouillon cube, crumbled
3 Tbs. rice wine or dry sherry	3 Tbs. rice wine or dry sherry

Melt the butter with the oil in a large frying-pan. When it is hot, add the cabbage and turn it in the mixture until thoroughly coated. Reduce the heat to low, cover and simmer for 5 minutes. Stir in the sugar, soy sauce, water, stock (bouillon) cube, wine and sherry and simmer, covered, for a further 5 minutes.

Transfer the mixture to a warmed serving dish and serve at once.

Serves 6
Preparation and cooking time: 20 minutes

Bamboo Shoot with Mushrooms

Metric/Imperial	American
350g./12oz. bamboo shoot, thinly sliced	2 cups thinly sliced bamboo shoot
50ml./2fl.oz. peanut oil	¼ cup peanut oil
10 dried mushrooms, soaked in cold water for 30 minutes, drained and sliced	10 dried mushrooms, soaked in cold water for 30 minutes, drained and sliced
2 Tbs. rice wine or dry sherry	2 Tbs. rice wine or dry sherry
4 Tbs. soya sauce	4 Tbs. soy sauce
1 Tbs. sugar	1 Tbs. sugar
75ml./3fl.oz. water	⅓ cup water
½ Tbs. cornflour, mixed to a paste with 2 Tbs. water	½ Tbs. cornstarch, mixed to a paste with 2 Tbs. water

Bean Curd, cakes of cooked, puréed soya beans and seen here with Bean Curd Skin (strips of dried curd), is one of the most important products made from the soya bean. It is used extensively throughout the Orient.

Heat a large frying-pan over moderate heat for 30 seconds. Add the oil and swirl it around the pan. Add the bamboo shoots and mushrooms and fry for 5 minutes, stirring frequently.

Stir in all the remaining ingredients and bring to the boil, stirring constantly. Cook, stirring constantly, until the sauce thickens and becomes translucent.

Transfer the mixture to a warmed serving dish and serve at once.

Serves 4
Preparation and cooking time: 30 minutes

Bean Curd with Spiced Meat and Vegetables

Metric/Imperial	American
50ml./2fl.oz. peanut oil	¼ cup peanut oil
1 garlic clove, crushed	1 garlic clove, crushed
7½cm./3in. piece of fresh root ginger, peeled and chopped	3in. piece of fresh green ginger, peeled and chopped
4 spring onions, chopped	4 scallions, chopped
4 dried mushrooms, soaked in cold water for 30 minutes, drained and chopped	4 dried mushrooms, soaked in cold water for 30 minutes, drained and chopped
1 tsp. red pepper flakes	1 tsp. red pepper flakes
2 dried chillis, chopped	2 dried chillis, chopped
175g./6oz. minced beef	6oz. ground beef
2 Tbs. soya sauce	2 Tbs. soy sauce
250ml./8fl.oz. chicken stock	1 cup chicken stock
3 bean curd cakes, mashed	3 bean curd cakes, mashed
1 Tbs. cornflour, mixed to a paste with 2 Tbs. stock	1 Tbs. cornstarch, mixed to a paste with 2 Tbs. stock

Heat the oil in a large saucepan. When it is hot, add the garlic, ginger, spring onions (scallions) and mushrooms and stir-fry for 3 minutes. Stir in the red pepper flakes and chillis and stir-fry for a further 1 minute. Add the minced (ground) meat and fry until it loses its pinkness. Pour over the soy sauce and stock and bring to the boil, stirring constantly.

Stir in the bean curd and stir-fry for 3 minutes. Add the cornflour (cornstarch) mixture and cook, stirring constantly, until the sauce thickens.

Transfer the mixture to a warmed serving dish and serve at once.

Serves 6
Preparation and cooking time: 30 minutes

Stir-Fried Mixed Vegetables with Egg

Metric/Imperial	American
3 Tbs. peanut oil	3 Tbs. peanut oil
5cm./2in. piece of fresh root ginger, peeled and chopped	2in. piece of fresh green ginger, peeled and chopped
5 spring onions, chopped	5 scallions, chopped
125g./4oz. mushrooms, sliced	1 cup sliced mushrooms
125g./4oz. bean sprouts	½ cup bean sprouts
salt and pepper to taste	salt and pepper to taste
1½ Tbs. soya sauce	1½ Tbs. soy sauce
3 eggs, lightly beaten	3 eggs, lightly beaten

Heat the oil in a large frying-pan. When it is hot, add the ginger and stir-fry for 1 minute. Add the spring onions (scallions) and mushrooms and stir-fry for 2 minutes. Stir in the bean sprouts, seasoning and soy sauce and stir-fry for a further 2 minutes.

Pour over the eggs, stir them with a fork and leave for a few seconds to allow the bottom to set. Stir again with the fork and leave until the eggs are creamy.

Transfer the mixture to a warmed serving dish and serve at once.

Serves 4
Preparation and cooking time: 20 minutes

Stir-Fried Mixed Vegetables

Metric/Imperial	American
4 Tbs. sesame oil	4 Tbs. sesame oil
4cm./1½in. piece of fresh root ginger, peeled and chopped	1½in. piece of fresh green ginger, peeled and chopped
1 large leek, cleaned and cut into 2.5cm./1in. lengths	1 large leek, cleaned and cut into 1in. lengths
2 large carrots, thinly sliced	2 large carrots, thinly sliced
1 large red pepper, pith and seeds removed and cut into thin strips	1 large red pepper, pith and seeds removed and cut into thin strips
½ cucumber, halved lengthways, seeds removed and cut into 2.5cm./1in. lengths	½ cucumber, halved lengthways, seeds removed and cut into 1in. lengths
4 button mushrooms, sliced	4 button mushrooms, sliced

Heat the oil in a large, deep frying-pan. When it is hot, add the ginger and stir-fry for 2 minutes. Add the leek and carrots and stir-fry for 2 minutes.

Add the remaining ingredients and stir-fry for 3 minutes, or until all the vegetables are just cooked but still crisp.

Serve at once.

Serves 4-6
Preparation and cooking time: 25 minutes

Stir-Fried Broccoli

Metric/Imperial	American
75ml./3fl.oz. sesame oil	⅓ cup sesame oil
1kg./2lb. broccoli, broken into flowerets, then cut on the diagonal into 2cm./1in. lengths	2lb. broccoli, broken into flowerets, then cut on the diagonal into 1in. lengths
1 tsp. salt	1 tsp. salt
½ tsp. sugar	½ tsp. sugar
300ml./10fl.oz. chicken stock	1¼ cups chicken stock
2 tsp. cornflour, mixed to a paste with 1 Tbs. water	2 tsp. cornstarch, mixed to a paste with 1 Tbs. water

Heat the oil in a large saucepan. When it is hot, add the broccoli and stir-fry for 2 minutes.

Add the salt, sugar and chicken stock and stir well. Bring to the boil, cover the pan and cook for 8 minutes, or until the broccoli is cooked but still crisp.

Stir in the cornflour (cornstarch) mixture and cook, stirring constantly, until the sauce thickens and becomes translucent.

Transfer to a warmed serving dish and serve at once.

Serves 6
Preparation and cooking time: 25 minutes

Stir-Braised Cauliflower with Parsley

Metric/Imperial	American
50ml./2fl.oz. peanut oil	4 Tbs. peanut oil
1 medium cauliflower, broken into flowerets	1 medium cauliflower, broken into flowerets
1 medium onion, chopped	1 medium onion, chopped
1 garlic clove, crushed	1 garlic clove, crushed
½ tsp. ground ginger	½ tsp. ground ginger
¼ tsp. 5-spice powder	¼ tsp. 5-spice powder
150ml./5fl.oz. vegetable or beef stock	⅔ cup vegetable or beef stock
2 Tbs. rice wine or dry sherry	2 Tbs. rice wine or dry sherry
4 Tbs. chopped parsley	4 Tbs. chopped parsley

A delicious dish of Stir-Fried Mixed Vegetables cooked in the traditional Chinese way to keep their goodness and crispness.

105

Heat the oil in a large frying-pan. When it is hot, add the cauliflower, onion, garlic and ginger and stir-fry for 5 minutes. Pour over the stock and wine or sherry, then stir in the parsley.

Bring to the boil, cover the pan and cook the mixture over moderate heat for 7 minutes, stirring occasionally.

Transfer the mixture to a warmed serving dish and serve at once.

Serves 6
Preparation and cooking time: 20 minutes

Ginger, famous for its sweet flavour, is an extremely important cooking ingredient throughout the Orient, used not only in curries and in almost all Chinese recipes, but also as a garnish especially in Japan. If buying fresh, the woody husk should be removed and the yellow, succulent flesh should be sliced or finely chopped before use.

Stir-Fried Spinach with Water Chestnuts

Metric/Imperial	American
50ml./2fl.oz. vegetable oil	$\frac{1}{4}$ cup vegetable oil
50g./2oz. bamboo shoot, sliced	$\frac{1}{4}$ cup sliced bamboo shoot
4 dried mushrooms, soaked in cold water for 30 minutes, drained and sliced	4 dried mushrooms, soaked in cold water for 30 minutes, drained and sliced

Metric/Imperial	American
125g./4oz. water chestnuts, sliced	½ cup water chestnuts, sliced
½kg./1lb. fresh leaf spinach, chopped	2 cups chopped leaf spinach
2 pieces star anise	2 pieces star anise
1 Tbs. oyster sauce	1 Tbs. oyster sauce
1 tsp. sugar	1 tsp. sugar

Heat the oil in a large, deep frying-pan. When it is hot, add the vegetables, except the spinach, and stir-fry for 3 minutes. Add the spinach and remaining ingredients and stir-fry for a further 2 minutes.

Transfer the mixture to a warmed serving dish and serve at once.

Serves 6
Preparation and cooking time: 40 minutes

Gingered Vegetables

Metric/Imperial	American
3 Tbs. peanut oil	3 Tbs. peanut oil
10cm./4in. piece of fresh root ginger, peeled and chopped	4in. piece of fresh green ginger, peeled and chopped
1 leek, white part only, thinly sliced on the diagonal	1 leek, white part only, thinly sliced on the diagonal
1 green pepper, pith and seeds removed and chopped	1 green pepper, pith and seeds removed and chopped
1 red pepper, pith and seeds removed and chopped	1 red pepper, pith and seeds removed and chopped
75g./3oz. bamboo shoots, sliced	½ cup sliced bamboo shoots
125g./4oz. bean sprouts	½ cup bean sprouts
50ml./2fl.oz. chicken stock	¼ cup chicken stock
2 Tbs. soya sauce	2 Tbs. soy sauce
½ tsp. sugar	½ tsp. sugar
2 tsp. cornflour, mixed to a paste with 2 Tbs. water	2 tsp. cornstarch mixed to a paste with 2 Tbs. water

Heat the oil in a large frying-pan. When it is hot, add the ginger and stir-fry for 2 minutes. Stir in the vegetables and stir-fry for 5 minutes. Pour over the stock, soy sauce and sugar, and bring to the boil. Add the cornflour (cornstarch) mixture and cook, stirring constantly, until the sauce thickens and becomes translucent.

Transfer the mixture to a warmed serving dish and serve at once.

Serves 6
Preparation and cooking time: 30 minutes

Bean Sprouts with Green Pepper

Metric/Imperial	American
50ml./2fl.oz. vegetable oil	¼ cup vegetable oil
2 large green peppers, pith and seeds removed and cut into thin strips	2 large green peppers, pith and seeds removed and cut into thin strips

1kg./2lb. bean sprouts	4 cups bean sprouts
3 Tbs. rice wine or dry sherry	3 Tbs. rice wine or dry sherry
2 tsp. salt	2 tsp. salt
$\frac{1}{4}$ tsp. monosodium glutamate (optional)	$\frac{1}{4}$ tsp. MSG (optional)

Heat the oil in a large, deep frying-pan. When it is hot, add the peppers and stir-fry for 2 minutes. Add the bean sprouts and stir-fry for a further 2 minutes.

Add the remaining ingredients and stir-fry for 2 minutes. Transfer the mixture to a warmed serving dish and serve at once.

Serves 6-8
Preparation and cooking time: 20 minutes

Quick-Fried Bean Sprouts

Metric/Imperial	American
$\frac{1}{2}$kg./1lb. bean sprouts	2 cups bean sprouts
3 Tbs. sesame oil	3 Tbs. sesame oil
2 spring onions, finely chopped	2 scallions, finely chopped
4 Tbs. Chinese cabbage, finely chopped	4 Tbs. Chinese cabbage, finely chopped
1 tsp. salt	1 tsp. salt
2$\frac{1}{2}$ Tbs. chicken stock	2$\frac{1}{2}$ Tbs. chicken stock

Heat the oil in a large frying-pan. When it is very hot, add the onion and stir-fry for 30 seconds. Stir in the bean sprouts and cabbage and stir-fry until they are translucent. Sprinkle over the salt and stir-fry for a further 1$\frac{1}{2}$ minutes. Add the stock and stir-fry for 1 minute.

Transfer to a warmed serving dish and serve.
Serves 4
Preparation and cooking time: 15 minutes

As fresh beansprouts are difficult to obtain, growing your own offers an easy solution: a glass jar, covered with a piece of cheesecloth secured by a rubber band and containing 10ml. (2 teaspoons) of thoroughly rinsed seed, should be put on its side in a dark place and taken out, thereafter, twice daily to be rinsed. The beansprouts will be ready to eat (see right) within a few days and make a nutritious accompaniment to most Chinese meals, as with this dish (far right) of quick-fried beansprouts.

SWEETS

Honey Apples

Metric/Imperial	American
5 medium cooking apples, peeled, cored and cut into 4 rings	5 medium cooking apples, peeled, cored and cut into 4 rings
SYRUP	SYRUP
125g./4oz. soft brown sugar	⅔ cup soft brown sugar
4 Tbs. clear honey	4 Tbs. clear honey
250ml./8fl.oz. water	1 cup water
juice of 2 lemons	juice of 2 lemons
BATTER	BATTER
125g./4oz. flour	1 cup flour
⅛ tsp. salt	⅛ tsp. salt
2 tsp. sugar	2 tsp. sugar
3 egg yolks	3 egg yolks
75ml./6fl.oz. water	¾ cup water
3 egg whites, stiffly beaten	3 egg whites, stiffly beaten
vegetable oil for deep-frying	vegetable oil for deep-frying
DECORATION	DECORATION
75g./3oz. icing sugar	¾ cup confectioners' sugar
1 lemon, sliced	1 lemon, sliced

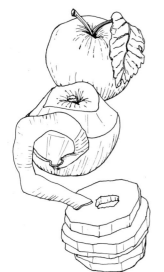

To make the syrup, put the sugar, honey and water in a large saucepan and bring to the boil. Boil for 5 minutes. Remove from the heat and stir in the lemon juice. Drop the apple rings into the syrup and carefully stir to coat them thoroughly. Set aside for 1 hour.

Meanwhile, to make the batter sift the flour and salt into a large bowl. Stir in the sugar. Beat in the egg yolks and water, then fold in the egg whites. Using a slotted spoon, transfer the apple rings to the batter and stir well to coat them completely. Discard the syrup. Set the batter mixture aside.

Fill a large saucepan one-third full with oil and heat until it is hot. Carefully drop in the apple rings, a few at a time, and fry for 2 to 3 minutes, or until they are crisp and golden brown. Remove the apple rings from the pan and drain on kitchen towels.

Put the icing (confectioners') sugar in a deep dish. Dip the apples in the sugar and arrange them on a warmed serving dish. Decorate with the lemon slices and serve at once.

Serves 5
Preparation and cooking time: 1½ hours

Pineapple and Ginger Ice-Cream

Metric/Imperial	American
½ small fresh pineapple, peeled, cored and cut into chunks (reserve any juice)	½ small fresh pineapple, peeled, cored, and cut into chunks (reserve any juice)
4 Tbs. rice wine or dry sherry	4 Tbs. rice wine or dry sherry
600ml./1 pint vanilla ice-cream	2½ cups vanilla ice-cream
25g./1oz. candied ginger, chopped	1oz. crystallized ginger, chopped

A sweetmeat stuffed with dates, almonds and finely grated orange rind, Wontons with Almonds and Dates is a delicious, crunchy dessert to serve at the end of a Chinese dinner.

Mix the pineapple juice and rice wine or sherry in a bowl. Add the pineapple chunks and set aside for 10 minutes.

Beat the ice-cream in a serving bowl until it has softened slightly. Gently fold in the pineapple chunks mixture and candied (crystallized) ginger until they are well mixed. Serve at once.

Serves 4-6

Preparation time: 15 minutes

Wontons with Almonds and Dates

Metric/Imperial	American
175g./6oz. stoned dates, finely chopped	1 cup finely chopped pitted dates
50g./2oz. slivered almonds	⅓ cup flaked almonds
2 tsp. sesame seeds	2 tsp. sesame seeds
grated rind of 1 orange	grated rind of 1 orange
2 Tbs. orange-flower water	2 Tbs. orange-flower water
225g./8oz. wonton dough (see page 39), thinly rolled and cut into 36 squares, or 36 bought wonton wrappers	8oz. wonton dough (see page 39), thinly rolled and cut into 36 squares, or bought wonton wrappers
vegetable oil for deep-frying	vegetable oil for deep-frying
2 Tbs. icing sugar	2 Tbs. confectioners' sugar
1 orange, thinly sliced	1 orange, thinly sliced

Put the dates, almonds, sesame seeds, orange rind and orange-flower water in a bowl and knead the mixture until the ingredients are combined.

Lay the wonton wrappers on a flat surface and put a little filling just below the centre. Wet the edges of the dough, then fold over one corner to make a triangle, pinching the edges together to seal. Pull the corners at the base of the triangle together and pinch to seal.

Fill a large saucepan one-third full with oil and heat until it is very hot. Carefully lower the wontons into the oil, a few at a time, and fry for 2 minutes, or until they are golden brown and crisp. Remove from the oil and drain on kitchen towels.

Arrange the cooked wontons on a warmed serving dish. Sprinkle over the icing (confectioners') sugar and garnish with the orange slices. Serve at once.
Serves 4-6
Preparation and cooking time: 25 minutes

Peking Dust

This is a simplified version of a classic dessert; traditionally fresh chestnuts are used and cooked then puréed. In the recipe below the dish is garnished with preserved ginger and almonds, but halved walnuts or kumquats could also be used.

Metric/Imperial	American
300ml./10fl.oz. double cream	1¼ cups heavy cream
150ml./5fl.oz. single cream	⅔ cup light cream
450g./1lb. canned unsweetened chestnut purée	1lb. canned unsweetened chestnut purée
2 Tbs. water	2 Tbs. water
6 whole almonds	6 whole almonds
50g./2oz. preserved ginger, chopped	⅓ cup chopped crystalized ginger

Put the creams into a bowl and beat until they form stiff peaks. Transfer the mixture to a serving dish, piling up into a dome shape.

Beat the purée and water smooth and soft. Using a flat-bladed knife or the back of a spoon, gradually smooth the purée mixture over the cream mixture until it completely encloses it.

Garnish with the almonds and preserved (candied) ginger and serve at once.
Serves 6
Preparation time: 15 minutes

How To Use Chopsticks

Chopsticks, the traditional way of eating Chinese food, adds excitement to Chinese meals. Once mastered, chopsticks contribute much to the authenticity of Chinese luncheons and dinners. These three photographs illustrate the basic stages of eating with chopsticks.

To start, hold one chopstick between thumb and index finger, against the middle and ring fingers.

The second chopstick should be placed under the thumb against the index finger.

The final positioning of both chopsticks culminates in picking up the food. The second chopstick should be flexible and able to move easily and should be able to support the food with the first.

GLOSSARY

Bamboo shoot
The cone-shaped shoot of tropical bamboo. It is usually sold canned in the West, packed in water. Leftover bean shoot should be stored in fresh water in the refrigerator, changing water frequently. It will keep for about 2 weeks in this way. Obtainable from any oriental store and most larger supermarkets.

Bean curd
One of the most important products of the soya bean. It is sold fresh, in white, shimmering 'cakes' that look somewhat similar to a soft cheese. Fresh bean curd should be stored in fresh cold water in the refrigerator; it will keep for about 2-3 days. Also available canned, in small cubes. When opened, treat as fresh bean curd. Red bean curd is a variety of the above only sold in cans. It is much stronger and should be used sparingly. Available fresh or canned from oriental stores.

Bean sprouts
Sprouts from the mung bean, a plant which also produces the bean from which soy sauce and bean curd are made. Used extensively in Chinese cooking. Available fresh, usually in plastic packs, or canned. Use the fresh variety if possible. If necessary, use canned but always refresh under cold running water to remove excess salt before adding to recipes. To store, either keep unopened in a plastic bag in the refrigerator or immerse in water, changing daily. They will keep for up to 15 days. Fresh bean sprouts are available from oriental stores and health food shops. Canned from oriental stores and most larger supermarkets.

Black beans
Fermented, heavily salted black beans form an important part of Chinese regional cooking in Szechwan and Canton. Sold in cans and sometimes jars. Refresh under cold running water to remove any excess salt before adding to recipes. To store leftover black beans, put in a covered container and keep in the refrigerator. They will keep for about 6 months. Available from oriental stores.

Cellophane noodles
Fine vermicelli made from the starch of the mung bean. Often require only soaking in hot water before use, although they are sometimes deep-fried. Substitute rice vermicelli if unobtainable. Available only from oriental stores.

Chilli sauce
A popular mixture used throughout Chinese cooking, made from a mixture of chillies, salt and vinegar. Quite hot, so use sparingly. Sold in jars and keeps indefinitely. Obtainable from stores and most supermarkets.

Dried mushrooms
Edible fungi of all types are popular in Chinese cooking. Chinese-type dried mushrooms are black and are usually sold by weight in oriental stores. They will keep for up to 1 year. Always soak for at least 30 minutes, before using, to soften and remove the rather hard, woody stalks if necessary. Do not substitute European dried mushrooms if they are unavailable – the flavour is very different.

Five spice powder
A popular seasoning in Chinese cooking, a mixture of ground cinnamon, cloves, Szechwan pepper, fennel and star anise. It is reddish brown in colour and available from oriental stores. Omit from the recipe if unobtainable, or substitute cloves or allspice.

Ginger
One of the most necessary ingredients in all oriental cooking. Fresh ginger is knobbly and light brown in colour. To use, peel the skin and remove the woody pieces. To store leftover ginger, either wrap tightly, unpeeled, in plastic film or cover with dry sherry. Always store in the refrigerator. Keeps for about six weeks. If fresh ginger is unavailable, ground ginger can be substituted but the taste will be very much inferior. Use about $\frac{1}{2}$ teaspoon ground ginger in place of 4cm./$1\frac{1}{2}$in. piece of fresh (green) ginger. Available from all oriental stores and some specialty vegetable shops.

Hoi Sin sauce
Chinese barbecue sauce, reddish brown in colour and of thick, pouring consistency. Used in cooking as a marinade and sauce thickener and often added as a condiment to cooked food. Keeps indefinitely. Available from oriental stores.

Monosodium glutamate (MSG)
A powder of white crystals, somewhat resembling salt in appearance. Used extensively in both Chinese and Japanese cooking, although its use is somewhat frowned upon in the West. Generally supposed to act as a catalyst for other flavours in a dish, rather than having a strong taste of its own but can easily be omitted from a recipe if you prefer. It is always given as an optional ingredient in this book. Available from supermarkets.

Oyster sauce
Delicate, brownish sauce made from a mixture of oysters and soy sauce. Available in cans or bottles from oriental stores. It will keep indefinitely. No substitute if unobtainable.

Rice vermicelli	A fine, white noodle used extensively throughout China and South-East Asia. Sometimes merely soaked in hot water before being used in specific recipes, although it is sometimes deep-fried to make crispy noodles. Available from oriental stores. No substitute – egg vermicelli is very different and should not be substituted in recipes which call for rice vermicelli.
Soy sauce	A condiment made from fermented soya beans, and one of the staple ingredients in Chinese, Japanese, Korean and South-East Asian cooking. Always use Chinese soy sauce for Chinese food. Light soy sauce is used basically for white meat and fish, dark, heavier soy sauce for dark meats. Stores indefinitely in the bottle or jar. Available from supermarkets and oriental stores.
Star anise	Pretty, black 8-pointed star shaped spice, which is used quite frequently in Chinese cooking. Available from oriental stores. If unavailable, omit from the recipe – there is no substitute.
Water chestnuts	Small white bulbs, usually available canned in the West. To store, put leftover water chestnuts in a covered container in the refrigerator, changing the water frequently. They will keep for about 1 month. Available from oriental stores and better supermarkets.

INTRODUCTION TO INDIA

Sharmini Tiruchelvam

Asked what single factor above others had formed the world of man as we know it, my father, a distinguished surgeon, answered unhesitatingly: 'Spices and the search for the Spice-lands'. An apparently flippant answer.

Yet not so on examination. For it was in attempting to discover the route to the fabled spice-rich Indies that the Old World mounted the greatest land search ever and discovered the two Americas, the West Indies and the two pre-canal routes round the Cape of Good Hope and Cape Horn. These discoveries of vast new land masses with their attendant wealth altered horizons in every sense; it changed the path of civilization. It also led Britain and Europe to the East and to the massive colonizing of the latter by the former. But, in the end and at least on the culinary level, it was the East which conquered the palate of the West, for 'curry' in some form or other has become a virtually universal dish.

It is one of the basic Western misconceptions about Indian cuisine that curry is the sum total of it – everything else being merely an extension or variation on the theme. Another is a curious belief that there is some magical, single, all-purpose mixture called a curry powder. A third, that spices are basically harmful, bad for the stomach, the liver, the kidneys, the complexion. (Nothing could be farther from the truth for, in fact, the original functions of spices in cooking were primarily as preservatives and medicinal cures.) In India, as elsewhere, their use gradually evolved from curative to aromatic so that it is now probably true to say that it is the proportionate assembling, method of preparation, combining techniques and blending with one another, and with other ingredients within each recipe, that is literally the very essence of the classic cooking of India and its neighbour Sri Lanka. This mixture of spices is called *masala*.

There is a great mystique about *masala* in the West although its combination is simplicity itself. At their most basic *masalas* are a combination of three types of aromatics – spices, herbs and seasonings. There are, of course, classic combinations but anyone can make up a *masala* with any combination – beginning with the simplest: a basic one-member-from-each-group arrangement (for example: fresh red chillis or paprika ground with crushed garlic, salt and lemon juice). You can then go on to more complex arrangements – and almost invariably discover that you have merely recreated an existing combination! But once certain traditional *masalas* have been mastered, there is nothing to stop you inventing your own dishes.

There is just one injunction: whether a dish be cooked or assembled raw, the *masala* must never taste 'raw'. This is simply a matter of knowing how much marinating or cooking time to allow for the spices especially, and experience will eventually teach when, with which and for how long; for different spices sometimes need attention separately depending on what they are being combined with. Often a quick, dry-pan roasting or 'tempering', in advance of use will suffice.

Some of India's finest cuisine has been developed, preserved and passed on from generation to generation, in fact within families. The recipes were taught practically; rarely, if ever, were they written down. There were of course the master-chefs who served in the palaces and with the great families. They were apprenticed for years to master-chefs before they qualified, so that once again the knowledge was handed down practically. Although considered great artists, even among them, there were almost none who could aspire to, far less claim, all-round proficiency, so great was the range. One man would specialize in *tandoor* cooking; another in the techniques of barbecuing and the preparation of the marinades; another would be a *korma* (considered the greatest art) expert, while yet another would excel in the cooking of *turrcurries* (curry cooking). Finally there was a whole magical world of the confectioner with his 'Arabian Nights' array of sweetmeats.

'The Hand Knows', they say, referring to that infallibility which usually develops with practice – if indeed it has not been there from the beginning – when almost without conscious thought an expert or experienced cook will stop adding a spice or condiment and proceed to the next stage of the work. Knowing the basic classic recipe is essential, but it is important, they say in the East, to know how the finished dish at its best should (a) smell (b) look like (c) taste and (d) have what texture – for instance, the meat of a *pasandah* should virtually melt in the mouth whereas the meat of a *tandoor* cooked chicken should be moist and tender but firm – in that order.

Regional Cooking

Setting aside personal variations, the subcontinent has as many different types of cooking as there are regions and provinces: Bengali, Punjabi (considered by many the best), Kashmiri, Sindhi, Asamese, Tamil, Hyderbadi, Goan to name only some. Each has its own favourite foods and idiosyncratic mixture of spices and other ingredients. The reasons for some are obvious: climate and terrain and the produce of that terrain according to the seasons; proximity to the seas, rivers and oceans and to the availability of foodstuffs from them. The people of Kerala for example, with a considerable sea coast, fisherfolk, have great sea-food cooks. The 'kool' of the South Indian (and Sri Lankan) Tamils is a rich bouillabaisse of sea foods, with powdered kernal of Palmyra palm – which grows in those lands – for thickening, together with diced, barely cooked, crunchy young green beans – probably plucked straight off their runners that morning by the cook. Travellers, traders and invaders influenced the cuisine, too, and undoubtedly the greatest single influence on the formation of an *haute cuisine* in India, was the Moghuls.

The Moghuls came from the north, and it is interesting that one can clearly trace, in the magnificence of Moghlai cooking, the cooking of their wild nomad ancestors, the earlier twelfth century Mongols (who incidentally also influenced Northern Chinese cuisine) with their preference for mutton, skewered marinated meats which were the forerunners of *tandoor* foods, hot pots and pot roasts, together with all-purpose soured milk, the ancestor of yogurt.

The Moghul also brought with him his food taboos. A Muslim, he forbade the eating of pork, also no sea scavengers, no crustacea: similar taboos to those of the Jews, from the same part of the world. One realizes that there were reasons more commonsensical than the mindless proscription of bigots to which these taboos were often attributed. The religious teachers and leaders were also their society's elders, the general law and health-law givers. Certain animals carried diseases which affected man when he ate their flesh. They banned his eating of them. Pork was the chief of these.

It is interesting to note that nowhere in the Vedic Law does it ban the eating of beef. But the elders of India saw the possible decimation of cattle from their land and feared that the pullers of their ploughs and carts, the givers of their precious milk, would be made extinct. So those ancient ecologists declared the cow sacred and banned the eating of its flesh! Buddhism came with its injunctions to take no life whatsoever. With it came into existence a great school of purely vegetarian cooking.

The Classic Methods and Styles

There are about fourteen main methods or techniques of cooking Indian dishes. Some of these, of course, have several subdivisions – for instance, there are four types of *bhuna*. Some also overlap one another as in the case of *dummed-bhuna* or *korma-dohpeeazah*, where each is a mixture of two or more techniques. To put it as simply as possible, they are: Currying – stewing; Dumming – steaming; Korma – braising (classically within a sealed pot); Bhuna – sautéeing and pot roasting; Talawa – deep-frying; Tandoori – *tandoor* oven cooking; Keebab – charcoal grilling (broiling); Oven baking and roasting of specially marinated foods and meat-stuffed breads; Tarka – a form of high-heat searing with ghee and glazing to finish; Parcha – rolled and stuffed meats; Dohpeeazah – the technique of adding onions, classically twice, (hence 'doh') but it can be three or more times throughout the cooking of a dish; Wrapped – 'en paupiette' – wrapped in smoked leaves such as banana leaves, or cooked encrusted in pastry as samosas; Bhogar – combining and assimilating the flavours belonging to two or more ingredients of a dish within a sealed pot; Koftas – minced (ground) meatballs.

Rice and Rice Cooking

There is no doubt that the most exquisitely assembled set of meat, vegetable and fish dishes can be ruined if the basis of the meal, the rice, is less than superb. As with everything else in life the quality of the starter materials matter. There are over a thousand varieties and sub-varieties of rice. The best for savoury rice cooking is Patna – a long-grain non-glutinous rice which cooks out each grain separately. The best again within this grouping are Basmati, Dehra Dun and Almora. There are all sorts of confusions about the various basic rice dishes. To summarize very simply: Plain boiled rice; Plain steamed rice; Mkhani or buttered rice. (The boiled or steamed rice, cooked, has ghee or butter and some delicate aromatics added to it. It is then put under foil or in a sealed dish and 'dummed' for a few minutes in the oven to allow the butter and aromatics to be absorbed.) A fourth type is *pulaus*, which range from plain to *shahi degh pulau*.

The basis of all *pulaus* is that the uncooked rice is first gently sautéed in ghee or butter until the grains become translucent. It is then always cooked in some sort of stock.

Classic *biryanis* are always flavoured and coloured with saffron. Turmeric is sometimes used as a substitute in cheaper versions. They always have the following combination of spices: cumin, coriander, cardamom seeds, whole black peppercorns, cinnamon and cloves. Twice as much butter

A busy, colourful scene in Calcutta where local delicacies can readily be obtained from street traders.

119

as for any of the other *pulaus* is used and twice as much meat or fish as the rice used for the dish.

Breads

Nan, the *tandoor* baked bread is the classic accompaniment for *tandoor* cooked meats. It is leavened bread made from white flour. The basic unleavened bread of the subcontinent – somewhat resembling the Mexican tortilla or a rough, very dry, thickish pancake and very tasty despite that description of it – is the *chapatti*. The thickest and coarsest form of it is called *roti*. The thin form of it is the classic *chapatti*. The thinnest and lightest form of it is the *phulka*. *Puris* are small round, sometimes merely bite-sized *phulkas* deep-fried until they are puffed out and airy light if done well. *Parathas* are heavier, layered, shallow-fried and may be either plain or stuffed with meats or vegetables, or both. All of the above are classically made with wholewheat flour (atar) or pounded barley, millet or buckwheat. They can also be made with rice flour, but this is less tasty and nutritious.

The South of India also boasts a fantastic array of breakfast 'breads' or hoppers, from the plain hopper to the milk hopper and the egg hopper. These are made with toddy leavening. String hoppers – like steamed platelets made of Chinese rice sticks – are made out of rice flour, as is *puttu*, a steamed unsweetened crumble pastry bread with coconut; *iddlis* – feather light, greyish, glancingly sour, soft crumpets are made of rice flour and lentils and *thosais* are like Scots oat-cakes. The list is endless.

Cooking ingredients

The Indians of the North, West and Central parts of India and the purist Jaffna Tamils of Sri Lanka all cook exclusively in ghee (clarified butter). The South Indians and Tamils of Sri Lanka generally use sesame seed, groundnut, coconut and other vegetable oils. The Sri Lankan Singhalese use coconut oil almost exclusively.

The Northern Indians, some South Indians and the Tamils of North Sri Lanka marinate their meats in yogurt, which also acts as a tenderizer. The South Indian Tamils, and the Tamils and Singhalese of Sri Lanka, also use asopfection perunkayam, vinegar, lime, lemon, tamarind, tomatoes, the crushed leaves of papaya or the juice of the raw fruit yielding papein, crushed pomegranate seeds and acid fruits such as young mangoes.

The Northern Indians, especially, are the makers of great stocks. The two classic ones are *akni* or vegetable stock – a court bouillon with a vegetable base and aromatics – and *yakni* or meat stock – a thick double-layered jelly of meat and vegetable stock with aromatics. These they use for the cooking of *pulaus* and *biryanis*. The South Indians and the Sri Lankan Tamils also make tasty stocks or 'soups' which they use as separate dishes within

(Above) Mustard is grown extensively in India and is a basic ingredient for many Indian recipes.

(Right) Women workers gather a rich crop of tea on a plantation in India.

the framework of a balanced meal when, for example, the main meat dish is a dry *korma*. Their *rasam* – coriander soup – and *mulliguthanni* or pepper-water soup (translated into mulligatawny soup by the British) are both famous.

The Northern Indians use cream and yogurt to thicken their sauces and gravies; the South Indians use yogurt and the first thick milk of coconuts, as do the Sri Lankans. However, in addition to their aromatizing effects, *masalas* are also used as thickening agents; as are crushed nuts such as cashewnuts, peanuts, almonds and pistachio nuts; poppy seed and jackfruit and breadfruit seeds powdered or pulverized; raw rice or parboiled rice roasted; fruits such as tomatoes; onions and garlic ground into pastes or finely pulverized; green and red chillis, ground; coriander, fenugreek, fennel, dill, mustard, mint, parsley or murunga leaves; chal and other lentils and pulses cooked to a pulp, roasted grated coconut, pounded maldive fish or the finely pulverized head and shells of shrimps and prawns for thickening seafood dishes.

In the North of India they powder and pound their spices. In the South and in Sri Lanka the cooking *masalas* are made up of ground spices and usually made up first into wet *masalas* – that is, as

pastes. The spices are ground daily, especially in the South, on a grinding stone using water, saltwater, coconutwater, lime or lemon juice, or tamarind or goraka water, according to the requirements of that day's recipes.

A dry-ground roasted *masala* mix called *garam masala* – for which various people have various recipes they swear by, is used as an aromatic garnish for certain dishes but it must never be treated as a cooking *masala*; it can give the dish a heavy and musty flavour.

Gold and silver foil so thin 'a breath could blow it away', is used both to beautify the dish and to act as a digestive, mostly by the Northern Indians. The Southerners make pretty patterns of the coloured powders of paprika, turmeric, chopped parsleys and spring greens (collards). Most important of all the actual laying out of the food in bowls and dishes should be the greatest appetizer of all: appealing to the 'senses of the eyes' – physical and spiritual!

Feasts of this fare are fun to make once one has learned a little about the cuisine.

Serving Indian Food
Whether one is ordering it in a restaurant or making it oneself the meal must always be balanced, not only from a point of dietary value – a fair balance of proteins, fats and carbohydrates – but from a point of view of texture and flavour. If a dryish *korma* is the main meat dish, the vegetable or fish dish accompanying it must be a gravy curry together with, say, a medium dry lentil dish. The Southerners, especially, consider a meal a success when one of the dishes causes 'the mouth to burn'. They will then 'balance' this with a cooling buttermilk or curd preparation such as a *raita*. They will probably also have a salad or fresh vegetable chutney. (Quite apart from the preserved variety of jam-like chutneys.) They will usually also have some fresh pickles or *achars*, *sambals* (pungent mixtures of meats, fish or vegetables ground finely or pounded together), *cachombars* (fresh mixed vegetables mixed with fresh herbs), fried bombay duck and fried or roasted poppadums and the preserved chutneys.

All the dishes are served at once and it is up to the person eating to serve themselves the meal with the flavours which they wish to predominate. In short, there are two levels of artistry involved: that of the chef and that of the diner. And perhaps even a third: that of the hostess who, once she has cooked her meal, will set it out in such a way and in such proportions, that the guests will be inclined to follow her lead and take the food as she has apportioned it.

A mouth watering selection
of typical Indians breads.

VEGETABLES & PULSES

Turkari Aloo

(Curried Potatoes)

Metric/Imperial	American
50g./2oz. ghee or clarified butter	¼ cup ghee or clarified butter
½ tsp. turmeric	½ tsp. turmeric
700g./1½lb. potatoes, cut into 2½cm./1in. cubes	1½lb. potatoes, cut into 1in. cubes
3 garlic cloves, crushed	3 garlic cloves, crushed
2 green chillis, chopped	2 green chillis, chopped
1 tsp. ground fenugreek	1 tsp. ground fenugreek
1 Tbs. ground coriander	1 Tbs. ground coriander
1 tsp. salt	1 tsp. salt
450ml./15fl.oz. yogurt, well beaten	2 cups yogurt, well beaten
1 Tbs. chopped coriander leaves	1 Tbs. chopped coriander leaves

Melt the ghee or clarified butter in a saucepan. Add the turmeric and potatoes and fry, turning the cubes frequently, until they are lightly and evenly browned. Stir in the garlic, chillis, spices and salt and fry for 3 minutes, striring constantly. Stir in the yogurt. Bring to the boil, reduce the heat to low and simmer the mixture for 30 minutes, or until the potatoes are tender.

Transfer the mixture to a warmed serving dish, and sprinkle over the coriander before serving.
Serves 4
Preparation and cooking time: 45 minutes

Gobi Ki Sabzi

(Spicy Cauliflower)

Metric/Imperial	American
5 Tbs. vegetable oil	5 Tbs. vegetable oil
1 tsp. mustard seeds	1 tsp. mustard seeds
2½cm./1in. piece of fresh root ginger, peeled and cut into thin strips	1in. piece of fresh green ginger, peeled and cut into thin strips
1 onion, sliced	1 onion, sliced
1 tsp. turmeric	1 tsp. turmeric
1 green chilli, chopped	1 green chilli, chopped
1 large cauliflower, separated into flowerets	1 large cauliflower, separated into flowerets
1 tsp. salt	1 tsp. salt
juice of ½ lemon	juice of ½ lemon
1 Tbs. chopped coriander leaves	1 Tbs. chopped coriander leaves

Heat the oil in a saucepan. When it is hot, add the mustard seeds and cover the

pan. When the seeds stop spattering, remove the lid and add the ginger, onion, turmeric and chilli. Fry for 3 minutes, stirring occasionally.

Stir in the cauliflower pieces and salt and sprinkle over the lemon juice. Cover the pan, reduce the heat to low and simmer for 20 minutes, or until the cauliflower is tender.

Transfer the mixture to a warmed serving dish and sprinkle over the coriander before serving.

Serves 4

Preparation and cooking time: 35 minutes

Gobi Ki Sabzi is a hot, spicy dish of cauliflower, well seasoned with mustard seeds.

Dum Gobi

(Cauliflower Baked in Yogurt)

Metric/Imperial	American
1 cauliflower, separated into flowerets	1 cauliflower, separated into flowerets
1 onion, finely chopped	1 onion, finely chopped
300ml./10fl.oz. yogurt	1¼ cups yogurt
2 Tbs. tomato purée	2 Tbs. tomato paste
1 tsp. ground coriander	1 tsp. ground coriander
1 tsp. garam masala	1 tsp. garam masala
¼ tsp. ground ginger	¼ tsp. ground ginger
½ tsp. turmeric	½ tsp. turmeric
½ tsp. salt	½ tsp. salt
1 Tbs. ghee or clarified butter, melted	1 Tbs. ghee or clarified butter, melted

Preheat the oven to fairly hot 190°C (Gas Mark 5, 375°F).

Arrange the cauliflower pieces in an ovenproof dish. Blend all the remaining ingredients, except the ghee, together, then pour the mixture over the cauliflower.

Put the dish into the oven and bake for 1 hour. Sprinkle the ghee or clarified butter over the cauliflower and return to the oven for a further 1 hour, adding more ghee if the cauliflower becomes too dry.

Transfer to a warmed serving dish and serve at once.

Serves 4
Preparation and cooking time: 2¼ hours

Khutti Dhal

(Spiced Lentils)

Metric/Imperial	American
25g./1oz. ghee or clarified butter	2 Tbs. ghee or clarified butter
1 onion, sliced	1 onion, sliced
1 garlic clove, crushed	1 garlic clove, crushed
1 green chilli, chopped	1 green chilli, chopped
½ tsp. ground cinnamon	½ tsp. ground cinnamon
½ tsp. hot chilli powder	½ tsp. hot chilli powder
225g./8oz. mixed dhal (lentils), washed and drained	1 cup mixed dhal (lentils), washed and drained
725ml./1¼ pints water	3 cups water
½ tsp. salt	½ tsp. salt
250ml./8fl.oz. coconut milk	1 cup coconut milk

Melt the ghee or clarified butter in a saucepan. Add the onion and garlic and fry, stirring occasionally, until the onion is golden brown. Add the chilli and fry for 2 minutes, stirring frequently. Add the cinnamon, chilli powder and dhal (lentils), then pour over the water and salt. Bring to the boil, stirring occasionally. Reduce the heat to low and simmer the mixture for 1 hour, stirring occasionally.

Purée the mixture in a blender, then return to the saucepan. Stir in the coconut milk and bring to the boil. Simmer for 10 minutes.

Transfer the mixture to a warmed serving bowl and serve at once.

Serves 4
Preparation and cooking time: 1½ hours

Sambar

(Lentils Cooked with Spices)

Metric/Imperial	American
225g./8oz. toovar dhal (lentils), soaked in cold water for 1 hour and drained	1 cup toovar dhal (lentils), soaked in cold water for 1 hour and drained
¼ tsp. ground fenugreek	¼ tsp. ground fenugreek
1¼l./2 pints water	5 cups water
1½ tsp. salt	1½ tsp. salt
50g./2oz. fresh coconut, chopped	⅓ cup chopped fresh coconut,
2 tsp. cumin seeds	2 tsp. cumin seeds
1 Tbs. coriander seeds	1 Tbs. coriander seeds
½ tsp. ground cinnamon	½ tsp. ground cinnamon
50g./2oz. tamarind	¼ cup tamarind
250ml./8fl.oz. boiling water	1 cup boiling water
2 tsp. soft brown sugar	2 tsp. soft brown sugar
1 tsp. hot chilli powder	1 tsp. hot chilli powder
2 Tbs. chopped coriander leaves	2 Tbs. chopped coriander leaves
2 Tbs. vegetable oil	2 Tbs. vegetable oil
1 tsp. mustard seeds	1 tsp. mustard seeds
1 tsp. turmeric	1 tsp. turmeric
¼ tsp. asafoetida	¼ tsp. asafoetida
2 garlic cloves, crushed	2 garlic cloves, crushed
1 green chilli, finely chopped	1 green chilli, finely chopped

Put the dhal, fenugreek, water and 1 teaspoon of salt into a saucepan and bring to the boil. Reduce the heat to low and simmer for 1 hour, or until the dhal is soft. Remove from the heat.

Meanwhile, cook the coconut, cumin, coriander and cinnamon in a frying-pan for 3 minutes, stirring constantly. Remove from the heat and cool. Purée the mixture in a blender with 4 tablespoons of water. Transfer to a bowl and set aside.

Put the tamarind into a bowl and pour over the water. Set aside until it is cool. Pour the contents of the bowl through a strainer into a saucepan, pressing as much of the pulp through as possible. Put the saucepan over moderate heat and stir in the sugar, chilli powder, coriander leaves and remaining salt. Simmer for 5 minutes. Remove from the heat and set aside.

Heat the oil in a small frying-pan. Add the mustard seeds and cover. When they begin to spatter, stir in the remaining spices, garlic and chilli. Reduce the heat to low and fry for 2 minutes, stirring constantly. Spoon the contents of the pan into the dhal with the tamarind mixture and coconut and spice purée. Stir to mix. Return the pan to low heat and simmer for 10 minutes, stirring frequently.

Transfer the mixture to a warmed serving bowl and serve at once.

Serves 4-6
Preparation and cooking time: 3 hours

(See over) Sambar, a dish originating from South India, is often served with boiled rice as part of an Indian meal.

Ekuri

(Scrambled Eggs with Chilli)
This is one of the specialities of the Parsees, a religious community on the west coast of India.

Metric/Imperial	American
40g./1½oz. butter	3 Tbs. butter
1 medium onion, chopped	1 medium onion, chopped
1cm./½in. piece of fresh root ginger, peeled and chopped	½in. piece of fresh green ginger, peeled and chopped
1 green chilli, chopped	1 green chilli, chopped
½ tsp. turmeric	½ tsp. turmeric
2 Tbs. chopped coriander leaves	2 Tbs. chopped coriander leaves
½ tsp. salt	½ tsp. salt
8 eggs, lightly beaten	8 eggs, lightly beaten
4 slices toast	4 slices toast
2 tomatoes, quartered	2 tomatoes, quartered

Melt the butter in a frying-pan. Add the onion and ginger and fry, stirring occasionally, until the onion is golden brown. Stir in the chilli, turmeric, 1½ tablespoons of coriander and the salt, and fry for 1 minute. Pour in the eggs, reduce the heat to low and cook the eggs until they are softly scrambled, stirring constantly.

Spoon the mixture on to the toast slices and garnish with the tomatoes and remaining coriander before serving.
Serves 4
Preparation and cooking time: 15 minutes

Mattar Pannir

(Peas and Cheese)

Metric/Imperial	American
50g./2oz. ghee or clarified butter	¼ cup ghee or clarified butter
4cm./1½in. piece of fresh root ginger, peeled and chopped	1½in. piece of fresh green ginger, peeled and chopped
2 garlic cloves, crushed	2 garlic cloves, crushed
1½ tsp. coriander seeds	1½ tsp. coriander seeds
½ tsp. cardamom seeds	½ tsp. cardamom seeds
½ tsp. hot chilli powder	½ tsp. hot chilli powder
1 tsp. turmeric	1 tsp. turmeric
½kg./1lb. peas, weighed after shelling	2⅔ cups peas, weighed after shelling
350g./12oz. feta or goat cheese	12oz. feta or goat cheese
3 tomatoes, blanched, peeled and chopped	3 tomatoes, blanched, peeled and chopped
1 Tbs. chopped coriander leaves	1 Tbs. chopped coriander leaves

Melt the ghee or clarified butter in a saucepan. Add the ginger and garlic and fry for 3 minutes, stirring constantly. Stir in the coriander and spices and fry for a further 1 minute, stirring constantly. Add a spoonful or two of water if the mixture becomes too dry. Stir in the peas and simmer for 10 minutes. Stir in the cheese and tomatoes and simmer for a further 10 minutes.

Transfer to a warmed serving dish and sprinkle over the coriander before serving.

Serves 6
Preparation and cooking time: 35 minutes

Tamatar Bharta

(Pureéd Tomatoes)

Metric/Imperial	American
700g./1½lb. tomatoes	1½lb. tomatoes
2 Tbs. vegetable oil	2 Tbs. vegetable oil
2 medium onions, chopped	2 medium onions, chopped
2 green chillis, chopped	2 green chillis, chopped
1cm./½in. piece of fresh root ginger, peeled and chopped	½in. piece of fresh green ginger, peeled and chopped
1 tsp. salt	1 tsp. salt
1 tsp. sugar	1 tsp. sugar
5 Tbs. yogurt	5 Tbs. yogurt
1 Tbs. chopped coriander leaves	1 Tbs. chopped coriander leaves

Blanch, peel and chop the tomatoes finely or, for a better flavour, put them under a hot grill (broiler) until the skins are scorched, then peel and chop them. Set aside.

Heat the oil in a saucepan. When it is hot, add the onions, chillis and ginger and fry, stirring frequently, until the onions are golden brown. Stir in the salt, sugar, yogurt and tomatoes and simmer, stirring occasionally, for 30 minutes, or until the mixture is thick.

Transfer the mixture to a warmed serving bowl and sprinkle over the coriander before serving.

Serves 4
Preparation and cooking time: 1 hour

Vendai Kai Kari

(Curried Okra)

Metric/Imperial	American
50g./2oz. tamarind	¼ cup tamarind
250ml./8fl.oz. boiling water	1 cup boiling water
5 Tbs. vegetable oil	5 Tbs. vegetable oil
700g./1½lb. okra, sliced	1½lb. okra, sliced
2 medium onions, sliced	2 medium onions, sliced
2½cm./1in. piece of fresh root ginger, peeled and chopped	1in. piece of fresh green ginger, peeled and chopped
2 garlic cloves, crushed	2 garlic cloves, crushed
2 green chillis, sliced	2 green chillis, sliced

Metric/Imperial	American
1 tsp. turmeric	1 tsp. turmeric
1 Tbs. ground coriander	1 Tbs. ground coriander
250ml./8fl.oz. coconut milk	1 cup coconut milk
1 tsp. salt	1 tsp. salt
1 tsp. mustard seeds	1 tsp. mustard seeds
4 curry or bay leaves	4 curry or bay leaves

Put the tamarind in a small bowl. Pour over the boiling water and set aside until it is cool. Pour the contents of the bowl through a strainer, pressing as much of the pulp through as possible.

Heat 4 tablespoons of the oil in a saucepan. When it is hot, add the okra and fry, stirring occasionally, until it is evenly browned. Using a slotted spoon, transfer the okra to a plate and set aside. Add the onions, ginger, garlic and chillis to the pan and fry, stirring occasionally, until the onions are golden brown. Stir in the spices and fry for 3 minutes, stirring constantly. Add a spoonful or two of water if the mixture becomes too dry.

Stir in the tamarind juice, return the okra to the pan and bring to the boil. Cover the pan, reduce the heat to low and simmer for 5 minutes. Stir in the coconut milk and salt and bring to the boil again. Reduce the heat to low again and simmer for 10 minutes.

Meanwhile, heat the remaining oil in a small frying-pan. When it is hot, add the mustard seeds and curry or bay leaves. Cover, and when the seeds stop spattering, stir the mixture into the okra mixture. Cook for 1 minute.

Transfer to a warmed serving dish and serve at once.

Serves 4
Preparation and cooking time: 1 hour

Khichri

(Rice with Lentils)

Metric/Imperial	American
65g./2½oz. butter	5 Tbs. butter
1 onion, finely chopped	1 onion, finely chopped
2½cm./1in. piece of fresh root ginger, peeled and chopped	1in. piece of fresh green ginger, peeled and chopped
1 garlic clove, crushed	1 garlic clove, crushed
6 peppercorns	6 peppercorns
1 bay leaf	1 bay leaf
225g./8oz. long-grain rice and 125g./4oz. yellow moong dhal (lentils), soaked together in cold water for 1 hour and drained	1⅓ cups long-grain rice and ½ cup yellow moong dhal (lentils), soaked together in cold water for 1 hour and drained
1 tsp. salt	1 tsp. salt
½ tsp. turmeric	½ tsp. turmeric
600ml./1 pint boiling water	2½ cups boiling water
fried onion slices	fried onion slices

Melt 40g./1½oz. (3 tablespoons) of the butter in a saucepan. Add the onion and fry, stirring occasionally, until it is soft. Stir in the ginger, garlic, peppercorns and bay leaf and fry for 3 minutes, stirring constantly. Add the rice, dhal, salt and turmeric and stir well. Simmer for 5 minutes, stirring frequently.

Pour in the water and stir once. Cover the pan, reduce the heat to low and simmer for 15 to 20 minutes, or until the rice is cooked and the liquid is absorbed. Stir in the remaining butter.

Transfer the mixture to a warmed serving dish, scatter over the fried onions and serve at once.

Serves 4

Preparation and cooking time: 1½ hours

Vegetable kitcheri

Metric/Imperial	American
2 tsp. salt	2 tsp. salt
225g./8oz. long-grain rice, soaked in cold water for 30 minutes and drained	1⅓ cups long-grain rice, soaked in cold water for 30 minutes and drained
75g./3oz. moong dhal (lentils), washed and drained	⅓ cup moong dhal (lentils), washed and drained
50g./2oz. tur dhal, washed and drained	¼ cup tur dhal, washed and drained
75g./3oz. masoor dhal, washed and drained	⅓ cup masoor dhal, washed and drained
65g./2½oz. butter	5 Tbs. butter
2 medium onions, sliced	2 medium onions, sliced
2 green chillis, chopped	2 green chillis, chopped
2½cm./1in. piece of fresh root ginger, peeled and chopped	1in. piece of fresh green ginger, peeled and chopped
2 garlic cloves, crushed	2 garlic cloves, crushed
1 Tbs. ground coriander	1 Tbs. ground coriander
½ tsp. turmeric	½ tsp. turmeric
1 potato, cubed	1 potato, cubed
1 large carrot, cubed	1 large carrot, cubed
1 small aubergine, cubed	1 small eggplant, cubed
125g./4oz. peas, weighed after shelling	⅔ cup peas, weighed after shelling
½ small cauliflower, separated into flowerets	½ small cauliflower, separated into flowerets
2 large tomatoes, blanched, peeled and chopped	2 large tomatoes, blanched, peeled and chopped
450ml./15fl.oz. chicken stock	2 cups chicken stock
25 g./1oz. butter, melted	2 Tbs. butter, melted

Half-fill a saucepan with boiling water and stir in ½ teaspoon of salt. Add the rice, bring to the boil again and boil the rice for 3 minutes. Remove from the heat and drain the rice. Set aside. Half-fill the same saucepan with boiling water again and stir in another ½ teaspoon of salt. Add the dhals (lentils), bring to the boil and boil for 5 minutes. Remove from the heat and drain the dhals. Set aside.

Melt 50g./2oz. (4 tablespoons) of the butter in a large frying-pan. Add the onions and fry, stirring occasionally, until they are golden brown. Add the chillis, ginger and garlic and fry for 2 minutes, stirring frequently. Stir in the coriander and turmeric and fry for 1 minute. Add the vegetables and remaining salt and stir well. Cover the pan, reduce the heat to moderately low and simmer for 20 to 30 minutes, or until the vegetables are tender.

Preheat the oven to very cool 140°C (Gas Mark 1, 275°F). Use the remaining butter to grease a large flameproof casserole. Make layers of the dhals, vegetables and rice in the casserole, in that order, ending with a layer of rice. Pour in the stock and cook the mixture for 1 minute. Cover and transfer to the oven. Cook for 45 minutes to 1 hour, or until the dhals and rice are cooked and the liquid is absorbed.

Remove from the oven, sprinkle over the melted butter and serve, straight from the dish.

Serves 6

Preparation and cooking time: 2½ hours

(See over) Vegetable Kitcheri, an imaginative mixture of rice and assorted vegetables, is a delicious and substantial vegetarian dish.

133

Wengyachen Bharit

(Curried Aubergines [Eggplants])

Metric/Imperial	American
1kg./2lb. aubergines	2lb. eggplants
40g./1½oz. butter	3 Tbs. butter
3 medium onions, chopped	3 medium onions, chopped
4 garlic cloves, crushed	4 garlic cloves, crushed
5cm./2in. piece of fresh root ginger, peeled and chopped	2in. piece of fresh green ginger, peeled and chopped
2 green chillis, seeded and chopped	2 green chillis, seeded and chopped
½ bunch chopped coriander leaves	½ bunch chopped coriander leaves
1 tsp. turmeric	1 tsp. turmeric

1 tsp. ground cumin	1 tsp. ground cumin
1 tsp. salt	1 tsp. salt
175ml./6fl.oz. yogurt	¾ cup yogurt
2 tsp. sugar	2 tsp. sugar

Preheat the oven to moderate 180°C (Gas Mark 4, 350°F).

Make three cuts in each aubergine (eggplant) and arrange on a baking sheet. Put the sheet into the oven and bake the aubergines (eggplants) for 45 minutes to 1 hour, or until they are soft. Remove from the oven and set aside until they are cool enough to handle. Peel and discard the skins and transfer the pulp to a bowl. Mash to a smooth purée.

Melt the butter in a saucepan. Add the onions and fry, stirring occasionally, until they are golden brown. Stir in the garlic, ginger and chillis and fry for 3 minutes, stirring frequently. Stir in the coriander, turmeric and cumin. Cook for 1 minute. Add the aubergine (eggplant) purée and salt and cook for 5 minutes, stirring frequently.

Stir in the yogurt and sugar, then transfer to a warmed serving dish and serve at once.
Serves 4
Preparation and cooking time: 2 hours

Wengi Bhat

(Aubergines [Eggplants] and Rice)

Metric/Imperial	American
6 small aubergines	6 small eggplants
2 dried red chillis	2 dried red chillis
2 garlic cloves	2 garlic cloves
1 tsp. mustard seeds	1 tsp. mustard seeds
1 tsp. turmeric	1 tsp. turmeric
4 cloves	4 cloves
6 black peppercorns	6 black peppercorns
1 tsp. cumin seeds	1 tsp. cumin seeds
1 tsp. white poppy seeds	1 tsp. white poppy seeds
3 Tbs. peanuts	3 Tbs. peanuts
4-6 Tbs. water	4-6 Tbs. water
75g./3oz. butter	6 Tbs. butter
1½ tsp. salt	1½ tsp. salt
2 medium onions, sliced	2 medium onions, sliced
350g./12oz. long-grain rice, soaked in cold water for 30 minutes and drained	2 cups long-grain rice, soaked in cold water for 30 minutes and drained
2 Tbs. desiccated coconut, blended with 2 Tbs. water	2 Tbs. shredded coconut, blended with 2 Tbs. water

Cut the aubergines (eggplants) in half, lengthways, and scoop out the flesh. Reserve the skins. Put the pulp in a bowl.

Blend the spices, peanuts and water to a smooth purée, adding the extra water if necessary. Transfer the purée to a small bowl.

Melt 25g./1oz. (2 tablespoons) of butter in a frying-pan. Add the spice purée and fry for 3 minutes, stirring constantly. Stir in the aubergine (eggplant) pulp and half the salt and fry for 7 minutes, stirring frequently. Spoon the mixture into the reserved skins and set aside.

Rinse and dry the frying-pan. Melt a further 25g./1oz. (2 tablespoons) of butter in the pan. Add the onions and fry, stirring occasionally, until they are golden brown. Add the stuffed aubergines (eggplants), reduce the heat to low and simmer for 5 minutes. Remove from the heat.

Preheat the oven to cool 150°C (Gas Mark 2, 300°F).

Melt the remaining butter in a saucepan. Add the rice and remaining salt and fry for 3 minutes, stirring constantly. Pour in enough boiling water to cover the rice by 1cm./½in. and bring to the boil. Cover the pan, reduce the heat to low and simmer for 15 to 20 minutes, or until the rice is cooked and the liquid is absorbed. Remove from the heat and stir in the coconut.

Arrange a third of the rice in a large baking dish and cover with half the aubergine (eggplant) halves, cut sides uppermost. Continue making layers in this way, ending with a layer of rice. Cover and put the dish into the oven. Bake for 25 minutes.

Remove from the oven and serve at once, from the dish.
Serves 4-6
Preparation and cooking time: 2 hours

Kabli Channa

(Whole Chick-Peas)

Metric/Imperial	American
225g./8oz. dried chick-peas, soaked overnight and drained	1⅓ cups dried chick-peas, soaked overnight and drained
600ml./1 pint water	2½ cups water
1 tsp. salt	1 tsp. salt
50ml./2fl.oz. vegetable oil	¼ cup vegetable oil
2 medium onions, sliced	2 medium onions, sliced
2 garlic cloves, chopped	2 garlic cloves, chopped
2½cm./1in. piece of fresh root ginger, peeled and cut into thin strips	1in. piece of fresh green ginger, peeled and cut into thin strips
1 tsp. turmeric	1 tsp. turmeric
1 tsp. ground cumin	1 tsp. ground cumin
2 tsp. ground coriander	2 tsp. ground coriander
4 green chillis, slit open	4 green chillis, slit open
1 large tomato, blanched, peeled, seeded and chopped	1 large tomato, blanched, peeled, seeded and chopped
1 green pepper, pith and seeds removed and cut into strips	1 green pepper, pith and seeds removed and cut into strips
juice of 1½ lemons	juice of 1½ lemons
1 tsp. garam masala	1 tsp. garam masala
2 Tbs. chopped coriander leaves	2 Tbs. chopped coriander leaves

Put the chick-peas into a saucepan and add the water and ¼ teaspoon of salt. Bring to the boil, cover and reduce the heat to low. Simmer for 1½ hours, or until the peas are tender. Drain and reserve 300ml./10fl.oz. (1¼ cups) of the cooking liquid.

Heat the oil in a frying-pan.

When it is hot, add the onions and garlic and fry, stirring occasionally, until the onions are golden brown. Add the ginger and fry for 1 minute, then stir in the spices and fry for 5 minutes, stirring constantly. Add a spoonful or two of water if the mixture becomes too dry. Add the chillis, tomato and pepper and cook for 5 minutes. Stir in the chick-peas and cook for a further 7 minutes. Stir in the reserved cooking liquid, the remaining salt and the lemon juice, and bring to the boil.

Cover the frying-pan and reduce the heat to low. Simmer for 15 minutes, uncover and simmer for a further 10 minutes.

Transfer the mixture to a warmed serving dish and sprinkle over the garam masala and coriander before serving.

Serves 4
Preparation and cooking time: 2¼ hours

Sabzi Pulao

(Vegetable Pilaff)

Metric/Imperial	American
125g./4oz. butter	8 Tbs. butter
1 medium onion, sliced	1 medium onion, sliced

2 garlic cloves, crushed
2½cm./1in. piece of fresh root ginger,
   peeled and chopped
1 green chilli, seeded and chopped
1 tsp. turmeric
½ tsp. hot chilli powder
225g./8oz. cauliflower, separated into
   flowerets
125g./4oz. peas, weighed after shelling
125g./4oz. carrots, sliced
1 small aubergine, cubed
1 small green pepper, pith and seeds
   removed and chopped
2 potatoes, cubed
2 tomatoes, blanched, peeled and
   chopped
175ml./6fl.oz. chicken stock
1 Tbs. chopped coriander leaves
1 tsp. salt
350g./12oz. long-grain rice, cooked
   until just tender

2 garlic cloves, crushed
1in. piece of fresh green ginger, peeled
   and chopped
1 green chilli, seeded and chopped
1 tsp. turmeric
½ tsp. hot chilli powder
8oz. cauliflower, separated into
   flowerets
⅔ cup peas, weighed after shelling
⅔ cup sliced carrots
1 small eggplant, cubed
1 small green pepper, pith and seeds
   removed and chopped
2 potatoes, cubed
2 tomatoes, blanched, peeled and
   chopped
¾ cup chicken stock
1 Tbs. chopped coriander leaves
1 tsp. salt
2 cups long-grain rice, cooked until
   just tender

Aviyal, a versatile curry, can be made from any combination of vegetables.

GARNISH
1 Tbs. butter
2 Tbs. slivered almonds
2 Tbs. raisins

GARNISH
1 Tbs. butter
2 Tbs. slivered almonds
2 Tbs. raisins

Melt the butter in a frying-pan. Add the onion, garlic, ginger and chilli and fry, stirring occasionally, until the onion is golden brown. Stir in the turmeric and chilli powder and fry for 1 minute, stirring constantly. Add the remaining vegetables, one at a time, stirring well before adding the next. Pour in the stock and bring to the boil. Stir in the coriander and salt, cover and reduce the heat to low. Simmer for 25 to 30 minutes, or until the vegetables are tender. Remove from the heat.

Preheat the oven to warm 170°C (Gas Mark 3, 325°F). Layer the rice and vegetable mixture in a well-greased baking dish, beginning and ending with a layer of rice. Cover and put the dish into the oven. Bake for 25 minutes.

Meanwhile, to prepare the garnish, melt the butter in a frying-pan. Add the almonds and raisins and fry, stirring constantly, until they are lightly browned. Remove from the heat.

Remove the dish from the oven and scatter over the garnish before serving.
Serves 6
Preparation and cooking time: 1½ hours

Aviyal

(Vegetable Curry)

You can use any combination of vegetables you wish in this spicy dish – carrots, beans, aubergine (eggplant), turnip, cauliflower, green pepper, potatoes and spring onions (scallions) were used in the version photographed below.

Metric/Imperial	American
50ml./2fl.oz. vegetable oil	¼ cup vegetable oil
1 tsp. mustard seeds	1 tsp. mustard seeds
5cm./2in. piece of fresh root ginger, peeled and minced	2in. piece of fresh green ginger, peeled and ground
2 garlic cloves, quartered	2 garlic cloves, quartered
1 onion, grated	1 onion, grated
1 green chilli, minced	1 green chilli, ground
1½ tsp. turmeric	1½ tsp. turmeric
1 Tbs. ground coriander	1 Tbs. ground coriander
700g./1½lb. mixed vegetables, sliced	1½lb. mixed vegetables, sliced
1 tsp. salt	1 tsp. salt
225g./8oz. fresh coconut or 2½cm./1in. slice creamed coconut, puréed with 175ml./6fl.oz. water.	8oz. fresh coconut or 1in. slice creamed coconut, puréed with ¾ cup water
2 Tbs. chopped coriander leaves	2 Tbs. chopped coriander leaves

Heat the oil in a large saucepan. When it is hot, add the mustard seeds, ginger and garlic and fry for 30 seconds, stirring constantly. Add the onion and chilli and fry until the onion is golden brown. Stir in the turmeric and coriander and cook for 1 minute. Add the vegetables and stir to mix. Stir in the salt and coconut purée. Add a spoonful or two of water if the mixture becomes too dry. Cover the pan and simmer for 30 minutes, or until the vegetables are tender.

Transfer the mixture to a warmed serving dish and sprinkle over the chopped coriander before serving.
Serves 4
Preparation and cooking time: 40 minutes

MEAT

Kheema

(Curried Minced [Ground] Lamb)

Metric/Imperial	American
50ml./2fl.oz. vegetable oil	¼ cup vegetable oil
3 large onions, sliced	3 large onions, sliced
2½cm./1in. piece of fresh root ginger, peeled and chopped	1in. piece of fresh green ginger, peeled and chopped
2 garlic cloves, crushed	2 garlic cloves, crushed
1 tsp. turmeric	1 tsp. turmeric
1 tsp. hot chilli powder	1 tsp. hot chilli powder
1 tsp. ground coriander	1 tsp. ground coriander
700g./1½lb. minced lamb	1½lb. ground lamb
1 tsp. salt	1 tsp. salt
3 tomatoes, blanched, peeled, seeded and chopped	3 tomatoes, blanched, peeled, seeded and chopped
2 Tbs. chopped coriander leaves	2 Tbs. chopped coriander leaves

Heat the oil in a deep frying-pan. When it is hot, add the onions, ginger and garlic and fry, stirring occasionally, until the onions are soft. Stir in the spices and fry for 3 minutes, stirring frequently. Add the meat and fry until it loses its pinkness. Stir in the salt and tomatoes and bring to the boil. Cover the pan, reduce the heat to low and simmer for 15 minutes. Uncover and simmer for a further 5 minutes, or until the meat is cooked through.

Transfer the mixture to a warmed serving dish and sprinkle over the coriander before serving.

Serves 4
Preparation and cooking time: 35 minutes

Roghan Gosht

(Curried Lamb)

Metric/Imperial	American
250ml./8fl.oz. yogurt	1 cup yogurt
¼ tsp. asafoetida	¼ tsp. asafoetida
½ tsp. cayenne pepper	½ tsp. cayenne pepper
1kg./2lb. lean lamb, cubed	2lb. lean lamb, cubed
4cm./1½in. piece of fresh root ginger, peeled and chopped	1½in. piece of fresh green ginger, peeled and chopped
4 garlic cloves	4 garlic cloves
1 tsp. white poppy seeds	1 tsp. white poppy seeds
1 tsp. cumin seeds	1 tsp. cumin seeds
1 Tbs. coriander seeds	1 Tbs. coriander seeds
4 cloves	4 cloves
2 Tbs. cardamom seeds	2 Tbs. cardamom seeds
8 peppercorns	8 peppercorns

2 Tbs. unblanched almonds	2 Tbs. unblanched almonds
50g./2oz. ghee or clarified butter	4 Tbs. ghee or clarified butter
1 medium onion, chopped	1 medium onion, chopped
1 tsp. turmeric	1 tsp. turmeric
250ml./8fl.oz. water	1 cup water
1 tsp. garam masala	1 tsp. garam masala
1 Tbs. chopped coriander leaves	1 Tbs. chopped coriander leaves

Roghan Gosht is a delicately flavoured lamb curry and very popular among the inhabitants of North India.

Combine the yogurt, asafoetida and cayenne in a large bowl and stir in the meat cubes. Cover and set aside.

Put the ginger, garlic, spices and almonds in a blender with 4 tablespoons of water and blend to a smooth purée. Transfer to a small bowl.

Melt the ghee or clarified butter in a flameproof casserole. Add the onion and fry, stirring occasionally, until it is golden brown. Stir in the turmeric and spice purée and fry for 8 minutes, stirring constantly. Add a spoonful or two of water if the mixture becomes too dry. Add the lamb cubes and yogurt mixture and fry until the cubes are evenly browned. Cover the casserole, reduce the heat to low and simmer for 45 minutes.

Preheat the oven to very cool 140°C (Gas Mark 1, 275°F).

Uncover the casserole and stir in 50ml./2fl.oz. ($\frac{1}{4}$ cup) of water. Add another 50ml./2fl.oz. ($\frac{1}{4}$ cup) of water and stir until it has been absorbed. Pour in the remaining water, cover the casserole and reduce the heat to low. Simmer for a further 15 minutes.

Stir in the garam masala and coriander leaves. Cover the casserole and put it into the oven. Cook for 25 minutes.

Transfer the mixture to a warmed serving dish and serve at once.

Serves 4-6

Preparation and cooking time: $1\frac{3}{4}$ hours

Lamb and Cashew Nut Curry can be served either with rice or chapattis and makes a substantial meal.

Lamb and Cashew Nut Curry

Metric/Imperial	American
4cm./1½in. piece of fresh root ginger, peeled and chopped	1½in. piece of fresh green ginger, peeled and chopped
3 garlic cloves	3 garlic cloves
2 green chillis	2 green chillis
50g./2oz. unsalted cashewnuts	½ cup unsalted cashewnuts
50-75ml./2-3fl.oz. water	¼-⅓ cup water
4 cloves	4 cloves
¼ tsp. cardamom seeds	¼ tsp. cardamom seeds
1 Tbs. coriander seeds	1 Tbs. coriander seeds
1 Tbs. white poppy seeds	1 Tbs. white poppy seeds
50g./2oz. butter	4 Tbs. butter
2 onions, finely chopped	2 onions, finely chopped
1kg./2lb. lean lamb, cubed	2lb. lean lamb, cubed
300ml./10fl.oz. yogurt	1¼ cups yogurt
¼ tsp. saffron threads, soaked in 2 Tbs. boiling water	¼ tsp. saffron threads, soaked in 2 Tbs. boiling water
1 tsp. salt	1 tsp. salt
juice of ¼ lemon	juice of ¼ lemon
1 Tbs. chopped coriander leaves	1 Tbs. chopped coriander leaves
1 lemon, sliced	1 lemon, sliced

Put the ginger, garlic, chillis, cashewnuts and half the water in a blender and blend to a smooth purée. Add the cloves, cardamom, coriander and poppy seeds, and enough of the remaining water to prevent the blender from sticking, and blend. Transfer the purée to a bowl.

Melt the butter in a large saucepan. Add the onions and fry, stirring occasionally, until they are golden brown. Stir in the spice purée and fry for 3 minutes, stirring constantly. Add the lamb cubes and fry until they are evenly browned.

Beat the yogurt with the saffron and salt, then stir the mixture into the pan. Bring to the boil, reduce the heat to low and simmer the curry for 1 hour. Stir in the lemon juice and sprinkle over the coriander. Cover and simmer for a further 20 minutes, or until the lamb is cooked through and tender.

Serve at once, garnished with the lemon slices.

Serves 4-6

Preparation and cooking time: 1½ hours

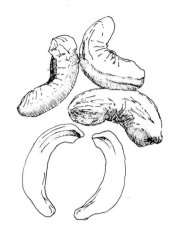

Talawa Gosht

(Deep-Fried Lamb and Potatoes)

Metric/Imperial	American
25g./1oz. butter	2 Tbs. butter
4cm./1½in. piece of fresh root ginger, peeled and chopped	1½in. piece of fresh green ginger, peeled and chopped
3 garlic cloves, crushed	3 garlic cloves, crushed
700g./1½lb. lean lamb, cubed	1½lb. lean lamb, cubed
1 tsp. turmeric	1 tsp. turmeric
2 tsp. hot chilli powder	2 tsp. hot chilli powder
½ tsp. salt	½ tsp. salt
50ml./2fl.oz. yogurt	¼ cup yogurt
vegetable oil for deep-frying	vegetable oil for deep-frying
½kg./1lb. potatoes, boiled until nearly tender, drained and cubed	1lb. potatoes, boiled until nearly tender, drained and cubed
2 lemons, cut into wedges	2 lemons, cut into wedges
BATTER	BATTER
225g./8oz. besan or chick-pea flour	2 cups besan or chick-pea flour
1 tsp. salt	1 tsp. salt
½ tsp. hot chilli powder	½ tsp. hot chilli powder
75ml./3fl.oz. yogurt	⅓ cup yogurt
250ml./8fl.oz. water	1 cup water

Melt the butter in a deep frying-pan. Add the ginger and garlic and fry for 3 minutes, stirring frequently. Add the meat cubes and fry until they are evenly browned.

Meanwhile, combine the spices and yogurt in a small bowl. Stir into the pan and cook, uncovered, for 40 minutes, or until the lamb is just cooked through. Set aside to cool.

To make the batter, sift the flour, salt and chilli powder into a large bowl. Beat in the yogurt and stir in the water, a little at a time, until the mixture forms a smooth batter. Set aside for 30 minutes.

Fill a deep-frying pan one-third full with oil and heat until it is hot. Dip the lamb and potato cubes into the batter, then carefully lower them, a few at a time, into the hot oil. Fry for 3 to 4 minutes, or until they are golden brown and crisp. Drain on kitchen towels.

Serve at once, garnished with lemon wedges.

Serves 4

Preparation and cooking time: 1¼ hours

Huseini Kabab

(Marinated Lamb on Skewers)

Metric/Imperial	American
150ml./5fl.oz. yogurt	⅔ cup yogurt
2 green chillis	2 green chillis
4cm./1½in. piece of fresh root ginger, peeled and chopped	1½in. piece of fresh green ginger, peeled and chopped
1 onion, quartered	1 onion, quartered
1 Tbs. chopped coriander leaves	1 Tbs. chopped coriander leaves
3 garlic cloves	3 garlic cloves
1 tsp. turmeric	1 tsp. turmeric
1 tsp. salt	1 tsp. salt
1kg./2lb. lean lamb, cubed	2lb. lean lamb, cubed
1 tsp. garam masala	1 tsp. garam masala

Put the yogurt, chillis, ginger, onion, coriander, garlic, turmeric and salt into a blender and blend to a smooth purée. Transfer to a large bowl. Stir in the lamb cubes to coat them thoroughly. Cover the bowl and chill in the refrigerator for 6 hours. Remove from the refrigerator and toss and turn the cubes in the marinade. Thread the cubes on to skewers and discard the marinade.

Preheat the grill (broiler) to high.

Arrange the skewers on the grill (broiler) rack and grill (broil) for 10 minutes, turning occasionally, or until the kebabs are cooked through.

Slide the cubes off the skewers on to a warmed serving dish and sprinkle over the garam masala before serving.

Serves 4-6

Preparation and cooking time: 6½ hours

A mildly spiced dish, Tikka Kabab is delicious served with chapattis and various chutneys.

Tikka Kabab

(Spiced Lamb Kebabs)

Metric/Imperial	American
10cm./4in. piece of fresh root ginger, peeled and chopped	4in. piece of fresh green ginger, peeled and chopped
3 medium onions, chopped	3 medium onions, chopped
1 small bunch coriander leaves	1 small bunch coriander leaves
1 Tbs. coriander seeds	1 Tbs. coriander seeds
juice of 1 lemon	juice of 1 lemon
2 green chillis	2 green chillis
½ tsp. black peppercorns	½ tsp. black peppercorns
1kg./2lb. lean lamb, cubed	2 lb. lean lamb, cubed
1 tsp. salt	1 tsp. salt
25g./1oz. butter, melted	2 Tbs. butter, melted

Put the ginger, onions, coriander leaves and seeds, lemon juice, chillis and peppercorns into a blender and blend to a smooth purée. Transfer the puree to a large bowl and stir in the lamb cubes. Cover and set aside at room temperature for 4 hours.

Preheat the grill (broiler) to high. Thread the meat on to skewers and sprinkle over the salt and melted butter. Arrange the skewers on a lined grill (broiler) pan and grill (broil) for 10 to 12 minutes, turning occasionally, or until the cubes are cooked through.

Slide the meat off the skewers on to a warmed serving dish and serve at once.
Serves 4-6
Preparation and cooking time: 4¼ hours

Thayir Kari

Metric/Imperial	American
4 garlic cloves	4 garlic cloves
5cm./2in. piece of fresh root ginger, peeled and chopped	2in. piece of fresh green ginger, peeled and chopped
2 green chillis, chopped	2 green chillis, chopped
6 Tbs. chopped coriander leaves	6 Tbs. chopped coriander leaves
1½ tsp. turmeric	1½ tsp. turmeric
1 tsp. salt	1 tsp. salt
50ml./2fl.oz. lemon juice	¼ cup lemon juice
1kg./2lb. lean lamb, cubed	2lb. lean lamb, cubed
50ml./2fl.oz. vegetable oil	¼ cup vegetable oil
2 medium onions, chopped	2 medium onions, chopped
600ml./1 pint yogurt	2½ cups yogurt
1½ tsp. aniseed, toasted	1½ tsp. aniseed, toasted

Put the garlic, ginger, chillis, coriander leaves, turmeric and salt into a blender with the lemon juice and blend to a smooth purée. Transfer the purée to a large bowl and stir in the lamb cubes. Set aside at room temperature for 1 hour.

Heat the oil in a large saucepan. When it is hot, add the onions and fry, stirring occasionally, until they are golden brown. Add the lamb cubes and spice purée and fry until the cubes are evenly browned. Stir the yogurt into the lamb mixture and add the aniseed. Bring to the boil, cover the pan and reduce the heat to low. Simmer for 1¼ hours, or until the lamb is cooked through and tender. Cook uncovered for the last 20 minutes.

Transfer the curry to a warmed serving bowl and serve at once.
Serves 4-6
Preparation and cooking time: 2½ hours

Shakooti Rassa

(Lamb Cooked with Coconut)

Metric/Imperial	American
6 green chillis, seeded	6 green chillis, seeded
6 Tbs. chopped coriander leaves	6 Tbs. chopped coriander leaves
3 garlic cloves	3 garlic cloves
5cm./2in. piece of fresh root ginger, peeled and chopped	2in. piece of fresh green ginger, peeled and chopped

1 tsp. salt	1 tsp. salt
450ml./15fl.oz. thick coconut milk	2 cups thick coconut milk
1kg./2lb. lean lamb, cubed	2lb. lean lamb, cubed
5 Tbs. ghee or clarified butter	5 Tbs. ghee or clarified butter
½ fresh coconut, grated	½ fresh coconut, grated
1 Tbs. cumin seeds	1 Tbs. cumin seeds
1 Tbs. white poppy seeds	1 Tbs. white poppy seeds
1 tsp. black peppercorns	1 tsp. black peppercorns
1 tsp. turmeric	1 tsp. turmeric
½ tsp. grated nutmeg	½ tsp. grated nutmeg
2 medium onions, chopped	2 medium onions, chopped
½kg./1lb. potatoes, cubed	1lb. potatoes, cubed

Thayir Kari is a traditional dish made with lamb and yogurt.

Put the chillis, coriander leaves, garlic, ginger and salt into a blender and blend with 2 to 3 tablespoons of the coconut milk to a smooth purée. Transfer to a large bowl and stir in the meat cubes. Set aside at room temperature for 6 hours.

Melt 2 tablespoons of ghee or clarified butter in a frying-pan. Add the grated coconut and spices and fry for 5 minutes, stirring constantly. Remove from the heat and set the mixture aside to cool. Put into the blender with 125ml./4fl.oz. (½ cup) of the remaining coconut milk and blend to a smooth purée. Set aside.

Melt the remaining ghee in a large saucepan. Add the onions and fry, stirring occasionally, until they are brown. Add the coconut and spice purée and fry for 5 minutes, stirring constantly. Add the meat and chilli mixture and fry until the cubes are evenly browned. Pour in the remaining coconut milk and bring to the boil. Cover the pan, reduce the heat to low and simmer for 45 minutes.

Add the potatoes and simmer, uncovered, for a further 30 minutes, or until the meat and potatoes are cooked through and tender, and the sauce has thickened.

Transfer the shakooti to a warmed serving dish and serve at once.

Serves 4-6
Preparation and cooking time: 7¾ hours

Sag Gosht

(Spinach with Meat)

Metric/Imperial	American
50g./2oz. butter	4 Tbs. butter
1½ tsp. mustard seeds	1½ tsp. mustard seeds
2 garlic cloves, crushed	2 garlic cloves, crushed
1 Tbs. cardamom seeds	1 Tbs. cardamom seeds
1 Tbs. ground coriander	1 Tbs. ground coriander
4cm./1½in. piece of fresh root ginger, peeled and chopped	1½in. piece of fresh green ginger, peeled and chopped
1kg./2lb. lean lamb, cubed	2lb. lean lamb, cubed
1 medium onion, chopped	1 medium onion, chopped
3 green chillis, chopped	3 green chillis, chopped
1 tsp. sugar	1 tsp. sugar
1 tsp. turmeric	1 tsp. turmeric
1kg./2lb. spinach, washed and chopped	2lb. spinach, washed and chopped
1½ tsp. salt	1½ tsp. salt
½ tsp. black pepper	½ tsp. black pepper
3 Tbs. yogurt	3 Tbs. yogurt

Melt the butter in a flameproof casserole. Add the mustard seeds and cover. When they begin to spatter, stir in the garlic, cardamom, coriander and ginger. Fry for 1 minute, stirring constantly. Add the lamb cubes and fry until they are evenly browned. Add the onion, chillis and sugar and fry, stirring occasionally, until the onions are golden brown. Stir in the turmeric and spinach and cook for 3 minutes. Stir in the remaining ingredients. Cover the casserole, reduce the heat to low and simmer for 1 hour. Uncover and stir well to mix.

Preheat the oven to cool 150°C (Gas Mark 2, 300°F). Transfer the casserole to the oven and cook for 25 minutes, or until the lamb is cooked through and tender.

Serve at once, from the casserole.

Serves 4-6
Preparation and cooking time: 1¾ hours

Zeera Gosht

(Cumin Lamb)

Metric/Imperial	American
1 Tbs. cumin seeds	1 Tbs. cumin seeds
2½cm./1in. piece of fresh root ginger, peeled and chopped	1in. piece of fresh green ginger, peeled and chopped
2 garlic cloves	2 garlic cloves
2 tsp. cardamom seeds	2 tsp. cardamom seeds
2 cloves	2 cloves
10 blanched almonds	10 blanched almonds
2 tsp. sesame seeds	2 tsp. sesame seeds
1 tsp. cayenne pepper	1 tsp. cayenne pepper
1 tsp. salt	1 tsp. salt
1 tsp. soft brown sugar	1 tsp. soft brown sugar
175ml./6fl.oz. yogurt	¾ cup yogurt

Metric/Imperial	American
40g./1½oz. butter	3 Tbs. butter
1 medium onion, chopped	1 medium onion, chopped
2 large green peppers, pith and seeds removed and chopped	2 large green peppers, pith and seeds removed and chopped
1kg./2lb. lean lamb, cubed	2lb. lean lamb, cubed
¼ tsp. ground saffron	¼ tsp. ground saffron

Put the cumin seeds, ginger, garlic, cardamom seeds, cloves, almonds, sesame seeds, cayenne, salt, sugar and 2 tablespoons of yogurt into a blender and blend to a smooth purée, adding more yogurt if necessary. Transfer to a small bowl.

Melt the butter in a large flameproof casserole. Add the onion and fry, stirring occasionally, until it is golden brown. Stir in the spice paste and fry for 5 minutes, stirring constantly. Add a spoonful or two of water if the mixture becomes too dry. Add the peppers and fry for 2 minutes. Add the lamb and fry for 10 minutes, turning frequently.

Meanwhile, beat the yogurt and saffron together, then pour into the meat mixture and mix well. Bring to the boil, cover and reduce the heat to very low. Simmer for 50 minutes.

Meanwhile, preheat the oven to cool 150°C (Gas Mark 2, 300°F). Transfer the casserole to the oven and cook the lamb for 25 minutes. Remove from the oven and serve at once.

Serves 4-6
Preparation and cooking time: 2 hours

Nargisi Koftas

(Meatballs Stuffed with Hard-boiled Eggs)

Metric/Imperial	American
575g./1¼lb. minced lamb	1¼lb. ground lamb
2½cm./1in. piece of fresh root ginger, peeled and chopped	1in. piece of fresh green ginger, peeled and chopped
½ tsp. hot chilli powder	½ tsp. hot chilli powder
1 tsp. ground cumin	1 tsp. ground cumin
1 Tbs. ground coriander	1 Tbs. ground coriander
1 onion, finely chopped	1 onion, finely chopped
2 garlic cloves, crushed	2 garlic cloves, crushed
40g./1½oz. gram or chick-pea flour	⅓ cup gram or chick-pea flour
1 tsp. salt	1 tsp. salt
½ tsp. black pepper	½ tsp. black pepper
1 egg	1 egg
8 hard-boiled eggs	8 hard-boiled eggs
vegetable oil for deep-frying	vegetable oil for deep-frying

Combine all the ingredients, except the hard-boiled eggs and oil, together until they are well blended. Divide the mixture into eight equal portions. Using damp hands, roll each portion into a ball, then flatten with the palm of your hands. Put a hard-boiled egg in the centre of the meat and bring the meat up and around it, to enclose it completely. Put the balls in a greased dish and chill in the refrigerator for 30 minutes.

Fill a large deep-frying pan one-third full with oil and heat until it is hot. Carefully lower the meatballs into the oil, a few at a time, and fry for 2 to 3 minutes, or until they are crisp and golden brown. Transfer to kitchen towels to drain.

Arrange the koftas on a warmed serving dish and serve hot.
Serves 4
Preparation and cooking time: 30 minutes

Turkari Molee

(Lamb and Coconut Curry)

Metric/Imperial	American
50g./2oz. butter	4 Tbs. butter
2 medium onions, sliced	2 medium onions, sliced
6 garlic cloves, crushed	6 garlic cloves, crushed
5cm./2in. piece of fresh root ginger, peeled and chopped	2in. piece of fresh green ginger, peeled and chopped
1½ tsp. turmeric	1½ tsp. turmeric
2 tsp. hot chilli powder	2 tsp. hot chilli powder
½ tsp. black pepper	½ tsp. black pepper
½ tsp. ground fenugreek	½ tsp. ground fenugreek
2 tsp. ground coriander	2 tsp. ground coriander
1 tsp. ground cumin	1 tsp. ground cumin
2 tsp. paprika	2 tsp. paprika
1kg./2lb. lean lamb, cubed	2lb lean lamb, cubed
600ml./1 pint coconut milk	2½ cups coconut milk
1½ tsp. salt	1½ tsp. salt
2 curry leaves (optional)	2 curry leaves (optional)

Melt the butter in a large saucepan. Add the onions and fry, stirring occasionally, until they are golden brown. Add the garlic, ginger and spices and fry for 5 minutes, stirring frequently. Add a spoonful or two of water if the mixture becomes too dry.

Add the lamb cubes and fry until they are evenly browned. Pour over the coconut milk, salt and curry leaves, if used, and bring to the boil. Cover the pan, reduce the heat to low and simmer for 1¼ hours, or until the lamb is cooked through and tender.

Transfer to a warmed serving dish and serve at once.
Serves 4-6
Preparation and cooking time: 1½ hours

Jal Farazi

(Curried Lamb and Potatoes)

This spicy lamb curry, Turkari Molee, should be served with rice and chutneys and an interesting accompaniment is Turkari Aloo, a hot vegetable dish made with potatoes.

Metric/Imperial	American
50ml./2fl.oz. vegetable oil	¼ cup vegetable oil
2 onions, sliced	2 onions, sliced
1 garlic clove, crushed	1 garlic clove, crushed
2½cm./1in. piece of fresh root ginger, peeled and chopped	1in. piece of fresh green ginger, peeled and chopped

Metric/Imperial	American
2 green chillis, finely chopped	2 green chillis, finely chopped
1 tsp. turmeric	1 tsp. turmeric
1 tsp. mustard seeds	1 tsp. mustard seeds
700g./1½lb. cooked lamb, cubed	1½lb. cooked lamb, cubed
½kg./1lb. potatoes, cooked and cubed	1lb. potatoes, cooked and cubed
1 tsp. salt	1 tsp. salt
juice of ½ lemon	juice of ½ lemon

Heat the oil in a large frying-pan. When it is hot, add the onions and garlic and fry, stirring occasionally, until the onions are soft. Add the ginger and chillis and fry for 2 minutes. Stir in the turmeric and mustard seeds and fry for 1 minute, stirring frequently.

Stir in the lamb, potatoes and salt and fry, stirring constantly, until they are well coated in the spices. Stir in the lemon juice and a spoonful or two of water if the mixture becomes too dry. Cook for 3 to 5 minutes, or until the mixture is quite dry and very hot.

Serves 4
Preparation and cooking time: 15 minutes

Biryani

(Spiced Rice with Lamb)

Metric/Imperial	American
125g./4oz. ghee or clarified butter	8 Tbs. ghee or clarified butter
2 garlic cloves, crushed	2 garlic cloves, crushed
2½cm./1in. piece of fresh root ginger, peeled and chopped	1in. piece of fresh green ginger, peeled and chopped
¼ tsp. cayenne pepper	¼ tsp. cayenne pepper
1½ tsp. cumin seeds	1½ tsp. cumin seeds
1kg./2lb. lean lamb, cubed	2lb. lean lamb, cubed
10cm./4in. cinnamon stick	4in. cinnamon stick
10 cloves	10 cloves
8 peppercorns	8 peppercorns
1 tsp. cardamom seeds	1 tsp. cardamon seeds
300ml./10fl.oz. yogurt	1¼ cups yogurt
2 tsp. salt	2 tsp. salt
450g./1lb. long-grain rice, soaked in cold water for 30 minutes and drained	2⅔ cups long-grain rice, soaked in cold water for 30 minutes and drained
½ tsp. saffron threads, soaked in 2 Tbs. boiling water	½ tsp. saffron threads, soaked in 2 Tbs. boiling water
2 onions, thinly sliced	2 onions, thinly sliced
40g./1½oz. slivered almonds	⅓ cup slivered almonds
40g./1½oz. pistachio nuts	⅓ cup pistachio nuts
50g./2oz. sultanans	⅓ cup seedless raisins

Melt half the ghee or clarified butter in a large saucepan. Add the garlic, ginger, cayenne and cumin seeds and fry for 3 minutes, stirring frequently. Add the lamb cubes and fry until they are deeply and evenly browned. Stir in the spices, yogurt and 1 teaspoon of salt. Add 150ml./5fl.oz. (⅔ cup) of water and bring to the boil, stirring occasionally. Cover the pan, reduce the heat to low and simmer for 1 hour, or until the lamb is cooked through and tender.

Bring 1¾l./3 pints (7½ cups) of water to the boil in a large saucepan. Add the remaining salt and the rice and boil briskly for 1½ minutes. Remove from the

heat, drain the rice thoroughly and set aside.

Preheat the oven to moderate 180°C (Gas Mark 4, 350°F).

Put 1 tablespoon of ghee or clarified butter into a large ovenproof casserole. Put one-third of the rice over the bottom and sprinkle one-third of the saffron mixture over it. Cover with a layer of one-third of the lamb. Continue making layers in this way until the ingredients are used up, ending with a layer of rice sprinkled with saffron. Pour all the liquid remaining in the pan containing the meat over the casserole mixture. Cover and put the dish into the oven. Cook for 20 to 30 minutes, or until the rice is cooked and the liquid is absorbed.

Melt the remaining ghee or clarified butter in a frying-pan. Add the onions and fry, stirring occasionally, until they are golden brown. Using a slotted spoon, transfer them to drain on kitchen towels. Add the remaining ingredients to the pan and fry for 3 minutes, or until the nuts are lightly browned. Set aside.

Remove the casserole from the oven and sprinkle the onions, nuts and sultanas (raisins) over the top before serving.

Serves 6
Preparation and cooking time: $2\frac{1}{4}$ hours

Biryani is a delicate mixture of lamb, spices, nuts and saffron rice and forms a complete meal in itself.

155

Raan is a very exotic, Indian dish made with leg of lamb marinated in spiced yogurt for 45 hours.

Raan

(Leg of Lamb Marinated in Spiced Yogurt)

Metric/Imperial	American
1 x 3kg./6lb. leg of lamb	1 x 6lb. leg of lamb
125g./4oz. fresh root ginger, peeled and chopped	4oz. fresh green ginger, peeled and chopped
12 large garlic cloves, crushed	12 large garlic cloves, crushed
thinly pared rind of 1 lemon	thinly pared rind of 1 lemon
5 Tbs. lemon juice	5 Tbs. lemon juice
2 tsp. cumin seeds	2 tsp. cumin seeds
2 Tbs. cardamom seeds	2 Tbs. cardamom seeds
8 cloves	8 cloves
1 tsp. turmeric	1 tsp. turmeric
1½ tsp. hot chilli powder	1½ tsp. hot chilli powder
1 Tbs. salt	1 Tbs. salt
150g./5oz. unblanched almonds	1 cup unblanched almonds
4 Tbs. soft brown sugar	4 Tbs. soft brown sugar
300ml./10fl.oz. yogurt	1¼ cups yogurt

$\frac{1}{2}$ tsp. saffron threads, soaked in
  2 Tbs. boiling water

$\frac{1}{2}$ tsp. saffron threads, soaked in
  2 Tbs. boiling water

Prick the lamb all over, then make several deep slits in the flesh. Put the lamb in a deep roasting pan.

Put the ginger, garlic, lemon rind and juice, spices and salt in a blender and blend to a smooth purée. Spread the purée all over the meat and set aside at room temperature for 1 hour.

Meanwhile, put the almonds, 2 tablespoons of sugar and half the yogurt into the blender and blend to a smooth purée. Transfer the purée to a bowl and stir in the remaining yogurt. Spread the mixture all over the lamb, on top of the spice purée. Cover the pan and put into the refrigerator for 45 hours.

Preheat the oven to hot 220°C (Gas Mark 7, 425°F). Remove the roasting pan from the refrigerator and allow the meat to warm to room temperature. Sprinkle over the remaining sugar.

Put the pan into the oven and roast, uncovered, for 20 minutes. Reduce the temperature to moderate 180°C (Gas Mark 4, 350°F) and roast for 1 hour. Reduce the temperature to warm 170°C (Gas Mark 3, 325°F), cover the pan and cook, basting occasionally, for 4 hours. Remove from the oven and very carefully transfer the meat to a large piece of foil. Cover completely and return to the oven.

Skim any scum from the surface of the cooking liquid and stir in the saffron mixture. Set the pan over moderately high heat and boil briskly for 15 to 20 minutes, or until the sauce has reduced by about half.

Remove the lamb from the oven and discard the foil. Arrange on a warmed serving dish, spoon over the sauce and serve.

Serves 8

Preparation and cooking time: 54 hours

Badami Gosht

(Lamb Cooked with Almonds)

Metric/Imperial	American
5 Tbs. vegetable oil	5 Tbs. vegetable oil
2 cinnamon sticks	2 cinnamon sticks
6 cloves	6 cloves
1 Tbs. cardamom seeds	1 Tbs. cardamom seeds
1 large onion, chopped	1 large onion, chopped
2 garlic cloves, crushed	2 garlic cloves, crushed
4cm./1½in. piece of fresh root ginger, peeled and chopped	1½in. piece of fresh green ginger, peeled and chopped
700g./1½lb. lean lamb, cubed	1½lb. lean lamb, cubed
300ml./10fl.oz. yogurt	1¼ cups yogurt
1 tsp. saffron threads, soaked in 2 Tbs. boiling water	1 tsp. saffron threads, soaked in 2 Tbs. boiling water
½ tsp. hot chilli powder	½ tsp. hot chilli powder
75g./3oz. ground almonds	½ cup ground almonds
1 tsp. salt	1 tsp. salt
350ml./12fl.oz. coconut milk	1½ cups coconut milk
2 dried red chillis	2 dried red chillis

Heat the oil in a saucepan. When it is hot, add the cinnamon, cloves and cardamom and fry for 1 minute. Add the onion and fry, stirring occasionally, until it is soft. Add the garlic and ginger and fry for 3 minutes, stirring frequently. Add the lamb cubes and fry until they are evenly browned.

Beat the yogurt, saffron mixture and chilli powder together, then stir mixture into the lamb cubes. Cook for 1 minute.

Beat the almonds with enough water to form a thick paste, then stir the paste into the lamb cubes, with the salt. Simmer for 15 minutes. Stir in the coconut milk and chillis and reduce the heat to low. Simmer for 1 hour, or until the lamb is cooked through and tender. Uncover the pan for the last 10 minutes of cooking.

Transfer to a warmed serving dish and serve at once.

Serves 4

Preparation and cooking time: 1½ hours

Samosas

(Stuffed Savoury Pastries)

Metric/Imperial	American
PASTRY	PASTRY
225g./8oz. flour	2 cups flour
½ tsp. salt	½ tsp. salt
25g./1oz. butter	2 Tbs. butter

Samosas, crisp pastry balls with a spicy meat or vegetable filling, are delicious either as a snack or as an accompaniment to a meal.

50-75ml./2-3fl.oz. water	$\frac{1}{4}$-$\frac{1}{3}$ cup water
FILLING	FILLING
25g./1oz. butter	2 Tbs. butter
1 small onion, chopped	1 small onion, chopped
2 garlic cloves, crushed	2 garlic cloves, crushed
2 green chillis, chopped	2 green chillis, chopped
2½cm./1in. piece of fresh root ginger, peeled and chopped	1in. piece of fresh green ginger, peeled and chopped
½ tsp. turmeric	½ tsp. turmeric
½ tsp. hot chilli powder	½ tsp. hot chilli powder
350g/12oz. minced lamb	12oz. ground lamb
1 tsp. salt	1 tsp. salt
2 tsp. garam masala	2 tsp. garam masala
juice of ½ lemon	juice of ½ lemon
vegetable oil for deep-frying	vegetable oil for deep-frying

First make the pastry. Sift the flour and salt into a bowl. Add the butter and rub it into the flour until the mixture resembles fine breadcrumbs. Pour in 50ml./ 2fl.oz. (¼ cup) of water and mix to a smooth dough. Add a little more water if the dough is too dry. Pat into a ball and turn out on to a lightly floured surface. Knead for 10 minutes, or until the dough is smooth and elastic. Return to the bowl, cover and set aside.

Melt the butter in a frying-pan. Add the onion, garlic, chillis and ginger and fry, stirring occasionally, until the onions are golden brown. Stir in the spices, then add the meat and salt and fry until the meat loses its pinkness. Stir in the garam masala and lemon juice and cook for 5 minutes, stirring occasionally. Remove from the heat and set aside to cool.

Divide the dough into 15 equal portions. Roll each portion into a ball, flatten and roll out to a circle about 10cm./4in. in diameter. Cut each circle in half. Dampen the cut edges of the semi-circles and shape into cones. Fill the cones with a little of the filling, dampen the top and bottom edges and pinch together to seal.

Fill a deep-frying pan one-third full with oil and heat until it is hot. Carefully lower the samosas into the oil, a few at a time, and fry for 2 to 3 minutes, or until they are golden brown and crisp. Drain on kitchen towels.

Pile into a warmed serving dish and serve at once.

Makes 30 Samosas
Preparation and cooking time: 45 minutes

Kamargaah

(Lamb Chops in Batter)

Metric/Imperial	American
8 lamb chops or cutlets	8 lamb chops or cutlets
350ml./12fl.oz. milk	1½ cups water
175ml./6fl.oz. water	¾ cup water
½ tsp. salt	½ tsp. salt
2 tsp. crushed cardamom seeds	2 tsp. crushed cardamom seeds
6 whole cloves	6 whole cloves
1 tsp. crushed black peppercorns	1 tsp. crushed black peppercorns
125ml./4fl.oz. vegetable oil	½ cup vegetable oil
BATTER	BATTER
50g./2oz. chick-pea flour	½ cup chick-pea flour
½ tsp. hot chilli powder	½ tsp. hot chilli powder
1 tsp. ground coriander	1 tsp. ground coriander
1 tsp. garam masala	1 tsp. garam masala
1 Tbs. melted ghee or clarified butter	1 Tbs. melted ghee or clarified butter
2 Tbs. yogurt	2 Tbs. yogurt
125ml./4fl.oz. water	½ cup water

First make the batter. Combine the chick-pea flour, chilli powder, coriander and garam masala in a medium bowl. Gradually stir in the melted ghee, yogurt and water until the mixture forms a smooth, fairly thick batter. Set aside at room temperature for 20 minutes.

Meanwhile, put the meat into a large saucepan and add all the remaining ingredients except the oil. Bring to the boil, reduce the heat to low and simmer, uncovered, for 30 to 40 minutes, or until the chops are cooked through and tender and the liquid evaporates. Remove from the heat and remove the chops from the pan.

Heat the oil in a large frying-pan. When it is very hot, dip the chops in the batter to coat them thoroughly, then arrange them in the pan. Fry for 5 minutes on each side, or until they are golden brown. Remove them from the pan and drain on kitchen towels.

Serve at once.

Serves 4-8
Preparation and cooking time: 1½ hours

Dry Beef Curry

Metric/Imperial	American
1kg./2lb. braising steak, cut into cubes	2lb. chunk steak, cut into cubes
50g./2oz. seasoned flour	$\frac{1}{2}$ cup seasoned flour
1 Tbs. dried red chillis, crumbled	1 Tbs. dried red chillis, crumbled
1 Tbs. fennel seeds	1 Tbs. fennel seeds
1 whole bulb of garlic, crushed	1 whole bulb of garlic, crushed
4cm./1$\frac{1}{2}$in. piece of fresh root ginger, peeled and chopped	1$\frac{1}{2}$in. piece of fresh green ginger, peeled and chopped
2 Tbs. ground coriander	2 Tbs. ground coriander
1 tsp. ground cumin	1 tsp. ground cumin
1 Tbs. ground cloves	1 Tbs. ground cloves
1 Tbs. ground cinnamon	1 Tbs. ground cinnamon
1 tsp. ground fenugreek	1 tsp. ground fenugreek
3 Tbs. white wine vinegar	3 Tbs. white wine vinegar
50g./2oz. ghee or clarified butter	4 Tbs. ghee or clarified butter
2 onions, chopped	2 onions, chopped
600ml./1 pint beef stock	2$\frac{1}{2}$ cups beef stock

Roll the beef cubes in the seasoned flour, shaking off any excess. Set aside.

Combine the chillis, fennel seeds, garlic and ginger and put them into a blender. Blend to a smooth purée. Transfer the purée to a small bowl and stir in the coriander, cumin, cloves, cinnamon and fenugreek until they are well blended. Stir in the vinegar until the mixture forms a smooth paste.

Melt the ghee in a large saucepan. Add the spice paste and cook, stirring constantly, for 2 minutes. Reduce the heat to low and cook for a further 2 minutes, stirring constantly. Add the onions to the pan and cook, stirring occasionally, until they are soft.

Add the meat and cook until it is evenly browned. Pour over the beef stock and bring to the boil. Reduce the heat to low, cover the saucepan and simmer the mixture for 2 to 2$\frac{1}{2}$ hours, or until the beef is tender.

Transfer the mixture to a warmed serving bowl and serve at once.
Serves 4-6
Preparation and cooking time: 3 hours

Harak Muss

(Sri Lankan Beef Curry)

Metric/Imperial	American
50g./2oz. ghee or clarified butter	4 Tbs. ghee or clarified butter
2 medium onions, chopped	2 medium onions, chopped
2 garlic cloves, crushed	2 garlic cloves, crushed
4cm./1$\frac{1}{2}$in. piece of fresh root ginger, peeled and chopped	1$\frac{1}{2}$in. piece of fresh green ginger, peeled and chopped
1 tsp. chopped lemon grass or grated lemon rind	1 tsp. chopped lemon grass or grated lemon rind
1 Tbs. lemon juice	1 Tbs. lemon juice
1 tsp. turmeric	1 tsp. turmeric
2 red chillis, chopped	2 red chillis, chopped
1kg./2lb. braising steak, cut into cubes	2lb. chuck steak, cut into cubes

200g./7oz. tin tomatoes	7oz. can tomatoes
250ml./8fl.oz. thick coconut milk	1 cup thick coconut milk
MASALA	MASALA
2 tsp. coriander seeds	2 tsp. coriander seeds
1 tsp. cumin seeds	1 tsp. cumin seeds
½ tsp. fennel seeds	½ tsp. fennel seeds
2.5cm./1in. cinnamon stick	1in. cinnamon stick
5 whole cloves	5 whole cloves
¼ tsp. cardamom seeds	¼ tsp. cardamom seeds

First make the masala. Arrange the spices, except the chillis, separately on a large baking sheet and dry roast them for 5 minutes in a moderate preheated oven. Remove from the oven and transfer them to a blender. Alternatively, dry roast the spices separately in a frying-pan for 3 minutes over gentle heat. Remove from the pan and put into a blender. Blend the mixture to a powder and set aside.

Melt the ghee in a large saucepan. Add the onions, garlic and ginger and fry, stirring occasionally, until the onions are soft. Stir in the masala mixture, the lemon grass or rind, lemon juice, turmeric and chopped chillis and continue frying for 5 minutes, stirring frequently. Add a spoonful or two of water if the mixture becomes too dry. Add the beef cubes and fry until they are evenly browned and coated with the spice mixture.

Stir in the tomatoes and can juice and the coconut milk and bring to the boil. Reduce the heat to low, cover the pan and simmer the mixture for 2 to 2½ hours, or until the beef is cooked and tender.

Transfer the mixture to a warmed serving dish and serve at once.
Serves 6
Preparation and cooking time: 3¼ hours

Gosht Aur Aloo

(Beef and Potato Curry)

Metric/Imperial	American
50g./2oz. ghee or clarified butter	4 Tbs. ghee or clarified butter
2 onions, chopped	2 onions, chopped
1 garlic clove, crushed	1 garlic clove, crushed
4cm./1½in. piece of fresh root ginger, peeled and chopped	1½in. piece of fresh green ginger, peeled and chopped
2 green chillis, chopped	2 green chillis, chopped
1 tsp. turmeric	1 tsp. turmeric
1 Tbs. ground coriander	1 Tbs. ground coriander
¼ tsp. hot chilli powder	¼ tsp. hot chilli powder
1 tsp. ground cumin	1 tsp. ground cumin
2 Tbs. cardamom seeds, crushed	2 Tbs. cardamom seeds, crushed
½ tsp. ground cloves	½ tsp. ground cloves
1kg./2lb. stewing steak, cubed	2lb. chuck steak, cubed
450ml./15fl.oz. water	2 cups water
1 tsp. salt	1 tsp. salt
2 bay leaves	2 bay leaves
½kg. 1lb. potatoes, scrubbed	1lb. potatoes, scrubbed

Melt the ghee or clarified butter in a large saucepan. Add the onions and garlic and fry, stirring occasionally, until the onions are golden brown. Add the ginger and chillis and fry for 4 minutes, stirring frequently. Stir in the spices and fry for 6 minutes, stirring frequently. Add a spoonful or two of water if the mixture becomes too dry.

Gosht aur Aloo, pungent and filling, is made with beef and potatoes.

Stir in the meat cubes and fry until they are evenly browned. Stir in the water, salt and bay leaves and bring to the boil. Cover the pan, reduce the heat to low and simmer the mixture for 1¼ hours. Add the potatoes and bring to the boil again. Re-cover and simmer for a further 45 minutes, or until the meat is cooked through.

Transfer to a warmed serving dish and serve at once.

Serves 4-6

Preparation and cooking time: 2½ hours

Seekh Kabab

(Beef Kebabs)

Metric/Imperial	American
700g./1½lb. minced beef	1½lb. ground beef
50g./2oz. fresh breadcrumbs	1 cup fresh breadcrumbs
2½cm./1in. piece of fresh root ginger, peeled and chopped	1in. piece of fresh green ginger, peeled and chopped
1 green chilli, chopped	1 green chilli, chopped
2 garlic cloves, crushed	2 garlic cloves, crushed
1 tsp. ground cumin	1 tsp. ground cumin
½ tsp. hot chilli powder	½ tsp. hot chilli powder
½ tsp. salt	½ tsp. salt
1 tsp. grated lemon rind	1 tsp. grated lemon rind
1 tsp. lemon juice	1 tsp. lemon juice

Combine all the ingredients in a large bowl and knead to mix thoroughly.

Divide the meat mixture into 16 portions. With damp hands, press eight portions on to well-greased wooden skewers, into pencil shapes, gently pressing the meat mixture until the kebabs measure about 10cm./4in. in length.

Preheat the oven to cool 150°C (Gas Mark 2, 300°F) and then preheat the grill (broiler) to high.

Arrange the eight skewers beneath the heat and grill (broil) turning once, for 6 to 8 minutes, or until the kebabs are cooked through. Slide the kebabs off the skewers and put into an ovenproof dish. Cover and put into the oven while you cook the remaining kebabs in the same way.

Serve at once.

Serves 4

Preparation and cooking time: 20 minutes

Kofta-Kabab Khatai

(Meatballs in Yogurt)

Metric/Imperial	American
1kg./2lb. minced beef	2lb. ground beef
4cm./1½in. piece of fresh root ginger, peeled and chopped	1½in. piece of fresh green ginger, peeled and chopped
2 garlic cloves, crushed	2 garlic cloves, crushed
125g./4oz. gram or chick-pea flour	1 cup gram or chick-pea flour
1¼ tsp. salt	1¼ tsp. salt
½ tsp. hot chilli powder	½ tsp. hot chilli powder
1 egg	1 egg
50g./2oz. sultanas	⅓ cup seedless raisins
juice of ½ lemon	juice of ½ lemon
3 Tbs. water	3 Tbs. water
75ml./3fl.oz. vegetable oil	⅓ cup vegetable oil
SAUCE	SAUCE
50g./2oz. butter	4 Tbs. butter
2 medium onions, chopped	2 medium onions, chopped
2½cm./1in. piece of fresh root ginger, peeled and chopped	1in. piece of fresh green ginger, peeled and chopped
2 garlic cloves, crushed	2 garlic cloves, crushed
1 Tbs. ground coriander	1 Tbs. ground coriander
1 tsp. ground cumin	1 tsp. ground cumin
½ tsp. hot chilli powder	½ tsp. hot chilli powder
600ml./1 pint yogurt	2½ cups yogurt
1 tsp. salt	1 tsp. salt
2 Tbs. chopped coriander leaves	2 Tbs. chopped coriander leaves

Combine the meat, ginger, garlic, 50g./2oz. (½ cup) of flour, 1 teaspoon of salt, the chilli powder and egg in a bowl. Knead until the ingredients are blended. Divide the mixture into about 34 portions. Roll each portion into a small ball, flatten and put 4 to 5 sultanas (raisins) in the centre. Shape the mixture around the sultanas or raisins to enclose them completely. Roll lightly to make them round and set aside.

Sift the remaining flour and salt into a saucer. Mix into a thick batter with the lemon juice and as much of the water as is necessary. Coat the meatballs in a little of the batter.

Heat the oil in a large frying-pan. When it is hot, add the meatballs and fry until they are golden brown. (Fry in several batches if necessary).

To make the sauce, melt the butter in a large saucepan. Add the onions, ginger and garlic and fry, stirring occasionally, until the onions are golden brown. Stir in the spices and fry for 3 minutes, stirring frequently. Stir in the yogurt and salt and bring to the boil. Gently stir in the meatballs, coating them thoroughly in the sauce. Cover the pan, reduce the heat to low and simmer for 15 minutes.

Transfer the mixture to a warmed serving dish and sprinkle over the coriander leaves before serving.

Serves 4-6

Preparation and cooking time: 1 hour

An alternative way of cooking meatballs is Kofta-kabab Khatai which are beef and raisin meatballs cooked in an aromatic yogurt sauce.

Pork Vindaloo

(Pork Vinegar Curry)

Metric/Imperial	American
5cm./2in. piece of fresh root ginger, peeled and chopped	2in. piece of fresh green ginger, peeled and chopped
4 garlic cloves, chopped	4 garlic cloves, chopped
1½ tsp. hot chilli powder	1½ tsp. hot chilli powder
2 tsp. turmeric	2 tsp. turmeric
1 tsp. salt	1 tsp. salt
2 tsp. cardamom seeds	2 tsp. cardamom seeds
6 cloves	6 cloves
6 peppercorns	6 peppercorns
1 cinnamon stick	1 cinnamon stick
2 Tbs. coriander seeds	2 Tbs. coriander seeds
1 Tbs. cumin seeds	1 Tbs. cumin seeds
150ml./5fl.oz. wine vinegar	⅔ cup wine vinegar
1kg./2lb. pork fillet, cubed	2lb. pork tenderloin, cubed
4 curry or bay leaves	4 curry or bay leaves
3 Tbs. vegetable oil	3 Tbs. vegetable oil
1 tsp. mustard seeds	1 tsp. mustard seeds
150ml./5fl.oz. water	⅔ cup water

Put the spices and vinegar into a blender and blend to a smooth purée, adding more liquid if necessary to form a liquid paste. Put the pork cubes into a large bowl and stir in the spice paste. Cover and set aside to marinate at room temperature for 1 hour. Lay the curry or bay leaves on top, re-cover and chill in the refrigerator for 24 hours, turning and basting the meat from time to time. Two hours before cooking time, remove the bowl from the refrigerator and set aside at room temperature.

Heat the oil in a large saucepan. Add the mustard seeds and cover the pan. When the seeds begin to spatter, add the pork, marinade and the water and bring to the boil. Cover the pan, reduce the heat to low and simmer for 40 minutes. Uncover the pan and simmer for a further 30 minutes, or until the pork is cooked through and tender and the sauce is neither too thick nor too thin.

Transfer the vindaloo to a warmed serving dish and serve at once.

Serves 4-6
Preparation and cooking time: 26½ hours

Pork Korma

(Braised Sliced Pork)

Metric/Imperial	American
50g./2oz. butter	4 Tbs. butter
4cm./1½oz. piece of fresh root ginger, peeled and chopped	1½in. piece of fresh green ginger, peeled and chopped
3 garlic cloves, crushed	3 garlic cloves, crushed
2 medium onions, chopped	2 medium onions, chopped
½ tsp. hot chilli powder	½ tsp. hot chilli powder
2 Tbs. ground coriander	2 Tbs. ground coriander
1kg./2lb. pork fillet, cubed	2lb. pork tenderloin, cubed
1 tsp. salt	1 tsp. salt
300ml./10fl.oz. yogurt	1¼ cups yogurt
125g./4oz. ground almonds	⅔ cup ground almonds
300ml./10fl.oz. double cream	1¼ cups heavy cream
½ tsp. ground cinnamon	½ tsp. ground cinnamon
¼ tsp. ground mace	¼ tsp. ground mace
½ tsp. ground cardamom	½ tsp. ground cardamom
¼ tsp. saffron threads, soaked in 2 Tbs. boiling water	¼ tsp. saffron threads, soaked in 2 Tbs. boiling water
GARNISH	GARNISH
2 medium onions, thinly sliced into rings and fried until crisp	2 medium onions, thinly sliced into rings and fried until crisp

Melt the butter in a large flameproof casserole. Add the ginger, garlic and onions and fry, stirring occasionally, until the onions are golden brown. Stir in the chilli powder and coriander and fry for 1 minute. Add the pork cubes and fry until they are evenly browned. Increase the heat to high and cook for a further 8 to 10 minutes, stirring constantly, or until all the cooking juices have evaporated. Reduce the heat to moderate.

Stir in salt and 50ml./2fl.oz. (¼ cup) of the yogurt, then stir in 50ml./2fl.oz. (¼ cup) more until it evaporates. Continue adding the yogurt in this way until all the yogurt is used up and there is no liquid in the pan. Remove from the heat and stir in the ground almonds and cream. Stir in the cinnamon, mace and cardamom and bring to the boil. Cover the pan, reduce the heat to low and simmer for 35 minutes, stirring occasionally. Stir in the saffron mixture.

Meanwhile, preheat the oven to moderate 180°C (Gas Mark 4, 350°F).

Transfer the casserole to the oven and cook for 15 to 20 minutes, or until

the pork is cooked through and tender. Remove from the oven, garnish with the fried onions before serving.

Serves 4-6
Preparation and cooking time: $1\frac{3}{4}$ hours

Liver Dopeeazah

Metric/Imperial	American
10 cardamom pods	10 cardamom pods
2.5cm./1in. piece of fresh root ginger, peeled and chopped	1in. piece of fresh green ginger, peeled and chopped
$\frac{1}{4}$ tsp. cayenne pepper	$\frac{1}{4}$ tsp. cayenne pepper
2 Tbs. grated onion	2 Tbs. grated onion
4 garlic cloves, crushed	4 garlic cloves, crushed
200ml./7fl.oz. yogurt	1 cup yogurt
150g./5oz. ghee or clarified butter	10 Tbs. ghee or clarified butter
2kg./4lb. onions, half sliced and half minced	4lb. onions, half sliced and half minced
700g./1$\frac{1}{2}$lb. ox or lambs' liver, cut into strips $\frac{1}{2}$cm./$\frac{1}{4}$in. thick and 5cm./2in. long	1$\frac{1}{2}$lb. ox or lambs' liver, cut into strips $\frac{1}{4}$in. thick and 2in. long
2 Tbs. ground coriander	2 Tbs. ground coriander
$\frac{1}{4}$ tsp. salt	$\frac{1}{4}$ tsp. salt
150ml./5fl.oz. water	$\frac{2}{3}$ cup water
$\frac{1}{4}$ tsp. black pepper	$\frac{1}{4}$ tsp. black pepper
$\frac{1}{4}$ tsp. ground saffron	$\frac{1}{2}$ tsp. ground saffron
$\frac{1}{2}$ tsp. grated nutmeg	$\frac{1}{2}$ tsp. grated nutmeg

Split half the cardamom pods and put them in a mortar. Add the ginger, cayenne, grated onion and garlic and pound the mixture with a pestle. Add 1 teaspoon of yogurt and continue to pound until the mixture forms a smooth paste. Rub the paste all over the liver strips and set aside at room temperature for 2 hours.

Melt one-third of the ghee in a heavy-based saucepan. Add the minced onions and fry, stirring occasionally, until they are golden. Using a slotted spoon, transfer the onions to a pestle or to a chopping board. Pound into a paste with a pestle or the end of a rolling pin. Alternatively, they can be puréed in a blender. Set aside.

Add half the remaining ghee to the saucepan. When it has melted, add the liver strips and fry for 5 to 8 minutes, or until they are evenly browned.

Split the remaining cardamom pods and grind the seeds. Stir the ground seeds, the coriander and salt into the pan and cook for 3 minutes, stirring frequently.

Add the remaining ghee, then the sliced onions. Cook, stirring occasionally, until the onions are soft. Stir in the yogurt, about 2 tablespoons at a time and making each addition when the previous amount has been amalgamated. Add the water, stirring constantly until it forms a sauce. Reduce the heat to low, cover and simmer the mixture for 20 minutes, or until the sauce has almost disappeared.

Stir in the onion purée, black pepper, saffron and nutmeg and continue to simmer for a further 10 minutes.

Transfer the mixture to a warmed serving dish and serve at once.

Serves 4
Preparation and cooking time: $3\frac{1}{2}$ hours

(See over) Served with raita and naan, Pork Korma is a hot, spicy dish made with yogurt and cream.

167

Spiced Liver

Metric/Imperial	American
700g./1½lb. lamb's liver, thinly sliced	1½lb. lamb's liver, thinly sliced
5cm./2in. piece of fresh root ginger, peeled and chopped	2in. piece of fresh green ginger, peeled and chopped
4 garlic cloves, crushed	4 garlic cloves, crushed
1 tsp. salt	1 tsp. salt
1 tsp. hot chilli powder	1 tsp. hot chilli powder
½ tsp. black pepper	½ tsp. black pepper
juice of 1 lemon	juice of 1 lemon
75g./3oz. ghee or clarified butter	6 Tbs. ghee or clarified butter

Cut each liver slice in half lengthways and set aside.

Combine the ginger, garlic, salt, chilli powder, pepper and lemon juice together in a large bowl and add the liver slices. Turn and toss them in the mixture until they are thoroughly coated. Cover and set aside to marinate at room temperature for 1 hour.

Melt the ghee or clarified butter in a large frying-pan. Add the liver slices, a few at a time, and fry for 4 to 6 minutes, or until they are cooked through and evenly browned. Transfer to a warmed serving dish and serve at once.

Serves 4-6
Preparation and cooking time: 1½ hours

Gurda Korma

(Curried Kidneys)

Metric/Imperial	American
25g./1oz. butter	2 Tbs. butter
1 Tbs. vegetable oil	1 Tbs. vegetable oil
1 garlic clove, crushed	1 garlic clove, crushed
1cm./½in. piece of fresh root ginger, peeled and chopped	½in. piece of fresh green ginger, peeled and chopped
2 small onions, chopped	2 small onions, chopped
¼ tsp. hot chilli powder	¼ tsp. hot chilli powder
¼ tsp. turmeric	¼ tsp. turmeric
1 tsp. ground coriander	1 tsp. ground coriander
¼ tsp. ground cumin	¼ tsp. ground cumin
¼ tsp. salt	¼ tsp. salt
½ tsp. black pepper	½ tsp. black pepper
8 lambs' kidneys, cored and halved	8 lambs' kidneys, cored and halved
1 small green pepper, pith and seeds removed and sliced	1 small green pepper, pith and seeds removed and sliced

Melt the butter and oil in a frying-pan. Add the garlic and ginger and fry for 30 seconds, stirring constantly. Add the onions and fry, stirring occasionally, until they are golden brown. Stir in the spices and cook for 1 minute. Add the salt, pepper and kidneys and stir to coat them with the spices. Cook for 15 minutes, stirring occasionally, or until the kidneys are cooked and tender.

Transfer the mixture to a warmed serving dish and garnish with the pepper slices before serving.

Serves 4
Preparation and cooking time: 30 minutes

Gurda Korma, complemented by home-made chutneys, is an appetizing meal of curried kidneys and green peppers.

POVLTRY & GAME

Yogurt Chicken

Metric/Imperial	American
1 x 2kg./4lb. chicken, skinned	1 x 4lb. chicken, skinned
1 tsp. salt	1 tsp. salt
juice of ½ lemon	juice of ½ lemon
2 green chillis, finely chopped	2 green chillis, finely chopped
250ml./8fl.oz. yogurt	1 cup yogurt
½ bunch coriander leaves, finely chopped	½ bunch coriander leaves, finely chopped
5cm./2in. piece of fresh root ginger, peeled and chopped	2in. piece of fresh green ginger, peeled and chopped
4 garlic cloves, crushed	4 garlic cloves, crushed
50g./2oz. butter, melted	4 Tbs. butter, melted

Prick the chicken all over, then rub with the salt, lemon juice and chillis. Put into a large bowl and set aside for 30 minutes.

Combine the yogurt, coriander leaves, ginger and garlic, then rub the mixture all over the chicken. Cover and set aside for 8 hours.

Preheat the oven to fairly hot 200°C (Gas Mark 6, 400°F).

Pour half the butter into a roasting pan. Put the chicken and marinade into the pan and put into the oven. Roast for 20 minutes. Reduce the heat to moderate 180°C (Gas Mark 4, 350°F) and roast the chicken for a further 30 minutes, or until it is cooked through and tender, basting frequently with the remaining butter. Remove from the oven.

Transfer the chicken to a warmed serving dish. Put the pan over moderate heat and bring the juices to the boil, stirring constantly. Boil for about 5 minutes, or until they have thickened.

Pour the sauce over the chicken and serve at once.

Serves 4
Preparation and cooking time: 9¾ hours

Murg Tikka

(Chicken Kebabs)

Metric/Imperial	American
150ml./5fl.oz. yogurt	⅔ cup yogurt
4 garlic cloves, crushed	4 garlic cloves, crushed
4cm./1½in. piece of fresh root ginger, peeled and chopped	1½in. piece of fresh green ginger, peeled and chopped
1 small onion, grated	1 small onion, grated
1½ tsp. hot chilli powder	1½ tsp. hot chilli powder
1 Tbs. ground coriander	1 Tbs. ground coriander
1 tsp. salt	1 tsp. salt
3 chicken breasts, skinned and boned	3 chicken breasts, skinned and boned
GARNISH	GARNISH
1 large onion, sliced into rings	1 large onion, sliced into rings

Yogurt Chicken is roasted in yogurt and spices which combine to make a delightful North Indian meal.

173

2 large tomatoes, thinly sliced
2 Tbs. chopped coriander leaves

2 large tomatoes, thinly sliced
2 Tbs. chopped coriander leaves

Combine the yogurt, garlic, ginger, onion, chilli powder, coriander and salt. Cut the chicken meat into 2½cm./1in. cubes and stir into the marinade. Cover and chill in the refrigerator for at least 6 hours, or overnight, basting occasionally.

Preheat the grill (broiler) to high.

Thread the chicken cubes on to skewers and arrange them on the rack of the grill (broiler). Grill (broil) for 5 to 6 minutes, turning occasionally, or until they are cooked through. Remove from the heat.

Slide the chicken cubes from the skewers on to a warmed serving dish and garnish with the onion rings, tomato slices and chopped coriander before serving.

Serves 4

Preparation and cooking time: 7 hours

Chicken Vindaloo

Metric/Imperial	American
1 x 2½kg./5lb. chicken, skinned and cut into serving pieces	1 x 5lb. chicken, skinned and cut into serving pieces
1½ tsp. salt	1½ tsp. salt
½ tsp. cayenne pepper	½ tsp. cayenne pepper
2 tsp. lemon juice	2 tsp. lemon juice
2 dried red chillis	2 dried red chillis
4 garlic cloves	4 garlic cloves
4cm./1½in. piece of fresh root ginger, peeled and chopped	1½in. piece of fresh green ginger, peeled and chopped
1 tsp. cumin seeds	1 tsp. cumin seeds
2 tsp. coriander seeds	2 tsp. coriander seeds
1 tsp. black peppercorns	1 tsp. black peppercorns
1 cinnamon stick	1 cinnamon stick
4 cloves	4 cloves
2 Tbs. malt vinegar	2 Tbs. malt vinegar
3 Tbs. vegetable oil	3 Tbs. vegetable oil
2 medium onions, chopped	2 medium onions, chopped
1 tsp. turmeric	1 tsp. turmeric
300ml./10fl.oz. chicken stock	1¼ cups chicken stock

Rub the chicken pieces all over with half the salt, the cayenne and lemon juice. Set aside for 30 minutes.

Meanwhile put the spices and vinegar into a blender and blend to a purée, adding more vinegar if necessary. Transfer to a bowl.

Heat the oil in a saucepan. When it is hot, add the onions and fry, stirring occasionally, until they are golden brown. Stir in the turmeric and spice purée and fry for 5 minutes, stirring frequently. Add a spoonful or two of water if the mixture becomes too dry. Add the chicken pieces and fry until they are evenly browned. Pour in the stock and remaining salt and bring to the boil. Cover the pan, reduce the heat to low and simmer for 45 minutes, or until the chicken is cooked through and tender.

Spoon the vindaloo into a warmed serving dish and serve at once.

Serves 6

Preparation and cooking time: 1¾ hours

Derived from a traditional Indian dish, Chicken Vindaloo is a hot, colourful curry from Bombay.

Kashmiri Chicken

Metric/Imperial	American
1 medium onion, chopped	1 medium onion, chopped
5cm./2in. piece of fresh root ginger, peeled and chopped	2in. piece of fresh green ginger, peeled and chopped
2 garlic cloves, crushed	2 garlic cloves, crushed
1 tsp. coriander seeds	1 tsp. coriander seeds
1½ tsp. anchovy essence	1½ tsp. anchovy essence
250g./9oz. ground almonds	1½ cups ground almonds
3 Tbs. vegetable oil	3 Tbs. vegetable oil
4 chicken pieces	4 chicken pieces
300ml./10fl.oz. chicken stock	1¼ cups chicken stock
300ml./10fl.oz. thick coconut milk	1¼ cups thick coconut milk
2 tsp. soft brown sugar	2 tsp. soft brown sugar
GARNISH	GARNISH
2 Tbs. finely chopped coriander leaves	2 Tbs. finely chopped coriander leaves
4 lemon wedges	4 lemon wedges

Combine the onion, ginger, garlic, coriander seeds and anchovy essence and put them into a blender. Blend to a smooth purée. Transfer the purée to a small bowl and stir in the ground almonds until the mixture is well blended.

Heat the oil in a saucepan. When it is hot, add the spice paste and fry, stirring constantly, for 5 minutes. Add a spoonful or two of water if the mixture becomes too dry.

Add the chicken pieces to the pan and turn until they are well coated with the spice mixture. Reduce the heat to moderately low and cook the chicken for 15 minutes, turning occasionally.

Pour over the chicken stock and bring to the boil, stirring constantly. Reduce the heat to low, cover the pan and simmer the mixture for 20 minutes. Stir in the coconut milk and brown sugar and continue to simmer the mixture for a further 20 minutes, or until the chicken is cooked through and tender.

Transfer the mixture to a warmed serving bowl and garnish with the coriander leaves and lemon wedges before serving.

Serves 4
Preparation and cooking time: 1¼ hours

Tandoori Murg is a very
popular chicken dish, traditionally served with mixed
salad.

Tandoori Murg

(Marinated Spiced Chicken)

Metric/Imperial	American
1 x 1½kg./3lb. chicken, skinned	1 x 3lb. chicken, skinned
1 tsp. hot chilli powder	1 tsp. hot chilli powder
1 tsp. salt	1 tsp. salt
½ tsp. black pepper	½ tsp. black pepper
2 Tbs. lemon juice	2 Tbs. lemon juice
50g./2oz. butter, melted	4 Tbs. butter, melted
MARINADE	MARINADE
3 Tbs. yogurt	3 Tbs. yogurt
4 garlic cloves	4 garlic cloves
1 Tbs. raisins	1 Tbs. raisins
5cm./2in. piece of fresh root ginger, peeled and chopped	2in. piece of fresh green ginger, peeled and chopped
1 tsp. cumin seeds	1 tsp. cumin seeds
1 Tbs. coriander seeds	1 Tbs. coriander seeds
2 dried red chillis	2 dried red chillis
½ tsp. red food colouring	½ tsp. red food coloring

Make gashes in the thighs and on each side of the breast of the chicken. Mix the
chilli powder, salt, pepper and lemon juice together, then rub the mixture all
over the chicken, especially into the gashes. Set aside for 20 minutes.

Meanwhile, prepare the marinade. Put all the ingredients, except the food
colouring, into the blender and blend to a smooth purée. Transfer to a bowl
and mix in the food colouring. Put the chicken into a large bowl, then spread
the mixture all over the chicken, rubbing it well into the gashes. Cover and chill
in the refrigerator for 24 hours.

Preheat the oven to fairly hot 200°C (Gas Mark 6, 400°F).

Put the chicken, on its back, on a rack in a roasting pan. Pour in enough water
just to cover the bottom of the pan (to prevent the drippings from burning).
Spoon the marinade in the bowl over the chicken, then a tablespoon of the melted
butter. Roast for 1 hour, or until it is cooked through and tender, basting frequently with the remaining melted butter and the pan drippings. Remove from
the oven.

Transfer the chicken to a carving board and carve into serving pieces. Arrange
them on a warmed serving dish and spoon the drippings over. Serve at once.
Serves 3
Preparation and cooking time: 26 hours

Madras Chicken Curry

Metric/Imperial	American
50ml./2fl.oz. vegetable oil	¼ cup vegetable oil
1 tsp. mustard seeds	1 tsp. mustard seeds
2 medium onions, finely chopped	2 medium onions, finely chopped
2½ cm./1in. piece of fresh root ginger, peeled and chopped	1in. piece of fresh green ginger, peeled and chopped
3 garlic cloves, crushed	3 garlic cloves, crushed
2 tsp. turmeric	2 tsp. turmeric

Metric/Imperial	American
1 Tbs. ground coriander	1 Tbs. ground coriander
1 tsp. hot chilli powder	1 tsp. hot chilli powder
¼ tsp. ground fenugreek	¼ tsp. ground fenugreek
2 tsp. ground cumin	2 tsp. ground cumin
1 tsp. black pepper	1 tsp. black pepper
8 chicken pieces, skinned	8 chicken pieces, skinned
600ml./1 pint coconut milk	2½ cups coconut milk
1 tsp. salt	1 tsp. salt
2 bay leaves	2 bay leaves
3 green chillis, slit lengthways and seeded	3 green chillis, slit lengthways and seeded
juice of ½ lemon	juice of ½ lemon

Heat the oil in a large saucepan. When it is hot, add the mustard seeds and fry until they begin to spatter. Add the onions, ginger and garlic and fry, stirring occasionally, until the onions are soft. Stir in the spices and fry for 5 minutes, stirring frequently. Add a tablespoonful or two of water if too dry.

Add the chicken pieces to the pan and turn them over to coat them thoroughly in the spices. Fry until they are evenly browned. Add all the remaining ingredients, except the lemon juice, and bring to the boil, stirring occasionally. Cover the pan, reduce the heat to low and simmer for 50 minutes, or until the chicken is cooked through and tender. After 30 minutes, uncover the pan and, if the curry is too liquid, simmer uncovered until it thickens. Stir in the lemon juice.

Remove from the heat and discard the bay leaves. Transfer to a warmed serving dish and serve at once.

Serves 4-6
Preparation and cooking time: 1¼ hours

Murg Kashmiri

(Chicken with Almonds and Raisins)

Metric/Imperial	American
1 x 2kg./4lb. chicken, skinned	1 x 4lb. chicken, skinned
juice of ½ lemon	juice of ½ lemon
1 Tbs. coriander seeds	1 Tbs. coriander seeds
1 tsp. black peppercorns	1 tsp. black peppercorns
1 tsp. cardamom seeds	1 tsp. cardamom seeds
6 cloves	6 cloves
4cm./1½in. piece of fresh root ginger, peeled and chopped	1½in. piece of fresh green ginger, peeled and chopped
1 tsp. salt	1 tsp. salt
½ tsp. hot chilli powder	½ tsp. hot chilli powder
75g./3oz. butter	6 Tbs. butter
2 medium onions, chopped	2 medium onions, chopped
300ml./10fl.oz. double cream	1¼ cups heavy cream
¼ tsp. saffron threads, soaked in 2 Tbs. boiling water	¼ tsp. saffron threads, soaked in 2 Tbs. boiling water
50g./2oz. slivered almonds	⅓ cup slivered almonds
50g./2oz. raisins	⅓ cup raisins

Preheat the oven to fairly hot 200°C (Gas Mark 6, 400°F). Prick the chicken all over, then rub over the lemon juice.

Put the spices into a mortar and grind coarsely with a pestle. Strain, discarding any husks left in the strainer, then mix in the ginger, salt and chilli powder. Cream half the butter to make a smooth paste, then beat into the spice mixture. Rub all over the chicken. Put the chicken into a flameproof casserole and put the casserole into the oven. Roast for 15 minutes.

Meanwhile, melt the remaining butter in a saucepan. Add the onions and fry, stirring occasionally, until they are golden brown. Remove from the heat and stir in the cream, saffron mixture, almonds and raisins.

Reduce the oven to moderate 180°C (Gas Mark 4, 350°F). Roast the chicken for 1 hour, or until it is cooked through, basting it every 10 minutes with the cream and almond mixture. Remove from the oven.

Transfer the chicken to a carving board and carve into serving pieces. Arrange the pieces in a warmed serving dish and keep hot.

Skim off most of the fat from the surface of the cooking liquid and set the casserole over moderate heat. Cook the sauce for 2 minutes, stirring constantly. Pour the sauce over the chicken pieces and serve at once.

Serves 4

Preparation and cooking time: $1\frac{1}{2}$ hours

Sindhi Chicken

Metric/Imperial	American
1 x 2kg./4lb. chicken, skinned	1 x 4lb. chicken, skinned
1½ tsp. salt	1½ tsp. salt
1 tsp. bicarbonate of soda	1 tsp. baking soda
75g./3oz. butter	6 Tbs. butter
STUFFING	STUFFING
40g.1½/oz. cooked rice	½ cup cooked rice
2 large tomatoes, blanched, peeled, seeded and chopped	2 large tomatoes, blanched, peeled, seeded and chopped
1 large onion, chopped	1 large onion, chopped
1cm./½in. piece of fresh root ginger, peeled and chopped	½in. piece of fresh green ginger, peeled and chopped
1 green chilli, chopped	1 green chilli, chopped
salt and pepper	salt and pepper
1 hard-boiled egg, chopped	1 hard-boiled egg, chopped
50ml./2fl.oz. yogurt	¼ cup yogurt
25g./1oz. butter, melted	2 Tbs. butter, melted

Rub the chicken all over with the salt and soda. Set aside for 1 hour. Wash the chicken, then dry on kitchen towels.

Preheat the oven to moderate 180°C (Gas Mark 4, 350°F).

Melt 25g./1oz. (2 tablespoons) of butter in a deep frying-pan. Add the chicken and fry until it is evenly browned. Remove the pan from the heat and set the chicken aside until is it cool enough to handle.

Meanwhile, prepare the stuffing. Combine all the ingredients and mix well. Spoon into the cavity of the chicken and close with a skewer or a trussing needle and thread.

Put the chicken in an ovenproof dish. Cut the remaining butter into small pieces and scatter over the chicken. Put into the oven and roast for $1\frac{1}{4}$ hours, basting the chicken regularly with the butter. Remove from the oven.

Transfer the chicken to a carving board and carve into serving pieces. Arrange in a warmed serving dish, with the stuffing and cooking juices, and serve at once.

Serves 4

Preparation and cooking time: $2\frac{1}{2}$ hours

Chicken Pulao

(Curried Rice with Chicken)

Metric/Imperial	American
50g./2oz. ghee or clarified butter	4 Tbs. ghee or clarified butter
1 large onion, sliced	1 large onion, sliced
2½cm./1in. piece of fresh root ginger, peeled and chopped	1in. piece of fresh green ginger, peeled and chopped
2 garlic cloves, crushed	2 garlic cloves, crushed
2 green chillis, chopped	2 green chillis, chopped
1 x 1½kg./3lb. chicken, cut into small serving pieces	1 x 3lb. chicken, cut into small serving pieces
1 tsp. turmeric	1 tsp. turmeric
½ tsp. hot chilli powder	½ tsp. hot chilli powder
1 Tbs. ground coriander	1 Tbs. ground coriander
1½tsp. salt	1½ tsp. salt
½ tsp. black pepper	½ tsp. black pepper
150ml./5fl.oz. yogurt	⅔ cup yogurt
juice of 1 small lemon	juice of 1 small lemon
350g./12oz. long-grain rice, soaked in cold water for 30 minutes and drained	2 cups long-grain rice, soaked in cold water for 30 minutes and drained
400ml./12fl.oz. boiling water	1½ cups boiling water

Melt the ghee or clarified butter in a saucepan. Add the onion and fry, stirring occasionally, until it is soft. Add the ginger, garlic and chillis and fry for 4 minutes, stirring occasionally. Add the chicken pieces and fry until they are evenly browned.

Combine the spices, salt, pepper, yogurt and lemon juice, then stir the mixture into the pan. Cover, reduce the heat to low and simmer for 40 minutes, or until the chicken is cooked through and tender. Uncover and stir in the rice and cook until most of the liquid has been absorbed. Pour over the water and cover the pan. Reduce the heat to low and simmer the pulau for 15 to 20 minutes, or until the rice is cooked and the liquid absorbed.

Serve at once.

Serves 4

Preparation and cooking time: $1\frac{3}{4}$ hours

White Chicken Curry

Metric/Imperial	American
1 cinnamon stick	1 cinnamon stick
2 tsp. cardamom seeds	2 tsp. cardamom seeds
4 peppercorns	4 peppercorns
4 cloves	4 cloves
50g./2oz. butter	4 Tbs. butter
3 garlic cloves, crushed	3 garlic cloves, crushed
5cm./2in. piece of fresh root ginger, peeled and chopped	2in. piece of fresh green ginger, peeled and chopped
4 medium onions, chopped	4 medium onions, chopped

1 x 2kg./4lb. chicken, cut into serving pieces	1 x 4lb. chicken, cut into serving pieces
450ml./15fl.oz. yogurt	2 cups yogurt
1 tsp. hot chilli powder	1 tsp. hot chilli powder
1 tsp. salt	1 tsp. salt
¼ tsp. saffron threads, soaked in 2 Tbs. boiling water	¼ tsp. saffron threads, soaked in 2 Tbs. boiling water
250ml./8fl.oz. thick coconut milk	1 cup thick coconut milk
3 Tbs. ground almonds	3 Tbs. ground almonds

Put the spices and peppercorns in a blender and blend to a powder. Set aside.

Melt the butter in a saucepan. Add the spice powder and fry for 1 minute, stirring constantly. Add the garlic, ginger and onions and fry, stirring frequently, until the onions are golden brown. Add the chicken pieces and fry until they are evenly browned.

Meanwhile, combine the yogurt with the chilli powder, salt and saffron mixture, then pour into the pan. Bring to the boil, cover the pan and reduce the heat to low. Simmer for 30 minutes. Stir in the coconut milk and ground almonds and bring to the boil again. Reduce the heat to low and simmer, uncovered, for 30 minutes, or until the chicken is cooked through and tender. (If the sauce is too thin, remove the chicken from the pan and boil the sauce for 10 to 15 minutes or until it thickens.)

Transfer the curry and chicken to a warmed serving dish and serve at once.
Serves 4
Preparation and cooking time: 1¾ hours

White Chicken Curry, accompanied by rice, chutneys and poppadums, makes a delicately flavoured dish.

Dhansak

(Chicken with Dhal [Lentils] and Vegetables)

Metric/Imperial	American
125g./4oz. tur dhal	½ cup tur dhal
25g./1oz. channa dhal	2 Tbs. channa dhal
50g./2oz. masoor dhal	¼ cup masoor dhal
25g./1oz. moong dhal	2 Tbs. moong dhal
900ml./1½ pints water	3¾ cups water
2 tsp. salt	2 tsp. salt
40g./1½oz. ghee or clarified butter	3 Tbs. ghee or clarified butter
2½cm./1in. piece of fresh root ginger, peeled and chopped	1in. piece of fresh green ginger, peeled and chopped
1 garlic clove, crushed	1 garlic clove, crushed
8 chicken pieces	8 chicken pieces
1 Tbs. chopped fresh mint	1 Tbs. chopped fresh mint
225g./8oz. aubergines, cubed	1 cup cubed, eggplants
225g./8oz. pumpkin, cubed	1 cup cubed, pumpkin
125g./4oz. chopped spinach	⅔ cup chopped spinach
1 large onion, sliced	1 large onion, sliced
½kg./1lb. tomatoes, blanched, peeled and chopped	1lb. tomatoes, blanched, peeled and chopped
MASALA	MASALA
50g./2oz. ghee or clarified butter	4 Tbs. ghee or clarified butter
1 large onion, sliced	1 large onion, sliced
4cm./1½in. piece of fresh root ginger, peeled and chopped	1½in. piece of fresh green ginger, peeled and chopped
3 green chillis, chopped	3 green chillis, chopped
3 garlic cloves, crushed	3 garlic cloves, crushed
½ tsp. ground cinnamon	½ tsp. ground cinnamon
½ tsp. ground cardamom	½ tsp. ground cardamom
½ tsp. ground cloves	½ tsp. ground cloves
1½ tsp. turmeric	1½ tsp. turmeric
1 tsp. ground coriander	1 tsp. ground coriander
¼ tsp. hot chilli powder	¼ tsp. hot chilli powder
3 Tbs. chopped coriander leaves	3 Tbs. chopped coriander leaves

Wash all the dhals (lentils) thoroughly in cold running water and soak for 30 minutes. Drain and transfer them to a saucepan. Add the water and salt and bring to the boil, skimming off any scum that rises to the surface. Cover the pan, reduce the heat to low and simmer for 40 minutes.

Meanwhile, melt the ghee or clarified butter in a large frying-pan. Add the ginger and garlic and fry for 2 minutes, stirring frequently. Add the chicken pieces and fry until they are evenly browned.

Transfer the chicken mixture to the dhal, then stir in the vegetables and tomatoes. Bring to the boil, reduce the heat to low and simmer for 45 minutes, or until the chicken is cooked through and tender.

Transfer the chicken to a plate. Purée the vegetables and dhal in a blender and set aside.

Rinse and dry the saucepan. To make the masala, melt the ghee or clarified butter in the saucepan. Add the onion and fry, stirring occasionally, until it is golden brown. Add the ginger, chillis and garlic and fry for 3 minutes, stirring frequently. Add all the remaining ingredients, except the coriander leaves, and fry for 8 minutes, stirring constantly. Add a spoonful or two of water if the mixture becomes too dry.

Stir the puréed vegetables and dhal into the pan and bring to the boil. Cover the pan, reduce the heat to low and simmer for 20 minutes. Stir in the chicken pieces and baste well with the sauce. Simmer for 10 minutes, or until they are heated through.

Transfer the dhansak to a warmed serving dish and sprinkle over the coriander before serving.

Serves 6
Preparation and cooking time: 3 hours

(See over) Dhansak combines chicken, lentils and vegetables to produce a delicious and filling meal.

Spiced Almond Chicken

Metric/Imperial	American
1 x 2kg./4lb. chicken	1 x 4lb. chicken
juice of 1½ lemons	juice of 1½ lemons
2 tsp. salt	2 tsp. salt
1 tsp. cayenne pepper	1 tsp. cayenne pepper
¼ tsp. saffron threads, soaked in 2 Tbs. boiling water for 10 minutes	¼ tsp. saffron threads, soaked in 2 Tbs. boiling water for 10 minutes
50g./2oz. butter, melted	4 Tbs. butter, melted
MARINADE	MARINADE
50g./2oz. raisins	⅓ cup raisins
75g./3oz. flaked almonds	½ cup slivered almonds
1 Tbs. clear honey	1 Tbs. clear honey
2 garlic cloves	2 garlic cloves
5cm./2in. piece of fresh root ginger, peeled and chopped	5cm./2in. piece of fresh green ginger, peeled and chopped
½ tsp. cardamom seeds	½ tsp. cardamom seeds
½ tsp. cumin seeds	½ tsp. cumin seeds
1 tsp. turmeric	1 tsp. turmeric
150ml./5fl.oz. yogurt	⅔ cup yogurt
125ml./4fl.oz. double cream	½ cup heavy cream

Make diagonal slits in the breast and thighs of the chicken. Combine the lemon juice, salt and cayenne then rub the mixture all over the chicken, especially into the slits. Put the chicken into a large bowl and set aside for 30 minutes.

Meanwhile, make the marinade. Put the raisins, almonds, honey, garlic, ginger and spices into a blender with 4 tablespoons of yogurt and blend to a smooth purée.

Transfer the purée to a bowl and beat in the remaining yogurt and the cream. Pour over the chicken, cover the bowl and chill in the refrigerator for 24 hours, turning occasionally. Remove from the refrigerator and set aside at room temperature for 1 hour.

Preheat the oven to fairly hot 200°C (Gas Mark 6, 400°F).

Put the chicken into a deep roasting pan. Combine the saffron mixture with the remaining marinade and pour over the chicken. Spoon a little of the melted butter over the top. Pour 150ml./5fl.oz. (⅔ cup) of water into the roasting pan and put the pan into the oven. Roast the chicken for 1 hour, or until it is cooked through and tender, basting frequently with the remaining melted butter and the liquid in the tin. Remove from the oven.

Transfer the chicken to a warmed serving dish. Spoon the tin juices over the chicken and serve at once.

Serves 4
Preparation and cooking time: 26 hours

Goan Vinegar Curry is a very spicy and hot chicken dish from the west coast of India.

Goan Vinegar Curry

Metric/Imperial	American
75ml./3fl.oz. vegetable oil	¾ cup vegetable oil
5cm./2in. piece of fresh root ginger, peeled and chopped	3in. piece of fresh root ginger, peeled and chopped
3 green chillis, chopped	3 green chillis, chopped
3 garlic cloves, crushed	3 garlic cloves, crushed
1 x 2kg./4lb. chicken, cut into serving pieces	1 x 4lb. chicken, cut into serving pieces
½ tsp. ground cardamom	½ tsp. ground cardamom
½ tsp. ground cloves	½ tsp. ground cloves
½ tsp. ground cinnamon	½ tsp. ground cinnamon
1½ tsp. turmeric	1½ tsp. turmeric
1 Tbs. ground coriander	1 Tbs. ground coriander
1 tsp. hot chilli powder	1 tsp. hot chilli powder
250ml./8fl.oz. vinegar	1 cup vinegar
4 large onions, sliced	4 large onions, sliced
150ml./5fl.oz. water	⅝ cup water
1 tsp. salt	1 tsp. salt

Heat the oil in a saucepan. When it is hot, add the ginger, chillis and garlic and fry for 2 minutes, stirring frequently. Add the chicken pieces and fry until they are evenly browned. Transfer the chicken to a plate.

Mix the spices with enough vinegar to make a smooth paste. Set aside.

Add the onions to the pan and fry, stirring occasionally, until they are golden brown. Add the spice paste and fry for 8 minutes, stirring frequently. Add a spoonful or two of water if the mixture becomes too dry.

Return the chicken pieces to the pan and pour in the remaining vinegar, the water and salt. Bring to the boil, cover the pan and reduce the heat to low. Simmer for 1 hour, or until the chicken is cooked through and tender.

Transfer the mixture to a warmed serving dish and serve at once.

Serves 4
Preparation and cooking time: 1¾ hours

Dopeeazah Chicken

(Chicken with Onions)

Metric/Imperial	American
1 x 2kg./4lb. chicken, skinned and cut into serving pieces	1 x 4lb. chicken, skinned and cut into serving pieces
1 tsp. salt	1 tsp. salt
50g./2oz. butter	4 Tbs. butter
1kg./2lb. onions, chopped	2lb. onions, chopped
2 garlic cloves, crushed	2 garlic cloves, crushed
5cm./2in. piece of fresh root ginger, peeled and chopped	2in. piece of fresh green ginger, peeled and chopped
1 green chilli, chopped	1 green chilli, chopped
½ tsp. cardamom seeds	½ tsp. cardamom seeds
1 tsp. turmeric	1 tsp. turmeric
1½ tsp. ground cumin	1½ tsp. ground cumin
1 tsp. ground coriander	1 tsp. ground coriander
450ml./15fl.oz. yogurt	2 cups yogurt
½ tsp. saffron threads, soaked in 2 Tbs. boiling water	½ tsp. saffron threads, soaked in 2 Tbs. boiling water
10 peppercorns	10 peppercorns

Preheat the oven to warm 170°C (Gas Mark 3, 325°F).

Rub the chicken pieces with salt and set aside. Melt the butter in a flameproof casserole. Add half the onions and fry, stirring occasionally, until they are soft. Add the garlic, ginger and chilli. Transfer the mixture to a bowl, draining off as much cooking liquid as possible.

Add the chicken pieces, cardamom, spices, yogurt and saffron mixture to the casserole and bring to the boil. Mash the cooked onion mixture to a pulp and return to the casserole. Arrange the uncooked onions and peppercorns on top. Cover the casserole and transfer to the oven. Bake for 1½ hours, or until the chicken is cooked through and tender.

Serve at once, straight from the casserole.

Serves 6
Preparation and cooking time: 2 hours

Kukul Murg

(Sri Lankan Chicken Curry)

Metric/Imperial	American
50g./2oz. ghee or clarified butter	4 Tbs. ghee or clarified butter
2 medium onions, chopped	2 medium onions, chopped

3 garlic cloves, crushed	3 garlic cloves, crushed
2.5cm./1in. piece of fresh root ginger, peeled and chopped	1in. piece of fresh green ginger, peeled and chopped
½ tsp. crushed fenugreek seeds	½ tsp. crushed fenugreek seeds
5 curry or bay leaves	5 curry or bay leaves
1 tsp. turmeric	1 tsp. turmeric
1 tsp. hot chilli powder	1 tsp. hot chilli powder
2 tsp. ground coriander	2 tsp. ground coriander
1 tsp. ground cumin	1 tsp. ground cumin
½ tsp. ground cardamom	½ tsp. ground cardamom
2 Tbs. vinegar	2 Tbs. vinegar
1 tsp. salt	1 tsp. salt
1 x 2kg./4lb. chicken, cut into serving pieces	1 x 4lb. chicken, cut into serving pieces
2 tomatoes, blanched, peeled and chopped	2 tomatoes, blanched, peeled and chopped
1 Tbs. tomato purée	1 Tbs. tomato paste
1 tsp. chopped lemon grass or grated lemon rind	1 tsp. chopped lemon grass or grated lemon rind
300ml./10fl.oz. thick coconut milk	1¼ cups thick coconut milk

Melt the ghee in a large saucepan. Add the onions, garlic and ginger and fry, stirring occasionally, until the onions are soft. Add the fenugreek and curry or bay leaves and fry for 1 minute. Stir in the ground spices, vinegar and salt and fry for 5 minutes, stirring constantly. Add the chicken pieces and cook until they are evenly browned and coated with the spice mixture. Stir in the tomatoes, tomato purée (paste) and lemon grass or rind and cook for 3 minutes. Pour over the coconut milk and bring to the boil.

Reduce the heat to low, cover the pan and simmer the mixture for 45 minutes to 1 hour, or until the chicken is cooked through and tender.

Transfer the mixture to a warmed serving dish and serve at once.

Serves 4-6
Preparation and cooking time: 1½ hours

Vath

(Roast Duck)

Metric/Imperial	American
1 x 2½kg./5lb. duck, oven-ready	1 x 5lb. duck, oven-ready
2 tsp. salt	2 tsp. salt
juice of 1 lemon	juice of 1 lemon
4 garlic cloves, crushed	4 garlic cloves, crushed
2 tsp. turmeric	2 tsp. turmeric
1 Tbs. ground coriander	1 Tbs. ground coriander
1 Tbs. garam masala	1 Tbs. garam masala
2 tsp. ground cumin	2 tsp. ground cumin
4 green chillis, chopped	4 green chillis, chopped
125ml./4fl.oz. sour cream	½ cup sour cream
175g./6oz. roasted cashewnuts, coarsely chopped	1 cup roasted cashewnuts, coarsely chopped
125g./4oz. pork sausagemeat	4oz. pork sausagemeat

2 small oranges, peeled, pith and
   seeds removed and chopped

2 small oranges, peeled, pith and
   seeds removed and chopped

Rub the duck all over with 1½ teaspoons of salt.

Combine the lemon juice, half the garlic, spices, chillis and sour cream. Put the duck in a shallow dish and spoon over the spice mixture. Rub all over the duck and set aside to marinate for 2 hours at room temperature.

Preheat the oven to very hot 230°C (Gas Mark 8, 450°F).

Combine the remaining salt, garlic, spices and sour cream. Add the cashewnuts, sausagemeat and oranges and beat until the mixture is thoroughly blended. Remove the duck from the marinade and put on a working surface. Stir any marinade remaining into the stuffing mixture, then spoon into the duck cavity. Secure with skewers or a trussing needle and thread.

Put the duck on a rack in a roasting pan. Put the pan into the oven and roast for 15 minutes. Reduce the oven to moderate 180°C (Gas Mark 4, 350°F) and roast the duck for a further 1¼ hours, or until it is cooked through and tender. Remove from the oven.

Transfer to a carving board, cut into serving pieces and serve at once.
Serves 4
Preparation and cooking time: 4¾ hours

Vath is a splendid dish of roast duck, stuffed with a mixture of pork sausage-meat, oranges and cashew nuts.

Served with plain boiled rice, home-made chutney and a tomato and onion salad, Duck Curry will make a rich meal.

Duck Curry

Metric/Imperial	American
5 Tbs. vegetable oil	5 Tbs. vegetable oil
1 x 3kg./6lb. duck, cut into serving pieces	1 x 6lb. duck, cut into serving pieces
1 tsp. mustard seeds	1 tsp. mustard seeds
3 medium onions, chopped	3 medium onions, chopped
2 garlic cloves, finely chopped	2 garlic cloves, finely chopped
4cm./1½in. piece of fresh root ginger, peeled and chopped	1½in. piece of fresh green ginger, peeled and chopped
1 green chilli, finely chopped	1 green chilli, finely chopped
1 tsp. ground cumin	1 tsp. ground cumin
1 tsp. hot chilli powder	1 tsp. hot chilli powder
1 Tbs. ground coriander	1 Tbs. ground coriander
1 Tbs. garam masala	1 Tbs. garam masala
1 tsp. turmeric	1 tsp. turmeric
½ tsp. salt	½ tsp. salt
3 Tbs. vinegar	3 Tbs. vinegar
350ml./12fl.oz. coconut milk	1½ cups coconut milk

Heat the oil in a large saucepan. When it is hot, add the duck pieces and fry until they are evenly browned. Transfer to a plate. Add the mustard seeds and cover the pan. When they have stopped spattering, stir in the onions and fry, stirring occasionally, until they are golden brown. Add the garlic, ginger, and chilli and fry for 2 minutes, stirring frequently.

Put the spices and salt in a small bowl and mix to a smooth paste with the vinegar. Stir into the saucepan and fry for 5 to 8 minutes, stirring constantly. Add the duck pieces and turn in the paste to coat them thoroughly. Fry for a further 3 minutes.

Pour over the coconut milk and bring to the boil. Cover the pan, reduce the heat to low and simmer for 1 hour, or until the duck is cooked through and tender and the gravy is thick.

Transfer to a warmed serving dish and serve at once.

Serves 4-5
Preparation and cooking time: 1½ hours

Curried Partridges

Metric/Imperial	American
4 partridges, oven-ready with the giblets reserved	4 partridges, oven-ready with the giblets reserved
1½ tsp. salt	1½ tsp. salt
900ml./1½ pints water	3¾ cups water
4 cloves	4 cloves
2½cm./1in. piece of fresh root ginger, peeled and chopped	1in. piece of fresh green ginger, peeled and chopped
4 garlic cloves, chopped	4 garlic cloves, chopped
1 onion, halved	1 onion, halved
50g./2oz. butter	4 Tbs. butter
3 medium onions, finely chopped	3 medium onions, finely chopped
2 tsp. ground coriander	2 tsp. ground coriander
1 tsp. cayenne pepper	1 tsp. cayenne pepper
300ml./10fl.oz. single cream	1¼ cups light cream
125g./4oz. ground almonds	⅔ cup ground almonds
1 tsp. crushed cardamom seeds	1 tsp. crushed cardamom seeds
¼ tsp. saffron threads, soaked in 2 Tbs. boiling water	¼ tsp. saffron threads, soaked in 2 Tbs. boiling water

Mix the lemon juice with 1 teaspoon of salt and rub all over the partridges. Set aside while you make the stock.

Put the giblets, water, spices and halved onion into a saucepan and bring to the boil. Cover the pan, reduce the heat to low and simmer for 1½ hours. Remove from the heat and strain the stock into a bowl. Rinse and dry the pan. Return the strained stock to the pan and bring to the boil. Boil until the stock reduces to about 300ml./10fl.oz. (1¼ cups).

Melt the butter in a flameproof casserole. Add the chopped onions and fry, stirring occasionally, until they are golden brown. Stir in the coriander and cayenne and fry for 3 minutes, stirring frequently. Add the partridges and fry until they are evenly browned. Pour over the reserved stock and the remaining salt and bring to the boil. Cover, reduce the heat to low and simmer for 20 minutes. Uncover and continue simmering for a further 30 to 35 minutes, or until the partridges are cooked through and tender and the liquid has evaporated.

Preheat the oven to cool 150°C (Gas Mark 2, 300°F).

Mix the cream, almonds, cardamom and saffron mixture together and pour over the partridges. Bring to the boil, cover and transfer to the oven. Bake for 20 minutes. Remove from the oven and serve at once, straight from the casserole.

Serves 4
Preparation and cooking time: 3 hours

FISH & SEAFOOD

Sondhia

(Spiced Prawns or Shrimps)

Metric/Imperial	American
1kg./2lb. uncooked Dublin Bay Prawns	2lb. uncooked large Gulf shrimps
1 tsp. hot chilli powder	1 tsp. hot chilli powder
1 tsp. ground cumin	1 tsp. ground cumin
2 tsp. turmeric	2 tsp. turmeric
1½ tsp. salt	1½ tsp. salt
3 garlic cloves, crushed	3 garlic cloves, crushed
3 green chillis, chopped	3 green chillis, chopped
50ml./2fl.oz. lemon juice	¼ cup lemon juice
300ml./10fl.oz. water	1¼ cups water
50ml./2fl.oz. vegetable oil	¼ cup vegetable oil
2 Tbs. chopped coriander leaves	2 Tbs. chopped coriander leaves

Shell the prawns (shrimps) and reserve the shells. Devein the prawns (shrimps) and wash under cold running water. Dry and transfer to a large bowl.

Combine the spices, salt, garlic and chillis with just enough of the lemon juice to make a paste. Rub the paste into the prawns (shrimps) and set aside for 1 hour.

Meanwhile, put the raw (shrimp) shells into a saucepan and pour over the water. Bring to the boil, cover and reduce the heat to low. Simmer for 20 minutes, then strain the stock into a jug, reserving about 250ml./8fl.oz. (1 cup).

Heat the oil in a large frying-pan. When it is hot, add the prawns (shrimps) and simmer for 5 minutes, or until they turn evenly pink. Stir in the reserved stock, and bring to the boil. Reduce the heat to low and simmer for 20 minutes, or until the prawns (shrimps) are cooked and tender. Stir in the remaining lemon juice and coriander leaves. Remove from the heat.

Transfer to a warmed serving dish and serve at once.
Serves 4-6
Preparation and cooking time: 2 hours

Jhinga Pakoras

(Shrimp and Chick-Pea Fritters)

Metric/Imperial	American
125g./4oz. chick-pea flour	1 cup chick-pea flour
½ tsp. hot chilli powder	½ tsp. hot chilli powder
½ tsp. salt	½ tsp. salt
¼ tsp. turmeric	¼ tsp. turmeric
250-300ml./8-10fl.oz. water	1-1¼ cups water
350g./12oz. shelled shrimps	12oz. shelled shrimps
vegetable oil for deep-frying	vegetable oil for deep-frying

Sondhia, an exotic blend of prawns or shrimps and spices, makes an appetizing main course.

Sift the flour and spices into a bowl. Make a well in the centre and pour in enough of the water to beat to a smooth batter, the consistency of thick cream. (If the

192

batter is too thick, add more water.) Cover and set aside to 'rest' at room temperature for 30 minutes. Just before frying, mix in the shrimps.

Fill a large deep-frying pan one-third full with oil and heat until it is hot. Drop tablespoonfuls of the batter into the oil and fry for 4 minutes, or until they are crisp and golden brown. As they cook, transfer them to kitchen towels to drain.

Serve hot.

Serves 4

Preparation and cooking time: 50 minutes

Jhinga Kari 1

(Prawn or Shrimp Curry)

Jinga Kari I, a colourful and tasty way of cooking prawns or shrimps, is very palatable served with boiled rice and Chapatti.

Metric/Imperial	American
4cm./1½in. piece of fresh root ginger, peeled and chopped	1½in. piece of fresh green ginger, peeled and chopped
3 garlic cloves	3 garlic cloves
4 green chillis, seeded	4 green chillis, seeded
6 Tbs. chopped coriander leaves	6 Tbs. chopped coriander leaves

1 Tbs. coriander seeds	1 Tbs. coriander seeds
juice of 1 lemon	juice of 1 lemon
450ml./15fl.oz. thick coconut milk	2 cups thick coconut milk
75ml./3fl.oz. vegetable oil	⅓ cup vegetable oil
700g./1½lb. large prawns, shelled	1½lb. large shrimps, shelled
2 medium onions, chopped	2 medium onions, chopped
1 tsp. turmeric	1 tsp. turmeric
1 tsp. mustard seeds	1 tsp. mustard seeds
1 tsp. salt	1 tsp. salt

Put the ginger, garlic, chillis, coriander leaves and seeds into a blender with the lemon juice and 4 tablespoons of coconut milk. Blend to form a thick paste, adding more milk if necessary. Transfer the paste to a small bowl.

Heat 50ml./2fl.oz. (¼ cup) of oil in a large saucepan. When it is hot, add the prawns or shrimps and fry, turning frequently, for 5 minutes. Transfer to a plate and set aside.

Add the remaining oil to the pan. Add the onions and fry until they are golden. Stir in the turmeric, mustard seeds and salt and fry for 1 minute, stirring constantly. Add the spice paste and fry for 5 minutes, stirring constantly. Return the prawns or shrimps to the pan and coat them thoroughly in the paste. Pour in the remaining coconut milk and bring to the boil. Cover the pan, reduce the heat to low and simmer for 30 minutes.

Transfer the curry to a warmed serving bowl and serve at once.
Serves 4-6
Preparation and cooking time: 50 minutes

Jhinga Kari II

(Prawn or Shrimp Curry)

Metric/Imperial	American
50g./2oz. butter	4 Tbs. butter
1 medium onion, chopped	1 medium onion, chopped
2 garlic cloves, crushed	2 garlic cloves, crushed
2½cm./1in. piece of fresh root ginger, peeled and chopped	1in. piece of fresh green ginger, peeled and chopped
1kg./2lb. Dublin Bay prawns, shelled	2lb. large Gulf shrimps, shelled
1 tsp. turmeric	1 tsp. turmeric
1 tsp. hot chilli powder	1 tsp. hot chilli powder
1 Tbs. ground coriander	1 Tbs. ground coriander
1 tsp. ground cumin	1 tsp. ground cumin
1 tsp. salt	1 tsp. salt
½ tsp. black pepper	½ tsp. black pepper
150ml./5fl.oz. yogurt or sour cream	⅔ cup yogurt or sour cream

Melt the butter in a saucepan. Add the onion, garlic and ginger and fry, stirring occasionally, until the onion is golden brown. Add the prawns or shrimps and fry for 5 minutes, stirring occasionally. Stir in the spices, seasoning and yogurt or cream. Bring to the boil, reduce the heat to low and simmer for 30 minutes, stirring frequently, or until the sauce has thickened.

Transfer the mixture to a warmed serving dish and serve at once.
Serves 6
Preparation and cooking time: 1 hour

Jhinga Kari III

(Prawn or Shrimp Curry)

Metric/Imperial	American
50ml./2fl.oz. vegetable oil	¼ cup vegetable oil
4cm./1½in. piece of fresh root ginger, peeled and chopped	1½in. piece of fresh green ginger, peeled and chopped
2 garlic cloves, crushed	2 garlic cloves, crushed
2 large onions, finely chopped	2 large onions, chopped
3 green chillis, finely chopped	3 green chillis, finely chopped
2 Tbs. ground coriander	2 Tbs. ground coriander
2 tsp. turmeric	2 tsp. turmeric
3 Tbs. wine vinegar	3 Tbs. wine vinegar
1 tsp. salt	1 tsp. salt
1kg./2lb. large cooked prawns, shelled	2lb. large cooked shrimps, peeled
450ml./15fl.oz. hot coconut milk	2 cups hot coconut milk

Heat the oil in a large saucepan. When it is hot, add the ginger and garlic and fry for 1 minute, stirring constantly. Add the onions and fry until they are golden brown. Stir in the chillis and fry for 30 seconds. Stir in the spices, reduce the heat to low and simmer for 4 minutes, stirring constantly. Stir in the vinegar and salt and fry for 30 seconds.

Stir in the prawns (shrimps) and fry for 2 to 3 minutes, tossing until they are completely coated in the spices. Pour over the milk and bring to the boil. Cover the pan, reduce the heat to low and simmer for 5 minutes.

Transfer to a warmed serving dish and serve at once.

Serves 6
Preparation and cooking time: 30 minutes

Jhinga Tikka

(Prawn or Shrimp Patties)

Metric/Imperial	American
275g./10oz. prawns, shelled	10oz. shrimp, shelled
1 medium onion	1 medium onion
1cm./½in. piece of fresh root ginger, peeled	½in. piece of fresh green ginger, peeled
1 green chilli	1 green chilli
1 Tbs. chopped coriander leaves	1 Tbs. chopped coriander leaves
¾ tsp. salt	¾ tsp. salt
1 Tbs. lemon juice	1 Tbs. lemon juice
2 Tbs. fresh white breadcrumbs	2 Tbs. fresh white breadcrumbs
¼ tsp. turmeric	¼ tsp. turmeric
¼ tsp. black pepper	¼ tsp. black pepper
1 egg	1 egg
75g./3oz. dry breadcrumbs	1 cup dry breadcrumbs
50ml./2fl.oz. vegetable oil	¼ cup vegetable oil

Finely chop the prawns (shrimp), onion, ginger and chilli and put into a bowl. Mix in the coriander, salt, lemon juice, breadcrumbs, turmeric, pepper and the egg. Knead to blend thoroughly. Divide into eight equal portions and shape them into flat round patties. Dip the patties into the dry breadcrumbs to coat them thoroughly.

Heat the oil in a large frying-pan. When it is hot, add the patties and fry for 5 to 7 minutes on each side, or until they are golden brown.

Transfer to a warmed serving dish and serve at once.

Serves 4
Preparation and cooking time: 30 minutes

Shrimp Pulao

(Curried Rice with Shrimps)

Metric/Imperial	American
½kg./1lb. uncooked prawns, shelled	1lb. uncooked shrimps, shelled
1½ tsp. salt	1½ tsp. salt
½ tsp. cayenne pepper	½ tsp. cayenne pepper
juice of ½ lemon	juice of ½ lemon
40g./1½oz. butter	3 Tbs. butter
2 medium onions, sliced	2 medium onions, sliced
2 garlic cloves, crushed	2 garlic cloves, crushed
1 tsp. cumin seeds	1 tsp. cumin seeds
1 tsp. turmeric	1 tsp. turmeric
125g./4oz. French beans, sliced	⅔ cup sliced green beans
3 carrots, sliced	3 carrots, sliced
2 small courgettes, sliced	2 small zucchini, sliced
350g./12oz. long-grain rice, soaked in cold water for 30 minutes and drained	2 cups long-grain rice, soaked in cold water for 30 minutes and drained
SAUCE	SAUCE
2 Tbs. vegetable oil	2 Tbs. vegetable oil
1 medium onion, chopped	1 medium onion, chopped
1 garlic clove, crushed	1 garlic clove, crushed
4cm./1½in. piece of fresh root ginger, peeled and chopped	1½in. piece of fresh green ginger, peeled and chopped
2 green chillis, chopped	2 green chillis, chopped
1 tsp. turmeric	1 tsp. turmeric
1 Tbs. ground coriander	1 Tbs. ground coriander
½ tsp. cayenne pepper	½ tsp. cayenne pepper
2 tsp. paprika	2 tsp. paprika
700g./1½lb. canned peeled tomatoes rubbed through a sieve with the can juice	1½lb. canned peeled tomatoes, rubbed through a strainer with the can juice
1 tsp. sugar	1 tsp. sugar
1 tsp. salt	1 tsp. salt
4cm./1½in. slice creamed coconut	1½in. slice creamed coconut

Put the prawns or shrimps on a plate and rub them all over with ½ teaspoon of salt, the cayenne and lemon juice. Set aside for 30 minutes.

Meanwhile, make the sauce. Heat the oil in a saucepan. When it is hot, add the onion, garlic, ginger and chillis and fry, stirring occasionally, until the onion is golden brown. Stir in the spices and fry for 2 minutes, then stir in the strained tomatoes, sugar and salt. Bring to the boil, cover and reduce the heat to low. Simmer for 20 minutes. Stir in the creamed coconut and bring to the boil again when it has dissolved. Cover and simmer for a further 20 minutes.

Meanwhile, melt the butter in a large saucepan. Add the prawns or shrimps and fry for 5 minutes, or until they become slightly pink. Transfer to a plate

A wide variety of accompaniments, such as Poppadums, chutneys and salads, are suitable to serve with Shrimp Pulao, a tasty combination of curried rice with shrimps.

and set aside.

Add the onions and garlic to the pan and fry, stirring occasionally, until the onions are golden brown. Stir in the cumin and turmeric and add the vegetables. Cover the pan, reduce the heat to low and simmer for 10 minutes. Stir in the rice and remaining salt and fry for 2 minutes, stirring constantly. Return the prawns or shrimps to the pan and pour in enough boiling water to cover by about 1cm./½in. When the liquid is boiling vigorously, cover the pan, reduce the heat to low and simmer for 15 to 20 minutes, or until the rice is cooked and the liquid absorbed.

Remove from the heat and spoon the rice on to a warmed serving dish. Pour the sauce into a bowl and serve, with the rice.

Serves 4-6

Preparation and cooking time: 2½ hours

Bangra Masala

(Spiced Fish)

Metric/Imperial	American
4 herrings, cleaned and gutted	4 herrings, cleaned and gutted
2½ tsp. salt	2½ tsp. salt
juice of ½ lemon	juice of ½ lemon
3 Tbs. flour	3 Tbs. flour
1 tsp. turmeric	1 tsp. turmeric
4-6 Tbs. cooking oil	4-6 Tbs. cooking oil
FILLING	FILLING
3 Tbs. cooking oil	3 Tbs. cooking oil
2 small onions, minced	2 small onions, ground
1 tsp. turmeric	1 tsp. turmeric
1 tsp. ground coriander	1 tsp. ground coriander
1 tsp. hot chilli powder	1 tsp. hot chilli powder
1 Tbs. garam masala	1 Tbs. garam masala
1 large garlic clove, crushed	1 large garlic clove, crushed
4cm./1½in. piece of fresh root ginger, peeled and chopped	1½in. piece of fresh green ginger, peeled and chopped
juice of ½ lemon	juice of ½ lemon
75g./3oz. tomato purée	3oz. tomato paste

Sprinkle the inside of each fish with ½ teaspoon of salt and set aside.

To make the filling, heat the oil in a frying-pan. When it is hot, add the onions and fry, stirring occasionally, until they are golden brown. Add the spices and fry for 8 minutes, stirring occasionally. Add the garlic and ginger and fry for 2 minutes, stirring frequently. Add the spices and fry for 8 minutes, stirring constantly. Add a spoonful or two of water if the mixture becomes too dry. Stir in the lemon juice and tomato purée (paste) and cook for 3 minutes. Remove from the heat and divide the filling between the fish. Close the openings, then gash the sides of the fish with a sharp knife and rub in a little lemon juice. Mix the flour, turmeric and remaining salt on a plate, then dip the fish into the mixture, one by one.

Heat the oil in a large frying-pan. When it is hot, add the fish and fry for about 10 minutes, turning occasionally, or until the fish is cooked and flakes easily.

Serves 4

Preparation and cooking time: 45 minutes

Fish Molee

Any type of firm, white fish can be used in this recipe – cheaper fish such as coley and huss could be substituted for the whiting suggested below.

Metric/Imperial	American
3 Tbs. peanut oil	3 Tbs. peanut oil
2 garlic cloves, crushed	2 garlic cloves, crushed
8 shallots, peeled and chopped	8 shallots, peeled and chopped
2.5cm./1in. piece of fresh root ginger, peeled and chopped	1in piece of fresh green ginger, peeled and chopped
juice of 2 lemons	juice of 2 lemons
150ml./5fl.oz. water	⅔ cup water
grated rind of 1 lemon	grated rind of 1 lemon
1 red chilli, chopped	1 red chilli, chopped
1 tsp. turmeric	1 tsp. turmeric
300ml./10fl.oz. thin coconut milk	1¼ cups thin coconut milk
700g./1½lb. whiting fillets, skinned and cut into 2½cm./1in. pieces	1½ lb. whiting fillets, skinned and cut into 1in. pieces
300ml./10fl.oz. thick coconut milk	1¼ cups thick coconut milk

Heat the oil in a large frying-pan. When it is hot, add the garlic and shallots and fry, stirring occasionally, for 1 minute. Add the ginger and fry for a further 1 minute, stirring occasionally. Mix the lemon juice and water together, then pour into the pan. Reduce the heat to low, then stir in the lemon rind, chilli and turmeric. Bring to the boil.

Reduce the heat to low and pour in the thin coconut milk. When the milk is bubbling gently, add the fish pieces and thick coconut milk. Reduce the heat to low, cover the pan and simmer for 20 minutes, or until the fish is cooked through.

Transfer the mixture to a warmed serving bowl and serve at once.

Serves 4
Preparation and cooking time: 45 minutes

White Fish Curry

Metric/Imperial	American
3 Tbs. vegetable oil	3 Tbs. vegetable oil
2 medium onions, chopped	2 medium onions, chopped
4 garlic cloves, crushed	4 garlic cloves, crushed
2½cm./1in. piece of fresh root ginger, peeled and chopped	1in. piece of fresh green ginger, peeled and chopped
6 green chillis, chopped	6 green chillis, chopped
1 tsp. turmeric	1 tsp. turmeric
2 tsp. ground coriander	2 tsp. ground coriander
¼ tsp. black pepper	¼ tsp. black pepper
300ml./10fl.oz. thin coconut milk	1¼ cups thin coconut milk
1kg./2lb. cod steaks	2lb. cod steaks
450ml./15fl.oz. thick coconut milk	2 cups thick coconut milk
1 tsp. salt	1 tsp. salt
2 Tbs. lemon juice	2 Tbs. lemon juice
1 tsp. sugar	1 tsp. sugar
1 Tbs. chopped coriander leaves	1 Tbs. chopped coriander leaves

Heat the oil in a saucepan. When it is hot, add the onions and fry, stirring occasionally, until they are golden brown. Add the garlic, ginger and chillis and fry for 3 minutes, stirring frequently. Add the spices and pepper and fry for 2 minutes. Pour in the coconut milk and stir well. Add the fish, bring to the boil and cook for 5 minutes. Pour in the thick coconut milk and salt and reduce the heat to low.

Simmer for 20 minutes, or until the fish is cooked and flakes easily. Remove from the heat and stir in the lemon juice and sugar.

Transfer to a warmed serving dish and sprinkle over the coriander before serving.
Serves 6
Preparation and cooking time: 45 minutes

Machee Kabab

(Fish Kebabs)

Metric/Imperial	American
300ml./10fl.oz. yoghurt	1¼ cups yogurt
2 Tbs. flour	2 Tbs. flour
2 garlic cloves, crushed	2 garlic cloves, crushed
2 tsp. crushed coriander seeds	2 tsp. crushed coriander seeds
1 small dried chilli, crushed	1 small dried chilli, crushed
½ tsp. garam masala	½ tsp. garam masala
juice of 1 lemon	juice of 1 lemon
1kg./2lb. firm white fish fillets, cubed	2lb. firm white fish fillets, cubed

Combine all the ingredients, except the fish, in a large shallow bowl. Stir in the fish gently and set aside to marinate at room temperature for 30 minutes, basting occasionally.

Preheat the grill (broiler) to moderate. Thread the cubes on to skewers and reserve the marinade. Arrange the skewers in a lined grill (broiler) pan and grill (broil) for 10 to 12 minutes, turning occasionally and basting with the marinade, or until the cubes are cooked through.

Slide the cubes off the skewers on to a warmed serving dish and serve at once.
Serves 4-6
Preparation and cooking time: 50 minutes

Tandoori Machee

(Marinated Spiced Fish)

Metric/Imperial	American
4 large red mullets, or any similar oily fish, cleaned and gutted	4 large red mullets, or any similar oily fish, cleaned and gutted
juice of 2 lemons	juice of 2 lemons
75g./3oz. butter, melted	6 Tbs. butter, melted
2 tsp. ground cumin	2 tsp. ground cumin
1 lemon, thinly sliced	1 lemon, thinly sliced

MARINADE	MARINADE
50ml./2fl.oz. yogurt	¼ cup yogurt
2 garlic cloves, crushed	2 garlic cloves, crushed
4cm./1½in. piece of fresh root ginger, peeled and chopped	1½in. piece of fresh green ginger, peeled and chopped
1 Tbs. coriander seeds	1 Tbs. coriander seeds
1 tsp. garam masala	1 tsp. garam masala
2 dried red chillis	2 dried red chillis
red food colouring	red food coloring

Make slits along both sides of the fish, about 2½cm./1in. apart. Rub all over with the lemon juice and set aside for 10 minutes.

To make the marinade, combine all the ingredients, except the food colouring, in a blender and blend to a paste. Stir in the food colouring. Put the fish in a shallow bowl and spoon over the marinade, turning to coat the fish thoroughly. Set aside to marinate at room temperature for 6 hours, basting occasionally. Remove from the marinade and arrange the fish on individual skewers. Arrange the skewers on the rack of a roasting tin and put the tin into the oven. Bake for 10 minutes. Combine the melted butter and ground cumin together, then brush over the fish. Return to the oven and cook for a further 5 to 8 minutes, or until the fish is cooked and flakes easily.

Remove from the oven and slide the fish on to a warmed serving dish. Garnish with the lemon slices before serving.

Serves 4
Preparation and cooking time: 6¾ hours

Tali Machee

(Deep-Fried Spiced Fish)

Metric/Imperial	American
8 lemon sole fillets	8 lemon sole fillets
salt and pepper	salt and pepper
juice of 2 lemons	juice of 2 lemons
vegetable oil for deep-frying	vegetable oil for deep-frying
BATTER	BATTER
75g./3oz. besan or chick-pea flour	¾ cup besan or chick-pea flour
25g./1oz. rice flour	¼ cup rice flour
1 tsp. turmeric	1 tsp. turmeric
1 tsp. hot chilli powder	1 tsp. hot chilli powder
125ml./4fl.oz. water	½ cup water

Cut each fillet in half, then rub all over with salt and pepper. Transfer the pieces to a large bowl. Sprinkle over the lemon juice and set aside for 1 hour.

Meanwhile, prepare the batter. Combine all the ingredients, beating until they form a smooth batter the consistency of single (light) cream.

Remove the fish from the lemon juice and pat dry with kitchen towels. Dip each piece into the batter to coat it thoroughly.

Fill a large deep-frying pan one-third full with oil and heat it until it is hot. Carefully lower the fish pieces into the oil, a few at a time, and fry for 5 minutes, or until they are crisp and golden brown. Drain on kitchen towels and transfer to a warmed serving dish before serving.

Serves 4
Preparation and cooking time: 1½ hours

Tali Machee is a delicious, savoury dish comprising sole fillets coated in batter and deep-fried until golden brown.

ACCOMPANIMENTS

Basic Basmati Rice

Metric/Imperial	American
275g./10oz. basmati or other long-grain rice, soaked in cold water for 30 minutes and drained	1⅔ cups basmati or other long-grain rice, soaked in cold water for 30 minutes and drained
600ml./1 pint water	2½ cups water
1 tsp. salt	1 tsp. salt

Put the rice in a saucepan and pour over the water and salt. Bring to the boil, cover the pan and reduce the heat to low. Simmer for 15 to 20 minutes, or until the rice is cooked and the liquid is absorbed.

Remove from the heat and serve at once.

Serves 4
Preparation and cooking time: 1 hour

Kaha Buth

(Sri Lankan Yellow Rice)

Metric/Imperial	American
50g./2oz. ghee or clarified butter	4 Tbs. ghee or clarified butter
2 medium onions, chopped	2 medium onions, chopped
1 garlic clove, crushed	1 garlic clove, crushed
4 curry or bay leaves	4 curry or bay leaves
450g./1lb. long-grain rice, washed, soaked in cold water for 30 minutes and drained	2⅔ cups long-grain rice, washed, soaked in cold water for 30 minutes and drained
10 black peppercorns	10 black peppercorns
1 tsp. chopped lemon grass or grated lemon rind	1 tsp. chopped lemon grass or grated lemon rind
5 whole cloves	5 whole cloves
1 tsp. crushed cardamom seeds	1 tsp. crushed cardamom seeds
½ tsp. saffron threads, soaked in 2 Tbs. boiling water for 10 minutes	½ tsp. saffron threads, soaked in 2 Tbs. boiling water for 10 minutes
1¼l./2 pints coconut milk	5 cups coconut milk
GARNISH	GARNISH
1 Tbs. ghee or clarified butter	1 Tbs. ghee or clarified butter
1 tomato, sliced	1 tomato, sliced
4 Tbs. sultanas	4 Tbs. seedless raisins
2 Tbs. cashewnuts	2 Tbs. cashewnuts
1 hard-boiled egg, sliced	1 hard-boiled egg, sliced

Melt the ghee in a large saucepan. Add the onions, garlic and curry or bay leaves and fry, stirring occasionally, until the onions are soft. Add the rice and fry for 3 minutes, stirring frequently. Stir in the peppercorns, lemon grass or rind, cloves, cardamom seeds and saffron threads until the mixture is slightly yellow. Pour over the coconut milk and bring to the boil.

Reduce the heat to low, cover the pan and simmer the rice for 15 to 20 minutes, or until it is cooked and tender and the liquid absorbed.

Meanwhile, make the garnish. Melt the ghee in a small frying-pan. Add the tomato, sultanas (raisins) and cashews and fry gently for 2 to 3 minutes, or until they are just beginning to turn brown. Remove from the heat.

Remove the whole spices from the rice and transfer it to a warmed serving dish. Arrange the tomatoes, sultanas (raisins) cashewnuts and egg slices decoratively over the top and sides and serve at once.

Serves 6
Preparation and cooking time: 45 minutes

Saffron Rice

Metric/Imperial	American
50g./2oz. butter	4 Tbs. butter
2 tsp. cardamom seeds	2 tsp. cardamom seeds
4 cloves	4 cloves
3 cinnamon sticks	3 cinnamon sticks
1 medium onion, chopped	1 medium onion, chopped
350g./12oz. long-grain rice, soaked in cold water for 30 minutes and drained	2 cups long-grain rice, soaked in cold water for 30 minutes and drained
725ml./1¼ pints boiling chicken stock	3 cups boiling chicken stock
1 tsp. salt	1 tsp. salt
¾ tsp. crushed saffron threads, soaked in 2 Tbs. boiling water	¾ tsp. crushed saffron threads, soaked in 2 Tbs. boiling water

Melt the butter in a saucepan. Add the spices and fry for 2 minutes, stirring constantly. Add the onion and fry, stirring occasionally, until it is golden brown. Add the rice, reduce the heat to moderately low and simmer for 5 minutes, stirring constantly. Pour over the boiling stock, and stir in the salt and saffron mixture. Cover the pan, reduce the heat to low and simmer for 15 to 20 minutes, or until the rice is cooked and the water absorbed.

Remove from the heat and serve at once.

Serves 4-6
Preparation and cooking time: 1 hour

Cachoombar

(Onion Salad)

Metric/Imperial	American
2 medium onions, very finely chopped	2 medium onions, very finely chopped
2 large tomatoes, finely chopped	2 large tomatoes, finely chopped
½ medium cucumber, very finely chopped	½ medium cucumber, very finely chopped
2 green chillis, seeded and finely chopped	2 green chillis, seeded and finely chopped
1 Tbs. chopped coriander leaves	1 Tbs. chopped coriander leaves
75ml./3fl.oz. wine vinegar	6 Tbs. wine vinegar

Combine the onions, tomatoes, cucumber and chillis in a shallow bowl. Sprinkle over the coriander and vinegar and toss gently to coat. Cover and chill in the refrigerator for 20 minutes before serving.

Serves 3-4
Preparation time: 30 minutes

Vellarikai Pachadi

(Cucumber and Yogurt Salad)

Metric/Imperial	American
1 cucumber, peeled and finely chopped	1 cucumber, peeled and finely chopped
½ fresh coconut	½ fresh coconut
2 green chillis	2 green chillis
450ml./15fl.oz. yogurt	2 cups yogurt
1 tsp. salt	1 tsp. salt
2 tsp. vegetable oil	2 tsp. vegetable oil
1 tsp. mustard seeds	1 tsp. mustard seeds

Vellarikai Pachadi is a refreshing salad made with cucumber and yogurt and suitable for serving with most curries.

Put the cucumber into a colander and drain for 1 hour.

Pare the thin brown skin of the coconut and cut the flesh into pieces. Put the

coconut pieces and chillis into a blender with 2 to 3 tablespoons of water and blend to form a smooth purée. Transfer to a serving bowl and beat in the yogurt, cucumber and salt.

Heat the oil in a small frying-pan. When it is hot, add the mustard seeds. Cover and fry until they begin to spatter. Stir the seeds and oil into the yogurt. Cover and chill in the refrigerator for 1 hour.

Serve chilled.

Serves 4-6
Preparation and cooking time: 1 hour 10 minutes

Cucumber Raita

(Cucumber and Yogurt Salad)

Metric/Imperial	American
600ml./1 pint yogurt	2½ cups yogurt
½ cucumber, washed and diced	½ cucumber, washed and diced
4 spring onions, finely chopped	4 scallions, finely chopped
salt and pepper	salt and pepper
1 green chilli finely chopped	1 green chilli, finely chopped
¼ tsp. paprika	¼ tsp. paprika

Beat the yogurt until it is smooth, then beat in the cucumber, spring onions (scallions) and seasoning. Spoon into a serving bowl, cover and chill in the refrigerator for 1 hour.

Sprinkle over the chilli and paprika before serving.

Serves 4-6
Preparation time: 1 hour 10 minutes

Banana Raita

(Banana and Yogurt Salad)

Metric/Imperial	American
600ml./1 pint yogurt	2½ cups yogurt
4 bananas, sliced	4 bananas, sliced
2 green chillis, finely chopped	2 green chillis, finely chopped
1 Tbs. lemon juice	1 Tbs. lemon juice
1 tsp. garam masala	1 tsp. garam masala
¼ tsp. ground coriander	¼ tsp. ground coriander
½ tsp. salt	½ tsp. salt
2 tsp. chopped coriander leaves	2 tsp. chopped coriander leaves

Beat the yogurt until it is smooth, then beat in the bananas, chillis, lemon juice, spices and salt. Spoon into a serving bowl, cover and chill for 1 hour.

Sprinkle over the coriander before serving.

Serves 4-6
Preparation time: 1 hour 10 minutes

Guava Raita

(Guava and Yogurt Salad)

Metric/Imperial	American
600ml./1 pint yogurt	2½ cups yogurt
2 canned guavas, drained and diced	2 canned guavas, drained and diced
½ tsp. salt	½ tsp. salt
1 Tbs. ghee or clarified butter	1 Tbs. ghee or clarified butter
1 tsp. mustard seeds	1 tsp. mustard seeds
1 green chilli, finely chopped	1 green chilli, finely chopped
2 tsp. coriander leaves	2 tsp. chopped coriander leaves

Beat the yogurt until it is smooth, then beat in the cucumber, guavas and salt. Melt the ghee or clarified butter in a small frying-pan. Add the mustard seeds, cover and cook until the seeds begin to spatter. Add the chilli and fry for 10 seconds, stirring constantly. Stir the contents of the pan into the yogurt mixture. Spoon into a serving bowl, cover and chill in the refrigerator for 1 hour.

Sprinkle over the coriander before serving.

Serves 4-6

Preparation and cooking time: 1 hour 10 minutes

Shrimp Sambal is a fiery side dish made with shrimps and is generally served with vegetable or fish curries.

Pol Sambola 1

Metric/Imperial	American
2 medium tomatoes, blanched, peeled and chopped	2 medium tomatoes, blanched, peeled and chopped
2 small onions, finely chopped	2 small onions, finely chopped
1 green chilli, finely chopped	1 green chilli, finely chopped
2 Tbs. lime or lemon juice	2 Tbs. lime or lemon juice
2 Tbs. desiccated coconut	2 Tbs. shredded coconut

Combine the tomatoes, onions and chilli, then pour over the lime or lemon juice. Spoon the mixture into a shallow serving bowl. Sprinkle over the coconut, cover and chill in the refrigerator until ready to serve.

Serves 3-4
Preparation and cooking tiem: 10 minutes

Pol Sambola 11

In Sri Lanka, Maldive fish, a dried tuna delicacy, is added to this sambal – if you wish to be authentic and add it or an equivalent (and if Maldive fish is unavailable) dried prawns (available from Chinese stores) or Japanese katsuobushi (dried bonito fish) can be substituted. For convenience, however, it is omitted from the recipe as given below.

Metric/Imperial	American
125g./4oz. desiccated coconut	1 cup shredded coconut
$\frac{1}{2}$ tsp. hot chilli powder	$\frac{1}{2}$ tsp. hot chilli powder
1 tsp. paprika	1 tsp. paprika
$\frac{1}{4}$ tsp. finely chopped lemon grass or finely grated lemon rind	$\frac{1}{4}$ tsp. finely chopped lemon grass or finely grated lemon rind
1 Tbs. lemon juice	1 Tbs. lemon juice
3 Tbs. grated onion	3 Tbs. grated onion
3 Tbs. coconut milk	3 Tbs. coconut milk

Combine the coconut, chilli powder, paprika and lemon rind in a small serving bowl. Gradually stir in the lemon juice, grated onion and coconut milk until the mixture is moistened.

Serve at once.

Serves 4
Preparation time: 5 minutes

Shrimp Sambal

Metric/Imperial	American
175g./6oz. cooked shrimps, chopped	6oz. cooked shrimps, chopped
2 hard-boiled eggs, sliced	2 hard-boiled eggs, sliced
1 medium onion, finely chopped	1 medium onion, finely chopped

Metric/Imperial	American
1 green chilli, chopped	1 green chilli, chopped
2½cm./1in. piece of fresh root ginger, peeled and chopped	1in. piece of fresh green ginger, peeled and chopped
½ tsp. hot chilli powder	½ tsp. hot chilli powder
2 Tbs. thick coconut milk	2 Tbs. thick coconut milk
¼ tsp. cumin seeds, coarsely crushed	¼ tsp. cumin seeds, coarsely crushed

Combine all the ingredients except the cumin seeds, then spoon the mixture into a shallow serving bowl. Sprinkle over the cumin, cover and chill in the refrigerator until ready to serve.
Serves 3-4
Preparation time: 10 minutes

Pipinge Sambal

(Cucumber Sambal)

Metric/Imperial	American
1 large cucumber	1 large cucumber
1½ Tbs. salt	1½ Tbs. salt
2 spring onions, very finely chopped	2 scallions, very finely chopped
2 red chillis, very finely chopped	2 red chillis, very finely chopped
½ tsp. turmeric	½ tsp. turmeric
1 Tbs. lemon juice	1 Tbs. lemon juice
125ml./4fl.oz. very thick coconut milk	½ cup very thick coconut milk

Peel the cucumber, then chop into small dice. Transfer to a colander and sprinkle liberally with the salt. Set aside at room temperature for 30 minutes. Rinse the cucumber under cold running water, then pat dry with kitchen towels.

Transfer the cucumber to a medium serving bowl. Gradually add all the remaining ingredients until the mixture is thoroughly blended.

Chill in the refrigerator until ready to use.
Serves 4-6
Preparation time: 35 minutes

BREAD

Chapatti

(Unleavened Bread)

Metric/Imperial	American
225g./8oz. wholewheat flour	2 cups wholemeal flour
salt	salt
50g./2oz. butter	4 Tbs. butter
150ml./5fl.oz. water	$\frac{2}{3}$ cup water
1 Tbs. ghee or clarified butter	1 Tbs. ghee or clarified butter

Sift the flour and a little salt into a large bowl. Add the butter and rub into the flour. Make a well in the centre and pour in 75ml./3fl.oz. ($\frac{1}{3}$ cup) of water. Gradually add the rest of the water, mixing it in with your fingers. Form the dough into a ball and transfer to a floured board. Knead for about 10 minutes, or until elastic. Put the dough in a bowl, cover and set aside at room temperature for 30 minutes.

Divide the dough into eight portions. Roll out each portion into a thin, round shape, about 15cm./6in. in diameter.

Meanwhile, heat a heavy frying-pan over moderate heat. When it is hot, put one dough shape into the pan. When small blisters appear on the surface, press to flatten the dough. Turn over and cook until it is pale golden. Remove from the pan and brush with a little ghee or clarified butter. Arrange on a plate and cook the other chapattis in the same way.

Serve warm.

Serves 8

Preparation and cooking time: 55 minutes

Chapatti, the staple cereal food of Northern India, is one of the most common accompaniments to Indian meals.

Puris are deep-fried whole meal (wholewheat) breads and are delicious served with dry Indian vegetable or meat dishes.

Puris

(Deep-Fried Wholemeal Bread)

Metric/Imperial	American
225g./8oz. wholewheat flour	2 cups wholemeal flour
salt	salt
1 Tbs. butter	1 Tbs. butter
50ml./2fl.oz. tepid water	¼ cup tepid water
vegetable oil for deep-frying	vegetable oil for deep-frying

Combine the flour and a little salt in a bowl. Add the ghee or clarified butter and rub into the flour until it is absorbed. Add the water and mix and knead the ingredients to make a firm dough.

Turn the dough out on to a floured surface and knead for about 10 minutes, or until elastic. Pat into a ball and return to the bowl. Cover and set aside at room temperature for 30 minutes.

Remove the dough from the bowl. Pinch off small pieces of the dough and shape into balls. Flatten the balls and roll them out into circles, about 12cm./5in. in diameter.

Fill a large deep-frying pan one-third full with oil and heat until it is hot. Drop the pieces, one at a time, into the oil. Using a spatula or fish slice, press down and fry for 1 minute. Turn over and press down again. Fry for 30 seconds or until the puri is puffed up and golden.

Remove the puri from the pan and keep warm while you cook the remaining puris in the same way. Serve hot or warm.

Makes about 12
Preparation and cooking time: 1½ hours

Paratha

(Fried Wholemeal Bread)

Metric/Imperial	American
225g./8oz. wholewheat flour	2 cups wholemeal flour
salt	salt
125g./4oz. ghee or clarified butter, melted	8 Tbs. ghee or clarified butter, melted
50-125ml./2-4fl.oz. water	¼-½ cup water

Combine the flour and a little salt in a bowl. Add about a quarter of the ghee or clarified butter and rub into the flour until it is absorbed. Pour in 50ml./2fl.oz. (¼ cup) of the water and knead until the mixture forms a soft dough. If it is too dry mix in the remaining water, a little at a time, until the dough is soft and comes away from the sides of the bowl.

Turn the dough out on to a floured surface and knead for about 10 minutes, or until elastic. Pat into a ball and return to the bowl. Cover and set aside at room temperature for 1 hour.

Remove the dough from the bowl and knead lightly. Divide into four equal portions and shape each portion into a ball. Roll out into a thin circle. Brush each circle with a little of the remaining ghee or clarified butter. Fold the circles in half, then into quarters. Roll out into circles again, brush again with ghee or clarified butter and repeat the process again until all but 2 tablespoons of the ghee or clarified butter has been used up. Roll out each dough portion into a circle, about 18cm./7in. in diameter.

Lightly grease a heavy frying-pan with a little of the remaining ghee or clarified butter. When it is hot, add a paratha and cook, moving with your fingers occasionally, for 3 to 4 minutes, or until the underside is lightly browned. Brush the top with a little of the remaining ghee or clarified butter and, using your fingers, turn over and continue cooking for a further 3 minutes, or until the paratha is browned all over.

Remove from the pan and keep warm while you cook the remaining parathas in the same way. Serve hot.

Makes 4
Preparation and cooking time: 2 hours

CHUTNEY

Mango Chutney

Metric/Imperial	American
1½kg./3lb. mangoes, peeled, halved and stoned	3lb. mangoes, peeled, halved and pitted
75g./3oz. salt	¾ cup salt
450g./1lb. sugar	2 cups sugar
600ml./1 pint white wine vinegar	2½ cups white wine vinegar
5cm./2in. piece of fresh root ginger, peeled and chopped	2in. piece of fresh green ginger, peeled and chopped
6 garlic cloves, crushed	6 garlic cloves, crushed
2 tsp. hot chilli powder	2 tsp. hot chilli powder
1 cinnamon stick	1 cinnamon stick
125g./4oz. stoned dates	⅔ cup pitted dates
125g./4oz. raisins	⅔ cup raisins

Chop the mangoes finely and put in a bowl. Add the salt and about 2l./3½ pints (8¾ cups) of water. Cover and set aside for 24 hours.

Put the sugar and vinegar into a saucepan and bring to the boil. stirring until the sugar has dissolved. Stir in the mangoes, then add all the remaining ingredients and bring to the boil, stirring occasionally. Reduce the heat to low and simmer for about 1½ hours, stirring occasionally, or until the chutney is very thick.

Remove the cinnamon stick and ladel the chutney into warmed, sterilized jars. Cover, label and set aside until ready to use.

Makes about two 1kg./2lb. jars

Preparation and cooking time: 25½ hours

Date Chutney

Metric/Imperial	American
450g./1lb. canned peeled tomatoes	1lb. canned peeled tomatoes
225g./8oz. stoned dates, chopped	1⅓ cups pitted dates, chopped
125g./4oz. raisins	⅔ cup raisins
125g./4oz. currants	⅔ cup currants
125ml./4fl.oz. vinegar	½ cup vinegar
1 tsp. salt	1 tsp. salt
1 tsp. cayenne pepper	1 tsp. cayenne pepper

Put all the ingredients into a saucepan and bring slowly to the boil, stirring occasionally. Reduce the heat to very low and simmer for 1 to 1½ hours, stirring occasionally, or until it is very thick.

Ladle the chutney into warmed, sterilized jars. Cover, label and set aside until ready to use.

Makes about 1kg./2lb.

Preparation and cooking time: 1¾ hours

(1) Chillis sold whole or ground.
(2) Peppercorns – buy fresh and grind only when required.
(3) Turmeric available in sticks or as ground seeds.
(4) Cardamom sold as pods or as ground seeds.
(5) Paprika – ground seeds of the red pepper.
(6) A mineral – Salt found in coarse or fine form.
(7) Cumin seeds – heat before use for flavour.
(8) Coriander leaves used as a garnish; its seeds sold whole or ground.
(9) Saffron available whole, in threads, or ground.
(10) Nutmeg sold whole or ground.
(11) Ginger found fresh (green), crystallized or dried.
(12) Green chillis (see 1)
(13) Garlic sold in bulbs.
(14) Mace, outer shell of Nutmeg, available as blades or in powdered form.
(15) Turmeric (see 3)
(16) Red chillis (see 1)
(17) Red chillis (see 1)
(18) Cinnamon sold in bark form as sticks or as powder.
(19) Coriander (see 8)

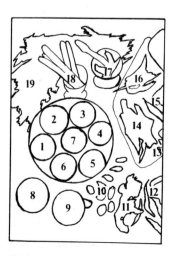

Lemon & Mustard Seed Chutney

Metric/Imperial	American
3 lemons, chopped and seeds removed	3 lemons, chopped and seeds removed
1 Tbs. salt	1 Tbs. salt
3 small onions, finely chopped	3 small onions, finely chopped
300ml./10fl.oz. vinegar	1¼ cups vinegar
1 tsp. garam masala	1 tsp. garam masala
2 Tbs. mustard seeds	2 Tbs. mustard seeds
225g./8oz. sugar	1 cup sugar
50g./2oz. raisins	⅓ cup raisins

Put the lemons into a bowl and sprinkle with salt. Cover and set aside for 10 hours.

Transfer the salted lemons to a saucepan and add all the remaining ingredients. Bring to the boil, reduce the heat to low, cover and simmer for 1 hour, or until the lemons are very soft.

Ladle the chutney into warmed, sterilized jars. Cover, label and set aside until ready to use.

Makes about 1kg./2lb.

Preparation and cooking time: 1½ hours

Tamatar Chatni

Metric/Imperial	American
1kg./2lb. tomatoes, blanched, peeled and chopped	2lb. tomatoes, blanched, peeled and chopped
450ml./15fl.oz. white vinegar	2 cups white vinegar
2 onions, finely chopped	2 onions, finely chopped
1 Tbs. salt	1 Tbs. salt
350g./12oz. soft brown sugar	2 cups soft brown sugar
4cm./1½in. piece of fresh root ginger, peeled and chopped	1½in. piece of fresh green ginger, peeled and chopped
3 garlic cloves, finely chopped	3 garlic cloves, finely chopped
3 dried red chillis, finely chopped	3 dried red chillis, finely chopped
10 cloves	10 cloves
2 cinnamon sticks	2 cinnamon sticks
½ tsp. crushed cardamom seeds	½ tsp. crushed cardamom seeds
50ml./2fl.oz. vegetable oil	¼ cup vegetable oil
1 Tbs. mustard seeds	1 Tbs. mustard seeds

Combine all the ingredients, except the oil and mustard seeds, in a saucepan and bring slowly to the boil, stirring occasionally. Reduce the heat to low and simmer for 5 hours, stirring occasionally, or until the mixture is very thick.

Meanwhile, heat the oil in a small frying-pan. When it is hot, add the mustard seeds and cover. When they stop spattering, turn the mixture into the pan with the other ingredients, stirring constantly. Simmer for a further 15 minutes.

Ladle the chutney into warmed, sterilized jars. Cover, label and set aside until ready to use.

Makes about ½kg.1lb.
Preparation and cooking time: 5½ hours

Banana and Raisin Chutney

Metric/Imperial	American
1½kg./3lb. bananas, chopped	3lb. bananas, chopped
700g./1½lb. onions, chopped	1½lb. onions, chopped
2 large garlic cloves, crushed	2 large garlic cloves, crushed
1 tsp. salt	1 tsp. salt
juice and grated rind of 1 orange	juice and grated rind of 1 orange
450g./1lb. raisins	2⅔ cups raisins
2 Tbs. ground cumin	2 Tbs. ground cumin
2 Tbs. ground cardamom	2 Tbs. ground cardamom
2 Tbs. ground coriander	2 Tbs. ground coriander
1 tsp. cayenne pepper	1 tsp. cayenne pepper
600ml./1 pint white wine vinegar	2½ cups white wine vinegar

Put all the ingredients into a saucepan and bring slowly to the boil, stirring occasionally. Reduce the heat to very low and simmer for 1¼ hours, stirring occasionally.

Ladle the chutney into warmed, sterilized jars. Cover, label and set aside until ready for use.
Makes five ½kg./1lb. jars
Preparation and cooking time: 1½ hours

Nariel Chatni

Metric/Imperial	American
50g./2oz. desiccated coconut, soaked in 150ml./5fl.oz. yogurt for 1 hour	½ cup shredded coconut, soaked in ⅔ cup yogurt for 1 hour
juice and grated rind of 1 lemon	juice and grated rind of 1 lemon
2½cm./1in. piece of fresh root ginger, peeled and chopped	1in. piece of fresh root ginger, peeled and chopped
1 green chilli, chopped	1 green chilli, chopped
1 garlic clove, chopped	1 garlic clove, chopped
1 medium onion, chopped	1 medium onion, chopped

Put the coconut mixture and lemon juice in a blender and blend to a smooth purée. Stir in the remaining ingredients and blend for 1 minute more.

Spoon into a small serving bowl and chill in the refrigerator until ready to serve.
Makes about 125g./4oz. (1 cup)
Preparation time: 10 minutes

Apricot, Carrot and Swede (Rutabaga) Chutney

Metric/Imperial	American
450g./1lb. dried apricots	2⅔ cups dried apricots
900ml./1½ pints distilled malt vinegar	3¾ cups distilled malt vinegar
½kg./1lb. swedes, peeled and chopped	1lb. rutabagas, peeled and chopped
½kg./1lb. carrots, chopped	1lb. carrots, chopped
½kg./1lb. onions, chopped	1lb. onions, chopped
225g./8oz. Demerara sugar	1⅓ cups light brown sugar
2 tsp. ground mace	2 tsp. ground mace
2 tsp. cayenne pepper	2 tsp. cayenne pepper

Put the apricots in a bowl and pour over 600ml./1 pint (2½ cups) of the vinegar. Set aside to soak overnight. Drain, reserve the vinegar and chop the apricots finely. Put all the ingredients into a saucepan and bring slowly to the boil. Reduce the heat to very low and simmer for 1 hour, stirring occasionally.

   Ladle the chutney into warmed, sterilized jars. Cover, label and set aside until ready to use.
Makes five ½kg./1lb. jars
Preparation and cooking time: 14 hours

Adrak Chatni

(Ginger Chutney)

This chutney does not keep well and should be eaten within two days of making.

Metric/Imperial	American
juice of 2 lemons	juice of 2 lemons
4 tsp. sugar	4 tsp. sugar
125g./4oz fresh root ginger, peeled and chopped	4oz. fresh green ginger, peeled and chopped
75g./3oz. sultanas	½ cup seedless raisins
1 garlic clove	1 garlic clove
1½ tsp. salt	1½ tsp. salt

Put the juice of 1½ lemons, 2 teaspoons of sugar and all the other ingredients into a blender and blend to a smooth purée. Add the remaining lemon juice and the sugar and stir well.

   Spoon into a small serving bowl and chill in the refrigerator until ready to serve.
Serves 6
Preparation time: 10 minutes

Date and Banana Chutney

Metric/Imperial	American
6 bananas, sliced	6 bananas, sliced
4 medium onions, chopped	4 medium onions, chopped
225g./8oz. stoned dates, chopped	$1\frac{1}{3}$ cups chopped pitted dates
300ml./10fl.oz. vinegar	$1\frac{1}{4}$ cups vinegar
1 tsp. curry powder	1 tsp. curry powder
125g./4oz. crystallized ginger, chopped	$\frac{2}{3}$ cup chopped candied ginger
$\frac{1}{2}$ tsp. salt	$\frac{1}{2}$ tsp. salt
250ml./8fl.oz. dark treacle	1 cup molasses

Put the bananas, onions, dates and vinegar into a saucepan and cook for about 15 minutes, or until the onions are tender. Remove from the heat and mash the mixture to a pulp, or purée the mixture in a blender. Stir in the curry powder, ginger, salt and treacle (molasses).

Return the ingredients to the saucepan and return the pan to moderate heat. Cook for 15 to 20 minutes, stirring occasionally, or until the mixture is a rich brown colour.

Remove from the heat and ladle the chutney into warmed, sterilized jars. Cover, label and set aside until ready to use.

Makes about $1\frac{1}{2}kg./1$ lb.

Preparation and cooking time: 1 hour

Chutneys are ideal to serve as accompaniments to Indian meals as they add variety of flavour, texture and taste.

Tamarind Sauce

Metric/Imperial	American
225g./8oz. tamarind	1 cup tamarind
900ml./1½ pints boiling water	3¾ cups boiling water
1 tsp. salt	1 tsp. salt
4cm./1½in. piece of fresh root ginger, peeled and chopped	1½in. piece of fresh green ginger, peeled and chopped
2 Tbs. jaggery or raw sugar	2 Tbs. jaggery or raw sugar
½ tsp. hot chilli powder	½ tsp. hot chilli powder

Put the tamarind into a bowl and pour over the boiling water. Set aside for 1 hour. Break up the pulp slightly with your fingers, then push through a fine strainer held over a small saucepan, rubbing as much of the pulp through as possible with the back of a wooden spoon. Discard the contents of the strainer.

Place the pan over moderate heat and stir in the remaining ingredients. Reduce the heat to low and simmer for 20 minutes, stirring occasionally.

Pour into a warmed sauceboat and set aside to cool slightly before serving.
Makes about 425ml./14fl.oz. (1¾ cups)
Preparation and cooking time: 1½ hours

Lime Pickle

Metric/Imperial	American
10 limes	10 limes
10 green chillis	10 green chillis
3 Tbs. coarse rock salt	3 Tbs. coarse rock salt
2 bay leaves, crumbled	2 bay leaves, crumbled
75g./3oz. fresh root ginger, peeled and cut into strips	3oz. fresh green ginger, peeled and cut into strips
300ml./10fl.oz. lime juice	1¼ cups lime juice

Wash the limes and dry on kitchen towels. Using a stainless steel knife, make four cuts through the limes to quarter them to within ½cm./¼in. of the bottom. Remove the pips (stones). Slit the chillis, lengthways, and scrape out the seeds, leaving the chillis whole with the stalks.

Arrange a layer of limes on the bottom of a pickling jar. Sprinkle with salt and bay leaves, then add 1 to 2 chillis and about 1 tablespoon of ginger. Repeat these layers until all the ingredients, except half the salt, are used up. Pour in the lime juice and give the jar a good shake to settle the contents. Cover the mouth of the jar with a clean cloth and tie down with string. Put the jar in a sunny place for at least 6 days, adding half a tablespoon of the remaining salt each day. Shake the jar at least twice a day. Each night place the jar in a dry place in the kitchen. Be sure to turn the jar each day so that all sides are exposed to the sun's rays.

After all this, keep the pickle on a kitchen shelf for 10 days. Cover with a lid and shake the jar every day. After 10 days the pickle is ready to eat.
Makes about 900g./1½ lbs
Preparation time: 16 days

SWEETS

Nariel Samosas

(Coconut Turnovers)

Metric/Imperial	American
50g./2oz. desiccated coconut, soaked in 75ml./3fl.oz. milk	½ cup shredded coconut, soaked in ⅓ cup milk
½ tsp. crushed cardamom seeds	½ tsp. crushed cardamom seeds
50g./2oz. sultanas	⅓ cup seedless raisins
50g./2oz. soft brown sugar	⅓ cup soft brown sugar
1 egg white, lightly beaten	1 egg white, lightly beaten
350g./12oz. frozen puff pastry, thawed	12oz. frozen puff pastry, thawed

Preheat the oven to hot 220°C (Gas Mark 7, 425°F).

To make the filling, combine the coconut, cardamom and sultanas (raisins) and stir to mix.

Roll out the dough on a lightly floured surface and, using a 7½cm./3in. pastry cutter, cut the dough into about 24 thin circles. Put a spoonful of the coconut mixture in the centre of each circle and dampen the edges with water. Fold the dough over and crimp to seal.

Transfer the turnovers to a lightly greased baking sheet and brush with a little egg white. Bake for 15 to 20 minutes, or until the turnovers are crisp and golden brown.

Transfer to a wire rack to cool and serve slightly warm.

Makes 24

Preparation and cooking time: 45 minutes to 1 hour

Halva

(Semolina Dessert)

Metric/Imperial	American
350g./14oz. sugar	1¾ cups sugar
900ml./1½ pints water	3¾ cups water
2 tsp. cardamom seeds	2 tsp. cardamom seeds
3 cinnamon sticks	3 cinnamon sticks
225g./8oz. butter	1 cup butter
225g./8oz. semolina	2 cups semolina
125g./4oz. sultanas	⅔ cup seedless raisins
125g./4oz. slivered almonds	⅔ cup slivered almonds

Put the sugar and water into a large saucepan and put over high heat. Bring to the boil, stirring constantly until the sugar has dissolved. Stir in the cardamom and cinnamon. Remove from the heat.

Melt the butter in a saucepan. Stir in the semolina and reduce the heat to low. Simmer for 20 minutes, then stir in the remaining ingredients and the sugar syrup. Boil for 5 minutes, stirring constantly. Discard the cardamom and cinnamon.

Turn the mixture into a greased shallow dish or pan and set aside to cool. When the fudge is completely cool, cut into bars or other serving shapes.
Makes about 350g./10oz.
Preparation and cooking time: 2 hours

Rava Kheer

(Semolina and Milk Dessert)

Metric/Imperial	American
900ml./1½ pints milk	3¾ cups milk
2 Tbs. semolina	2 Tbs. semolina
2 Tbs. sugar	2 Tbs. sugar
1 Tbs. melted butter	1 Tbs. melted butter
1 Tbs. crushed cardamom seeds	1 Tbs. crushed cardamom seeds
½ tsp. grated nutmeg	½ tsp. grated nutmeg
1 tsp. rose water	1 tsp. rose water
2 Tbs. toasted flaked almonds	2 Tbs. toasted slivered almonds

Put the milk and semolina into a saucepan and bring to the boil, stirring constantly. Reduce the heat to low and simmer for 5 to 7 minutes, stirring constantly, or until the mixture is thick. Stir in the sugar and cook for 5 minutes, stirring constantly until the sugar has dissolved. Stir in the butter. Remove from the heat and stir in the cardamom, nutmeg and rose water.

Spoon into a greased shallow dish or pan and set aside to cool completely. Sprinkle over the almonds before serving.
Serves 6
Preparation and cooking time: 1¼ hours

Barfi

(Milk and Coconut Fudge)

Metric/Imperial	American
1 tsp. butter, softened	1 tsp. butter, softened
1¼l./2 pints milk	5 cups milk
125g./4oz. desiccated coconut	1 cup shredded coconut
125g./4oz. sugar	½ cup sugar
¼ tsp. carmine food colouring	¼ tsp. carmine food coloring
1 tsp. crushed cardamom seeds	1 tsp. crushed cardamom seeds

Bring the milk to the boil very slowly in a large, heavy saucepan. When it is bubbling, increase the heat and boil briskly, stirring constantly, for about 40 minutes, or until the milk is reduced by about half. Stir in the coconut and sugar, reduce the heat to low and cook for 10 minutes, stirring constantly, or until the mixture is very thick. Stir in the remaining ingredients.

Turn the mixture into a greased shallow dish or pan and set aside to cool. When the fudge is completely cool, cut into bars or other serving shapes.
Makes 350g./12oz.
Preparation and cooking time: 2 hours

Shrikhand

(Curd with Sugar and Saffron)

Metric/Imperial	American
2¼l./4 pints yogurt	5 pints yogurt
castor sugar	superfine sugar
½ tsp. ground saffron	½ tsp. ground saffron
1 Tbs. rose water	1 Tbs. rose water
2 Tbs. crushed cardamom seeds	2 Tbs. crushed cardamom seeds
15 pistachio nuts, blanched and sliced	15 pistachio nuts, blanched and sliced

Put the yogurt in a cheesecloth bag and tie over a mixing bowl. Drain for 2 hours, or until the whey has drained out. Discard the whey.

Weigh the curd left in the bag and transfer to a large bowl. For every 225g./8oz. (1 cup) of curd, stir in 175g./6oz. (¾ cup) of sugar. Stir in the remaining ingredients, reserving a few nuts for garnish. The mixture should have the consistency of thick cream.

Cover the bowl and chill in the refrigerator for 1 hour. Spoon into individual bowls, and sprinkle over the reserved nuts before serving.
Serves 8-10
Preparation time: 3¼ hours

Kulfi

(Ice-Cream)

Metric/Imperial	American
450ml./15fl.oz. mango juice	2 cups mango juice
150ml./5fl.oz. single cream	⅔ cup light cream
2 Tbs. castor sugar	2 Tbs. superfine sugar

Combine all the ingredients, then spoon into six small moulds. Tightly cover and freeze, shaking the moulds about three times during the first hour of freezing.

To serve, dip the bottoms of the moulds into boiling water for 2 seconds, then invert giving the moulds a sharp shake. The ice-cream should slide out easily. Serve at once.
Serves 6
Preparation time: 3 hours

BASIC RECIPES

Ghee

(Clarified Butter)

Metric/Imperial	American
450g./1lb. butter	2 cups butter

Put the butter into a heavy-based saucepan and melt very slowly over low heat. Be careful not to let the butter burn. Heat to just below boiling point, then simmer for 30 minutes, or until the moisture in the butter evaporates and the protein sinks to the bottom of the pan. Remove from the heat and carefully strain the clear fat through several thicknesses of cheesecloth into a jar.

Cover tightly and store in a cool, dry place. It will solidify as it cools.

Makes 350g./12oz. (1½ cups)
Preparation and cooking time: 45 minutes

Coconut Milk

Coconut milk is an important ingredient in many Indian recipes and this is a substitute if you cannot obtain fresh coconut milk. This recipe will produce a medium milk – add a little more creamed coconut for thick, and a little less for thin.

Metric/Imperial	American
7½cm./3in. slice creamed coconut	3in. slice creamed coconut
450ml./15fl.oz. boiling water	2 cups boiling water

Combine the ingredients together, stirring constantly until the coconut dissolves.

Makes about 500ml./18fl.oz. (2¼ cups)
Preparation time: 5 minutes

Home-Made Yogurt

Metric/Imperial	American
725-900ml./1¼-1½ pints milk	3-3¼ cups milk
2 Tbs. yogurt or yogurt culture	2 Tbs. yogurt or yogurt culture

Pour the milk into a saucepan and bring to the boil. Remove from the heat and allow to cool to 43°C (110°F) on a sugar thermometer, or until you can immerse a finger for 10 seconds without discomfort.

Meanwhile, beat the yogurt or yogurt culture in a glass or earthenware bowl to smooth. Add 3 tablespoons of the warmed milk, a little at a time, beating constantly until the mixture is blended. Beat in the remaining milk until the mixture is thoroughly blended. Cover, wrap in a towel and keep in a warm, draught-free place for 8 hours, or until it has thickened.

Store in the refrigerator until you are ready to use.

Makes 1¼l./2 pints (5 cups)
Preparation time: 8¼ hours

Garam Masala

(Mixed Ground Spices)
Garam masala can be bought commercially but in India it is often made at home. There are many versions -- this is a basic one.

Metric/Imperial	American
3 Tbs. black peppercorns, ground	3 Tbs. black peppercorns, ground
1 Tbs. ground cumin	1 Tbs. ground cumin
1 tsp. ground cinnamon	1 tsp. ground cinnamon
2 tsp. ground cardamom	2 tsp. ground cardamom
3 Tbs. ground coriander	3 Tbs. ground coriander
1 tsp. ground cloves	1 tsp. ground cloves
1½ tsp. ground mace	1½ tsp. ground mace
½ tsp. grated nutmeg	½ tsp. grated nutmeg

Combine all the ingredients together and store, covered, in a cool, dry place.

Makes about 50g./2oz. (½ cup)
Preparation time: 2 minutes

Curry Powder 1

Curry powder as it is known in the west is merely a dry 'masala' or concoction of mixed ground spices. Most recipes in this book conform to the standard Indian practice of adding several spices to any given dish, but you can prepare your own powder which can be used for basic meat or fish curries. If you use root ginger in the recipe, omit the ground ginger below.

Metric/Imperial	American
1 Tbs. ground coriander	1 Tbs. ground coriander
1 tsp. ground cumin	1 tsp. ground cumin
1 tsp. turmeric	1 tsp. turmeric
½ tsp. ground ginger	½ tsp. ground ginger
½ tsp. hot chilli powder	½ tsp. hot chilli powder

Combine all the ingredients in a small bowl. Add to the recipe in appropriate amounts.

Makes about 25g./1oz. (¼ cup)
Preparation time: 2 minutes

Curry Powder II

This is a slightly sweeter, milder version and could be used for fish or shellfish, or vegetable dishes.

Metric/Imperial	American
1 Tbs. ground coriander	1 Tbs. ground coriander
½ tsp. ground cumin	½ tsp. ground cumin
1 tsp. turmeric	1 tsp. turmeric
½ tsp. garam masala	½ tsp. garam masala
¼ tsp. ground fenugreek	¼ tsp. ground fenugreek
¼ tsp. ground cardamom	¼ tsp. ground cardamom
¼ tsp. hot chilli powder	¼ tsp. hot chilli powder

Combine all the ingredients in a small bowl. Add to the recipe in appropriate amounts.

Makes about 15g./½oz. (2 tablespoons)
Preparation time: 2 minutes

GLOSSARY

Asafoetida

A dried gum resin, sometimes used as a spice in Indian cooking. It can be one of the spices used to make up the western 'curry' powder. Not easily obtainable in the West, although many oriental stores stock it. If unobtainable, omit from the recipe – there is no substitute.

Besan or Chick-pea flour

(Sometimes known as gram) used extensively in India, especially for batters for deep-frying. Oriental or Indian stores are the most likely stockists. If unobtainable, you *could* grind chick-peas in a blender, then sift to refine them sufficiently, or substitute ordinary flour or cornflour (cornstarch).

Cardamom

A spice widely used in Indian and Sri Lankan cooking. A member of the ginger family and one of the most expensive spices in the world. Used in both seed and ground form – the outer pods are usually discarded and the seeds bruised and added to recipes whole, or the seeds are ground to a powder. Obtainable from oriental stores and also from any good Scandinavian store.

Chilli

Used in Indian cooking either fresh or dried, to add 'heat' to recipes. Obtainable from oriental or Mexican stores. The seeds are the hottest part of the chilli, so if you wish to reduce the firiness of a dish, remove them and add only the chopped outer part. If fresh or dried chillis are difficult to obtain, substitute dried chilli powder – but make sure it is hot chilli powder and not the much milder chilli seasoning. About ½ teaspoon ground chilli is a rough equivalent of one chopped chilli.

Coconut milk

Used as a cooking stock all over India. If fresh coconut is not available a good substitute can be made from creamed coconut (see recipes). If creamed coconut is unavailable, then use desiccated (shredded) coconut instead. Put about 125g./4oz. of desiccated (shredded) coconut into a blender and pour over 300ml./10fl.oz./1¼ cups of boiling water. Soak for 10 minutes, then blend the mixture and strain through cheesecloth into a jug or bowl.

Coriander

Used in many ways in Indian cooking: as a ground spice, one of the necessary ingredients in a 'curry' sauce; as a seed used in many savoury recipes and as chopped leaves used as a garnish on almost everything. It is a member of the parsley family and if coriander leaves are unobtainable, fresh chopped parsley can be substituted. Ground and seeded coriander are available from most supermarkets. Coriander leaves can be bought from oriental, Greek or Mexican stores.

Curry leaves

Used fresh in India as either a garnish to curries, or as an ingredient to be added towards the end of cooking. Can be obtained dried from Indian provision stores. If unobtainable, either omit from the recipe or substitute bay leaves.

Dhal

The collective word for legumes or pulses. Lentils are the most popular form of dhal, and there are many varieties and colours found in India. In the sourthen part of the country, where many people are vegetarian, it forms an important part of the diet. If you cannot obtain the Indian varieties of lentil mentioned in the recipes, substitute the orange lentils widely available in the West. In some cases the authenticity will be a little impaired but the results are good.

Fenugreek

A spice used both in seed and ground form in Indian dishes, especially fish dishes. Obtainable from better supermarkets or oriental stores – but if you cannot obtain it omit from the recipe.

Garam masala

Literally 'dried spice mixture' in India, although a commercial preparation is now sold (see recipe). Garam masala is usually added to dishes towards the end of cooking – otherwise it can become slightly bitter.

Ghee

A type of clarified butter widely used in India as a cooking agent (see recipe). Butter or vegetable oil can be substituted.

Ginger

The root of the ginger plant is probably the single most important flavouring used in all oriental cooking – it is found in China, India, Japan and most of South-East Asia. Most recipes in this book call for fresh (green) ginger. To peel, scrape off the skin and any woody pieces and chop or grate the moist flesh. To store fresh ginger, wrap tightly, unpeeled, in plastic film or cover with dry sherry and leave in the refrigerator; it will keep for about six weeks. Although the taste is not really the same, *in extremis* ground ginger can be substituted for fresh – use about ½ teaspoon to 4cm./1½in. piece of fresh (green) ginger root. Obtainable from oriental stores and some specialty fruit and vegetable shops.

Lime	Sometimes used to provide a slightly sour flavour in Indian savoury dishes. If unobtainable lemon may be substituted.
Poppy seeds	Small seeds, both black and white, often used to thicken sauces slightly in Indian cooking. When added to a dish, they should first be cooked until they spatter slightly before adding other ingredients to the pan. Obtainable from oriental stores and better supermarkets.
Saffron	The world's most expensive spice and as a consequence perhaps used lovingly by almost every cuisine in the world. Made from the dried stamens of the crocus flower. It can be obtained in both strand and ground form – the strands should be soaked in warm water before using (see specific recipes for instructions). As a substitute for colour, turmeric can be used, but the flavour is very different.
Tamarind	The dried fruit of the tamarind tree, sold commercially in blocks. Used extensively in southern Indian cooking. Since the plant is somewhat fibrous, it is always soaked first, then strained and the tamarind water used rather than the fibrous pulp. See specific recipes for instructions on how to use.
Yogurt	One of the most popular cooking stocks in all of India. Commercial yogurt is perfectly acceptable but home-made is cheaper – and tastes better (see recipe). Always use plain yogurt as specified in the recipes.

INTRODUCTION Derek Davies

TO JAPAN & KOREA

Neither Japanese nor Korean cuisine is much known outside its own shores, although with increasing travel, especially to Japan, this will probably change. Those lucky enough to have tasted food from Japan and Korea know them to be delicious and unique, but the majority, who have not, assume them to be more or less the same and both rather poor relations of the magnificent cuisine of China. Nothing could be farther from the truth for while there are similarities (many ingredients are common to all three, they all use chopsticks and rice is the basic staple), there are also enormous differences (methods of preparation and cooking, the flavours preferred). They are related to one another, in fact, only as the French, British and Spanish cuisines are inter-related.

In general, Japanese food is delicate and refined, with an emphasis on freshness and clean, sharp, natural tastes: hot, spicy flavourings, popular in India and Malaysia are not used. Many ingredients, fish in particular, are eaten uncooked, and dipping sauces are used extensively to enhance the flavours. Not only are subtleties of taste all important, but the appearance of the dish should satisfy the eye just as much as the flavours satisfy the palate. Korean food, with a strong, rather spicy character of its own, also 'borrows' what is considered to be the best of neighbouring cuisines – so you will find Chinese noodles happily married to a dish containing Japanese soy sauce, and even a dish called 'curry', which turns out to be hot and spicy and with a chilli base.

The two most important ingredients in both cuisines are rice and soya beans. Plain rice is served with all meals. In Japan it has an almost religious significance and shrines to the rice god, *Inari*, can be seen throughout the country. Historically, it was used as a unit of taxation and as a measure of man's wealth; even today, so important is its preparation, that a women's skill at cooking is judged according to how well she makes it. Rice is also used to make wine: in Korea, known as *mah koli*, and in Japan, *sake* and *mirin*, not only drunk but also used extensively in cooking.

The versatile soya bean makes its appearance in several forms: it is the basic ingredient of soy sauce, which is the foundation of all Korean and Japanese cooking (it is used not only as a dipping sauce and as a seasoning, but as part of the base mixture in which many ingredients are cooked); it is con-verted into the white, jelly-like bean curd cake called *tofu* in Japan, which turns up in all sorts of dishes and in many different forms; and it is made into *miso*, a fermented paste used to marinate and dress fish and vegetables, and as a base for a whole range of soups.

Meat has always been part of the Korean diet, if something of a luxury, and several national dishes boast beef in various guises, but the Japanese ate it only rarely until about a hundred years ago. Partly, this was the result of Buddhist proscriptions against eating anything that had 'received the breath of life' and partly because the mountainous islands of Japan lacked suitable grazing land for the breeding of cattle. At the end of the nineteenth century, however, Japan was opened to the West after more than 200 years of isolation and the diet, among many other things, changed dramatically. As part of the general adoption of Western ways, people were positively encouraged to eat meat. Most Japanese meat dishes, in fact, date from this time, including the popular *sukiyaki*. Reservations about meat do still remain in respect to lamb, which is rarely eaten.

For both the Japanese and Koreans, the most important source of protein is the sea. Favourable currents in the surrounding waters, long coastlines and numerous islands endow both with a wealth of marine life. The Japanese eat more fish per head of the population than any other people in the world: nearly half a kilo or a pound each per week. They also eat a wide variety including, on occasions, strange species such as sea-urchins and deadly blow-fish (*fugu*). (Blow-fish are prepared in restaurants specially licensed to remove the poison – but even so a number of Japanese people die from *fugu* poisoning each year.) The Japanese are particuarly ingenious at cooking and preparing fish and shell-fish: an old text describes a hundred ways of preparing one fish alone, the *tai*, or sea bream, much appreciated by the Japanese and always eaten on festive occasions.

Fish is not the only seafood eaten in Japan, however, seaweeds – or more accurately sea vegetables such as *nori* (laver) and *kombu* (kelp) – are used extensively. They are eaten primarily for their flavour which is rich and subtle, but they also contain a high proportion of iodine and vitamins, which makes them beneficial to health as well. *Nori* is specially prepared in thin, dried sheets which

*Seaweed is a very
important part of the
Japanese diet.*

can be used as a sort of delicate wrapping material for many foods, or as a garnish for soups and rice dishes. Its flavour is enhanced when heated until dry and brittle, and then it is quite delicious simply dipped in a soy sauce and eaten with rice. *Kombu* is also dried into sheets, but thicker and harder ones than *nori* and they are used mainly in soups and stocks – Japanese *dashi* (stock) is made from *kombu* and the flakes of dried bonito fish (*katsuobushi*). In contrast, the Koreans usually make soups and stocks with a meat base. Seaweed is not part of their diet, though it is cultivated for export to Japan.

Apart from their great range of seafoods, Japan and Korea also possess a wealth of fruit and vegetables. Korea is a mainly agricultural country where most of the world's common vegetables are grown, as well as some unusual roots, leaves and edible mosses. Koreans say that without vegetables, no meal is complete. As for Japan, the sheer length of the country – over a thousand miles from north to south – as well as a varied topography and pronounced seasons, create climatic differences conducive to great variety.

In keeping with their love of nature, the Japanese pay great attention to seasonal changes. Not only do fruit and vegetables have their seasons, but even cakes and tea.

Winter is the time for tangerines, hot noodles and warming one-pot dishes cooked on the table; in February the world's largest and most succulent strawberries make their appearance; with the spring and the first sound of the nightingale come cakes shaped like nightingales; and as the cherry blossom begins to flower, cakes flavoured with cherry blossoms also appear. Spring is also the time for tender bamboo shoots and the mellow flavour of new tea, *shincha*.

May sees the opening of the season for the *ayu*, a small, delicious and delicately flavoured river trout. In one part of Japan, Gifu, there is an ingenious method of catching *ayu*: cormorants tethered to fishing boats snatch the fish from the water, and are then pulled back on to the boats by the fishermen where they disgorge their catch. Summer is also the time for chilled noodles, chilled *tofu* and hot eels.

Autumn (fall) is the season for pickle making. In Korea, the markets are laden with large, white radishes, Chinese cabbages, hot red peppers and dozens of other vegetables that go into the many varieties of *kim chee*. All domestic activity centres on the business of chopping and sorting vegetables and filling the pickle pots for winter. 'When the

*Fish and octopus on sale
in a seafood market in
Korea.*

kim chee is prepared for the winter,' they say, 'half the harvest is done.' The Japanese also make and eat many pickles, although generally they are gentler than the Korean variety. In Japan, autumn is also the season for what are said to be the world's most delicious mushrooms, the *matsutake*. During the season, city dwellers equipped with cooking gear converge on the forests where the mushrooms grow to picnic on them.

One of the great pleasures of travelling in both countries is the variety of their regional specialities. Each town or area has its own products, from handicrafts such as lacquerware or pottery, to various foods, such as cakes, pickles and fish. A Japanese island might be noted for abalone (*awabe*), which is collected from the seabed by specially-trained diving girls; or a mountain village might be famous for its young fern shoots (*warabi*). But apart from such special products, the taste of food varies from region to region. In Japan, the food of Kyoto tends to be lighter and more subtle than that of Tokyo, reflecting perhaps the tastes of the old Kyoto court. With its many Buddhist temples, Kyoto is also famous for its vegetarian dishes, while Tokyo, with its huge fish market, is known for the flavour of its seafood. The long trading history of Nagasaki in the southern island has left strong Chinese influences on the food of that region.

It was in the imperial courts of Kyoto and Nara that the tea ceremony was developed from its Chinese origins into a stylized ritual. Today, the tea ceremony is still widely practised, and knowledge of it is considered to be an important qualification for prospective Japanese brides. Essentially, the tea ceremony is the art of preparing tea as gracefully as possible, but the manner in which it is done is highly formalized. Practitioners must strictly observe the correct procedures, such as how to pour the water and hold the tea bowl. Tea ceremony food, *kaiseki*, is the most refined of the Japanese cuisine, with great emphasis being placed upon simplicity and harmony. The tastes, textures and colours of the food should balance one another, and the containers in which it is served should enhance its appearance. *Kaiseki* food reflects the seasons and, if possible, is locally produced; it should not be expensive or extravagant, but should be imaginative and in good taste. The tea used for the tea ceremony is a special type of powdered green tea, *matcha*. After adding hot water to the powder, it is whipped with a bamboo whisk which looks rather like a shaving brush. The taste is bitter, but refreshing.

The Koreans have no equivalent of the Japanese tea ceremony, though they are enthusiastic tea drinkers. They do, however, have a special tea made from the roots of the *ginsing* plant. *Ginsing* tea is rich to taste and is reputed to have many medicinal properties. They also make a rice tea from the grains remaining in the saucepan after the

231

rice has been cooked.

To describe the ingredients of a nation's cooking, particularly when many of them are strange to the western palate, can be misleading – the thought of eating uncooked fish, for example, is repugnant to many, but when it is eaten absolutely fresh, in the Japanese manner, you can almost forget that it is fish at all; the tastes and textures might best be compared to chilled, very tender, rare beef. And many who have tried uncooked fish dishes, such as *sushi* and *sashimi*, consider them to be among the greatest delicacies in Japan's vast cuisine.

Other dishes are less difficult: *tempura*, for example, deep-fried vegetables and fish in the lightest of batters, is popular throughout the world. Properly prepared, it is succulent and crisp with only the slightest hint of oil. Strangely enough although it is one of the country's best-known dishes, it is not strictly speaking Japanese at all – but an adaptation of a Portuguese dish. (It arrived with Western traders and missionaries over four hundred years ago and the name itself comes from the Latin word for time – a reference to those certain days of the year on which the Portuguese, as good Catholics, could not eat meat.) Another dish easy to appreciate is *sukiyaki*, thinly sliced beef cooked in one-pot style on the table.

Sukiyaki and *tempura* are served both at home and in restaurants, or are delivered from the restaurants to the home – a common practice in Japan. This is because, on the whole, restaurants are better equipped to prepare the food properly – the cutting of the fish for *sushi*, for example, requires great skill, and *sushi* cooks are required to spend many years in apprenticeship. Some restaurants serve only one type of food, such as *tempura*, *noodles* or *sushi*, and there are even some which serve only *tofu* dishes. The Japanese never drink without eating and many dishes can therefore be regarded primarily as snacks with alcohol – even the smallest bars serve their own specialities. The Koreans also make many snack dishes to be served with drinks, some of them quite unusual – bulls' testicles, which are thought to be a powerful aphrodisiac, are very popular!

For both Japanese and Korean meals, the dishes are not served consecutively in courses as they are in the West, but are placed together on the table. The Koreans arrange the dishes on low tables in the kitchen and then carry them to the eating area. Almost invariably every Japanese and Korean meal includes rice and soup, perhaps a main dish of meat or fish, dipping sauces and various side dishes. Usually there will be separate dishes and bowls for each person. There are no rules about the order in which the food is eaten, though it is customary to sip a little of the soup first. Some hot dishes, such as *tempura* or *shin-sol-lo* should be eaten as soon as they are served. Very often, if people are drinking *sake* with the meal, they will not eat rice until they

Dinner – in the traditional Japanese way, cross-legged on the floor below a low table.

have finished drinking. The meal is usually completed by rice, pickles and tea. Desserts are not a part of either Japanese or Korean cooking, though sometimes fresh fruit will be served at the end of a meal.

The style of a one-pot meal is somewhat different, however, for all the ingredients are prepared in the kitchen in advance and the cooking done on a portable burner on the centre of the dining table. Each person selects what he or she wants from the plates of uncooked ingredients and places them in the communal pot. After brief cooking, the food is transferred to a dipping sauce before eating. The cooking time is so short that the flavour, texture and essential nutrients of the ingredients are not destroyed. A one-pot meal is ideal for dinner parties since it does not take long to prepare or cook, and is informal to eat. A selection of ingredients to make up a first batch to be put in the pot, is put on the table and, when these are eaten, there is traditionally a pause while conversation and drinking take over from food. Later, more rounds can be cooked, with further rests between them. The portable burner may be of any type, so long as it is powerful enough to bring the cooking liquid to boiling point. The Japanese have a variety of dishes known as *nabes* (pots), after which many one-pot dishes are named, but any type of flameproof pot, or fondue pot is equally suitable. The Koreans have a special charcoal stove, called *shin-sol-lo*, used to cook their national dish. It is shaped rather like a hat: the charcoal is placed in the middle and the cooking liquid in the surrounding brim.

In spite of the emphasis that is placed on appearance, it is a mistake to assume that Japanese and Korean food is expensive to prepare at home. Elaborate garnishes and beautiful pottery are not necessary, and more often than not they can be omitted from home cooking: you can improvise very well with soup or cereal bowls, or even decorative ashtrays. Many of the ingredients are relatively cheap, though obviously some special ones are necessary for certain dishes. Very often substitutes are quite acceptable, while other dishes can be made from ingredients commonly available at grocery stores and supermarkets. But it is advisable for someone interested in making Japanese and Korean food to stock up with some standard items, such as soy sauce – for Japanese dishes, make sure it is the Japanese variety — *mirin* (sweet

A family from the Ainu, an important sub-group from the northern archipelago of Japan.

232

cooking wine), *sake* (dry rice wine), *miso* paste and perhaps sesame oil. All can be kept for long periods, and can be obtained from Japanese food stores; some are stocked by general Oriental or Chinese stores.

The preparation of Japanese and Korean food is not as difficult as it might seem: the cutting of vegetables, particularly, is considered to be very important and something of an art form. There are no set rules for menus: but dishes are usually chosen to give variety in taste and colour. Remember that in Japanese and Korean meals the side dishes might not seem very substantial, but the volume is made up with rice; about half a cup of uncooked rice is usually allowed for each person.

Do not be afraid to vary the proportions of ingredients in the recipes which follow, or to adapt them to your own requirements. The important thing is to find the tastes which suit you best — and the recipes you enjoy most.

The face of Japan is delicate, beautiful and full of ceremony and grace.

SOUPS & NOODLES

Dashi

(Basic Stock)

Dashi is used extensively in Japanese cooking, and is the base for almost every soup and noodle dish. There are several types, but the simplest way to make it is with instant dashi powder (dashi-no-moto), which is obtainable from Japanese and some general Oriental stores. If all else fails, a chicken stock (bouillon) cube can be used as a substitute – although this does of course affect the authenticity (not to mention the taste) of the cooked dish.

Metric/Imperial	American
⅓ tsp. instant dashi powder (dashi-no-moto)	⅓ tsp. instant dashi powder (dashi-no-moto)
250ml./8fl.oz. water	1 cup water

Add the dashi powder to boiling water and set over moderately low heat. Boil for about 1 minute, stirring gently to blend. Remove from the heat and use as described in the various recipes.
Makes 250ml./8fl. oz. (1 cup) stock
Preparation and cooking time: 2 minutes

Kombo to Katsuobushi no Dashi

(Home-made Stock)

If you prefer to make your own dashi, the recipe which follows is one version. Kombo (dried kelp) and katsuobushi (dried bonito fish [tuna]) are essential ingredients and both can be bought in Japanese or Oriental stores, or in the case of kombu, in many health food stores. Kombu is sold in sheets and the katsuobushi either in flakes or in a solid block, which then has to be flaked.

Metric/Imperial	American
5cm./2in. piece of kombu	2in. piece of kombu
250ml./8fl.oz. water	1 cup water
1 tsp. katsuobushi	1 tsp. katsuobushi

Put the kombu and water into a small saucepan and bring to the boil, stirring constantly to release the flavour of the kelp. Remove from the heat and drain the water into a second saucepan, discarding the kombu pieces. Add the katsuobushi flakes and set the saucepan over moderate heat. Bring to the boil and boil for 1 minute. Remove the pan from the heat and set aside until the flakes settle. Strain the liquid, discarding the flakes.
The stock is now ready to use.
Makes 250ml./8fl.oz. (1 cup) stock
Preparation and cooking time: 5 minutes

Hamaguri Sumashi-Jiru

(Clam and Mushroom Soup)

Oysters can be substituted for the clams in this recipe. If used, omit the soaking period and add straight to the water.

Metric/Imperial	American
8 clams, soaked in salt water for 3 hours and drained	8 clams, soaked in salt water for 3 hours and drained
salt	salt
8 small button mushroom caps	8 small button mushroom caps
8 watercress sprigs	8 watercress sprigs
1 tsp. soya sauce	1 tsp. soy sauce
monosodium glutamate (optional)	MSG (optional)
125ml./4fl.oz. sake or dry sherry	½ cup sake or dry sherry
4 pieces of lemon rind	4 pieces of lemon rind

Put the clams and about 900ml./1½ pints (3¾ cups) of water into a large saucepan. Bring to the boil, then continue to boil until the shells open. Discard any that do not open. Remove any scum which rises to the surface and stir in salt to taste, the mushroom caps and watercress. Cook for 1 minute. Stir in soy sauce, monosodium glutamate to taste and the sake or sherry and return the soup to the boil.

Put one piece of lemon rind into each of four serving bowls, then divide the soup among the bowls. Serve at once.
Serves 4
Preparation and cooking time: 3¼ hours

Yakinasu no Miso Shiru

(Miso Soup with Fried Aubergine [Eggplant])

Metric/Imperial	American
125ml./4fl.oz. vegetable oil	½ cup vegetable oil
2 medium aubergines, sliced and dégorged	2 medium eggplants, sliced and dégorged
1.2l./2 pints dashi	5 cups dashi
4 Tbs. miso paste	4 Tbs. miso paste
2 mint leaves, thinly sliced	2 mint leaves, thinly sliced
mustard to taste	mustard to taste

Heat the oil in a frying-pan. When it is hot, add the aubergine (eggplant) slices and fry over moderately high heat until the skin begins to burn and peel. Remove from the heat and transfer the aubergines (eggplants) to a chopping board. Carefully peel off the skin and chop the flesh into bite-sized pieces. Divide the pieces among 4 to 6 soup bowls and keep hot.

Heat the dashi in a saucepan until it comes to the boil. Stir in the miso paste until it melts, forming a suspension in the liquid.

Pour the liquid over the aubergine (eggplant) pieces and add some mint leaf slices and mustard to taste to each bowl. Serve at once.
Serves 4–6
Preparation and cooking time: 35 minutes

Iwashi no Tsumire Jiru

(Clear Soup with Sardine Balls)

Metric/Imperial	American
5 fresh sardines, cleaned and with the heads removed	5 fresh sardines, cleaned and with the heads removed
2 Tbs. miso paste	2 Tbs. miso paste
1cm./½in. piece of fresh root ginger, peeled and grated	½in. piece of fresh green ginger, peeled and grated
1 Tbs. flour	1 Tbs. flour
1.2 l./2 pints water	5 cups water
2 Tbs. soya sauce	2 Tbs. soy sauce
¼ tsp. salt	¼ tsp. salt
1 medium turnip, thinly sliced then quartered	1 medium turnip, thinly sliced then quartered
4 small pieces of lemon rind	4 small pieces of lemon rind

Remove the main bones from the sardines and clean them in salted water. Dry on kitchen towels and chop into small pieces. Put the sardines into a blender and blend until smooth. Alternatively, pound in a mortar with a pestle until smooth. Stir the miso paste, grated ginger and flour into the sardines and beat until they are thoroughly combined. Using the palm of your hands, gently roll small pieces of the mixture into balls.

Bring the water to the boil in a large saucepan. Drop in the fish balls and cook until they rise to the surface. Using a slotted spoon, transfer the fish balls to a plate and strain the liquid into a fresh pan. Stir in the soy sauce and salt.

In the meantime, cook the turnip in boiling water for about 5 minutes, or until the pieces are crisp. Drain and reserve.

Reheat the strained soup liquid and add the fish balls. Bring to the boil, then stir in the turnip.

Transfer to soup bowls and garnish with lemon rind.

Serves 4–6
Preparation and cooking time: 40 minutes

Tofu no Miso Shiru

(Bean Paste Soup with Bean Curd)

Metric/Imperial	American
1.2 l./2 pints dashi	5 cups dashi
4 Tbs. miso paste	4 Tbs. miso paste
2 bean curd cakes (tofu), cut into small cubes	2 bean curd cakes (tofu), cut into small cubes
2 spring onions, finely chopped	2 scallions, finely chopped

Put the dashi into a large saucepan and set over moderate heat. Stir in the miso paste until it melts. Raise the heat to high and add the bean curd pieces. Boil until the bean curd rises to the surface of the liquid.

Serve at once, garnished with the spring onions (scallions).

Serves 4–6
Preparation and cooking time: 10 minutes

Kong-Na-Mool Kuk

(Bean Sprout Soup)   (Korea)

Metric/Imperial	American
225g./8oz. lean beef, cut into thin strips	8oz. lean beef, cut into thin strips
2 garlic cloves, crushed	2 garlic cloves, crushed
2 tsp. roasted sesame seeds, ground	2 tsp. roasted sesame seeds, ground
2 spring onions, green part only, finely chopped	2 scallions, green part only, finely chopped
salt and pepper	salt and pepper
3 Tbs. soya sauce	3 Tbs. soy sauce
1½ Tbs. sesame oil	1½ Tbs. sesame oil
700g./1½lb. bean sprouts	3 cups bean sprouts
1.75l./3 pints water	1½ quarts water

Mix the beef, garlic, sesame seeds, half the spring onions (scallions), the salt and pepper and half the soy sauce together. Heat the oil in a saucepan. When it is hot, add the meat and stir-fry until it is evenly browned .Stir in the bean sprouts and stir-fry for a further 3 minutes.

Pour in the water and remaining soy sauce and bring to the boil. Cover and simmer for 30 minutes. Stir in the remaining spring onion (scallion) and simmer for a further 5 minutes.

Serves 4–6
Preparation and cooking time: 40 minutes

Sumashi Jiru

(Chicken and Noodle Soup)

The type of noodle most commonly used in this soup is udon, *which somewhat resembles spaghetti in appearance. If* udon *is not available, then spaghetti vermicelli or any similar noodle may be substituted.*

Metric/Imperial	American
350g./12oz. udon	12oz. udon
1 large chicken breast, skinned, boned and cut into thin strips	1 large chicken breast, skinned, boned and cut into thin strips
1.2l./2 pints dashi	5 cups dashi
6 dried mushrooms, soaked in cold water for 30 minutes, drained and sliced	6 dried mushrooms, soaked in cold water for 30 minutes, drained and sliced
2 tsp. soya sauce	2 tsp. soy sauce
2 spring onions, chopped	2 scallions, chopped
6 strips of lemon rind	6 strips of lemon rind

Cook the noodles in boiling salted water for 5 to 12 minutes, or until they are just tender. Drain and keep hot.

Put the chicken meat strips into a large saucepan and pour over the dashi. Bring to the boil, then reduce the heat to moderate. Cook for 3 minutes. Add the mushrooms and soy sauce and cook for a further 2 minutes. Stir in the udon and return to the boil. Cook for 1 minute, then remove the pan from the heat.

Pour the soup either into a large warmed tureen, or into six individual small soup bowls. Garnish with spring onions (scallions) and lemon before serving.
Serves 6
Preparation and cooking time: 1 hour

Tofu No Ankake (Bean Curd Soup) and Chawan Mushi (Chicken and Steamed Vegetables in Egg) are both served as soup courses in Japan – although Chawan Mushi is also a popular breakfast dish.

Tofu no Ankake

(Bean Curd Soup)

Metric/Imperial	American
1.2 l./2 pints dashi	5 cups dashi
3 Tbs. soya sauce	3 Tbs. soy sauce
½ tsp. salt	½ tsp. salt
2 Tbs. mirin or sweet sherry	2 Tbs. mirin or sweet sherry
2 Tbs. cornflour, mixed to a paste with 2 Tbs. water	2 Tbs. cornstarch, mixed to a paste with 2 Tbs. water
2 Tbs. water	2 Tbs. water
4 dried mushrooms, soaked in cold water for 30 minutes, drained and sliced	4 dried mushrooms, soaked in cold water for 30 minutes, drained and sliced
350g./12oz. bean curd cakes (tofu), diced	2 cups diced bean curd cakes (tofu)
1cm./½in. piece of fresh root ginger, peeled and grated	½in. piece of fresh green ginger, peeled and grated

Put the dashi, soy sauce, salt, mirin or sherry, cornflour (cornstarch) mixture and mushrooms into a large saucepan and bring to the boil, stirring constantly. Reduce the heat to low, cover and simmer the soup for 15 minutes. Stir in the bean curd and simmer for a further 5 minutes.

Ladle the soup into individual soup bowls, dividing the bean curd pieces equally among them. Garnish each bowl with a little grated ginger and serve.
Serves 4–6
Preparation and cooking time: 1 hour

Chawan Mushi

(Chicken and Steamed Vegetables in Egg)

Metric/Imperial	American
1 small chicken breast, boned and diced	1 small chicken breast, boned and diced
soya sauce	soy sauce
50g./2oz. firm white fish, skinned and cut into 4 pieces	2oz. firm white fish, skinned and cut into 4 pieces
salt	salt
8 prawns, shelled	8 shrimp, shelled
4 mushrooms caps, quartered	4 mushroom caps, quartered
50g./2oz. French beans, thinly sliced and parboiled	⅓ cup green beans, thinly sliced and parboiled
EGG MIXTURE	EGG MIXTURE
900ml./1½ pints dashi	3¾ cups dashi
1½ tsp. salt	1½ tsp. salt
1½ tsp. soya sauce	1½ tsp. soy sauce
monosodium glutamate (optional)	MSG (optional)
1 tsp. mirin or sweet sherry	1 tsp. mirin or sweet sherry
4 eggs, plus 2 egg yolks, lightly beaten	4 eggs, plus 2 egg yolks, lightly beaten

Sprinkle the chicken pieces with soy sauce and set aside for 5 minutes. Sprinkle the fish pieces with salt and set aside.

Meanwhile, to make the egg mixture, mix the dashi, salt, soy sauce, monosodium glutamate to taste and mirin or sherry together. Pour the beaten eggs slowly into the mixture, stirring gently. Set aside.

Divide the chicken dice, fish pieces, prawns or shrimp and mushrooms among four small ovenproof bowls. Pour the egg mixture on top and cover, leaving the covers slightly ajar.

Arrange the bowls in the top of a double boiler and half fill the bottom with boiling water. (If you do not have a double boiler, improvise by using a small baking dish set in a deep roasting pan. Fill the pan with water until it comes halfway up the sides of the baking dish.) Steam the mixture for 25 minutes, or until the eggs have set. (The surface should be yellow not brown and although the egg will be set on the outside it should still contain some liquid inside.)

About 5 minutes before the end of the cooking time, remove the covers from the bowls and garnish with the sliced beans. Serve hot, either as a soup course or as a breakfast dish.

Serves 4
Preparation and cooking time: 1¼ hours

Mandoo

(Meat Dumpling Soup)   (Korea)

Metric/Imperial	American
SOUP	SOUP
1.75 l./3 pints beef stock	7½ cups beef stock
2 Tbs. soya sauce	2 Tbs. soy sauce
1 Tbs. roasted sesame seeds, ground	1 Tbs. roasted sesame seeds, ground
1 large spring onion, chopped	1 large scallion, chopped
DUMPLING DOUGH	DUMPLING DOUGH
350g./12oz. flour	3 cups flour
250ml./8fl.oz. water	1 cup water
DUMPLING FILLING	DUMPLING FILLING
2 Tbs. vegetable oil	2 Tbs. vegetable oil
225g./8oz. minced beef	8oz. ground beef
1 onion, finely chopped	1 onion, finely chopped
1 garlic clove, crushed	1 garlic clove, crushed
50g./2oz. button mushrooms, chopped	½ cup chopped button mushrooms
225g./8oz. bean sprouts, chopped	1 cup chopped bean sprouts
2 spring onions, finely chopped	2 scallions, finely chopped
2 Tbs. soya sauce	2 Tbs. soy sauce
1 Tbs. roasted sesame seeds, ground	1 Tbs. roasted sesame seeds, ground
½ tsp. salt	½ tsp. salt

First make the dumpling dough. Put the flour into a mixing bowl and make a well in the centre. Gradually pour in the water, beating with a wooden spoon until the mixture forms a smooth dough. Turn the dough out on to a lightly floured board and knead for 5 minutes. Return to the bowl, cover with a damp cloth and set aside to 'rest' for 15 minutes while you prepare the filling.

Heat the oil in a frying-pan. When it is hot, add the beef, onion and garlic and fry for 5 minutes, stirring occasionally, or until the beef loses its pinkness. Stir in the mushrooms, bean sprouts, half the spring onions (scallions), soy sauce, sesame seeds and salt and bring to the boil. Cook for 1 minute, stirring frequently, then remove the pan from the heat.

To make the soup, pour the stock and soy sauce into a large saucepan and bring to the boil. Reduce the heat to moderately low and stir in the sesame seeds. Cook for 10 minutes.

Meanwhile, assemble the dumplings. Roll out the dough very thinly, then, using a 7.5cm./3in. pastry cutter, cut into circles. Spoon about 1 tablespoonful of filling on to the lower half of the circle, then fold over to make a semi-circle, pressing the edges firmly together so that the filling is completely enclosed.

Carefully add the dumplings to the soup and continue to cook until they come to the surface. Cook for 2 minutes longer, then transfer the mixture to a warmed tureen or ladle into individual soup bowls. Garnish the soup with the remaining chopped spring onion (scallion) before serving.

Serves 6–8
Preparation and cooking time: 45 minutes

Kitsune Donburi

('Fox' Noodles)

The unusual name of this dish (kitsune is the Japanese word for fox) comes about because, so folklore has it, the fox is very partial to bean curd which, with udon noodles, is the main ingredient of the dish. Udon noodles greatly resemble spaghetti in shape and texture though they are lighter coloured – spaghetti, or even vermicelli or tagliatelle can therefore be substituted if Japanese-style noodles are not available.

Metric/Imperial	American
BEAN CURD	BEAN CURD
175g./6oz. bean curd cakes (tofu), cut into six pieces	6oz. bean curd cakes (tofu), cut into six pieces
125ml./4fl.oz. dashi	$\frac{1}{2}$ cup dashi
75ml./3fl.oz. soya sauce	$\frac{1}{3}$ cup soy sauce
2 Tbs. mirin or sweet sherry	2 Tbs. mirin or sweet sherry
2 Tbs. sugar	2 Tbs. sugar
$\frac{1}{4}$ tsp. monosodium glutamate (optional)	$\frac{1}{4}$ tsp. MSG (optional)
NOODLES	NOODLES
1.2l./2 pints water	5 cups water
1 tsp. salt	1 tsp. salt
225g./8oz. udon	8oz. udon
KAKEJIRU SOUP	KAKEJIRU SOUP
1.2l./2 pints dashi	5 cups dashi
125ml./4fl.oz. soya sauce	$\frac{1}{2}$ cup soy sauce
125ml./4fl.oz. mirin or sweet sherry	$\frac{1}{2}$ cup mirin or sweet sherry
$\frac{1}{2}$ tsp. salt	$\frac{1}{2}$ tsp. salt
$\frac{1}{4}$ tsp. monosodium glutamate	$\frac{1}{4}$ tsp. MSG
2 spring onions, thinly sliced	2 scallions, thinly sliced

To make the bean curd, put the bean curd, dashi, soy sauce, mirin or sherry, sugar and monosodium glutamate into a saucepan and bring to the boil, stirring occasionally. Reduce the heat to low and simmer for 20 to 25 minutes, or until the bean curd has absorbed most of the liquid.

Meanwhile, prepare the noodles. Cook the udon in boiling, salted water for 10 to 12 minutes, or until they are just tender. Drain and return them to the saucepan. Set aside and keep hot.

To make the soup, put the dashi, soy sauce, mirin or sherry, salt, monosodium glutamate and spring onions (scallions) into a second large saucepan. Bring to the boil, reduce the heat to low and simmer the soup for 10 minutes.

To serve, divide the noodles between individual soup bowls. Place some bean curd on top and spoon over any remaining bean curd liquid. Pour over the soup, then serve at once.
Serves 6–8
Preparation and cooking time: 1 hour

Wu-Dung

(Fried Noodles)   (Korea)

Chinese rice noodles would probably be the most authentic type of pasta to use in this dish, but if they are unavailable, egg noodles or vermicelli can be substituted.

Metric/Imperial	American
350g./12oz. rice vermicelli	12oz. rice vermicelli
50ml./2fl.oz. vegetable oil	¼ cup vegetable oil
225g./8oz. rump steak, cut into strips	8oz. rump steak, cut into thin strips
3 spring onions, chopped	3 scallions, chopped
1 garlic clove, crushed	1 garlic clove, crushed
125g./4oz. button mushrooms, sliced	1 cup sliced button mushrooms
125g./4oz. peeled prawns	4oz. peeled shrimp
1 bean curd cake (tofu), chopped	1 bean curd cake (tofu), chopped
2 Tbs. soya sauce	2 Tbs. soy sauce
1 tsp. sugar	1 tsp. sugar
1 Tbs. roasted sesame seeds, ground	1 Tbs. roasted sesame seeds, ground

Cook the vermicelli in boiling, salted water for 5 minutes. Drain and keep warm.

Heat the oil in a large, deep frying-pan. When it is hot, add the steak strips and stir-fry until they lose their pinkness. Add the spring onions (scallions) and garlic to the pan and stir-fry for 2 minutes. Add the mushrooms, prawns (shrimp) and bean curd and stir-fry for a further 2 minutes. Add the soy sauce, sugar and sesame seeds, then stir in the vermicelli. Cook the mixture for a further 2 minutes, or until the vermicelli is heated through.

Transfer the mixture to a warmed serving bowl and serve at once.
Serves 4
Preparation and cooking time: 20 minutes

Hiyashi Somen

(Iced Noodles)

Metric/Imperial	American
450g./1lb. somen or noodles	1lb. somen or noodles
2 hard-boiled eggs, thinly sliced	2 hard-cooked eggs, thinly sliced
2 tomatoes, thinly sliced	2 tomatoes, thinly sliced
⅓ medium cucumber, peeled and cubed	⅓ medium cucumber, peeled and cubed
175g./6oz. lean cooked ham, cubed	1 cup lean cooked ham cubes
4 mint leaves, cut into strips	4 mint leaves, cut into strips

SAUCE	SAUCE
900ml./1½ pints dashi	3¾ cups dashi
150ml.5fl.oz. soya sauce	⅔ cup soy sauce
2 Tbs. sugar	2 Tbs. sugar
150ml./5fl.oz. sake or dry sherry	⅔ cup sake or dry sherry
monosodium glutamate (optional)	MSG (optional)
2 dried mushrooms, soaked in cold water for 30 minutes, drained and chopped	2 dried mushrooms, soaked in cold water for 30 minutes, drained and chopped

Cook the somen or noodles in boiling salted water for 5 minutes, or until they are just tender. Drain and rinse under cold running water. Transfer to a bowl and put into the refrigerator for 30 minutes.

Meanwhile, make the sauce. Put the dashi into a large saucepan and add all the remaining sauce ingredients. Bring to the boil and cook briskly for 8 minutes. Remove from the heat and set aside to cool.

Arrange the eggs, tomatoes, cucumber and ham decoratively on a large serving platter and sprinkle over the mint strips.

To serve, put the somen noodles over a bed of ice cubes, or sprinkle them with ice chips. Pour the sauce mixture into individual serving bowls. Traditionally, each guest helps himself to a portion of each dish, dipping the noodles into the sauce before eating.

Serves 6
Preparation and cooking time: 1¼ hours

Buta Udon

(Noodles with Pork)

Metric/Imperial	American
1.2l./2 pints dashi	5 cups dashi
275g./10oz. lean pork meat, cut into thin strips	10oz. lean pork meat, cut into thin strips
2 leeks, cleaned and cut into 2½cm./1in. lengths	2 leeks, cleaned and cut into 1in. lengths
150ml./5fl.oz. soya sauce	⅔ cup soy sauce
1½ Tbs. sugar	1½ Tbs. sugar
½ tsp. monosodium glutamate (optional)	½ tsp. MSG (optional)
salt	salt
350g./12oz. udon or spaghetti	12oz. udon or spaghetti
2 spring onions, finely chopped	2 scallions, finely chopped
paprika or hichimi togarashi	paprika or hichimi togarashi

Pour the dashi into a large saucepan and bring to the boil. Add the pork strips and leeks and cook the meat for 5 to 8 minutes, or until they are cooked through. Remove the pan from the heat and stir in the soy sauce, sugar and monosodium glutamate. Keep hot.

Meanwhile, cook the noodles in boiling salted water for 5 to 12 minutes, or until they are just tender. Drain and stir them into the soup. Return to moderate heat and bring to the boil.

To serve, divide the soup among 4 to 6 serving bowls and garnish with spring onions (scallions) and paprika or hichimi togarashi to taste.

Serve at once.

Serves 4–6
Preparation and cooking time: 30 minutes

RICE

Gohan

(Plain Boiled Rice, Japanese Style)

Short-grain rice is the closest Western equivalent to Japanese rice and has therefore been suggested here; long-grain can, of course, be substituted, but the texture will be a little different. The proportion of water to rice is always vital in rice cooking but it does tend to vary a little according to the age and quality of the rice grains. The amounts given below, therefore, are approximate and should be taken as a guide only. The finished product should be white, shiny, soft and moist; never wet and sticky.

Metric/Imperial	American
450g./1lb. short-grain rice	2⅔ cups short-grain rice
600ml./1 pint water	2½ cups water

Wash the rice to remove the starch, under cold running water. Alternatively, put the rice into a bowl, add water and stir and drain. Repeat two or three times until the water is almost clear.

Put the rice into a large, heavy saucepan and pour over the water. Bring to the boil, cover the pan and reduce the heat to low. Simmer for 15 to 20 minutes, or until the rice is cooked and the liquid absorbed. Reduce the heat to an absolute minimum and leave for 15 minutes. Turn off the heat but leave the saucepan on the burner for a further 10 minutes.

Transfer to a warmed serving bowl. The rice is now ready to serve.

Serves 4-6
Preparation and cooking time: 1 hour

Kuri Gohan

(Chestnut Rice)

Metric/Imperial	American
450g./1lb. short-grain rice	2⅔ cups short-grain rice
½kg./1lb. chestnuts	2⅔ cups chestnuts
900ml./1½ pints water	3¾ cups water
1½ Tbs. sake or dry sherry	1½ Tbs. sake or dry sherry
1 tsp. salt	1 tsp. salt

Wash the rice, then soak it for 1 hour.

Meanwhile, put the chestnuts into a saucepan and pour over the water. Bring to the boil, then parboil for 15 minutes. Drain and remove the skins from the chestnuts. Quarter them if they are large; keep them whole if they are not.

Add the chestnuts, sake or sherry and salt to the drained rice and cook, following the instructions given in *Gohan*.

Serve at once.

Serves 4-6
Preparation and cooking time: 1¾ hours
Note: You can cheat on this recipe by substituting a 450g./1lb. can of whole chestnuts for the fresh chestnuts above. In this case, the parboiling can be omitted and the chestnuts should be added straight to the rice.

Maze Gohan

(Mixed Vegetables and Rice)

Metric/Imperial	American
1 large dried mushroom, soaked in cold water for 30 minutes, drained and finely chopped	1 large dried mushroom, soaked in cold water for 30 minutes, drained and finely chopped
2 carrots, sliced	2 carrots, sliced
2½cm./1in. piece of fresh root ginger, peeled and chopped	1in. piece of fresh green ginger, peeled and chopped
12 tinned ginko nuts, drained	12 canned ginko nuts, drained
2 celery stalks, chopped	2 celery stalks, chopped
2 Tbs. soya sauce	2 Tbs. soy sauce
1 Tbs. sake or dry sherry	1 Tbs. sake or dry sherry
½ tsp. salt	½ tsp. salt
700g./1½lb. short-grain rice, soaked in cold water for 1 hour and drained	4 cups short-grain rice, soaked in cold water for 1 hour and drained
900ml./1½ pints water	3¾ cups water
125g./4oz. green peas, weighed after shelling	½ cup green peas, weighed after shelling
125g./4oz. shelled shrimps	½ cup shelled shrimp

Maze Gohan is a superb mixture of rice, peas, carrots, peas and shrimps, delicately flavoured with ginger, sake and ginko nuts.

Put the mushroom, carrots, ginger, ginko nuts, celery, soy sauce, sake, salt and rice into a large, heavy saucepan. Pour over the water and bring to the boil. Cover the pan, reduce the heat to low and simmer the rice for 15 to 20 minutes, or until it is cooked and the water absorbed.

Stir in the peas and shrimps and simmer for a further 10 minutes. (If the mixture becomes a little dry during this period add a tablespoonful or two of water.)

Transfer to a warmed serving dish and serve at once.

Serves 4
Preparation and cooking time: 1½ hours

Song i Pahb

(Rice and Mushrooms)   (Korea)

Metric/Imperial	American
1 Tbs. sesame oil	1 Tbs. sesame oil
4 spring onions, chopped	4 scallions, chopped
225g./8oz. mushrooms, thinly sliced	2 cups thinly sliced mushrooms
175g./6oz. lean cooked meat, very finely chopped	1 cup very finely chopped lean cooked meat
2 Tbs. soya sauce	2 Tbs. soy sauce
2 tsp. roasted sesame seeds, ground	2 tsp. roasted sesame seeds, ground
salt and pepper	salt and pepper
350g./12oz. long-grain rice, soaked in cold water for 30 minutes and drained	2 cups long-grain rice, soaked in cold water for 30 minutes and drained
725ml./1¼ pints water	3 cups water

Heat the oil in a large frying-pan. When it is hot, stir in the spring onions (scallions), mushrooms, meat, soy sauce, sesame seeds and salt and pepper, and cook for 3 minutes, stirring constantly. Stir the mixture into the rice and transfer to a saucepan. Pour over the water and bring to the boil. Cover, reduce the heat to very low and simmer for 30 minutes, or until the rice is very dry and fluffy and the liquid completely absorbed; do not remove the lid during the cooking period.
Serves 4-6
Preparation and cooking time: 1 hour

Katsudon

(Pork Cutlets with Rice)

Metric/Imperial	American
450g./1lb. short-grain rice	2⅔ cups short-grain rice
600ml./1 pint water	2½ cups water
575g./1¼lb. pork fillet, cut into 4 cutlets	1¼lb. pork tenderloin, cut into 4 cutlets
4 eggs, lightly beaten	4 eggs, lightly beaten
50g./2oz. flour	½ cup flour
75g./3oz. dry breadcrumbs	1 cup dry breadcrumbs
vegetable oil for deep-frying	vegetable oil for deep-frying
650ml./1¼ pints dashi	3 cups dashi
150ml./5fl.oz. soya sauce	⅔ cup soy sauce
1½ Tbs. mirin or sweet sherry	1½ Tbs. mirin or sweet sherry
2 medium onions, thinly sliced into rings	2 medium onions, thinly sliced into rings

Cook the rice, following the instructions given in *Gohan*.

Meanwhile, coat the pork cutlets first in half the eggs, then in the flour and finally in the breadcrumbs, coating thoroughly and shaking off any excess.

Fill a large saucepan one-third full with oil and heat until it is very hot. Carefully lower the cutlets, two at a time, into the oil and fry until they are golden brown. Drain on kitchen towels. Set aside and keep hot.

Put the dashi, soy sauce and mirin into a pan and bring to the boil. Reduce the heat to low, add the onion rings and simmer for 10 minutes, or until the rings are soft. When the pork is cool enough to handle, slice into thin strips and add to the saucepan with the onion rings. Pour in the remaining beaten egg and simmer the mixture gently for 3 minutes. Remove from the heat.

Transfer the cooked rice into individual serving bowls. Top with the egg, onion and pork mixture and pour over any remaining liquid from the pan. Serve at once.
Serves 4
Preparation and cooking time: 50 minutes

Tendon

(Tempura with rice)

The 'tempura' offerings in Tendon always include fish and/or seafood but other than this, can be tailored to suit your taste and purse! The items listed below are therefore suggestions rather than ethnically essential.

Metric/Imperial	American
450g./1lb. short-grain rice	2⅔ cups short-grain rice
600ml./1 pint water	2½ cups water
TEMPURA	TEMPURA
4 large Dublin Bay prawns, shelled	4 large Gulf shrimp, shelled
3 small plaice fillets, quartered	3 small flounder fillets, quartered
1 red pepper, pith and seeds removed and cut into squares	1 red pepper, pith and seeds removed and cut into squares
6 button mushrooms	6 button mushrooms
50g./2oz. flour	½ cup flour
75ml./3fl.oz. water	⅓ cup water
1 small egg, lightly beaten	1 small egg, lightly beaten
vegetable oil for deep-frying	vegetable oil for deep-frying
SAUCE	SAUCE
175ml./6fl.oz. dashi	¾ cup dashi
3 Tbs. sake or dry sherry	3 Tbs. sake or dry sherry
3 Tbs. soya sauce	3 Tbs. soy sauce
½ tsp. sugar	½ tsp. sugar
monosodium glutamate (optional)	MSG (optional)
1cm./½in. piece of fresh root ginger, peeled and grated	½in. piece of fresh green ginger, peeled and grated
2 spring onions, chopped (to garnish)	2 scallions, chopped (to garnish)

Cook the rice, following the instructions given in *Gohan*.

Meanwhile, prepare the tempura. Arrange the seafood and vegetables on a platter. Beat the flour, water and egg together to make a light, thin batter, then dip the seafood and vegetable pieces into it to coat them thoroughly. Set aside.

Fill a large deep-frying pan about one-third full of vegetable oil and heat it until it is very hot. Carefully lower the seafood and vegetable pieces into the oil, a few at a time, and fry until they are crisp and golden brown. Using a slotted spoon, transfer the pieces to kitchen towels to drain, then keep hot while you prepare the sauce.

Put the dashi, sake or dry sherry, soy sauce, sugar and monosodium glutamate to taste into a saucepan and gently bring to the boil, stirring until the sugar has dissolved. Stir in the grated ginger and remove from the heat.

To serve, transfer the rice to a warmed serving bowl and arrange the tempura pieces decoratively over the top. Pour over the sauce and garnish with the chopped spring onions (scallions) before serving.
Serves 4-6
Preparation and cooking time: 1 hour

(See previous page) *The translation of Mi-Iro Gohan is 'three-coloured rice'—so called because of the pretty pattern made by the three main ingredients, the rice, minced (ground) beef and green peas.*

Mi-Iro Gohan

(Three-Coloured Rice)

Metric/Imperial	American
450g./1lb. short-grain rice	2⅔ cups short-grain rice
225g./8oz. green peas, weighed after shelling	1 cup green peas, weighed after shelling
MEAT	MEAT
275g./10oz. minced beef	10oz. ground beef
3 Tbs. soya sauce	3 Tbs. soy sauce
1 tsp. salt	1 tsp. salt
3 Tbs. sugar	3 Tbs. sugar
150ml./5fl.oz. dashi	⅔ cup dashi
4 Tbs. sake or dry sherry	4 Tbs. sake or dry sherry
EGGS	EGGS
5 eggs, lightly beaten	5 eggs, lightly beaten
1 Tbs. sugar	1 Tbs. sugar
1 Tbs. vegetable oil	1 Tbs. vegetable oil
¼ tsp. salt	¼ tsp. salt

Cook the rice, following the instructions given in *Gohan*.

Meanwhile, prepare the meat. Combine all the meat ingredients in a small saucepan and set over moderate heat. Cook, stirring constantly, until the meat loses its pinkness and is broken up into small grains. Cook for a further 5 minutes, or until the meat is cooked through. Remove from the heat and keep hot.

Beat all the egg ingredients together and put into a small saucepan. Set over low heat and cook, stirring constantly, until the eggs scramble and become dry. Remove from the heat and keep hot.

Cook the peas in boiling salted water for 5 minutes, or until they are just cooked. Remove from the heat, drain and set aside.

To assemble, fill individual serving bowls with rice. Level the top and arrange the meat mixture, egg mixture and peas decoratively on top, in three sections. Pour over any juices from the meat bowl and serve at once.
Serves 4-6
Preparation and cooking time: 1 hour

Iwashi no Kabayaki

(Sardines with Rice)

Metric/Imperial	American
450g./1lb. short-grain rice, soaked in cold water for 1 hour and drained	2⅔ cups short-grain rice, soaked in cold water for 1 hour and drained
12 sardines, cleaned, gutted and with the head removed	12 sardines, cleaned, gutted and with the head removed
3 Tbs. soya sauce	3 Tbs. soy sauce
4cm./1½in. piece of fresh root ginger, peeled and grated	1½in. piece of fresh green ginger, peeled and grated
50g./2oz. cornflour	½ cup cornstarch
50ml./2fl.oz. vegetable oil	¼ cup vegetable oil
225g./8oz. cooked green peas, weighed after shelling	1 cup cooked green peas, weighed after shelling

SAUCE	SAUCE
150ml./5fl.oz. soya sauce	⅔ cup soy sauce
4 Tbs. mirin or sweet sherry	4 Tbs. mirin or sweet sherry
2 Tbs. sugar	2 Tbs. sugar
3 Tbs. water	3 Tbs. water
monosodium glutamate (optional)	MSG (optional)
2 tsp. miso paste	2 tsp. miso paste

Cook the rice, following the instructions given in *Gohan*.

Meanwhile, remove the main bones from the sardines and splay open. Wash in lightly salted water then transfer to a shallow dish. Pour over the soy sauce and ginger and set aside at room temperature for 20 minutes, turning the fish from time to time. Remove the fish from the marinade and pat dry with kitchen towels.

Dip the fish in the cornflour (cornstarch), shaking off any excess. Heat the oil in a large frying-pan. When it is hot, add the sardines, in batches, and fry for 6 to 8 minutes or until they are golden and the flesh flakes.

Meanwhile, combine all the sauce ingredients, except the miso paste, and bring to the boil. Stir in the miso paste and continue cooking until it melts. Remove from the heat.

Pour off the oil from the sardines and add the sauce mixture. Bring to the boil then remove from the heat.

When the rice is cooked, arrange in deep serving bowls and top with the sardines. Pour over the soy sauce mixture and garnish with cooked green peas. Serve at once.

Serves 4
Preparation and cooking time: 1¾ hours

Nigiri Zushi

(Rice and Fish 'Sandwiches')

Metric/Imperial	American
700g./1½lb. short-grain rice	4 cups short-grain rice
8 large prawns, in the shell	8 large shrimp, in the shell
1 lemon sole fillet, skinned	1 lemon sole fillet, skinned
1 mackerel fillet, skinned	1 mackerel fillet, skinned
40g./1½oz. smoked salmon	⅙ cup smoked salmon
1 medium squid, cleaned, skinned and boned	1 medium squid, cleaned, skinned and boned
3 tsp. green horseraish (wasabi), mixed to a paste with 1 Tbs. water	3 tsp. green horseradish (wasabi), mixed to a paste with 1 Tbs. water
parsley or mint	parsley or mint
350ml./12fl.oz. soy sauce	1½ cups soy sauce
VINEGAR SAUCE	VINEGAR SAUCE
125ml./4fl.oz. white wine vinegar	½ cup white wine vinegar
1½ Tbs. sugar	1½ Tbs. sugar
1½ tsp. salt	1½ tsp. salt
monosodium glutamate (optional)	MSG (optional)

Cook the rice, following the instructions given in *Gohan*. Transfer the drained rice to a warmed bowl and set aside. To make the vinegar sauce, combine the vinegar, sugar, salt and monosodium glutamate to taste, then pour the mixture over the rice. Stir gently with a wooden spoon and set aside to cool at room temperature.

Cook the prawns (shrimp) in boiling water until they turn pink. Drain and

remove the shell and heads. Gently cut along the underside of the prawns (shrimp) and splay them open. Set aside. Sprinkle the sole with salt, then neatly cut the flesh into rectangles about 5cm by 2½cm./2in. by 1in. and just under 1cm./½in. thick. Cut the mackerel, smoked salmon and boned squid into pieces about the same size as the sole.

Using the palm of your hand, gently shape about 1 tablespoon of the rice mixture into a wedge, about the size of your thumb. Smear a small amount of horseradish paste on to the middle of one piece of fish and press the fish and rice gently together to form a 'sandwich', with the horseradish in the centre. Continue this procedure, using up the remaining fish pieces and the remaining rice, but omitting the horseradish mixture for the prawns (shrimp). (You will probably find that the rice will stick to your hands slightly, so rinse them regularly in a bowl of water to which a dash of vinegar has been added.)

When the 'sandwiches' have been made, arrange them decoratively on a large flat dish and garnish with parsley or mint. Pour the soy sauce into individual small dipping bowls, and dip the 'sandwiches' into the soy sauce before eating. This is usually served as a snack or hors d'oeuvre in Japan.

Serves 6-8
Preparation and cooking time: 1 hour

Sashimi Gohan

(Prepared Fish and Rice)

Metric/Imperial	American
1 large mackerel, cleaned, gutted, then filleted	1 large mackerel, cleaned, gutted, then filleted
1 tsp. salt	1 tsp. salt
450ml./15fl.oz. white wine vinegar	2 cups white wine vinegar
350g./12oz. short-grain rice, soaked in cold water for 1 hour and drained	2 cups short-grain rice, soaked in cold water for 1 hour and drained
600ml./1 pint water	2½ cups water
GARNISH	GARNISH
4cm./1½in. piece of fresh root ginger, peeled and grated	1½in. piece of fresh green ginger, peeled and grated
5 spring onions, finely chopped	5 scallions, finely chopped
350ml./12fl.oz. soya sauce	1½ cups soy sauce
2 tsp. green horseradish (wasabi), mixed to a paste with 2 tsp. water	2 tsp. green horseradish (wasabi), mixed to a paste with 2 tsp. water

Sprinkle the mackerel fillets with salt and put into the refrigerator to chill for 1 hour. Remove from the refrigerator and soak in the vinegar for a further 1 hour.

Meanwhile, put the rice into a saucepan and cover with the water. Bring to the boil, reduce the heat to low and cover the pan. Simmer for 15 to 20 minutes, or until the rice is cooked and the water absorbed. Remove from the heat and transfer to a warmed serving bowl. Set aside and keep hot.

Remove the fish from the vinegar and pat dry with kitchen towels. Cut vertically into 1cm./½in. pieces, removing any bones. Arrange the fish decoratively on a serving dish and surround with the grated ginger and spring onions (scallions). Pour the soy sauce into small, individual dipping bowls and serve individual portions of the horseradish mixture.

To eat, mix horseradish to taste into the soy sauce and dip the mackerel pieces into the sauce before eating with the rice.

Serves 4
Preparation and cooking time: 2½ hours

Sashimi Gohan (Sliced Raw Fish with Rice) is so popular in Japan that there are restuarants devoted exclusively to preparing it. This version is simplicity itself, and the result is guaranteed to make a convert of even the most doubtful eater of uncooked fish!

255

Seki Han

(Red Cooked Rice)

This special festival dish is most authentic when the small red Japanese azuki beans are used. They can be obtained from many health food stores and oriental delicatessens. However, if they are not available, dried red kidney beans can be substituted successfully.

Metric/Imperial	American
275g./10oz. dried azuki beans, soaked overnight in cold water	1½ cups dried azuki beans, soaked overnight in cold water
350g./12oz. short-grain rice	2 cups short-grain rice
1 tsp. salt	1 tsp. salt
2 Tbs. sake or dry sherry	2 Tbs. sake or dry sherry
1 Tbs. soya sauce	1 Tbs. soy sauce

Put the beans and their soaking liquid into a saucepan and bring to the boil (top up with water if necessary, so that the beans are completely covered). Cover the pan, reduce the heat to low and cook the beans for 1 hour, or until they are just tender. Remove the pan from the heat and drain and reserve the bean cooking liquid. Transfer the beans to a bowl and set aside and keep hot.

Cook the rice, following the instructions given in *Gohan*, except that instead of using all water to cook the rice, use the bean cooking liquid and make up any extra liquid needed with water.

About 5 minutes before the rice is ready to serve, stir in the reserved beans, the salt, sake or sherry and soy sauce and cook until they are all heated through.

Transfer the mixture to a warmed serving bowl and serve at once.
Serves 3-4
Preparation and cooking time: 14 hours

Nori Maki

(Rice Rolls Wrapped in Seaweed)

Metric/Imperial	American
900g./2lb. short-grain rice	5⅓ cups short-grain rice
1.2l./2 pints water	5 cups water
¼ large mackerel, filleted	¼ large mackerel, filleted
150ml./5fl.oz. white wine vinegar	⅔ cup white wine vinegar
1 Tbs. kanpyo, soaked in cold salted water for 1 hour and drained	1 Tbs. kanpyo, soaked in cold salted water for 1 hour and drained
1 Tbs. soya sauce	1 Tbs. soy sauce
50ml./2fl.oz. water	¼ cup water
2 tsp. sugar	2 tsp. sugar
½ cucumber	½ cucumber
125g./4oz. fresh tuna fish	4oz. fresh tuna fish
4 sheets of nori (seaweed)	4 sheets of nori (seaweed)
3 tsp. green horseradish (wasabi), mixed to a paste with 1 Tbs. water	3 tsp. green horseradish (wasabi), mixed to a paste with 1 Tbs. water
350ml./12fl.oz. soya sauce	1½ cups soy sauce

VINEGAR SAUCE	VINEGAR SAUCE
125ml./4fl.oz. white wine vinegar	½ cup white wine vinegar
1½ Tbs. sugar	1½ Tbs. sugar
1½ tsp. salt	1½ tsp. salt
monosodium glutamate (optional)	MSG (optional)

Cook the rice, following the instructions given in *Gohan*. Transfer the drained rice to a warmed bowl and set aside. To make the vinegar sauce, combine the vinegar, sugar, salt and monosodium glutamate to taste, then pour the mixture over the rice. Stir gently with a wooden spoon and set aside to cool at room temperature.

Meanwhile, soak the mackerel in the vinegar for 1 hour. Put the kanpyo into a saucepan and just cover with water. Bring to the boil and cook briskly until it is just tender. Drain then return the kanpyo to the saucepan and add the soy sauce, water, and sugar. Cook over moderate heat for 10 minutes, to ensure that the flavours are absorbed into the kanpyo. Set aside.

Remove the mackerel from the vinegar and pat dry on kitchen towels. Cut the flesh vertically into long strips. Slice the cucumber and tuna fish into long thin strips, about the same length as the nori. Set aside.

Preheat the grill (broiler) to moderately high. Place the nori sheets on the rack and grill (broil) until it is crisp on one side. Remove from the heat and cut each sheet into half.

Place one half nori sheet on a flexible bamboo mat or heavy cloth napkin. Spread a handful of sushi rice over the top of the nori, to within about 5cm./2in. of all the edges. Smear a little horseradish over the sushi. Arrange two or three strands of mackerel across the centre of the rice and roll up the mat or napkin gently but firmly so that the mixture will stick together and form a long cylinder. Remove the mat and, in the same way, make cylinders of the remaining nori, sushi rice and fish. Omit the horseradish from the kanpyo mixture.

When all the cylinders have been formed, gently slice across them to form sections about 2½cm./1in. wide.

Pour the soy sauce into small individual dipping bowls and dip the nori sections into the sauce before eating.

Serve the nori maki either on its own as an hors d'oeuvre or as a light snack, or with nigiri zushi as a light meal.

Serves 8
Preparation and cooking time: 2½ hours

Chirashi Zushi

(Rice Salad with Fish)

Metric/Imperial	American
125g./4oz. French beans, sliced	⅔ cup sliced green beans
2 sheets of nori (seaweed)	2 sheets of nori (seaweed)
sprinkling of shredded ginger	sprinkling of shredded ginger
MACKEREL	MACKEREL
1 small mackerel, filleted	1 small mackerel, filleted
1 Tbs. salt	1 Tbs. salt
450ml./15fl.oz. white wine vinegar	2 cups white wine vinegar
RICE	RICE
450g./1lb. short-grain rice, soaked in cold water for 1 hour and drained	2⅔ cups short-grain rice, soaked in cold water for 1 hour and drained

75ml./3fl.oz. white wine vinegar	⅓ cup white wine vinegar
1½ Tbs. sugar	1½ Tbs. sugar
1 Tbs. salt	1 Tbs. salt
KANPYO	KANPYO
handful of kanpyo, soaked in cold, salted water for 1 hour and drained	handful of kanpyo, soaked in cold, salted water for 1 hour and drained
3 Tbs. soya sauce	3 Tbs. soy sauce
2 Tbs. sugar	2 Tbs. sugar
250ml./8fl.oz. water	1 cup water
MUSHROOMS	MUSHROOMS
5 dried mushrooms, soaked in 450ml./ 15fl.oz. cold water for 30 minutes, stalks removed and caps sliced	5 dried mushrooms, soaked in 2 cups cold water for 30 minutes, stalks removed and caps sliced
1½ Tbs. soya sauce	1½ Tbs. soy sauce
3 Tbs. sugar	3 Tbs. sugar
1½ Tbs. sake or dry sherry	1½ Tbs. sake or dry sherry
½ tsp. salt	½ tsp. salt
CARROTS	CARROTS
1 large carrot, sliced	1 large carrot, sliced
2 tsp. sugar	2 tsp. sugar
¼ tsp. salt	¼ tsp. salt
EGGS	EGGS
3 eggs, lightly beaten	3 eggs, lightly beaten
few drops soya sauce	few drops soy sauce
½ tsp. salt	½ tsp. salt
½ Tbs. vegetable oil	2 Tbs. vegetable oil

Sprinkle the mackerel fillets with salt and put into the refrigerator to chill for 1 hour. Remove from the refrigerator and soak in the vinegar for a further 1 hour.

Cook the rice, following the instructions given in *Gohan*. Transfer the drained rice to a warm bowl and set aside. To make the vinegar sauce, combine the vinegar, sugar and salt, then pour the mixture over the rice. Stir gently with a wooden spoon and set aside to cool at room temperature.

Put the kanpyo into a saucepan and just cover with water. Bring to the boil and cook briskly until it is just tender. Drain, then return to the saucepan with the soy sauce, sugar and water. Cook over moderate heat for 10 minutes, to ensure that the flavours are absorbed into the kanpyo. Set aside.

Reserve the mushroom draining liquid and add to a small saucepan with the soy sauce, sugar, sake or sherry and salt. Stir in the mushroom pieces and bring to the boil. Cook over moderate heat for 15 minutes, then transfer the mushrooms to a plate with a slotted spoon. Add the carrots to the saucepan, with the sugar and salt. Reduce the heat to low and simmer until all of the sauce has evaporated. Remove from the heat and set aside.

Beat the eggs, soy sauce and salt together. Heat a little of the oil in a small frying-pan. When it is hot, add some of the egg mixture and fry until it forms a wafer-thin pancake. Using a spatula, carefully remove from the pan. Continue to cook the egg mixture in this way until it is all used up. When all the pancakes are cooked, roll them up together and slice them into thin strips. Set aside.

Cook the beans in boiling salted water for 5 minutes, or until they are just tender. Drain and set aside.

Remove the mackerel fillets from the vinegar and pat dry on kitchen towels. Cut vertically into thin strips and set aside.

Preheat the grill (broiler) to moderately high. Place the nori sheets on the rack and grill (broil) until crisp on both sides. Remove from the heat and set aside.

To assemble, arrange the rice in a large serving bowl. Combine the mushrooms, carrots and kanpyo and stir gently into the rice. Arrange the beans, eggs and sliced mackerel on top and sprinkle over the ginger. Crumble over the nori and serve at once.

Serves 4-6

Preparation and cooking time: 2¾ hours

Zushi rice (rice mixed with vinegar and sugar) forms the basis of Chirashi Zushi. It is garnished with nori, a type of seaweed popular in Japan.

Oyako Donburi

(Chicken and Eggs with Rice)

Metric/Imperial	American
450g./1lb. short-grain rice, soaked in cold water for 1 hour and drained	2⅔ cups short-grain rice, soaked in cold water for 1 hour and drained
3 Tbs. vegetable oil	3 Tbs. vegetable oil
2 small chicken breasts, skinned, boned and cut into thin strips	2 small chicken breasts, skinned, boned and cut into thin strips
2 medium onions, thinly sliced	2 medium onions, thinly sliced
4 eggs, lightly beaten	4 eggs, lightly beaten
2 sheets of nori (seaweed)	2 sheets of nori (seaweed)
SAUCE	SAUCE
4 Tbs. water	4 Tbs. water
4 Tbs. soya sauce	4 Tbs. soy sauce
4 Tbs. dashi	4 Tbs. dashi

Cook the rice, following the instructions given in *Gohan*.

Meanwhile, heat the oil in a frying-pan. When it is hot, add the chicken pieces and fry until they are just cooked through. Remove from the heat and, using a slotted spoon, transfer to a plate.

Combine the sauce ingredients together.

Put about a quarter of the sauce mixture into a small frying-pan and bring to the boil. Add about a quarter of the onions and fry briskly for 3 minutes. Add quarter of the chicken slices and quarter of the eggs. Reduce the heat to low and stir once. Leave until the egg has set then cover the pan and steam for 1 minute.

Spoon about a quarter of the rice into an individual serving bowl and top with the egg mixture. Repeat this process three more times, using up the remaining ingredients.

Meanwhile, preheat the grill (broiler) to moderately high. Place the nori on the rack of the grill (broiler) pan and grill (broil) until it is crisp. Remove from the heat and crumble over the rice and egg mixture. Serve at once.

Serves 4
Preparation and cooking time: 1¾ hours

Oboro

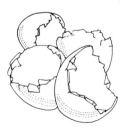

(Chicken and Rice)

Metric/Imperial	American
450g./1lb. short-grain rice	2⅔ cups short-grain rice
6 dried mushrooms, soaked in cold water for 30 minutes and drained	6 dried mushrooms, soaked in cold water for 30 minutes and drained
75ml./3fl.oz. soya sauce	⅓ cup soy sauce
75ml./3fl.oz. sake or dry sherry	⅓ cup sake or dry sherry
1 tsp. sugar	1 tsp. sugar
2 chicken breasts, skinned, boned and cut into strips	2 chicken breasts, skinned, boned and cut into strips
225./8oz. frozen green peas	1 cup frozen green peas
50ml./2fl.oz. vegetable oil	¼ cup vegetable oil
2 eggs, beaten	2 eggs, beaten

Cook the rice, following the instructions given in *Gohan*.

Remove the stalks from the mushrooms and cook the caps in boiling water for 5 minutes, drain then cut into slices. Set aside.

Put the soy sauce, sake or sherry and sugar into a large saucepan and bring to the boil, stirring constantly until the sugar has dissolved. Add the chicken strips and peas to the pan and reduce the heat to low. Cover and simmer for 5 minutes, or until the chicken strips are cooked. Remove from the heat and set aside.

Heat the oil in a small frying-pan. When it is hot, add the eggs and cook for 2 minutes, or until the bottom has set and is browned. Turn over the omelet and cook for 2 minutes on the other side. Slide the omelet on to a plate and cut into strips. Set aside.

When the rice is cooked, transfer it to a warmed serving bowl. Arrange the chicken strips and peas on top and pour over the chicken cooking liquid. Scatter over the mushrooms and omelet strips and serve at once.

Serves 4–6
Preparation and cooking time: 1 hour

Gyu Donburi

(Beef on Rice)

Metric/Imperial	American
450g./1lb. short-grain rice, soaked in cold water for 1 hour and drained	2⅔ cups short-grain rice, soaked in cold water for 1 hour and drained
175ml./6fl.oz. soya sauce	¾ cup soy sauce
175ml./6fl.oz. dashi	¾ cup dashi
3 Tbs. sugar	3 Tbs. sugar
½kg./1lb. rump steak, thinly sliced	1lb. rump steak, thinly sliced
50ml./2fl.oz. vegetable oil	¼ cup vegetable oil
2 green peppers, pith and seeds removed and cut into bite-sized pieces	2 green peppers, pith and seeds removed and cut into bite-sized pieces
½kg./1lb. leeks, cleaned and cut diagonally into 1cm./½in. lengths	1lb. leeks, cleaned and cut diagonally into ½in. lengths
4cm./1½in. piece of fresh root ginger, peeled and grated	1½in. piece of fresh green ginger, peeled and grated

Cook the rice, following the instructions given in *Gohan*.

Meanwhile, combine the soy sauce, dashi and sugar together in a large shallow dish. Add the beef slices and set aside to marinate at room temperature for 15 minutes, basting occasionally. Remove from the marinade and pat dry with kitchen towels. Reserve the marinade.

Heat half the oil in a large frying-pan. When it is hot, add the beef slices and cook for 2 minutes on each side. Reduce the heat to moderately low and cook for a further 2 minutes on each side. Stir in the reserved marinade and remove from the heat. Keep hot.

Heat the remaining oil in a second frying-pan. When it is hot, add the peppers and leeks and fry gently for 8 to 10 minutes, or until they are just cooked. Remove from the heat and set aside.

When the rice is cooked, transfer it to individual serving bowls. Either cut the beef into thin strips or serve it as it is. Arrange the peppers and leeks and beef to make three sections on top of the rice. Pour over the meat cooking juices and sprinkle with grated ginger.

Serve at once.

Serves 4
Preparation and cooking time: 1 hour

MEAT & POULTRY

Kushi Dango

(Meatballs)

Metric/Imperial	American
575g./1¼lb. minced beef	1¼lb. ground beef
4 spring onions, finely chopped	4 scallions, finely chopped
4cm./1½in. piece of fresh root ginger, peeled and grated	1½in. piece of fresh green ginger, peeled and grated
3 Tbs. flour	3 Tbs. flour
1 Tbs. soya sauce	1 Tbs. soy sauce
3 eggs, lightly beaten	3 eggs, lightly beaten
monosodium glutamate (optional)	MSG (optional)
vegetable oil for deep-frying	vegetable oil for deep-frying

Combine the beef, spring onions (scallions), ginger, flour, soy sauce, eggs and monosodium glutamate to taste in a large bowl. Using the palm of your hands, gently shape the mixture into small balls, about 2½cm./1in. in diameter.

Fill a large deep-frying pan about one-third full with vegetable oil and heat it until it is very hot. Carefully lower the meatballs, a few at a time, into the hot oil and fry until they are golden brown. Using a slotted spoon, remove the meatballs from the pan and drain on kitchen towels. Keep hot while you fry the remaining meatballs in the same way.

To serve, thread three or four meatballs each on to short skewers and serve as an hors d'oeuvre.
Serves 4–6
Preparation and cooking time : 40 minutes

San Juhk

(Beef Kebabs)   (Korea)

Metric/Imperial	American
½kg./1lb. rump steak, cut into 5cm./2in. strips	1lb. rump steak, cut into 2in. strips
1 green pepper, pith and seeds removed and cut into strips	1 green pepper, pith and seeds removed and cut into strips
4 spring onions, cut into 2½cm./1in. lengths	4 scallions, cut into 1in. lengths
2 eggs, beaten	2 eggs, beaten
50g./2oz. flour	½ cup flour
125ml./4fl.oz. vegetable oil	½ cup vegetable oil
MARINADE	MARINADE
2 Tbs. soya sauce	2 Tbs. soy sauce
1 Tbs. sesame oil	1 Tbs. sesame oil
1 garlic clove, crushed	1 garlic clove, crushed
1 tsp. sugar	1 tsp. sugar
1 Tbs. roasted sesame seeds, ground	1 Tbs. roasted sesame seeds, ground

First, make the marinade. Put the soy sauce, sesame oil, garlic clove, sugar and half the ground sesame seeds into a large, shallow bowl. Add the beef strips to the bowl and turn to baste thoroughly. Set aside at room temperature for 30 minutes. Remove the strips from the bowl and pat dry with kitchen towels. Discard the marinade.

Thread the beef on to skewers, alternating them with the pepper and spring onion (scallion) pieces. Carefully dip the skewers into the beaten eggs, then coat in the flour, shaking off any excess.

Heat the oil in a large frying-pan. When it is hot, carefully arrange the skewers in the pan. Fry, turning the skewers occasionally, for 8 to 10 minutes, or until the beef is brown and crisp. Remove from the heat and drain on kitchen towels.

Transfer the skewers to a warmed serving dish, sprinkle over the remaining sesame seeds and serve at once.
Serves 4
Preparation and cooking time: 1 hour

Gyuniku no Amiyaki

(Steak Marinated in Sesame)

Metric/Imperial	American
4 x 225g./8oz. rump steaks	4 x 8oz. rump steaks
MARINADE	MARINADE
1½ Tbs. sesame seeds	1½ Tbs. sesame seeds
1 garlic clove, crushed	1 garlic clove, crushed
1½ Tbs. soya sauce	1½ Tbs. soy sauce
1 Tbs. sake or dry sherry	1 Tbs. sake or dry sherry
1 tsp. sugar	1 tsp. sugar
DIPPING SAUCE	DIPPING SAUCE
2 spring onions, finely chopped	2 scallions, finely chopped
4cm./1½in. piece of fresh root ginger, peeled and grated	1½in. piece of fresh green ginger, peeled and grated
½ tsp. paprika or hichimi togarashi	½ tsp. paprika or hichimi togarashi
150ml./5fl.oz. soya sauce	⅔ cup soy sauce
2 Tbs. dashi	2 Tbs. dashi

First make the marinade. Fry the sesame seeds gently in a small frying-pan until they begin to 'pop'. Transfer them to a mortar and crush with a pestle to release the oil. Put the crushed seeds into a large shallow bowl and mix thoroughly with all the remaining marinade ingredients. Add the steaks to the dish and baste thoroughly. Set aside to marinate at room temperature for 30 minutes, turning the steaks and basting them occasionally.

Meanwhile, prepare the dipping sauce by mixing all the ingredients together. Pour the sauce into individual dipping bowls and set aside.

Preheat the grill (broiler) to moderately high.

Remove the steaks from the marinade and arrange on the rack of the grill (broiler). Grill (broil) for 2 minutes on each side, then reduce the heat to moderate. Grill (broil) for a further 2 minutes on each side for rare steaks; double the cooking time for medium.

Remove the steaks from the heat, transfer to a chopping board and carefully cut into strips. Arrange the strips on individual serving plates. Serve at once, with the dipping sauce.
Serves 4
Preparation and cooking time: 1 hour

Bul-Ko-Kee

(Barbecued Beef)   (Korea)

Metric/Imperial	American
½kg./1lb. topside of beef, very thinly sliced into strips	1lb. top round of beef, very thinly sliced into strips
3 Tbs. soft brown sugar	3 Tbs. soft brown sugar
125ml./4fl.oz. soya sauce	½ cup soy sauce
salt and pepper	salt and pepper
5 Tbs. roasted sesame seeds, ground	5 Tbs. roasted sesame seeds, ground
50ml./2fl.oz. sesame oil	4 Tbs. sesame oil
1 garlic clove, crushed	1 garlic clove, crushed
2 spring onions, green part only, finely chopped	2 scallions, green part only, finely chopped
½ tsp. monosodium glutamate (optional)	½ tsp. MSG (optional)

Mix the beef, sugar, soy sauce, salt and pepper to taste, half the sesame seeds, the oil, garlic, spring onions (scallions) and monosodium glutamate together. Set aside at room temperature for 2 hours, basting and turning the meat from time to time.

Preheat the grill (broiler) to hot.

Lay the beef strips on the lined grill (broiler) pan and grill (broil) for 5 to 8 minutes, or until the strips are cooked through and evenly browned. (If you prefer, the beef can be fried quickly in a little sesame oil until browned.)

Remove from the heat, sprinkle over the remaining sesame seeds and serve at once.

Serves 4
Preparation and cooking time: about 2¼ hours

Bul-Ko-Kee, a succulent mixture of beef strips, first marinated then barbecued and sprinkled with sesame seeds, is almost the Korean national dish. It is served here with Kim Chee, a popular Korean version of pickled cabbage.

Yuk-Kae-Jang-Kuk

(Beef Stew with Peppers)   (Korea)

Metric/Imperial	American
1kg./2lb. braising steak, cut into thin strips	2lb. chuck steak, cut into thin strips
3 green peppers, pith and seeds removed and cut into strips	3 green peppers, pith and seeds removed and cut into strips
3 red peppers, pith and seeds removed and cut into strips	3 red peppers, pith and seeds removed and cut into strips
3 spring onions, chopped	3 scallions, chopped
½ tsp. sugar	½ tsp. sugar
½ tsp. salt	½ tsp. salt
125ml./4fl.oz. soya sauce	½ cup soy sauce
175ml./6fl.oz. water	¾ cup water

Put all the ingredients into a heavy-bottomed saucepan and bring to the boil. Cover and simmer for 2 to 2½ hours, or until the beef is very tender. (Do not add any more liquid – enough is produced by the ingredients.)

Transfer to a warmed serving dish before serving.

Serves 4–6
Preparation and cooking time: 3 hours

Gyuniku no Kushiyaki

(Beef Kebabs with Green Pepper)

This dish is a sort of Japanese shashlik and the 'extra' fillings can be varied according to taste. The combination used here is particularly colourful, but you could substitute small whole onions, tomatoes, or mushrooms if you prefer.

Metric/Imperial	American
½kg./1lb. rump steak, cut into bite-sized cubes	1lb. rump steak, cut into bite -sized cubes
1 large green pepper, pith and seeds removed and cut into pieces about the same size as the meat cubes	1 large green pepper, pith and seeds removed and cut into pieces about the same size as the meat cubes
1 large red pepper, pith and seeds removed and cut into pieces about the same size as the meat cubes	1 large red pepper, pith and seeds removed and cut into pieces about the same size as the meat cubes
50g./2oz. flour	½ cup flour
2 eggs, beaten	2 eggs, beaten
75g./3oz. fine dry breadcrumbs	1 cup fine dry breadcrumbs
vegetable oil for deep-frying	vegetable oil for deep-frying
MARINADE	MARINADE
75ml./3fl.oz. soya sauce	⅓ cup soy sauce
3 Tbs. mirin or sweet sherry	3 Tbs. mirin or sweet sherry
2 spring onions, chopped	2 scallions, chopped
1 tsp. sugar	1 tsp. sugar
½ tsp. hichimi togarishi or paprika	½ tsp. hichimi togarishi or paprika

First, make the marinade. Put all the ingredients into a large, shallow dish and mix until they are thoroughly blended.

Thread the meat and pepper pieces on to skewers then arrange them carefully in the marinade mixture. Set aside at room temperature for at least 1 hour, turning the skewers from time to time so that all sides of the mixture become coated in the marinade. Remove from the marinade, then discard the marinade. Pat the cubes dry with kitchen towels and dip lightly in the flour, shaking off any excess. Dip the skewers into the beaten eggs, then coat thoroughly with the breadcrumbs, shaking off any excess.

Fill a large deep-frying pan about one-third full with vegetable oil and heat until it is very hot. Carefully lower the skewers, a few at a time, into the oil and fry the beef and peppers until they are crisp and golden brown. Remove from the oil and drain on kitchen towels.

Serve at once, piping hot.
Serves 4
Preparation and cooking time: 1½ hours

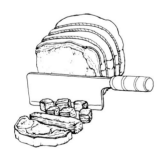

Bulgalbi

(Marinated Beef Spareribs)   (Korea)

Metric/Imperial	American
1kg./2lb. beef spareribs, cut into 7½cm./3in. pieces	2lb. beef spareribs, cut into 3in. pieces
1 Tbs. peanut oil	1 Tbs. peanut oil
MARINADE	MARINADE
4 Tbs. soya sauce	4 Tbs. soy sauce

Metric/Imperial	American
3 garlic cloves, crushed	3 garlic cloves, crushed
2 Tbs. sake or dry white wine	2 Tbs. sake or dry white wine
4 Tbs. water	4 Tbs. water
2 tsp. roasted sesame seeds, ground	2 tsp. roasted sesame seeds, ground
2 Tbs. sugar	2 Tbs. sugar
1 tsp. black pepper	1 tsp. black pepper
4 spring onions, chopped	4 scallions, chopped
1 onion, chopped	1 onion, chopped
1 large ripe pear, peeled and cored	1 large ripe pear, peeled and cored

First prepare the spareribs. Using a sharp knife, carefully open out the flesh to make three 'wings', then criss-cross all of the meat (and bone) with small, deep incisions, taking care not to cut through the meat entirely.

To make the marinade, combine all the ingredients, except the pear, in a large, shallow dish. Chop the pear roughly so that the flesh is crumbling, and stir into the marinade mixture. Add the ribs and set aside to marinate overnight at room temperature.

Preheat the grill (broiler) to moderately high.

Remove the beef from the marinade and transfer to the rack of the grill (broiler). Brush lightly with the oil. Grill (broil) the meat for 15 minutes, or until it is cooked through and golden brown.

Remove from the heat and serve at once.

Serves 4
Preparation and cooking time: 13 hours

Oyi Jim

(Beef with Cucumbers)   (Korea)

Metric/Imperial	American
50ml./2fl.oz. vegetable oil	¼ cup vegetable oil
350g./12oz. rump steak, cut into thin strips	12oz. rump steak, cut into thin strips
2 medium cucumbers, halved lengthways with the seeds removed, then cut into 1cm./½in. slices	2 medium cucumbers, halved lengthways with the seeds removed, then cut into ½in. slices
1 red chilli, finely chopped	1 red chilli, finely chopped
1 Tbs. roasted sesame seeds, ground	1 Tbs. roasted sesame seeds, ground
MARINADE	MARINADE
1 Tbs. sesame oil	1 Tbs. sesame oil
1 Tbs. soya sauce	1 Tbs soy sauce
1 garlic clove, crushed	1 garlic clove, crushed
½ tsp. sugar	½ tsp. sugar

First, prepare the marinade. Combine all the ingredients together, beating until they are thoroughly blended. Arrange the beef strips in the marinade and baste and turn until they are covered. Set aside at room temperature for 15 minutes, turning the strips from time to time.

Heat the oil in a large frying-pan. When it is hot, add the beef mixture and stir-fry for 1½ minutes. Add the cucumbers and chilli and stir-fry for a further 2 minutes, or until the cucmbers are cooked but still crisp.

Transfer the mixture to a warmed serving dish and sprinkle over the ground sesame seeds before serving.

Serves 3–4
Preparation and cooking time: 35 minutes

Beef Teriyaki I

Metric/Imperial	American
1kg./2lb. fillet steak, cut into ½cm./¼in. slices	2lb. fillet steak, cut into ¼in. slices
MARINADE	MARINADE
2½cm./1in. piece of fresh root ginger, peeled and chopped	1in. piece of fresh green ginger, peeled and chopped
2 garlic cloves, crushed	2 garlic cloves, crushed
4 spring onions, finely chopped	4 scallions, finely chopped
25g./1oz. soft brown sugar	2 Tbs. soft brown sugar
250ml./8fl.oz. soya sauce	1 cup soy sauce
125ml./4fl.oz. sake or dry sherry	½ cup sake or dry sherry
salt and pepper	salt and pepper

Combine all the marinade ingredients in a large shallow dish. Put the steak pieces into the marinade and set aside at room temperature to marinate for 2 hours, basting occasionally.

Preheat the grill (broiler) to high.

Remove the steaks from the marinade and arrange them on the rack of the grill (broiler). Brush them generously with the marinade mixture and grill (broil) for 2 minutes. Remove from the heat, turn the steak and brush with the marinade. Grill (broil) for a further 2 minutes. These will give you rare steaks; double the cooking time for medium.

Transfer the steaks to warmed serving dishes and either serve at once, or cut into thin strips before serving.

Serves 6
Preparation and cooking time: 2¼ hours

Beef Teriyaki II

Metric/Imperial	American
4 small fillet steaks, cut ½cm./¼in. thick	4 small fillet steaks, cut ¼in. thick
3 Tbs. vegetable oil	3 Tbs. vegetable oil
MARINADE	MARINADE
50ml./2fl.oz. sake or dry sherry	¼ cup sake or dry sherry
2 Tbs. soya sauce	2 Tbs. soy sauce
1 garlic clove, crushed	1 garlic clove, crushed
50ml./2fl.oz. dashi	¼ cup dashi

Combine all the marinade ingredients in a large, shallow dish. Arrange the steaks in the mixture and set aside at room temperature to marinate for 1 hour, basting occasionally. Remove the steaks from the marinade, drying on kitchen towels, and reserve the marinade.

Heat the oil in a large frying-pan. When it is hot, add the steaks and fry for 1 minute on each side. Pour off all but a thin film of fat from the pan and add the marinade. Cook the steaks for a further 3 minutes on each side, basting them occasionally with the pan juices. These times will give rare steaks; double the cooking time for medium.

Transfer the steaks to warmed individual serving plates and either serve as they are or cut them into thin strips. Pour a little of the pan juices over the meat before serving.

Serves 4
Preparation and cooking time: 1¼ hours

Juhn Kol

(Mixed Meats and Vegetables cooked at the Table) (Korea)

This popular dish has Japanese origins still represented today since the hibachi-type grill (broiler) plate on the table is a favourite way to present it. This is also a particularly suitable dish for barbecuing. The meats and vegetables suggested below are typical but any can be omitted or added to – the choice is yours.

Serve this superb Beef Teriyaki I with rice and bean sprouts for a delicious Japanese meal. If you wish to use chopsticks, you should cut the beef into thin strips before eating, as the Japanese do.

Metric/Imperial	American
½kg./1lb. rump steak or pork fillet (or a mixture of the two), cut into thin squares	1lb. rump steak or pork tenderloin (or a mixture of the two), cut into thin squares
2 large onions, sliced	2 large onions, sliced
3 celery stalks, cut into 2½cm./1in. lengths	3 celery stalks, cut into 1in. lengths
125g./4oz. small button mushrooms	1 cup small button mushrooms
2 carrots, thinly sliced diagonally	2 carrots, thinly sliced diagonally
MARINADE	MARINADE
125ml./4fl.oz. soya sauce	½ cup soy sauce
50g./2oz. sugar	¼ cup sugar
2 Tbs. vegetable oil	2 Tbs. vegetable oil
2 garlic cloves, crushed	2 garlic cloves, crushed
1 spring onion, finely chopped	1 scallion, finely chopped
1 chilli, finely chopped	1 chilli, finely chopped
1 Tbs. roasted sesame seeds, ground	1 Tbs. roasted sesame seeds, ground

269

First, prepare the marinade. Put all the marinade ingredients into a shallow mixing bowl and beat well until they are thoroughly blended. Add the meat squares to the mixture and baste well to cover them completely. Set aside for 2 hours, turning the squares from time to time.

Meanwhile, arrange all the vegetables attractively on a large platter and set on the table. Put the burner or electric plate on the table and warm up.

The meal is now ready to be cooked, ingredients requiring most cooking to be cooked first. The meat is first seared then cooked with enough of its marinade to keep from burning.

Serve hot.

Serves 4
Preparation and cooking time: $2\frac{1}{2}$ hours

Binatok

(Dried Green Pea Pancake with Filling)   (Korea)

Metric/Imperial	American
450g./1lb. dried split peas	$2\frac{2}{3}$ cups dried split peas
175g./6oz. long-grain rice	1 cup long-grain rice
2 garlic cloves, crushed	2 garlic cloves, crushed
2 spring onions, finely chopped	2 scallions, finely chopped
1 small onion, finely chopped	1 small onion, finely chopped
1 carrot, grated	1 carrot, grated
Water	Water
4 Tbs. peanut oil	4 Tbs. peanut oil
FILLING	FILLING
125g./4oz. rump steak, cut into thin strips	4oz. rump steak, cut into thin strips
3 spring onions, cut into $2\frac{1}{2}$cm./1in. lengths	3 scallions, cut into 1 in. lengths
2 carrots, thinly sliced on the diagonal	2 carrots, thinly sliced on the diagonal
1 red or green pepper, pith and seeds removed and cut into strips	1 red or green pepper, pith and seeds removed and cut into strips
1 dried red chilli, crumbled	1 dried red chilli, crumbled
black pepper	black pepper
DIPPING SAUCE	DIPPING SAUCE
250 ml./8fl.oz. soya sauce	1 cup soy sauce
2 spring onions, very finely chopped	2 scallions, very finely chopped

Put the split peas and rice into a large bowl and just cover with water. Set aside to soak overnight. Drain, then put the mixture into a blender. Grind until smooth. Transfer the mixture to a large bowl. Stir in the garlic, spring onions (scallions), onion and carrot until they are well blended, then stir in enough water to form a thick batter. Set aside to 'rest' at room temperature for 30 minutes.

Meanwhile, assemble the filling ingredients on a large plate, in the order of cooking, that is those to be cooked longest first.

Heat quarter of the oil in a small saucepan. When it is very hot, add about a quarter of the batter and fry until the edges curl slightly. Arrange about a quarter of the meat over the batter and cook for 1 minute. Arrange a quarter of the spring onions (scallions), carrots, pepper and chilli, with pepper to taste, in the same way. Cook for 3 minutes, carefully working around the edges occasionally with a spatula, or until the bottom is brown. Carefully turn the pancake over and fry on the other side until it is golden brown.

Slide the pancake on to a warmed serving plate and keep hot while you cook the remaining batter and the remaining filling ingredients in the same way.

To make the dipping sauce, combine the soy sauce and spring onions (scallions) and pour into small, individual dipping bowls. Serve at once, with the bintatok.

Serves 4
Preparation and cooking time: 12¾ hours

Kan Juhn

(Fried Liver)   (Korea)

Metric/Imperial	American
½kg./1lb. lamb's liver, thinly sliced	1lb. lamb's liver, thinly sliced
1 large garlic clove	1 large garlic clove
salt and pepper	salt and pepper
50g./2oz. flour	½ cup flour
2 eggs, lightly beaten	2 eggs, lightly beaten
50ml./2fl.oz. sesame oil	¼ cup sesame oil
SAUCE	SAUCE
125ml./4fl.oz. soya sauce	½ cup soy sauce
125ml./4fl.oz. wine vinegar	½ cup wine vinegar
1 Tbs. soft brown sugar	1 Tbs. soft brown sugar
2 tsp. chopped pine nuts	2 tsp. chopped pine nuts

Rub the liver gently with the garlic, then discard the clove. Sprinkle with salt and pepper to taste. Dip the slices in flour, shaking off any excess, then in the beaten eggs.

Heat the oil in a large frying-pan. When it is hot, add the liver slices and fry for 3 to 4 minutes on each side (depending on thickness), or until the meat is just cooked through.

Meanwhile, make the sauce by combining all the ingredients in a screw-top jar until they are thoroughly blended. Pour into a shallow dipping bowl.

Transfer the liver slices to a warmed serving platter and serve at once, with the dipping sauce.

Serves 4
Preparation and cooking time: 20 minutes

Buta no Kakuni

(Pork Cooked with Sake)

Metric/Imperial	American
575g./1¼lb. lean pork meat, cut into 4 pieces	1¼lb. lean pork meat, cut into 4 pieces
4cm./1½in. piece of fresh root ginger, peeled and sliced	1½in. piece of fresh green ginger, peeled and sliced
2 garlic cloves, sliced	2 garlic cloves, sliced
450ml./15fl.oz. sake or dry sherry	2 cups sake or dry sherry
4 Tbs. sugar	4 Tbs. sugar
5 Tbs. soya sauce	5 Tbs. soy sauce
½ tsp. salt	½ tsp. salt
1 Tbs. mustard	1 Tbs. mustard

Put the pork into a medium saucepan and just cover with water. Add the ginger and garlic. Bring to the boil, reduce the heat to low and simmer for 1 hour. Remove from the heat, cool, then skim any fat from the surface of the liquid. Add the sake or sherry and sugar and continue to simmer for about 1½ hours, or until the meat is so tender that it is almost coming apart. Stir in the soy sauce and salt and remove the pan from the heat.

To serve, put one piece of pork on four individual, deep serving plates and pour over the cooking liquid. Add a dash of mustard to each piece of meat and serve at once.

Serves 4
Preparation and cooking time: 3½ hours

Ton-Yuk-Kui

Ton-Yuk-Kui is a Korean dish of lean pork fillet (tenderloin), first marinated then baked until it is tender. It is tradionally served with a sauce made from the delicious marinade.

(Korean Pork Fillets)

Metric/Imperial	American
1kg./2lb. pork fillet, thinly sliced	2lb. pork tenderloin, thinly sliced
2 Tbs. sesame oil	2 Tbs. sesame oil
MARINADE	MARINADE
125ml./4fl.oz. soya sauce	½ cup soy sauce
50 ml./2fl.oz. water	¼ cup water
3 Tbs. sugar	3 Tbs. sugar
2 spring onions, finely chopped	2 scallions, finely chopped
2 garlic cloves, crushed	2 garlic cloves, crushed
5cm./2in. piece of fresh root ginger, peeled and finely chopped	2in. piece of fresh green ginger, peeled and finely chopped
salt and pepper	salt and pepper

Combine all the marinade ingredients in a shallow dish and add the pork slices. Baste well, then set aside at room temperature for 2 hours, basting occasionally.

Preheat the oven to fairly hot 190°C (Gas Mark 5, 375°F).

Remove the pork from the marinade and dry on kitchen towels. Reserve the marinade.

Coat the bottom and sides of a baking dish with the oil. Arrange the pork slices in the dish, in one layer. Cover and bake the meat for 45 minutes to 1 hour, or until it is tender.

Meanwhile, pour the marinade into a saucepan and bring to the boil. Reduce the heat to low and simmer for 10 to 15 minutes, or until it has reduced slightly.

Remove the meat from the oven and arrange it on a warmed serving dish. Pour the cooking juices into the saucepan with the marinade and bring to the boil again. Pour a little over the pork and serve the rest with the meat.

Serves 4–6
Preparation and cooking time: $3\frac{1}{4}$ hours

Tonkatsu

(Japanese Pork Schnitzel)

The schnitzels are divided into thin strips before serving in the recipe below to enable chop-stick users to pick up the meat easily. If you plan to eat your meal with a knife and fork, this step can be omitted.

Metric/Imperial	American
6 large slices of pork fillet, beaten thin	6 large slices of pork tenderloin, beaten thin
2 eggs, beaten	2 eggs, beaten
2 Tbs. finely chopped spring onion	2 Tbs. finely chopped scallion
125g./4oz. soft white breadcrumbs	2 cups soft white breadcrumbs
75ml./3fl.oz. vegetable oil	$\frac{1}{3}$ cup vegetable oil
hichimi togarishi or paprika (to garnish)	hichimi togarishi or paprika (to garnish)
MARINADE	MARINADE
6 Tbs. soya sauce	6 Tbs. soy sauce
4 Tbs. mirin or sweet sherry	4 Tbs. mirin or sweet sherry
2 garlic cloves, crushed	2 garlic cloves, crushed
1 tsp. hichimi togarishi or paprika	1 tsp. hichimi togarishi or paprika

To make the marinade, combine the soy sauce, mirin or sherry, garlic and hichimi togarishi or paprika together, beating until they are thoroughly blended. Arrange the pork slices in the marinade and set aside at room temperature for 20 minutes, basting and turning the pork occasionally. Remove from the marinade and pat dry with kitchen towels. Discard the marinade.

Beat the eggs and spring onion (scallion) together in a shallow bowl. Dip the pork, first in the egg then in the breadcrumbs, shaking off any excess. Arrange the coated pork pieces on a plate and chill in the refrigerator for 2 hours.

Heat the oil in a large frying-pan. When it is hot, add the schnitzels and fry for 3 to 4 minutes on each side, or until they are golden brown and crisp. Remove from the heat and drain on kitchen towels.

Cut the schnitzels, crosswise, into thin strips, then carefully reassemble into the schnitzel shape. Serve at once, garnished with hichimi togarishi to taste.

Serves 4
Preparation and cooking time: $2\frac{1}{2}$ hours

273

Kulbi Jim

(Spareribs with Sesame Seed Sauce)   (Korea)

This is a very basic version of a very popular dish. If you wish, vegetables can be added to the mixture – some sliced carrots or mushrooms, for instance, or even water chestnuts.

Metric/Imperial	American
3 Tbs. vegetable oil	3 Tbs. vegetable oil
1½kg./3lb. American-style spareribs, cut into 5cm./2in. pieces	3lb. spareribs, cut into 2-rib serving pieces
2 Tbs. sugar	2 Tbs. sugar
2 Tbs. sesame oil	2 Tbs. sesame oil
4 Tbs. soya sauce	4 Tbs. soy sauce
3 spring onions, chopped	3 scallions, chopped
2 garlic cloves, crushed	2 garlic cloves, crushed
2½cm./1in. piece of fresh root ginger, peeled and chopped	1in. piece of fresh green ginger, peeled and chopped
3 Tbs. roasted sesame seeds, ground	3 Tbs. roasted sesame seeds, ground
300ml./10fl.oz. water	1¼ cups water

Heat the oil in a large, shallow saucepan or frying-pan. When it is hot, add the spareribs and fry until they are evenly browned. (If necessary, fry the ribs in two or three batches.)

Stir in the sugar, sesame oil, soy sauce, spring onions (scallions), garlic, ginger and 2 tablespoons of the sesame seeds until they are thoroughly blended. Pour over the water and bring to the boil. Reduce the heat to low, cover the pan and simmer the mixture for 50 minutes, or until the spareribs are cooked and crisp.

Transfer the mixture to a warmed serving dish and sprinkle over the remaining roasted sesame seeds before serving.

Serves 6–8
Preparation and cooking time: 1½ hours

Seekumche Kuk

(Spinach with Pork)   (Korea)

Many Korean dishes, like most Chinese ones, are geared to make comparatively little meat go quite a long way – and this dish is a particularly good example. If you prefer, lean beef, such as rump steak, can be substituted for the pork.

Metric/Imperial	American
1kg./2lb. spinach, washed thoroughly and chopped	2lb. spinach, washed thoroughly and chopped
1 tsp. salt	1 tsp. salt
3 Tbs. vegetable oil	3 Tbs. vegetable oil
225g./8oz. pork fillet, cut into bite-sized pieces	8oz. pork tenderloin, cut into bite-sized pieces
1 garlic clove, crushed	1 garlic clove, crushed
¼ tsp. cayenne pepper	¼ tsp. cayenne pepper
2 spring onions, chopped	2 scallions, chopped
2 Tbs. soya sauce	2 Tbs. soy sauce
½ tsp. sugar	½ tsp. sugar
2 Tbs. roasted sesame seeds, ground	2 Tbs. roasted sesame seeds, ground

Put the spinach into a large saucepan with the salt and cook gently for 8 to 10 minutes, or until it is just tender. (Do not add water – there should be enough clinging to the leaves to provide moisture for cooking.) Drain, then transfer the spinach to a plate. Keep hot.

Heat the oil in a large frying-pan. When it is hot, add the pork pieces and garlic and stir-fry for 2 minutes. Stir in the cayenne, spring onions (scallions), soy sauce and sugar and continue to stir-fry for a further 2 minutes. Stir in the chopped spinach and heat it through.

Transfer the mixture to a warmed serving dish and sprinkle over the roasted sesame seeds before serving.

Serves 3–4
Preparation and cooking time: 25 minutes

Yakibuta

(Basted Pork)

Metric/Imperial	American
1kg./2lb. boned leg or loin of pork	2lb. boned leg or loin of pork
3 garlic cloves, crushed	3 garlic cloves, crushed
4cm./1½in. piece of fresh root ginger, peeled and sliced	1½in. piece of fresh green ginger, peeled and sliced
150ml./5fl.oz. sake or dry sherry	⅔ cup sake or dry sherry
150ml./5fl.oz. soya sauce	⅔ cup soy sauce
2 Tbs. sugar	2 Tbs. sugar
1½ tsp. salt	1½ tsp. salt

Put the pork piece in a large saucepan and just cover with water. Add the garlic and ginger. Bring to the boil, then cook over moderate heat for 1 hour, or until the water has evaporated and the oil on the bottom of the saucepan begins to bubble. Pour off the oil and turn the meat in the pan, slightly burning the outside.

Warm the sake or sherry to tepid then add to the saucepan. Continue cooking until the sake has boiled away. Turn the meat again, basting with the pan juices. Stir in the remaining ingredients and cook for a further 10 minutes.

Serve either hot or cold.

Serves 6–8
Preparation and cooking time: 1¾ hours

Goma Yaki

(Chicken with Sesame Seeds)

Metric/Imperial	American
2 large chicken breasts, skinned, boned and halved	2 large chicken breasts, skinned boned and halved
3 Tbs. sesame oil	3 Tbs. sesame oil
2 Tbs. roasted sesame seeds	2 Tbs. roasted sesame seeds
MARINADE	MARINADE
75ml./3fl.oz. sake or dry sherry	⅓ cup sake or dry sherry
2 tsp. soya sauce	2 tsp. soy sauce
monosodium glutamate (optional)	MSG (optional)
¼ tsp. hichimi togarishi or paprika	¼ tsp. hichimi togarishi or paprika

First, prepare the marinade. Combine all the ingredients in a medium-sized shallow bowl, beating until they are thoroughly blended. Add the chicken pieces and baste well. Set aside at room temperature for 20 minutes, turning and basting the chicken from time to time.

Heat the oil in a large frying-pan. When it is hot, add the chicken pieces and fry for 5 minutes on each side. Sprinkle over half the sesame seeds and stir and turn until the chicken is coated. Reduce the heat to low and cook the chicken for a further 6 to 8 minutes, or until the pieces are cooked through and tender.

Transfer the mixture to a warmed serving dish and sprinkle over the remaining sesame seeds before serving.

Serves 2-4
Preparation and cooking time: 50 minutes

Dak Jim

(Steamed Chicken and Vegetables) (Korea)

Metric/Imperial	American
1 x 2kg./4lb. chicken, cut into 8 or 10 serving pieces	1 x 4lb. chicken, cut into 8 or 10 serving pieces
2 carrots, cut into thin strips	2 carrots, cut into thin strips
3 dried mushrooms, soaked in cold water for 30 minutes, drained and thinly sliced	3 dried mushrooms, soaked in cold water for 30 minutes, drained and thinly sliced
1 bamboo shoot, sliced	1 bamboo shoot, sliced
2 spring onions, thinly sliced	2 scallions, thinly sliced
2 garlic cloves, crushed	2 garlic cloves, crushed
1 tsp. ground ginger	1 tsp. ground ginger
50g./2oz. walnuts, chopped	$\frac{1}{3}$ cup chopped walnuts
50ml./2fl. oz. soya sauce	$\frac{1}{4}$ cup soy sauce
2 Tbs. soft brown sugar	2 Tbs. soft brown sugar
1 Tbs. roasted sesame seeds, ground	1 Tbs. roasted sesame seeds, ground
salt and pepper	salt and pepper
GARNISH	GARNISH
2 eggs, separated	2 eggs, separated

Put the chicken pieces into a saucepan and cover with water. Bring to the boil, cover and simmer for 1 to 1½hours, or until the chicken is tender. Drain and reserve the stock. When the meat is cool enough to handle, cut the chicken into bite-sized strips.

Put all the remaining ingredients, except the garnish, into a large saucepan and bring to the boil. Stir in the chicken strips and reserved stock, cover and simmer for 15 to 20 minutes or until the vegetables are cooked but still crisp.

Meanwhile, make the garnish. Beat the egg yolks and whites separately until they are both well mixed. Lightly oil a heavy-bottomed frying-pan and heat it over moderate heat. Pour in the egg white and spread over the bottom in a thin layer. Cook until the bottom is firm, then turn over and cook until the other side is firm. Slide on to a warmed dish and cook the egg yolks in the same way. Cut the cooked eggs into strips.

Transfer the chicken and vegetables to a warmed serving bowl and scatter over the egg strips before serving.

Serves 6
Preparation and cooking time: 2½ hours

Chicken Teriyaki I

Metric/Imperial	American
125ml./4fl.oz. sake or dry sherry	½ cup sake or dry sherry
50ml./2fl.oz. soya sauce	¼ cup soy sauce
125ml./4fl.oz. dashi	½ cup dashi
2 tsp. sugar	2 tsp. sugar
2 tsp. cornflour	2 tsp. cornstarch
4 chicken breasts, skinned and boned	4 chicken breasts, skinned and boned
2 celery stalks, sliced lengthways	2 celery stalks, sliced lengthways
8 spring onions, trimmed	8 scallions, trimmed

The essence of Japanese cooking is well illustrated in this dish of Chicken Teriyaki I – the simpliclty of the presentation and the importance attached to the appearance of the dish. If you wish to eat with chopsticks, cut the meat (to the bone) into thin strips.

Warm the sake or sherry in a small saucepan. Remove from the heat and carefully ignite, allowing the sake to burn until the flames die down. Stir in the soy sauce and dashi. Put 3 tablespoons of the sake mixture into a small bowl and mix in the sugar and cornflour (cornstarch). Set aside. Pour the remaining sauce into a shallow dish.

Preheat the grill (broiler) to moderately high.

Dip the chicken pieces into the sauce to coat thoroughly, then arrange them on the rack in the grill (broiler). Grill (broil) for about 6 minutes, or until one side is golden brown. Remove the chicken from the heat, coat thoroughly in the sauce again and return to the rack. Grill (broil) the other side for 6 minutes, or until it is golden brown. Remove from the heat again and dip into the sauce then return to the grill (broiler). Brush generously with the cornflour (cornstarch) mixture and grill (broil) for a final 6 minutes, turning the chicken occasionally, or until the meat is cooked through.

Arrange the chicken pieces on a warmed serving plate and either serve as is, or cut into slices. Garnish with the celery and spring onions (scallions).

Serves 4
Preparation and cooking time: 45 minutes

Chicken Teriyaki II

Metric/Imperial	American
2 Tbs. clear honey	2 Tbs. clear honey
6 small chicken breasts, skinned and boned	6 small chicken breasts, skinned and boned
MARINADE	MARINADE
125ml./4fl. oz. soya sauce	½ cup soy sauce
salt and pepper	salt and pepper
4cm./1½in. piece of fresh root ginger, peeled and chopped	1½in. piece of fresh green ginger, peeled and chopped
1 garlic clove, crushed	1 garlic clove, crushed
125ml./4fl. oz. sake or dry white wine	½ cup sake or dry white wine

Combine all the marinade ingredients in a large shallow dish and set aside.

Heat the honey in a small saucepan until it liquefies slightly. Remove the pan from the heat and brush the honey mixture generously over the chicken breasts. Arrange the chicken in the marinade and set aside at room temperature to marinate for 2 hours, basting occasionally.

Preheat the oven to moderate 180°C (Gas Mark 4, 350°F).

Line a deep-sided baking pan with foil and arrange the chicken breasts on the foil. Pour over the marinade. Put the pan into the oven and bake, basting frequently, for 30 to 35 minutes, or until the chicken is cooked through and tender. Remove from the oven and, using a slotted spoon, transfer the chicken to a warmed serving dish. Pour the cooking juices into a warmed serving bowl and serve with the chicken.

Serves 6
Preparation and cooking time: 2¾ hours

Chicken Pokkum

(Stir-Fried Chicken)   (Korea)

Metric/Imperial	American
50ml./2fl.oz. sesame oil	¼ cup sesame oil
2 chicken breasts, skinned, boned and cut into strips	2 chicken breasts, skinned, boned and cut into strips
2 spring onions, chopped	2 scallions, chopped
1 garlic clove, crushed	1 garlic clove, crushed
4cm./1½in. piece of fresh root ginger, peeled and finely chopped	1½in. piece of fresh green ginger, peeled and finely chopped
50g./2oz. button mushrooms, sliced	½ cup sliced button mushrooms
3 Tbs. soya sauce	3 Tbs. soy sauce
2 Tbs. water	2 Tbs. water
1 Tbs. sugar	1 Tbs. sugar
1 Tbs. roasted sesame seeds, ground	1 Tbs. roasted sesame seeds, ground

Heat the oil in a large frying-pan. When it is hot, add the chicken strips and stir-fry for 3 minutes, or until they are just cooked through. Stir in the spring onions (scallions), garlic and ginger and stir-fry for 1 minute. Add the mushrooms and stir-fry for 2 minutes. Stir in the soy sauce, water, sugar and sesame seeds and bring to the boil. Cook for 1 minute.

Transfer the mixture to a warmed serving dish and serve at once.
Serves 3–4
Preparation and cooking time: 15 minutes

Yaki Tori

(Barbecued Chicken)

Metric/Imperial	American
½kg./1lb. chicken breast, skinned, boned and cut into bite-sized pieces	1lb. chicken breast, skinned, boned and cut into bite-sized pieces
½kg./1lb. leeks, cleaned, cut into 1cm./½in. lengths and parboiled	1lb. leeks, cleaned, cut into ½in. lengths and parboiled
SAUCE	SAUCE
175ml./6fl. oz. soya sauce	¾ cup soy sauce
175ml./6fl. oz. mirin or sweet sherry	¾ cup mirin or sweet sherry
monosodium glutamate (optional)	MSG (optional)

Thread the chicken pieces on to small skewers. Thread the leek pieces (pierce through the sides) on to separate small skewers. Set aside.

Preheat the grill (broiler) to moderately high.

Meanwhile, to make the sauce, put the soy sauce and mirin into a small saucepan and add monosodium glutamate to taste. Bring to the boil, then cook for a few minutes or until it begins to thicken slightly. Remove from the heat.

Arrange the chicken and leek skewers on the rack of the grill (broiler). (If possible put the leeks further away from the flame to avoid excessive charring.) Grill (broil) for 3 minutes. Remove the skewers from the heat and dip into the sauce mixture, to coat the food thoroughly. Return to the heat, turn the skewers and grill (broil) for a further 3 minutes. Repeat this once more, then cook until the chicken meat is cooked through.

Remove from the heat and dip the skewers once more in the sauce mixture before serving.

Serves 4
Preparation and cooking time: 40 minutes
Note: Lamb or calf's liver and green pepper pieces can also be cooked in this way.

Iri Dori

(Chicken Casserole)

Any vegetables can be used in this dish – variations could include onions, cauliflower and brussels sprouts.

Metric/Imperial	American
50ml./2fl.oz. vegetable oil	¼ cup vegetable oil
2 small chicken breasts, skinned, boned and cut into bite-sized pieces	2 small chicken breasts, skinned, boned and cut into bite-sized pieces
4 dried mushrooms, soaked in cold water for 30 minutes, drained, stalks removed and caps quartered	4 dried mushrooms, soaked in cold water for 30 minutes, drained, stalks removed and caps quartered
2 large carrots, diced	2 large carrots, diced
175g./6oz. tin bamboo shoot, drained and chopped	6oz. can bamboo shoot, drained and chopped
175ml./6fl.oz. dashi	¾ cup dashi
4 Tbs. mirin or sweet sherry	4 Tbs. mirin or sweet sherry
4 Tbs. sugar	4 Tbs. sugar
4 Tbs. soya sauce	4 Tbs. soy sauce
3 Tbs. green peas	3 Tbs. green peas

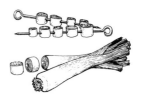

Heat the oil in a large, deep frying-pan. When it is hot, add the chicken pieces, mushrooms, carrots and bamboo shoot and fry, stirring occasionally, for 2 minutes. Add the dashi, mirin or sherry and sugar and cook for a further 10 minutes, stirring occasionally. Reduce the heat to low and stir in the soy sauce. Simmer the mixture until about three-quarters of the liquid has evaporated. Stir in the peas, then remove the pan from the heat.

Transfer the mixture to a warmed serving dish and serve at once.

Serves 4

Preparation and cooking time: 1 hour

Chicken Stew

(Korea)

Metric/Imperial	American
1 x 2kg./4lb. chicken, cut into 8 serving pieces	1 x 4lb. chicken, cut into 8 serving pieces
MARINADE	MARINADE
4 Tbs. soya sauce	4 Tbs. soy sauce
125ml./4fl.oz. water	½ cup water
½ small onion, chopped	½ small onion, chopped
2 spring onions, chopped	2 scallions, chopped
1 carrot, chopped	1 carrot, chopped
1 Tbs. sugar	1 Tbs. sugar
salt and pepper	salt and pepper
5cm./2in. piece of fresh root ginger, peeled and chopped	2in. piece of fresh green ginger, peeled and chopped
2 garlic cloves, crushed	2 garlic cloves, crushed

Put all the marinade ingredients into a saucepan and bring to the boil. Reduce the heat to moderately low and add the chicken pieces, basting thoroughly. Cover the pan and cook the mixture for 30 minutes. Remove from the heat and set aside to cool to room temperature. When the mixture is cool, chill in the refrigerator overnight.

Remove from the refrigerator and set over high heat. Bring to the boil. Reduce the heat to low and simmer the mixture for 20 to 30 minutes, or until the chicken is cooked through and tender.

Serve at once.

Serves 8

Preparation and cooking time: 13 hours

Tori no Sakamushi

(Sake-Steamed Chicken)

Metric/Imperial	American
4 chicken breasts, skinned, boned and cut into 2½cm./1in. slices	4 chicken breasts, skinned, boned and cut into 1in. slices
175ml./6fl.oz. sake or dry sherry	¾ cup sake or dry sherry
1 Tbs. sugar	1 Tbs. sugar
1 tsp. soya sauce	1 tsp. soy sauce
¼ tsp. monosodium glutamate (optional)	¼ tsp. MSG (optional)

Put the chicken meat slices into a shallow dish and pour over the sake or sherry. Set aside to marinate at room temperature for 1 hour, basting occasionally. Remove the chicken from the marinade and reserve the marinade. Pat the chicken dry with kitchen towels.

Arrange the chicken slices, in one layer, in the top part of a steamer, or on an ovenproof plate. Fill the base of the steamer (or a medium saucepan over which the plate will fit) about two-thirds full of boiling water and fit the top part over. Cover and steam the meat for 10 minutes. Remove the steamer from the heat and set aside.

Preheat the grill (broiler) to high.

Pour the reserved marinade into a small saucepan and stir in the sugar, soy sauce and monosodium glutamate. Bring to the boil, stirring constantly, then remove from the heat.

Arrange the chicken slices on the rack of the grill (broiler), brush with the marinade sauce and grill (broil) for 3 minutes on each side, basting occasionally with the sauce.

To serve, transfer the chicken slices to a warmed serving dish and pour over the remaining sauce.

Serves 4
Preparation and cooking time: 1½ hours.

Tori No Sakamushi (Sake-Steamed Chicken) is first steamed then barbecued to crisp perfection. Serve as either a first course or hors d'oeuvre in the West, or as part of an Oriental meal.

FISH

Shimesaba

(Marinated Mackerel)

Metric/Imperial	American
1 large fresh mackerel, cleaned, gutted and filleted	1 large fresh mackerel, cleaned, gutted and filleted
1 tsp. salt	1 tsp. salt
450ml./15fl.oz. white wine vinegar	2 cups white wine vinegar
4cm./1½in. piece of fresh root ginger, peeled and grated	1½in. piece of fresh green ginger, peeled and grated
4 spring onions, finely chopped	4 scallions, finely chopped
250ml./8fl.oz. soya sauce	1 cup soy sauce
2 tsp. green horseradish (wasabi), mixed to a paste with 2 tsp. water	2 tsp. green horseradish (wasabi), mixed to a paste with 2 tsp. water

Sprinkle the mackerel fillets liberally with salt and put into the refrigerator for 1 hour. Remove from the refrigerator and wash under cold running water. Arrange the fillets in a shallow dish and pour over the vinegar. Soak for 1 hour, turning at least once.

Remove the mackerel from the vinegar and pat dry on kitchen towels. Skin and remove any bones with your fingers. Cut across each fillet at about 2½cm./1in. intervals and arrange the pieces decoratively on a serving dish. Garnish with the grated ginger and spring onions (scallions).

Pour the soy sauce into individual dipping bowls and arrange the horseradish in individual small bowls. To make the dipping sauce, mix the horseradish and soy sauce together to taste and dip in the fish.
Serves 4
Preparation and cooking time: 2¼ hours

Hizakana

(Fish Simmered in Soy Sauce)

If you prefer, other fish such as mackerel, sole and sardine can be used instead of herrings in this dish.

Metric/Imperial	American
4 herrings, gutted and cleaned	4 herrings, gutted and cleaned
4cm./1½in. piece of fresh root ginger, peeled and sliced	1½in. piece of fresh green ginger, peeled and sliced
SAUCE	SAUCE
250ml./8fl.oz. dashi	1 cup dashi
250ml./8fl.oz. soya sauce	1 cup soy sauce
250ml./8fl.oz. sake or dry sherry	1 cup sake or dry sherry
3 tsp. sugar	3 tsp. sugar
monosodium glutamate (optional)	MAG (optional)

Put the fish on a chopping board and make two or three cuts through the belly of each one, to allow the sauce to be absorbed while cooking. Set aside.

Put the dashi, soy sauce, sake or sherry, sugar and monosodium glutamate to taste in a saucepan large enough to accommodate the fish. Bring to the boil. Arrange the fish in the bottom of the pan and sprinkle over the ginger slices. Return the dashi mixture to the boil, reduce the heat to low and simmer for 5 minutes. Reduce the heat to very low and continue to simmer for a further 15 minutes.

Transfer the fish to a warmed deep serving dish and pour over some of the cooking liquid. Serve at once.

Serves 4
Preparation and cooking time: 30 minutes

Sansuhn Jim

(Fish with Vegetables)   (Korea)

Metric/Imperial	American
225g./8oz. braising beef, cut into thin strips	8oz. chuck steak, cut into thin strips
125g./4oz. button mushrooms, sliced	1 cup sliced button mushrooms,
3 celery stalks, chopped	3 celery stalks, chopped
1 small turnip or large Japanese radish, chopped	1 small turnip or large Japanese radish, chopped
2 carrots, sliced	2 carrots, sliced
½kg./1lb. fish fillets, cut into small bite-sized pieces	1lb. fish fillets, cut into small bite-sized pieces
4 spring onions, chopped	4 scallions, chopped
2 green chillis, finely chopped	2 green chillis, finely chopped
3 Tbs. soya sauce	3 Tbs. soy sauce
MARINADE	MARINADE
2 tsp. sugar	2 tsp. sugar
2 Tbs. soya sauce	2 Tbs. soy sauce
1 garlic clove, crushed	1 garlic clove, crushed
2 Tbs. sesame oil	2 Tbs. sesame oil
1 Tbs. roasted sesame seeds, ground	1 Tbs. roasted sesame seeds, ground

First, prepare the marinade. Combine all the ingredients in a shallow bowl, beating until they are thoroughly blended. Arrange the beef strips in the marinade, basting and turning to coat them. Set aside at room temperature for 20 minutes, basting and turning the strips from time to time.

Preheat the oven to moderate 180°C (Gas Mark 4, 350°F).

Arrange the beef mixture in the bottom of a medium-sized flameproof casserole. Cover with a layer of mushrooms, then celery, turnip or radish and sliced carrots. Arrange the fish pieces on top and scatter over about three-quarters of the spring onions (scallions) and chillis. Pour just enough water into the casserole to come about half-way up the mixture then add the soy sauce. Bring to the boil on top of the stove, then cover and put into the oven. Cook for 15 to 20 minutes, or until the fish flakes easily.

Remove from the oven and garnish with the remaining spring onions (scallions) and chillis before serving.

Serves 4-6
Preparation and cooking time: 1 hour

(See previous page) Yok Kai Chi Sake (Marinated Salmon) is raw, delicate salmon marinated to the succulence of rare beef in a mixture of soy sauce and sake.

Yok Kai Sake

(Marinated Salmon)

Metric/Imperial	American
½kg./1lb. fresh salmon, thinly sliced then cut into strips	1lb. fresh salmon, thinly sliced then cut into strips
2½cm./1in. piece of fresh root ginger, peeled and chopped	1in. piece of fresh green ginger, peeled and chopped
1 garlic clove, crushed	1 garlic clove, crushed
2 spring onions, chopped	2 scallions, chopped
1 tsp. sugar	1 tsp. sugar
1 tsp. salt	1 tsp. salt
50ml./2fl.oz. soya sauce	¼ cup soy sauce
150ml./5fl.oz. sake or dry sherry	⅔ cup sake or dry sherry

Arrange the salmon strips in a large shallow serving dish. Combine all of the remaining ingredients in a mixing bowl, beating until they are well blended and the sugar has dissolved. Pour the mixture over the salmon strips and put the dish into the refrigerator for 1 hour.

Remove from the refrigerator and serve at once.

Serves 4
Preparation time: 1¼ hours

Fish in Wine Sauce

Metric/Imperial	American
4 large herrings, cleaned, gutted and filleted	4 large herrings, cleaned, gutted and filleted
4 Tbs. sake or dry sherry	4 Tbs. sake or dry sherry
4 Tbs. mirin or sweet sherry	4 Tbs. mirin or sweet sherry
125ml./4fl.oz. soya sauce	½ cup soy sauce
2 Tbs. sugar	2 Tbs. sugar
1 tsp. black pepper	1 tsp. black pepper
1 Tbs. chopped parsley	1 Tbs. chopped parsley
1 tsp. chopped chives	1 tsp. chopped chives

Wipe the herrings with damp kitchen towels and place on a chopping board. Cut each one in two lengthways. Make three cuts on the skin side of each fish, taking care not to cut through the flesh completely. Set aside.

Put the sake or sherry and mirin or sherry into a small saucepan and bring to the boil. Remove from the heat and ignite carefully. Leave until the flames have died down, then stir in the soy sauce and sugar. Pour the mixture into a shallow mixing bowl.

Preheat the grill (broiler) to moderate.

Dip the herring into the sauce mixture, then arrange them on the rack of the grill (broiler). Grill (broil) for 5 minutes. Remove the fish from the heat and dip into the sauce again. Return to the heat, turn the fish and grill (broil) for a further 5 minutes.

Transfer the fish to a warmed serving dish and garnish with the pepper, parsley and chives. Pour the basting liquid into a warmed serving bowl and serve with the fish.

Serves 4
Preparation and cooking time: 40 minutes

Misozuke

(Barbecued Mackerel with Miso)

Although mackerel has been suggested as the fish in the recipe given below, any similar, rather oily fish could be substituted – herrings, fresh large sardines, or even red mullet. This dish can be served either as an hors d'oeuvre (in which case it will serve 8) or as a main course.

Metric/Imperial	American
4 mackerel, cleaned, gutted and cut into 5cm./2in. pieces	4 mackerel, cleaned, gutted and cut into 2in. pieces
MARINADE	MARINADE
125g./4oz. miso paste	½ cup miso paste
50g./2oz. sugar	¼ cup sugar
2 Tbs. sake or dry sherry	2 Tbs. sake or dry sherry
2 Tbs. mirin or sweet sherry	2 Tbs. mirin or sweet sherry

First, make the marinade. Combine all the ingredients in a large shallow mixing bowl, beating until they are thoroughly blended. Arrange the fish pieces in the marinade, basting to coat them completely. Cover the dish and chill in the refrigerator for at least one day, turning the fish pieces from time to time. Remove the fish pieces from the marinade and pat dry with kitchen towels. Discard the marinade.

Preheat the grill (broiler) to moderate. Arrange the fish pieces on the rack of the grill (broiler) and grill (broil) for 5 minutes. Turn the fish over and grill (broil) for a further 5 to 8 minutes, or until the fish flesh flakes easily.

Transfer the fish pieces to a warmed serving dish and serve at once.

Serves 4
Preparation and cooking time: 24½ hours

Sakana Shioyaki

(Fish Barbecued with Salt)

This is another very simple yet very popular way of preparing fish in Japan, and is very healthy since the natural flavour of the fish is preserved. The salt is also said to break down the fats under the skin of the fish, and thereby moisten the flesh.

Metric/Imperial	American
4 herrings, cleaned and gutted	4 herrings, cleaned and gutted
3 Tbs. salt	3 Tbs. salt

Wash the fish under cold running water, then pat dry with kitchen towels. Cover liberally with salt (use more than suggested if you wish) and set aside at room temperature for at least 30 minutes.

Preheat the grill (broiler) to moderate.

Wipe any excess liquid from the fish and sprinkle with a little more salt, rubbing it well into the tail to prevent burning. Grill (broil) the fish for 15 to 20 minutes, turning occasionally, or until the flesh flakes easily.

Serve at once, with rice, soup and some vegetable side dishes.

Serves 4
Preparation and cooking time: 50 minutes

Washi no Su-Jyoyu Zuke

(Barbecued Sardines)

Metric/Imperial	American
150ml./5fl.oz. soya sauce	$\frac{2}{3}$ cup soy sauce
50ml./2fl.oz. vinegar	$\frac{1}{4}$ cup vinegar
2 Tbs. lemon juice	2 Tbs. lemon juice
2½cm./1in. piece of fresh root ginger, peeled and chopped	1in. piece of fresh green ginger, peeled and chopped
2 garlic cloves, crushed	2 garlic cloves, crushed
½kg./1lb. fresh sardines, cleaned and gutted	1lb. fresh sardines, cleaned and gutted
2 Tbs. vegetable oil	2 Tbs. vegetable oil

Washi No Su-Jyoyu Zuke is a delicious dish of sardines marinated first in a mixture of soy sauce, vinegar, lemon juice and ginger, then barbecued.

Combine the soy sauce, vinegar, lemon juice, ginger and garlic in a small bowl. Arrange the sardines in a large shallow dish and pour over the soy sauce mixture, basting to coat the fish thoroughly. Set aside at room temperature to marinate for 2 hours, basting the fish occasionally.

Preheat the grill (broiler) to high.

Remove the sardines from the marinade and dry them on kichen towels. Discard the marinade. Reduce the grill (broiler) to moderate.

Arrange the sardines on the rack of the grill (broiler) and brush the fish with half the oil. Grill (broil) for 4 minutes, then brush again with the remaining oil. Grill (broil) the other side for 3 minutes, or until the flesh flakes easily.

Remove from the heat and serve at once.

Serves 4

Preparation and cooking time: $2\frac{1}{4}$ hours

Ika no Tsukeyaki

(Gilled [Broiled] Squid)

Metric/Imperial	American
4 medium squid, cleaned, spinal bone removed	4 medium squid, cleaned, spinal bone removed
4 Tbs. grated radish	4 Tbs. grated radish
MARINADE	MARINADE
150ml./5fl.oz. soya sauce	⅔ cup soy sauce
150ml./5fl.oz. sake or dry sherry	⅔ cup sake or dry sherry
2 Tbs. sugar	2 Tbs. sugar

Remove the tentacles from the squid, then rub away the outer skin. Set side.

Put the soy sauce, sake or sherry and sugar into a small saucepan and bring to the boil. Remove the pan from the heat and pour the mixture into a large shallow dish. Arrange the squid in the dish and set aside at room temperature to marinate for 15 minutes.

Preheat the grill (broiler) to moderate.

Remove the squid from the marinade and pat dry with kitchen towels. Reserve the marinade. Score the surface of the fish and arrange them on the rack of the grill (broiler). Grill (broil) for 8 minutes on each side, basting occasionally with the marinating liquid.

Remove the squid to a chopping board and cut into strips about 2½cm./1in. wide. Arrange decoratively on a serving platter and pour over the remaining marinade. Garnish with grated radish and serve at once.

Serves 4

Preparation and cooking time: 30 minutes

Tarako to Tasai no Niawase

(Cod's Roes and Vegetables Cooked in Soy Sauce)

Metric/Imperial	American
3 Tbs. vegetable oil	3 Tbs. vegetable oil
1 large carrot, cut into matchstick strips	1 large carrot, cut into matchstick strips
50g./2oz. tin shirataki noodles, soaked in hot water for 3 minutes and cut into matchstick strips	2oz. can shirataki noodles, soaked in hot water for 3 minutes and cut into matchstick strips
1 Tbs. sake or dry sherry	1 Tbs. sake or dry sherry
monosodium glutamate (optional)	MSG (optional)
2 fresh cod's roes, skinned	2 fresh cod's roes, skinned
250ml./8fl.oz. dashi	1 cup dashi
2 Tbs. soya sauce	2 Tbs. soy sauce
1 Tbs. mirin or sweet sherry	1 Tbs. mirin or sweet sherry
1 leek, cleaned and finely chopped	1 leek, cleaned and finely chopped

Heat the oil in a deep frying-pan. When it is hot, add the carrot, shirataki, sake or sherry and monosodium glutamate to taste. Cook, stirring occasionally, for 5 minutes. Add the cod's roes, dashi, soy sauce and mirin and continue to cook until the roes turn white. Stir in the leek and cook for a further 2 minutes.

Transfer the mixture to a warmed serving bowl and serve.

Serves 4-6

Preparation and cooking time: 30 minutes

Sashimi

(Sliced Raw Fish)

Sashimi is one of the finest and simplest of Japanese fish dishes. Almost any type of fish can be used – dover sole, lemon sole, tuna, squid, abalone, bream or any type of shellfish – but it must be of the very highest quality and be as fresh as possible. To preserve freshness, it is better to buy a whole fish and have the fish merchant clean and fillet it for you, rather than purchase pre-filleted fish.

Metric/Imperial	American
½kg./1lb. firm fresh fish (as above)	1lb. firm fresh fish (as above)
1 Tbs. salt	1 Tbs. salt
SAUCE	SAUCE
2 tsp. green horseradish (wasabi), mixed to a paste with 2 tsp. water	2 tsp. green horseradish (wasabi), mixed to a paste with 2 tsp. water
125ml./4fl.oz. soya sauce	½ cup soy sauce

Sashimi (Sliced Raw Fish) – the dish that foreigners (rightly) think of as epitomizing Japanese cuisine. Here the fish is as fresh from the sea as possible, and served with a slightly piquant sauce made from horseradish and soy sauce.

Wash the fillets and sprinkle them lightly with salt. Cover and put into the refrigerator for 30 minutes. (Some people prefer to douse the fish in boiling water, then refresh in cold running water before putting into the refrigerator, to provide protection against surface bacteria.)

Remove the fish from the refrigerator and cut crosswise into bite-sized pieces. Arrange the pieces either on one large serving dish or on individual dishes.

To make the sauce, mix the horseradish into the soy sauce, then pour the mixture into individual dipping bowls. The fish should be dipped in the sauce before eating.

Serves 2-4

Preparation time: 40 minutes

Sushi

(Marinated Fish)

Metric/Imperial	American
½kg./1lb. mackerel fillets, skinned	1lb. mackerel fillets, skinned
GARNISH	GARNISH
125g./4oz. radish, grated	⅔ cup grated radish
1 red pepper, pith and seeds removed and chopped	1 red pepper, pith and seeds removed and chopped
2 Tbs. soya sauce mixed with 2 tsp. lemon juice	2 Tbs. soy sauce mixed with 2 tsp. lemon juice
SAUCE	SAUCE
2 tsp. green horseradish (wasabi), mixed to a paste with 2 tsp. water	2 tsp. green horseradish (washabi), mixed to a paste with 2 tsp. water
50ml./2fl.oz. soya sauce mixed with 2 Tbs. sake or dry sherry	¼ cup soy sauce mixed with 2 Tbs. sake or dry sherry

Put the mackerel fillets in a colander and pour over boiling water. Refresh the fish under cold running-water, then transfer them to a chopping board. Cut the fillets, crosswise, into very thin strips. Arrange the strips on a plate, cover with foil and chill in the refrigerator while you arrange the garnish.

Put the vegetables in a small serving bowl and pour over the soy sauce mixture. Toss gently so that all the vegetable pieces are coated.

Remove the fish from the refrigerator and divide it among six individual serving bowls. Arrange a portion of the garnish beside each bowl.

To make the sauce, stir the horseradish mixture into the soy sauce mixture and pour into individual dipping bowls.

Dip the fish into the sauce mixture before eating and eat at once, with the garnish.

Serves 6
Preparation time: 30 minutes

Kamaboko

(Small Fish Cakes)

Kamaboko are very popular in Japan as an hors d'oeuvre, but they can also form part of some one-pot meals as well. A canned version is widely used now, but as always, home-made varieties tend to have a much better taste and texture. Almost any type of firm white fish fillet could be used – or a mixture; this is an excellent way to use leftover fillet pieces. They can also be steamed for a more delicate taste.

Metric/Imperial	American
½kg./1lb. white fish fillets, skinned and chopped	1lb. white fish fillets, skinned and chopped
3 Tbs. flour	3 Tbs. flour
2 egg whites, beaten until frothy	2 egg whites, beaten until frothy
1 Tbs. mirin or sweet sherry	1 Tbs. mirin or sweet sherry
1 tsp. sugar	1 tsp. sugar
½ tsp. monosodium glutamate	½ tsp. MSG
50g./2oz. cornflour	½ cup cornstarch
75ml./3fl.oz. vegetable oil	⅓ cup vegetable oil

Put the fish pieces into a blender and blend until they form a fairly smooth purée. Transfer the purée to a mixing bowl and stir in the flour, egg whites, mirin or sherry, sugar and monosodium glutamate. Beat briskly until the mixture is thoroughly blended.

Take about 2 tablespoonfuls of the mixture and shape it into a small cake or patty shape with your hands. Dust it lightly with the cornflour (cornstarch) and set aside. Repeat the process until all of the mixture is used up.

Heat the oil in a large frying-pan. When it is hot, add the fish cakes (in batches if necessary) and fry gently for 5 minutes on each side, or until they are golden brown and crisp, and cooked through.

Remove from the pan and drain on kitchen towels. Serve hot.

Serves 4-6 as an hors d'oeuvre
Preparation and cooking time: 30 minutes

Shrimps with Bamboo Shoot

Metric/Imperial	American
50ml./2fl.oz. water	$\frac{1}{4}$ cup water
50ml./2fl.oz. soya sauce	$\frac{1}{4}$ cup soy sauce
350g./12oz. shelled prawns	12oz. shelled shrimp
400g./14oz. tin bamboo shoot, drained and sliced	14oz. can bamboo shoot, drained and sliced
2 Tbs. sake or dry sherry	2 Tbs. sake or dry sherry
2 Tbs. mirin or sweet sherry	2 Tbs. mirin or sweet sherry

Put the water and soy sauce into a shallow saucepan and bring to the boil. Reduce the heat to moderate and stir in the prawns (shrimp). Cook for 5 minutes. Using a slotted spoon, transfer the prawns (shrimp) to a warmed bowl and keep hot.

Add the bamboo shoot slices to the pan and return to the boil. Stir in the sake or sherry and mirin or sherry and cook for 3 minutes. Return the prawns (shrimp) to the pan and stir until the mixture is blended. Cook for 1 minute.

Transfer the mixture to a warmed serving dish and serve at once.

Serves 4
Preparation and cooking time: 15 minutes

Iri-Tamago

(Eggs with Shrimp and Peas)

Metric/Imperial	American
4 eggs, lightly beaten	4 eggs, lightly beaten
50ml./2fl.oz. dashi	$\frac{1}{4}$ cup dashi
1 tsp. sugar	1 tsp. sugar
2 tsp. soya sauce	2 tsp. soy sauce
2 tsp. sake or dry sherry	2 tsp. sake or dry sherry
monosodium glutamate (optional)	MSG (optional)
3 Tbs. vegetable oil	3 Tbs. vegetable oil
125g./4oz. frozen shelled shrimps	4 oz. frozen shelled shrimp
225g./8oz. frozen green peas	1 cup frozen green peas
3 dried mushrooms, soaked in cold water for 30 minutes, drained and sliced	3 dried mushrooms, soaked in cold water for 30 minutes, drained and sliced

Beat the eggs, dashi, sugar, soy sauce, sake or sherry and monosodium glutamate to taste together until they are thoroughly blended. Set aside.

Heat the oil in a large frying-pan. When it is hot, add the shrimps, peas and mushrooms and stir-fry for 3 to 4 minutes, or until the shrimps and peas are cooked through. Stir in the eggs and reduce the heat to moderately low. Cook the mixture, stirring the eggs from time to time to 'scramble' them, until the egg mixture has just lightly set.

Transfer the mixture to a warmed serving plate and serve at once.

Serves 2-3
Preparation and cooking time: 40 minutes

Mazezushi

(Vegetables and Seafood with Rice)

Metric/Imperial	American
450g./1lb. short-grain rice	2⅔ cups short-grain rice
600ml./1 pint water	2½ cups water
VINEGAR SAUCE	VINEGAR SAUCE
50ml./2fl.oz. white wine vinegar	¼ cup white wine vinegar
1 Tbs. sugar	1 Tbs. sugar
½ tsp. salt	½ tsp. salt
monosodium glutamate (optional)	MSG (optional)
VEGETABLES	VEGETABLES
2 carrots, thinly sliced	2 carrots, thinly sliced
1 tinned bamboo shoot, drained and thinly sliced	1 canned bamboo shoot, drained and thinly sliced
¼ small turnip, thinly sliced	¼ small turnip, thinly sliced
3 Tbs. frozen green peas	3 Tbs. frozen green peas
175ml./6fl.oz. dashi	¾ cup dashi
1 Tbs. sake or dry sherry	1 Tbs. sake or dry sherry
1 Tbs. sugar	1 Tbs. sugar
1 Tbs. vegetable oil	1 Tbs. vegetable oil
4 dried mushrooms, soaked in cold water for 30 minutes, drained and sliced	4 dried mushrooms, soaked in cold water for 30 minutes, drained and sliced
2 Tbs. soya sauce	2 Tbs. soy sauce
OMELET	OMELET
1 Tbs. vegetable oil	1 Tbs. vegetable oil
3 eggs, lightly beaten	3 eggs, lightly beaten
SEAFOOD	SEAFOOD
125g./4oz. cooked prawns	4oz. cooked shrimp
125g./4oz. crabmeat, shell and cartilage removed and flaked	4oz. crabmeat, shell and cartilage removed and flaked

First make the rice. Cook the rice, following the instructions given in *Gohan*. Transfer the drained rice to a warmed bowl and set aside. To make the vinegar sauce, combine the vinegar, sugar, salt and monosodium glutamate to taste, then pour the mixture over the rice. Stir gently with a wooden spoon and set aside to cool at room temperature.

Meanwhile, prepare the vegetables. Put the carrots, bamboo shoot, turnip and peas into a saucepan and pour over enough water to cover. Bring to the boil and blanch briskly for 2 minutes. Drain the vegetables. Put 125m./4fl. oz. (½ cup) of dashi, the sake or dry sherry and half the sugar in a small saucepan and bring to the boil. Add the drained vegetables and cook for a further 2 minutes. Transfer the vegetables to a bowl and drain and reserve the dashi liquid.

Heat the oil in a small frying-pan. When it is hot, add the mushrooms, the remaining dashi and sugar, and the soy sauce. Cook, stirring constantly, for 3 minutes. Remove from the heat and cool.

To make the omelets, brush the bottom of an omelet pan with some of the oil and pour in about a third of the egg mixture. Tilt the pan so that the mixture covers the bottom of the pan, then leave to cook until the omelet has set. Shake the pan slightly to loosen the omelet, then quickly turn over and cook the other side for 15 seconds. Slide on to a plate and cook the remaining egg mixture in the same way. When all the omelets have been cooked, pile them on top of one another and cut into thin strips.

To assemble, stir the vegetables and reserved cooking liquid gently into the vinegared rice with a wooden spoon. Then stir in the prawns (shrimp) and crabmeat. Arrange the egg strips decoratively over the top and serve at once.

Serves 6
Preparation and cooking time: 2 hours

Hamaguri Shigure-Ni

(Sake and Soy Sauce-Flavoured Clams)

Metric/Imperial	American
50ml./2fl.oz. sake or dry sherry	¼ cup sake or dry sherry
2 Tbs. sugar	2 Tbs. sugar
12 clams, removed from their shells	12 clams, removed from their shells
2 Tbs. soya sauce	2 Tbs. soy sauce

In a large, heavy frying-pan combine the sake or sherry, sugar and clams. Stir the mixture thoroughly with a wooden spoon. Bring to the boil and cook for 3 minutes, stirring constantly. Stir in the soy sauce and boil for a further 1 minute, stirring constantly. Using a slotted spoon, transfer the clams to a plate.

Boil the sauce for a further 10 minutes, or until it becomes thick and rather syrupy. Return the clams to the pan and stir them gently into the sauce. Cook the mixture for about 1 minute, or until the clams are thoroughly coated with the sauce.

Remove from the heat and spoon the mixture into a warmed serving dish. Serve at once.

Serves 4
Preparation and cooking time: 30 minutes

Kimini

(Glazed Prawns or Shrimp)

Metric/Imperial	American
12 medium prawns	12 medium shrimp
50g./2oz. cornflour	½ cup cornstarch
3½ Tbs. dashi	3½ Tbs. dashi
2 Tbs. sake or dry sherry	2 Tbs. sake or dry sherry
½ tsp. sugar	½ tsp. sugar
¼ tsp. salt	¼ tsp. salt
monosodium glutamate (optional)	MSG (optional)
3 egg yolks, well beaten	3 egg yolks, well beaten

Shell the prawns (shrimp), leaving the tails intact. Remove the veins at the head with the tip of a knife, then dip the prawns (shrimp) into the cornflour (cornstarch), shaking off any excess. Drop the prawns (shrimp) into a saucepan of boiling water and cook for about 10 seconds. Remove and rinse under cold running water. Set aside.

Pour the dashi into a small saucepan and stir in the sake or sherry, sugar, salt and monosodium glutamate to taste. Bring to the boil. Arrange the prawns (shrimp) in the pan and return the liquid to the boil, basting the prawns (shrimp). When the liquid boils, pour the beaten egg yolks slowly over the prawns (shrimp). Do not stir, cover the pan and simmer over low heat for 2 minutes. Remove from the heat but leave for a further 2 minutes before serving as a side dish, or as a main dish with vegetables.

Serves 2-4
Preparation and cooking time: 20 minutes

Clams are a popular ingredient in many Japanese dishes. In Hamaguri Shigure-Ni they are cooked in a very special mixture of sake and soy sauce.

Kani no Sunomono

(Crab and Cucumber with Vinegar Dressing)

Metric/Imperial	American
½ cucumber	½ cucumber
225g./8oz. crabmeat, shell and cartilage removed and flaked	8oz. crabmeat, shell and cartilage removed and flaked
VINEGAR DRESSING	VINEGAR DRESSING
2 Tbs. white wine vinegar	2 Tbs. white wine vinegar
2 Tbs. mirin or sweet sherry	2 Tbs. mirin or sweet sherry
2 Tbs. dashi	2 Tbs. dashi
1 Tbs. soya sauce	1 Tbs. soy sauce
2 tsp. sugar	2 tsp. sugar
monosodium glutamate (optional)	MSG (optional)

Partially peel the cucumber, leaving some long green strips for colour. Slice as thinly as possible, sprinkle with salt and leave to dégorge in a colander for about 30 minutes. Squeeze out any excess liquid gently with your hands, then dry on kitchen towels. Arrange the cucumber and crabmeat decoratively in a small shallow dish.

To make the vinegar dressing, combine all the ingredients, beating until they are well blended. Pour over the cucumber and crabmeat and toss gently so that they are well coated. Set the dish aside at room temperature to marinate for 30 minutes, tossing gently from time to time. Carefully drain off any excess dressing before serving.

Sunamon ('vinegared things') can accompany main dishes or be served as an hors d'oeuvre.

Serves 2
Preparation time: 1¼ hours

Hamaguri Sakani

(Sake-Flavoured Clams)

Metric/Imperial	American
50ml./2fl.oz. sake or dry sherry	¼ cup sake or dry sherry
12 clams, removed from the shells, half the shells scrubbed and reserved	12 clams, removed from the shells, half the shells scrubbed and reserved
GARNISH	GARNISH
12 lemon slices	12 lemon slices

Put the sake into a large saucepan and bring to the boil. Add the clams, stirring with a wooden spoon. Cover the pan and reduce the heat to low. Simmer for 5 minutes. Using a slotted spoon, remove the clams and arrange one on each of the reserved shells. Garnish each shell with a lemon slice.

Put the clams on a serving dish and allow them to cool to room temperature. Chill in the refrigerator for 30 minutes. Remove from the refrigerator and serve as an hors d'oeuvre.

Serves 4
Preparation and cooking time: 50 minutes

Torigai to Wakame no Nuta

(Cockles and Seaweed with Miso)

Metric/Imperial	American
1 Tbs. wakame or dried seaweed, soaked in water until soft	1 Tbs. wakame or dried seaweed, soaked in water until soft
8 spring onions, chopped and parboiled	8 scallions, chopped and parboiled

225g./8oz. cockles, washed	8oz. cockles, washed
1 celery stalk, chopped	1 celery stalk, chopped
MISO SAUCE	MISO SAUCE
2½ Tbs. white wine vinegar	2½ Tbs. white wine vinegar
2½ Tbs. sake or dry sherry	2½ Tbs. sake or dry sherry
2½ Tbs. sugar	2½ Tbs. sugar
5 Tbs. miso paste	5 Tbs. miso paste

Put the vinegar, sake and sugar into a saucepan and bring to the boil. Remove from the heat and stir in the miso paste until it melts. Pour into individual dipping bowls and set aside.

Chop the wakame into short lengths, then arrange all the remaining ingredients on one large serving platter or individual serving plates. The sauce can either be served separately or, alternatively, it can be mixed into the ingredients and tossed gently before serving.

This dish is usually served as a starter or a side dish.

Serves 3-4
Preparation and cooking time: 15 minutes

Prawns in Batter

(Korea)

Metric/Imperial	American
½kg./1lb. prawns	1lb. shrimp
vegetable oil for deep-frying	vegetable oil for deep-frying
BATTER	BATTER
50g./2oz. rice flour	½ cup rice flour
salt	salt
monosodium glutamate (optional)	MSG (optional)
1 egg, lightly beaten	1 egg, lightly beaten
125ml./4fl.oz. water	½ cup water
DIPPING SAUCE	DIPPING SAUCE
250ml./8fl.oz. soya sauce	1 cup soy sauce
3 spring onions, chopped	3 scallions, chopped

Remove the shells from the prawns (shrimp), leaving the tails intact. Remove the heads and any tentacles.

To make the batter, beat all of the ingredients together in a shallow bowl with a whisk or wooden spoon until they are thoroughly blended.

Set the bowl aside.

Fill a large deep-frying pan one-third full with oil and heat it until it is hot. Dip the prawns (shrimp) first in the batter, coating thoroughly but shaking off any excess, then carefully lower them into the oil, a few at a time. Deep-fry for 2 to 3 minutes, or until the prawns (shrimp) are golden brown. Remove from the oil and drain on kitchen towels. Keep hot while you cook the remaining prawns (shrimp) in the same way.

To make the dipping sauce, combine the soy sauce and spring onions (scallions) and pour into small, individual bowls.

Serve at once, with the prawns (shrimp).

Serves 4
Preparation and cooking time: 25 minutes

ONE-POT

Shin-Sol-Lo

(Korean Steamboat)

This exotic soup-like mixture is the 'royal' dish of Korea and, to be absolutely authentic, should be cooked in a special shin-sol-lo cooker as suggested below. They can be obtained from Chinese or other large Oriental stores. If you don't have one, however, a fondue pot or flameproof casserole makes a perfectly adequate substitute. In the latter case, just put all the ingredients into the pot together and bring to the boil before serving. Any vegetable of your choice can be substituted for those suggested below.

Metric/Imperial	American
FISH	FISH
225g./8oz. firm white fish fillet, skinned and cut into large bite-sized pieces	8oz. firm white fish fillet, skinned and cut into large bite-sized pieces
50g./2oz. cornflour, mixed to a paste with 125ml./4fl.oz. water	½ cup cornstarch, mixed to a paste with ½ cup water
4 Tbs. peanut oil	4 Tbs. peanut oil
VEGETABLES	VEGETABLES
¼ small Chinese cabbage, shredded	¼ small Chinese cabbage, shredded
225g./8oz. leaf spinach, chopped	1⅓ cups chopped leaf spinach
3 carrots, chopped or sliced	3 carrots, chopped or sliced
salt	salt
SHIN-SOL-LO	SHIN-SOL-LO
225g./8oz. cooked meat, such as ox tongue, cut into strips	8oz. cooked meat, such as ox tongue, cut into strips
1 large red pepper, pith and seeds removed and sliced	1 large red pepper, pith and seeds removed and sliced
4 large button mushrooms, sliced	4 large button mushrooms, sliced
2 spring onions, chopped	2 scallions, chopped
125g./4oz. Chinese fish cake, sliced (optional)	4oz. Chinese fish cake, sliced (optional)
125g./4oz. frozen peeled prawns	4oz. frozen peeled shrimp
1.21./2 pints boiling beef stock	5 cups boiling beef stock
salt and black pepper	salt and black pepper

First prepare the fish. Dip the fish pieces in the cornflour (cornstarch) batter and set aside for 5 minutes. Heat the oil in a large frying-pan. When it is hot, add the fish pieces and fry gently for 5 minutes on each side, or until the flesh just flakes. Remove the fish from the heat and drain on kitchen towels. Transfer the pieces to a plate.

Cook the cabbage, spinach and carrots separately in boiling salted water until they are just cooked but still crisp. Remove from the heat, drain and add to the fish pieces.

To prepare the shin-sol-lo, prepare the charcoal so that it is burning. Arrange the fish pieces, vegetables pieces, then meat, red pepper and mushroom slices around the sides of the pot. Scatter over the spring onions (scallions), fish cake and prawns (shrimp), then pour over the stock and season with salt and pepper to taste.

Put the embers from the charcoal into the centre of the pot, then cover with new charcoal, fanning the embers so that the new charcoal will ignite. Cover the pot and steam the shin-sol-lo for 3 to 5 minutes, or until the stock returns to the boil.

Traditionally, the pot is then brought to the table (with the embers still lit) and diners help themselves. Rice is usually served as an accompaniment, in the same bowl as the shin-sol-lo.

Serves 6–8
Preparation and cooking time: 45 minutes

Sukiyaki I

(Quick-Braised Beef and Vegetables)

Sukiyaki is one of the most popular one-pot dishes in Japan – and is probably the most famous Japanese dish outside the country. To eat it Japanese style, the ingredients for the dish should be arranged decoratively on a serving platter then cooked at the table, fondue-style, with each diner selecting his own food. The cooked food should be dipped in the lightly beaten egg before being eaten.

Metric/Imperial	American
1kg./2lb. fillet steak, cut across the grain into thin slices or strips	2lb. fillet steak, cut across the grain into thin slices or strips
225g./8oz. tin shirataki noodles	8oz. can shirataki noodles
225g./8oz. small spinach leaves	2 cups small spinach leaves
450g./1lb. mushrooms, stalks removed and caps halved	1lb. mushrooms, stalks removed and caps halved
1 large carrot, cut into strips	1 large carrot, cut into strips
12 spring onions, sliced	12 scallions, sliced
200g./7oz. tin bamboo shoot, drained and sliced	7oz. can bamboo shoot, drained and sliced
1 bean curd cake (tofu), cubed	1 bean curd cake (tofu), cubed
250ml./8fl.oz. dashi	1 cup dashi
125ml./4fl.oz. sake or dry sherry	½ cup sake or dry sherry
6 eggs	6 eggs
2 Tbs. beef suet or lard	2 Tbs. beef suet or lard
175ml./6fl.oz. soya sauce	¾ cup soy sauce
2 Tbs. soft brown sugar	2 Tbs. soft brown sugar

Arrange the steak pieces, shirataki noodles, spinach leaves, mushrooms, carrot, spring onions (scallions), bamboo shoot and bean curd cubes decoratively on a large serving platter. Set aside. Mix the dashi and sake together until they are well combined. Set aside. Break the eggs into individual serving bowls and beat lightly. Set aside.

Heat a heavy, flameproof casserole over low heat until it is hot. Spear the suet on a fork and rub gently over the bottom of the casserole, or allow the lard to melt. Discard the suet. Put about a sixth of the meat and vegetables into the casserole, adding about a sixth of the dashi mixture, a sixth of the soy sauce and a sixth of the sugar. Cook for 5 to 6 minutes, stirring and turning frequently, until all the ingredients are tender but still crisp. Using a slotted spoon, transfer the mixture to individual serving plates and serve with the beaten egg. Cook the remaining ingredients in the same way. The liquid should always be simmering. If the food begins to stick in the casserole, add 1 teaspoon of cold water to cool it or to reduce the heat to moderately low. The sauce becomes stronger as more liquid and sugar are added at each cooking stage so it may be necessary to reduce these amounts to your taste.

Serves 6
Preparation and cooking time: 45 minutes

(See over) Sukiyaki is what everyone thinks of when they think of Japanese food, and you can see why when you taste this version (Sukiyaki I). It is also one of the most hospitable of dishes – who can stand on ceremony when faced with a communal pot full of rich, cooking food?

Sukiyaki II

(Marinated Braised Beef and Vegetables)

Metric/Imperial	American
1kg./2lb. fillet steak, cut into thin strips	2lb. fillet steak, cut into thin strips
300ml./10fl.oz. sake or dry sherry	1¼ cups sake or dry sherry
4 Tbs. soya sauce	4 Tbs. soy sauce
salt and pepper	salt and pepper
8 spring onions, cut into 2½cm./1in. lengths	8 scallions, cut into 1in. lengths
12 button mushrooms, stalks removed	12 button mushrooms, stalks removed
2 large green peppers, pith and seeds removed and cut into strips	2 large green peppers, pith and seeds removed and cut into strips
225g./8oz. small spinach leaves	1 cup small spinach leaves
vegetable oil for deep-frying	vegetable oil for deep-frying
SAUCE	SAUCE
1 eating apple, cored and grated	1 eating apple, cored and grated
1 large leek, cleaned and chopped	1 large leek, cleaned and chopped
2 garlic cloves, crushed	2 garlic cloves, crushed
¼ tsp. cayenne pepper	¼ tsp. cayenne pepper
1 small red pepper, pith and seeds removed and finely chopped	1 small red pepper, pith and seeds removed and finely chopped

Put the beef strips into a large shallow dish and pour over the sake or sherry and soy sauce. Sprinkle over salt and pepper to taste. Set aside at room temperature to marinate for at least 4 hours, turning the meat occasionally. Using a slotted spoon, transfer the meat strips to a plate and reserve the marinade.

Arrange the spring onions (scallions), mushrooms, peppers, and spinach decoratively on a serving platter. Set aside.

Pour the reserved marinade into a serving bowl and stir in the grated apple, leek, garlic, cayenne and red pepper.

Fill a large deep-frying pan one-third full with oil and heat it until it is very hot. Either transfer the oil carefully to a fondue pot or Japanese cooking pot or continue cooking in the saucepan. Carefully lower a few pieces of meat and vegetables into the oil and cook for 1 to 2 minutes, or until they are just crisp. Remove from the oil and drain on kitchen towels. Keep hot while you cook the remaining ingredients in the same way.

The cooked food should be dipped into the sauce before eating.
Serves 6
Preparation and cooking time: 4½ hours

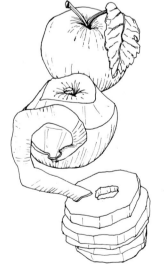

Chiri Nabe

(Fish and Vegetable Casserole)

Metric/Imperial	American
1 small Chinese cabbage, trimmed	1 small Chinese cabbage, trimmed
1 large bream or similar fish, cleaned, gutted and filleted	1 large bream, or similar fish, cleaned, gutted and filleted
3 leeks, cleaned and cut into 1cm./½in. lengths	3 leeks, cleaned and cut into ½in. lengths
3 bean curd cakes (tofu), cubed	3 bean curd cakes (tofu), cubed

1.21/2 pints dashi	5 cups dashi
150ml./5fl.oz. soya sauce	⅔ cup soy sauce
6 spring onions, chopped	6 scallions, chopped
1 small turnip, grated	1 small turnip, grated
juice of two lemons	juice of two lemons

Cook the cabbage in boiling water for 5 minutes. Drain, then chop diagonally into 5cm./2in. lengths. Cut the fish into large pieces and arrange the fish, cabbage, leeks and bean curd on a large serving platter.

Pour the dashi into a flameproof casserole or fondue pot and bring to the boil. Add the ingredients to the dashi, a few at a time, and cook for 3 to 5 minutes, or until they are cooked through.

Mix the soy sauce, spring onions (scallions), turnip and lemon juice together and divide among individual dipping bowls. The cooked food should be dipped in the sauce before eating.

Serves 4-6
Preparation and cooking time: 45 minutes

Botan Nabe

(Pork and Vegetables in Stock)

The name for this dish comes from the Japanese word for peony because the pork pieces are arranged in the shape of this flower before cooking.

Metric/Imperial	American
½kg./1lb. carrots, cut into ½cm./¼in. lengths	1lb. carrots, cut into ¼in. lengths
1 medium white cabbage, separated into leaves	1 medium white cabbage, separated into leaves
225g./8oz. mushrooms	2 cups mushrooms
700g./1½lb. lean pork, very thinly sliced	1½lb. lean pork, very thinly sliced
3 garlic cloves, crushed	3 garlic cloves, crushed
4cm./1½in. piece of fresh root ginger, peeled and chopped	1½in. piece of fresh green ginger, peeled and chopped
250ml./8fl.oz. soya sauce	1 cup soy sauce
6 spring onions, finely chopped	6 scallions, finely chopped
2 lemons, cut into small wedges	2 lemons, cut into small wedges
450ml./15fl.oz. dashi	2 cups dashi

Lightly cook the carrots and cabbage separately in boiling water for 3 minutes. Drain and roll up the cabbage leaves into rolls. Arrange the carrots, cabbage rolls and mushrooms decoratively on a serving platter.

Arrange the pork slices carefully in the shape of a flower on a serving plate and garnish with the garlic and ginger to make the centre of the flower.

Combine the soy sauce with about a quarter of the spring onions (scallions) and pour into individual dipping bowls. Arrange the lemon wedges and remaining spring onions (scallions) in separate serving bowls.

Pour the dashi into a saucepan or fondue pot and bring to the boil. Add a few pieces of the pork and cook until it is white. Cook the other ingredients in the same way. The cooked food should be dipped in the sauce before eating.

When all the ingredients have been cooked, the stock may be served as a soup.

Serves 6
Preparation and cooking time: 50 minutes

Tempura

(Deep-Fried Food Japanese Style)

Although tempura is one of the best known Japanese dishes outside Japan, it is not traditionally Japanese – but rather an adaptation of a Portuguese dish. (The name comes from the Latin word for time.) In Japan there are many restaurants devoted exclusively to tempura and in the West it has now become a popular party dish – and it does lend itself extremely well to fondue-style informality.

The oil used to fry the tempura is important; in Japan a mixture of cotton seed, sesame seed and groundnut oil is a favourite and we would suggest here that you use groundnut oil and sesame oil in the proportions of 4 to 1.

Metric/Imperial	American
12 fresh prawns, heads removed but still in shell	12 fresh shrimp, with the heads removed but still in shell
4 plaice fillets, skinned and cut into 2½cm./1in. pieces	4 flounder fillets, skinned and cut into 1in. pieces
1 medium squid, skinned and cut into 2½cm./1in. pieces	1 medium squid, skinned and cut into 1 in. pieces
225g./8oz. cod fillet, skinned and cut into 2½cm./1in. pieces	8oz. cod fillet, skinned and cut into 1in. pieces
1 large green pepper, pith and seeds removed and cut into 2½cm./1in. pieces	1 large green pepper, pith and seeds removed and cut into 1in. pieces
12 small button mushrooms	12 small button mushrooms
1 tinned bamboo shoot, drained and cut into ½cm./¼in. pieces	1 canned bamboo shoot, drained and cut into ¼in. pieces
12 cauliflower flowerets	12 cauliflower flowerets
mixed oil for deep-frying	mixed oil for deep-frying
BATTER	BATTER
1 egg, plus 1 egg yolk, lightly beaten	1 egg, plus 1 egg yolk, lightly beaten
175ml./6fl.oz. water	¾ cup water
125g./4oz. flour	1 cup flour
SAUCE	SAUCE
250ml./8fl.oz. soya sauce	1 cup soy sauce
250ml./8fl.oz. water	1 cup water
2 small turnips or large Japanese radishes, grated	2 small turnips or large Japanese radishes, grated

Put the prawns (shrimp) on a board and slit them lengthways, leaving the tails intact. Remove and discard the shells and open out the flesh so that they stay flat. Arrange the prawns (shrimp), plaice (flounder) pieces, squid, cod, green pepper, mushrooms, bamboo shoot and cauliflower flowerets on a large serving platter.

To make the batter, combine all the batter ingredients and beat with a fork until it forms a smooth paste.

Fill a large deep-frying pan one-third full with the oil and heat it until it is very hot. Either continue cooking in this pan or transfer the oil to a fondue pot and continue cooking over a spirit burner.

Using Japanese cooking chopsticks or a long-handled two-prong fork, spear a piece of food and dip it into the batter. Then carefully lower it into the oil and cook for 2 to 4 minutes, depending on the food being cooked, or until it is golden brown. Remove from the oil and transfer to kitchen towels to drain. Keep hot while you cook the remaining food in the same way.

To make the dipping sauce, combine all the ingredients and pour into individual dipping bowls. The cooked food should be dipped into the sauce before eating.
Serves 8
Preparation and cooking time: 1 hour

Mizataki

(Chicken and Vegetable One-Pot Dish)

Metric/Imperial	American
1 x 1½kg./3lb. chicken, cut through the bones with a cleaver into bite-sized pieces	1 x 3lb. chicken, cut through the bones with a cleaver into bite-sized pieces

1 bean curd cake (tofu), cubed	1 bean curd cake (tofu), cubed
225g./8oz. mushrooms, stalks removed	2 cups mushrooms, stalks removed
1 small cabbage, separated into leaves	1 small cabbage, separated into leaves
4 carrots, thinly sliced	4 carrots, thinly sliced
1 bunch of watercress	1 bunch of watercress
2 leeks, cleaned and cut diagonally into 2½cm./1in. lengths	2 leeks, cleaned and cut diagonally into 1in. lengths
450ml./15fl.oz. dashi	2 cups dashi
250ml./8fl.oz. soya sauce	1 cup soy sauce
lemon slices	lemon slices
grated radish	grated radish

Put the chicken and bean curd on a serving platter. Chop or shred the vegetables attractively and arrange them on a serving platter.

Pour the dashi into a flameproof casserole or fondue pot and bring to the boil. Keep it over low heat and add some chicken and vegetables. Cook for 3 to 5 minutes, or until the meat is just cooked through. Each guest should help himself individually, replenishing the pot as necessary.

Pour the soy sauce into individual dipping bowls and garnish with lemon slices and radish.

The cooked food should be dipped into the sauce before eating.

Serves 4
Preparation and cooking time: 1 hour

Shabu Shabu

(Beef with Cabbage and Spinach)

The name of this dish comes from the sound the ingredients make as they are being cooked in the soup.

Metric/Imperial	American
1 medium white cabbage, separated into leaves	1 medium white cabbage, separated into leaves
12 button mushroom caps	12 button mushroom caps
½kg./1lb. spinach, chopped	3 cups chopped spinach
1 bean curd cake (tofu), cubed	1 bean curd cake (tofu), cubed
700g./1½lb. rump steak, cut across the grain into thin strips	1½lb. rump steak, cut across the grain into thin strips
150ml./5fl.oz. soya sauce	⅔ cup soy sauce
2 radishes, grated	2 radishes, grated
4 spring onions, finely chopped	4 scallions, finely chopped
juice of 2 lemons	juice of 2 lemons
1.2l./2 pints dashi	5 cups dashi

Cook the cabbage leaves lightly for 3 minutes, then drain and remove from the pan. Roll up the leaves into rolls. Arrange all the vegetables and bean curd cubes decoratively on a serving platter. Arrange the beef slices decoratively on a second, smaller platter. Set aside.

Mix the soy sauce, radishes, spring onions (scallions) and lemon juice together and pour into individual dipping bowls.

Pour the dashi into a saucepan or fondue pot and bring to the boil. Cook the ingredients in the stock, a few at a time, until they are just cooked through.

The cooked food should be dipped into the sauce before eating.

Serves 4
Preparation and cooking time: 50 minutes

Yose Nabe

(Chicken and Oyster Casserole)

Yosenabe literally means 'a collection of everything', so the ingredients below are just that – suggestions. Almost anything suitable that takes your fancy could be substituted!

Metric/Imperial	American
900ml./1½ pints dashi	3¾ cups dashi
2 chicken breasts, skinned, boned and cubed	2 chicken breasts, skinned, boned and cubed
2 large carrots, sliced	2 large carrots, sliced
12 radishes, thinly sliced	12 radishes, thinly sliced
50ml./2fl.oz. soya sauce	¼ cup soy sauce
150ml/5fl.oz. sake or dry sherry	⅔ cup sake or dry sherry
225g./8oz. tin shirataki noodles	8oz. can shirataki noodles
3 sheets of nori (seaweed), cubed	3 sheets of nori (seaweed), cubed
8 spring onions, cut into small lengths	8 scallions, cut into small lengths
12 raw prawns, shelled	12 raw shrimp, shelled
18 oysters or clams, shells removed	18 oysters or clams, shells removed
225g./8oz. cod fillet, skinned and cubed	8oz. cod fillet, skinned and cubed
18 button mushroom caps	18 button mushroom caps

Pour the dashi into a large saucepan and bring to the boil. Reduce the heat to low, add the chicken cubes and simmer for 10 minutes, or until the cubes are almost tender. Add the carrots and radishes and simmer for a further 5 minutes. Remove the pan from the heat and transfer the chicken and vegetables to a plate. Strain the stock into a large fondue pot or flameproof casserole and stir in the soy sauce and sake or sherry. Bring to the boil.

Arrange all the remaining ingredients on a large serving platter.

Cook the ingredients in the hot stock for 1 to 2 minutes before eating. When all the ingredients have been cooked, the stock may be served as a soup.

Serves 4
Preparation and cooking time: 1 hour

Oden

(Tokyo Hotchpotch)

Street stalls selling this warming dish – which is supposed to have originated in Tokyo – are a common sight in Japan during winter. It is also an excellent dish for parties since it can be left on very low heat for guests to help themselves as and when they want to eat.

Metric/Imperial	American
2.5l./4 pints dashi	2½ quarts dashi
6 Tbs. soya sauce	6 Tbs. soy sauce
1½ Tbs. sugar	1½ Tbs. sugar
monosodium glutamate (optional)	MSG (optional)
1 large squid, cleaned and cut into rings	1 large squid, cleaned and cut into rings
2 medium turnips, cut into chunks	2 medium turnips, cut into chunks
2 large carrots, cut into chunks	2 large carrots, cut into chunks
4 medium potatoes, cut into chunks	4 medium potatoes, cut into chunks
2 pieces of konnyaku, cut into largish triangles	2 pieces of konnyaku, cut into largish triangles

| 4 pieces of abura age, cut into largish triangles and parboiled to remove excess oil | 4 pieces of abura age, cut into largish triangles and parboiled to remove excess oil |

Metric/Imperial	American
4 pieces of abura age, cut into largish triangles and parboiled to remove excess oil	4 pieces of abura age, cut into largish triangles and parboiled to remove excess oil
4 hard-boiled eggs	4 hard-cooked eggs
1 bean curd cake (tofu), cubed	1 bean curd cake (tofu), cubed
MEATBALLS	MEATBALLS
350g./12oz. minced beef	12oz. ground beef
2 spring onions, finely chopped	2 scallions, finely chopped
2½cm./1in. piece of fresh root ginger, peeled and grated	1in. piece of fresh green ginger, peeled and grated
1½ Tbs. flour	1½ Tbs. flour
2 tsp. soya sauce	2 tsp. soy sauce
2 small eggs, beaten	2 small eggs, beaten
monosodium glutamate (optional)	MSG (optional)
vegetable oil for deep-frying	vegetable oil for deep-frying

First prepare the meatballs. Combine the beef, spring onions (scallions), ginger, flour, soy sauce, eggs and monosodium glutamate to taste in a large bowl. Using the palm of your hand, gently shape the mixture into small balls, about 2½cm./1in. in diameter.

Fill a large deep-frying pan about one-third full with oil and heat it until it is very hot. Carefully lower the meatballs, a few at a time, into the oil and fry until they are golden brown. Using a slotted spoon, remove the meatballs from the oil and drain on kitchen towels. Keep hot while you fry the remaining meatballs in the same way. Set aside.

Pour the dashi into a large flameproof casserole and add the soy sauce, sugar and monosodium glutamate to taste. Add all the remaining ingredients, including the meatballs but excepting the bean curd, to the pan and bring to the boil. Reduce the heat to very low and simmer for 2 to 3 hours. Add the bean curd about 30 minutes before you wish to serve the dish.

Oden is usually served with mustard to taste.

Serves 8
Preparation and cooking time: 3½ hours

Tempura Harusame

(Deep-Fried Food coated in Harusame Noodle)

Harusame is a Japanese noodle somewhat similar in texture to Chinese cellophane noodles – and these latter can be substituted if harusame is difficult to obtain.

Metric/Imperial	American
8 large prawns, shelled	8 large shrimp, shelled
1 cod fillet, skinned and cut into 5cm./2in. pieces	1 cod fillet, skinned and cut into 2in. pieces
1 large plaice fillet, skinned and cut into 5cm./2in. pieces	1 large flounder fillet, skinned and cut into 2in. pieces
2 scallops, coral removed and quartered	2 scallops, coral removed and quartered
8 button mushrooms	8 button mushrooms
1 tinned bamboo shoot, drained and cut into 5cm./2in. pieces	1 canned bamboo shoot, drained and cut into 2in. pieces
1 carrot, sliced	1 carrot, sliced
50g./2oz. flour	½ cup flour
2 egg whites, well beaten	2 egg whites, well beaten

175g./6oz. harusame, cut into small
   pieces
vegetable oil for deep-frying
SAUCE
175ml./6fl.oz. dashi
2 Tbs. soya sauce
2 Tbs. mirin or sweet sherry
1 tsp. grated daikon or turnip

6oz. harusame, cut into small
   pieces
vegetable oil for deep-frying
SAUCE
¾ cup dashi
2 Tbs. soy sauce
2 Tbs. mirin or sweet sherry
1 tsp. grated daikon or turnip

Arrange the prawns (shrimp), cod, plaice (flounder), scallops, mushrooms, bamboo shoot and carrot on a large platter. Dip them, one by one, first in the flour, shaking off any excess, then in the egg whites and finally roll them in the chopped noodles to coat them thoroughly. Set aside.

Fill a large deep-frying pan about one-third full of vegetable oil and heat it until it is very hot. Carefully lower the food pieces, two or three at a time, into the oil and fry until they are golden brown and the noodles have expanded. Remove from the oil and transfer to kitchen towels to drain. Keep hot while you cook the remaining pieces in the same way.

To make the sauce, put the dashi, soy sauce and mirin or sherry into a saucepan. Bring to the boil, then stir in the grated daikon or turnip. Remove from the heat and pour into a dipping bowl.

Serve the tempura pieces while they are still piping hot, with the dipping sauce.

Serves 6
Preparation and cooking time: 40 minutes

The classic tempura batter contains egg, water and flour but sometimes in Japan there is another ingredient – harusame. Harusame are small white noodles which expand gloriously in the oil when frying and provide the most deliciously crunchy coating for the succulent fish and vegetables being cooked.

VEGETABLES & PICKLES

Tamago Dashimaki

(Rolled Omelet)

Japanese omelet pans (tamago pans) are rectangular in shape, not round as in the West, but a conventional rounded omelet pan can be substituted. If you have a rectangular flameproof griddle, this would be even better.

Metric/Imperial	American
4 eggs, beaten	4 eggs, beaten
125ml./4fl.oz. dashi	½ cup dashi
pinch of salt	pinch of salt
1 tsp. soya sauce	1 tsp. soy sauce
3 Tbs. vegetable oil	3 Tbs. vegetable oil
DIPPING SAUCE	DIPPING SAUCE
50ml./2fl.oz. soya sauce	¼ cup soy sauce
1 tsp. grated daikon, radish or turnip	1 tsp. grated daikon, radish or turnip

First, prepare the dipping sauce. Combine the ingredients together, beating until they are thoroughly blended. Pour into a small dipping bowl and set aside.

Combine the eggs, dashi, salt and soy sauce in a small bowl.

Using a pastry brush, generously brush the surface of an omelet pan with a little of the oil. When the pan is hot, pour in about a third of the egg mixture, tilting the pan so that the mixture runs over the bottom. Reduce the heat to low and cook until the omelet is set. Using tongs or a spatula, carefully roll up the omelet away from you, then slide on to the far side of the pan. Using the pastry brush, grease the vacant part of the pan with some more of the oil and, when it is hot, pour in half the remaining mixture, gently lifting the rolled omelet so that the mixture covers the entire bottom of the pan. Cook again until the omelet is set, then roll up the second omelet as before, enclosing the first omelet within the second one.

Repeat this process, using the remaining oil and remaining egg mixture and again enclosing the rolled-up omelet in a third roll. Carefully slide the completed omelet on to a flat serving dish and cut into thick slices.

Serve at once, with the dipping sauce.
Serves 2–3
Preparation and cooking time: 20 minutes

Cha Soh Juhn

(Vegetable Croquettes)   (Korea)

Metric/Imperial	American
1 large potato, very finely chopped	1 large potato, very finely chopped
2 carrots, coarsely grated	2 carrots, coarsely grated
1 large onion, very finely chopped	1 large onion, very finely chopped
1 garlic clove, crushed	1 garlic clove, crushed
2 eggs, lightly beaten	2 eggs, lightly beaten
50ml./2fl.oz. water	¼ cup water

1 Tbs. soya sauce	1 Tbs. soy sauce
½ tsp. salt	½ tsp. salt
75g./3oz. flour	¾ cup flour
50ml./2fl.oz. vegetable oil	¼ cup vegetable oil
SAUCE	SAUCE
50ml./2fl.oz. soya sauce	¼ cup soy sauce
50ml./2fl.oz. wine vinegar	¼ cup wine vinegar
1 Tbs. sugar	1 Tbs. sugar

Put the potato, carrots, onion and garlic into a medium mixing bowl and beat until they are thoroughly blended. In a second bowl, beat the eggs, water, soy sauce and salt together until they are thoroughly blended, then gradually fold in the flour until the mixture forms a smooth batter. Stir in the vegetable mixture until it is well blended.

Heat the oil in a large frying-pan. When it is hot, carefully arrange the mixture in the pan, in heaped tablespoons and fry gently until they are browned on one side. Carefully turn over and fry until the croquettes are golden brown on the other side.

Remove from the oil and drain on kitchen towels.

To make the sauce, combine all the ingredients together in a dipping bowl. Serve the croquettes at once, with the sauce.

Serves 4
Preparation and cooking time: 25 minutes

Ko Chooh Juhn

(Fried Green Peppers)   (Korea)

Metric/Imperial	American
4 green peppers, halved lengthwise and with pith and seeds removed	4 green peppers, halved lengthwise and with pith and seeds removed
225g./8oz. minced beef	8oz. ground beef
1 small onion, very finely chopped	1 small onion, very finely chopped
1 garlic clove, crushed	1 garlic clove, crushed
1 Tbs. soya sauce	1 Tbs. soy sauce
¼ tsp. hot chilli powder	¼ tsp. hot chilli powder
1 tsp. roasted sesame seeds, ground	1 tsp. roasted sesame seeds, ground
2 eggs, lightly beaten	2 eggs, lightly beaten
25g./1oz. flour	¼ cup flour
50ml./2fl.oz. vegetable oil	¼ cup vegetable oil
DIPPING SAUCE	DIPPING SAUCE
125ml./4fl.oz. soya sauce	½ cup soy sauce
125ml./4fl.oz. wine vinegar	½ cup wine vinegar
1 garlic clove, crushed	1 garlic clove, crushed

Put the pepper halves into a large saucepan and just cover with water. Bring to the boil and blanch the peppers for 5 minutes. Drain and set them aside while you make the filling.

Put the beef, onion, garlic, soy sauce, chilli powder and sesame seeds into a mixing bowl and beat them until they are thoroughly blended. Spoon the beef mixture into the pepper halves until they are level with the edges. Carefully dip the pepper halves in the beaten eggs, then in the flour, shaking off any excess. Set aside.

To make the dipping sauce, combine all the ingredients in a small bowl, beating until they are thoroughly blended. Pour into a dipping bowl.

Heat the oil in a large frying-pan. Fry gently for 10 to 15 minutes, turning the peppers occasionally, or until the meat is cooked through.

Remove from the pan and serve at once, accompanied by the dipping sauce.

Serves 4

Preparation and cooking time: 30 minutes

Kong-Na-Mool

(Bean Sprouts) (Korea)

Metric/Imperial	American
1kg./2lb. bean sprouts	4 cups bean sprouts
2 tsp. soya sauce	2 tsp. soy sauce
1 Tbs. roasted sesame seeds, ground	1 Tbs. roasted sesame seeds, ground
salt	salt
2 spring onions, green part only, finely chopped	2 scallions, green part only, finely chopped
1 tsp. sesame oil	1 tsp. sesame oil

Put the bean sprouts into a saucepan and cover with boiling water. Cook for 5 to 10 minutes, or until they are just tender. Drain and return the bean sprouts to the pan.

Stir in the remaining ingredients, a little at a time, and cook over moderate heat until all are combined.

Serve at once.

Serves 6

Preparation and cooking time: 15 minutes

Umani

(Vegetables Simmered in Soy Sauce)

Metric/Imperial	American
2 carrots, sliced diagonally into short lengths	2 carrots, sliced diagonally into short lengths
200g./7oz. tin bamboo shoot, drained and cut into 5cm./2in. lengths	7oz. can bamboo shoot, drained and cut into 2in. lengths
200g./7oz. tin konnyaku, cut into 5cm./2in. cubes	7 oz. can konnyaku, cut into 2in. cubes
600ml./1 pint dashi	2½ cups dashi
5 Tbs. soya sauce	5 Tbs. soy sauce
2 Tbs. sugar	2 Tbs. sugar
1 Tbs. mirin or sweet sherry	1 Tbs. mirin or sweet sherry
1 tsp. salt	1 tsp. salt
6 dried mushrooms, soaked in cold water for 30 minutes, drained, and stalks removed	6 dried mushrooms, soaked in cold water for 30 minutes, drained and stalks removed

125g./4oz. French beans, chopped	⅔ cup chopped green beans
MEATBALLS	MEATBALLS
½kg./1lb. minced beef	1lb. ground beef
1 Tbs. soya sauce	1 Tbs. soy sauce
1 Tbs. mirin or sweet sherry	1 Tbs. mirin or sweet sherry
2 Tbs. cornflour	2 Tbs. cornstarch
3 Tbs. dashi	3 Tbs. dashi

First make the meatballs. Combine all the ingredients in a large mixing bowl. Using the palm of your hands, gently shape the mixture into balls about 5cm./2in. in diameter. Set aside.

Put the carrots, bamboo shoot and konnyaku into a saucepan and add the dashi, soy sauce, sugar, mirin or sherry and salt. Bring to the boil, then reduce the heat to low. Add the meatballs to the pan, cover and simmer for 15 minutes. Add the mushroom caps and French (green) beans to the pan and simmer for a further 10 minutes.

Serve as a vegetable side dish, hot or cold.

Serves 4-6
Preparation and cooking time: 1¼ hours

Yasi no Kushiage

(Vegetable Shis-kebab)

Metric/Imperial	American
3 eggs, lightly beaten	3 eggs, lightly beaten
50g./2oz. dry breadcrumbs	⅔ cup dry breadcrumbs
flour for coating	flour for coating
½ medium cauliflower, separated into small flowerets	½ medium cauliflower, separated into small flowerets
125g./4oz. mushroom caps	1 cup button mushroom caps
2 courgettes, sliced	2 zucchini, sliced
2 onions, cut downwards into 8 pieces	2 onions, cut downwards into 8 pieces
vegetable oil for deep-frying	vegetable oil for deep-frying
SAUCE	SAUCE
1 Tbs. miso paste	1 Tbs. miso paste
1 tsp. vinegar	1 tsp. vinegar
150ml./5fl.oz. mayonnaise	⅔ cup mayonnaise

First make the sauce. Beat the miso paste and vinegar together until they are well blended, then stir into the mayonnaise. Set aside while you cook the vegetables.

Put the eggs, breadcrumbs and flour into separate, shallow bowls. Dip all of the vegetable pieces first in the eggs, then in the flour and finally in the breadcrumbs, shaking off any excess.

Arrange the pieces on to metal skewers, repeating on different skewers until they are used up. (The skewers will be put into a large saucepan, so make sure the vegetables are arranged in such a way that they can be deep-fried.)

Fill a large deep-frying pan about one-third full with oil and heat it until it is very hot. Carefully lower the skewers into the hot oil and fry until the vegetables are deep golden. Remove the skewers from the oil and drain on kitchen towels.

Arrange the vegetable kebabs on serving platters and either pour over the sauce or serve it as an accompaniment. Serve at once.

Serves 4
Preparation and cooking time: 45 minutes

(See over) Pride of place in this picture is given to Yasi no Kushiage (Vegetable Shis-kebab)– delightfully filling and savoury kebabs which can be a light meal on their own, or be served perhaps with some Sashimi or other light fish dish. Also in the picture are Carrot Salad and Goma Joyu Ae (Green Beans with Sesame Dressing).

Niyakko Tofu

(Cold Bean Curd)

Metric/Imperial	American
4 bean curd cakes (tofu)	4 bean curd cakes (tofu)
GARNISH	GARNISH
2 garlic cloves, crushed	2 garlic cloves, crushed
2½cm./1in. piece of fresh root ginger, peeled and grated	1in. piece of fresh green ginger, peeled and grated
4 mint leaves, chopped	4 mint leaves, chopped
½ leek, cleaned and sliced into thin strips	½ leek, cleaned and sliced into thin strips
DIPPING SAUCE	DIPPING SAUCE
75ml./3fl.oz. soya sauce	6 Tbs. soy sauce
1½ Tbs. sake or dry sherry	1½ Tbs. sake or dry sherry
monosodium glutamate (optional)	MSG (optional)

Cut the bean curd into small cubes and divide among individual serving bowls. Add chilled water, so that the bean curd cubes are floating.

Arrange the garlic, ginger, mint and leek decoratively on a small serving dish. Combine all the ingredients for the sauce in a small mixing bowl, then divide among individual small dipping bowls.

To serve, each diner sprinkles the garnish offerings to taste into the dipping sauce, and dips in the bean curd cubes before eating.

Serves 4
Preparation time: 10 minutes

Shirasu Ae

(Vegetables Mixed in White Sesame Sauce)

This dish originated with Zen monks in Japan and is considered an exercise in skill to prepare – but although it is a little time-consuming, the end result is well worth the effort. The 'secret' of making good Shirasu Ae is to remove as much water from the vegetables as possible.

Metric/Imperial	American
175g./6oz. dried broad white beans, soaked overnight	1 cup dried lima beans, soaked overnight
2 medium aubergines	2 medium eggplants
5 Tbs. water	5 Tbs. water
2 Tbs. soya sauce	2 Tbs. soy sauce
2 tsp. sugar	2 tsp. sugar
4 dried mushrooms, soaked in cold water for 30 minutes, drained, stalks removed and caps thinly sliced	4 dried mushrooms, soaked in cold water for 30 minutes, drained, stalks removed and caps thinly sliced
SESAME SAUCE	SESAME SAUCE
½ bean curd cake (tofu), boiled for 3 minutes and drained	½ bean curd cake (tofu), boiled for 3 minutes and drained
4 Tbs. white sesame seeds	4 Tbs. white sesame seeds
1 Tbs. sugar	1 Tbs. sugar

Metric/Imperial	American
3 Tbs. vinegar	3 Tbs. vinegar
1 Tbs. mirin or sweet sherry	1 Tbs. mirin or sweet sherry
½ tsp. salt	½ tsp. salt

First prepare the dressing. Put the drained bean curd into a cloth and gently squeeze out as much water as possible (the bean curd should break up). Set aside. Gently fry the sesame seeds in a small frying-pan until they begin to 'jump', taking care not to burn them too much. Remove from the heat and put them into a mortar. Grind with a pestle until the seeds form a paste (this may take some time – so be prepared!). Stir the bean curd into the mortar and continue to pound with the pestle for a further 3 minutes. Stir in the remaining sauce ingredients and continue pounding until the sauce is smooth and sticky and makes a sort of suction noise when the pestle is moved around the mortar. Set aside.

Meanwhile, prepare the vegetables. Put the beans and their soaking liquid into a small saucepan and bring to the boil. Reduce the heat to moderately low and cook for about 1 hour, or until they are tender. Replenish the liquid if necessary during cooking. Cook the aubergines (eggplants) in boiling salted water for 1 hour or until they are tender. Drain and transfer to a chopping board. Cut the aubergines (eggplants) lengthways into thin slices, then halve each round to make a half-moon shape. Set aside.

Put the water, soy sauce and sugar into a small saucepan and bring to the boil, stirring constantly until the sugar dissolves. Add the mushroom slices to the pan, reduce the heat to low and simmer for 10 minutes, so that the mushrooms absorb the flavour of the liquid. Drain the mushrooms and put into a cloth. Gently squeeze as much liquid as possible out of the mushrooms.

To serve, combine all the vegetables together, then pour over the sesame sauce. Stir gently to coat the vegetables in the sauce and serve the dish at room temperature.

Serves 6
Preparation and cooking time: 1½ hours

Carrot Salad

Metric/Imperial	American
4 carrots, scraped	4 carrots, scraped
2 Japanese radishes (daikon), peeled	2 Japanese radishes (daikon), peeled
1 tsp. salt	1 tsp. salt
150ml./5fl.oz. cider vinegar	10 Tbs. cider vinegar
2 Tbs. sugar	2 Tbs. sugar
1 Tbs. soya sauce	1 Tbs. soy sauce
1cm./½in. piece of fresh root ginger, peeled and chopped	½in. piece of fresh green ginger, peeled and chopped
monosodium glutamate (optional)	MSG (optional)

Carefully cut the carrots and radishes into long, thin strips. Arrange in a bowl, sprinkle with the salt and set aside for 45 minutes. Drain off any water which appears on the surface of the vegetables and dry on kitchen towels. Transfer the vegetable strips to a shallow serving bowl.

Put all the remaining ingredients into a screw-top jar and shake vigorously to mix. Pour the dressing over the salad and serve at once.

Serves 4
Preparation time: 1 hour
Note : Turnip can be substituted for the daikon if they are not available.

Goma Joyu Ae

(French [Green] Beans with Sesame Dressing)

Metric/Imperial	American
350g./12oz. French beans, chopped	2 cups chopped green beans
DRESSING	DRESSING
4 Tbs. sesame seeds	4 Tbs. sesame seeds
2 Tbs. soya sauce	2 Tbs. soy sauce
1 Tbs. sugar	1 Tbs. sugar
monosodium glutamate (optional)	MSG (optional)

Cook the beans in lightly salted boiling water for about 5 minutes, or until they are just tender. Drain, then rinse in cold water. Dry on kitchen towels and set aside.

Roast the sesame seeds gently in a small pan until they begin to 'jump' then pound in a mortar with a pestle to release the oil – this takes some time. When they form a reasonably smooth paste, stir in the soy sauce, sugar and monosodium glutamate to taste.

Arrange the beans in a serving dish and spoon over the dressing. Mix gently, making sure the beans are well coated. Serve at once, as a side dish.
Serves 4
Preparation and cooking time: 20 minutes

Mixed Vegetable Salad

(Korea)

Metric/Imperial	American
1 small turnip	1 small turnip
1 tsp. salt	1 tsp. salt
3 Tbs. sesame oil	3 Tbs. sesame oil
1 small onion, finely chopped	1 small onion, finely chopped
125g./4oz. mushrooms, sliced	1 cup sliced mushrooms
2 celery stalks, thinly sliced	2 celery stalks, thinly sliced
3 spring onions, thinly sliced	3 scallions, thinly sliced
1 carrot, cut into thin strips	1 carrot, cut into thin strips
DRESSING	DRESSING
3 Tbs. soya sauce	3 Tbs. soy sauce
1 Tbs. soft brown sugar	1 Tbs. soft brown sugar
1 Tbs. vinegar	1 Tbs. vinegar
½ tsp. ground ginger	½ tsp. ground ginger
1 Tbs. finely chopped pine nuts	1 Tbs. finely chopped pine nuts

Cut the turnip into long, thin strips, then sprinkle over the salt. Set aside for 15 minutes.

Heat the oil in a small frying-pan. When it is hot, add the turnip strips and fry for 3 to 4 minutes, turning occasionally, or until they are crisp. Transfer to kitchen towels to drain. Add the onion to the pan and fry until it is golden brown. Transfer to kitchen towels to drain. Add the mushrooms and fry them for 4 minutes, stirring frequently. Transfer to kitchen towels to drain. Finally, fry the celery in the pan for 3 minutes, then transfer to kitchen towels. Put all the vegetables in a bowl and leave until they are cold.

Stir in the spring onions (scallions) and carrot. Combine all the dressing

ingredients, then pour over the mixture. Toss lightly before serving.
Serves 4
Preparation and cooking time: 2 hours

Horeso no Chitashi

(Boiled Spinach)

Metric/Imperial	American
½kg./1lb. spinach leaves, washed	1lb. spinach leaves, washed
1 Tbs. katsuobushi or dried tuna	1 Tbs. katsuobushi or dried tuna
1 Tbs. soya sauce	1 Tbs. soy sauce
Monosodium glutamate (optional)	MSG (optional)

Put the spinach into a saucepan. Do *not* add water (the water clinging to the leaves will be sufficient). Cook gently for 6 to 8 minutes, or until the spinach is tender, taking care not to overcook. Drain, then arrange the spinach on a chopping board so that all the stalks are facing the same way. Shred the spinach, crosswise, into 2½cm./1in. sections. Section by section, gently squeeze out the water from the spinach.

Arrange the dry spinach on a serving plate and sprinkle over the katsuobushi, soy sauce and monosodium glutamate to taste. Serve cold, as a side dish with meat or fish.
Serves 4
Preparation and cooking time: 20 minutes
Note: Watercress or cos (romaine) lettuce can be cooked in this way.

A delicious, filling dish from Korea is Mixed Vegetable Salad. This version contains turnip, carrot, celery, mushrooms and spring onions (scallions), but you can add your favourite vegetables as you wish.

Kabu no Tsukemono

(Pickled Turnip)

Metric/Imperial	American
1 large turnip, sliced as thinly as possible	1 large turnip, sliced as thinly as possible
1 piece of kombu (seaweed), about 2½ x 5cm./1 x 2in.	1 piece of kombu (seaweed), about 1 x 2in.
4cm./1½in. piece of fresh root ginger, peeled and sliced	1½in. piece of fresh green ginger, peeled and sliced
2 dry red chillis, chopped	2 dry red chillis, chopped
chopped rind of ½ lemon	chopped rind of ½ lemon
½ carrot, cut into matchstick strips	½ carrot, cut into matchstick strips
2 tsp. salt	2 tsp. salt
DRESSING	DRESSING
1 Tbs. mirin or sweet sherry	1 Tbs. mirin or sweet sherry
1 Tbs. soya sauce	1 Tbs. soy sauce

Put the turnip, kombu, ginger, red chillis, lemon rind, carrot and salt into a deep plate. Cover and place a heavy object, such as an iron on top to compress the mixture. Leave for at least 12 hours.

To serve, remove the heavy object and uncover. Using your hands, gently squeeze any excess moisture from the pickle. Transfer to a serving bowl and pour over the soy sauce and mirin or sherry. Toss gently to mix and serve at once.

Serves 4
Preparation time: 12¼ hours

Kim Chee I

(Pickled Cabbage)

Metric/Imperial	American
1 large celery or Chinese cabbage, shredded	1 large celery or Chinese cabbage, shredded
125g./4oz. rock salt	½ cup rock salt
900ml./1½ pints water	3¼ cups water
6 spring onions, finely chopped	6 scallions, finely chopped
2 tsp. sugar	2 tsp. sugar
5cm./2in. piece of fresh root ginger, peeled and cut into strips	2in. piece of fresh green ginger peeled and cut into strips
2 chillis, finely chopped	2 chillis, finely chopped

Put the shredded cabbage in a large bowl and sprinkle over the salt. Pour over the water, cover and set aside overnight.

Combine the spring onions (scallions), sugar, ginger and chillis.

Drain, then rinse and drain the cabbage again. Put the cabbage in a fresh bowl and stir in the spring onion (scallion) mixture. Pack into sterilized pickling jars, cover and set aside for 4 to 5 days before using.

Makes about 1.2l./2 pints (5 cups)
Preparation time: 6 days

Kim Chee II

(Pickled Cabbage)   (Korea)

Metric/Imperial	American
1 Chinese cabbage, quartered	1 Chinese cabbage, quartered
3 Tbs. salt	3 Tbs. salt
2 tsp. hot chilli powder	2 tsp. hot chilli powder
2 garlic cloves, crushed	2 garlic cloves, crushed
4 spring onions, chopped	4 scallions, chopped
1 small onion, chopped	1 small onion, chopped
1 small carrot, chopped	1 small carrot, chopped
1 Tbs. sugar	1 Tbs. sugar
1 large ripe pear, peeled, cored and roughly chopped	1 large ripe pear, peeled, cored and roughly chopped
monosodium glutamate (optional)	MSG (optional)

Put the cabbage into a large shallow bowl and sprinkle over the salt. Leave overnight to dégorge.

Remove the cabbage from the bowl and wash under cold running water. Squeeze all the moisture from the cabbage with your hands, then shred finely.

Put the cabbage, and all the remaining ingredients, into a large jar or deep bowl and cover with a heavy weight. Set aside for 1 to 2 days before serving.

Serves 8
Preparation time: 3 days

Na-Moul

(Spinach Pickle)   (Korea)

Metric/Imperial	American
1kg./2lb. leaf spinach	2lb. leaf spinach
2 garlic cloves, crushed	2 garlic cloves, crushed
1 Tbs. roasted sesame seeds, ground	1 Tbs. roasted sesame seeds, ground
1 Tbs. sesame oil	1 Tbs. sesame oil
2 spring onions, finely chopped	2 scallions, finely chopped
1 tsp. hot chilli powder	1 tsp. hot chilli powder

Wash the spinach thoroughly in cold, running water. Put into a saucepan and bring to the boil (do not add any more water – the water clinging to the leaves will make enough liquid). Reduce the heat to low and cook the spinach for 5 to 8 minutes, or until it is tender. Remove the saucepan from the heat and drain the spinach very thoroughly, squeezing as much moisture from the leaves as possible.

Transfer the drained spinach to a shallow serving dish. Stir in all of the remaining ingredients until the mixture is well blended. Set aside at room temperature for 3 hours before serving.

Serves 8
Preparation and cooking time: 3¼ hours

GLOSSARY

Abure age Fried bean curd, usually sold in thin, frozen sheets. Obtainable from Japanese stores. Substitute other types of bean curd, as available – but the taste will be different.

Agar-agar A gelatinous substance obtained from seaweed, widely used in Japanese cooking. Used as a substitute setting gel in vegetarian cooking. Obtainable from oriental and health food stores. If unavailable (and you are not a vegetarian) substitute gelatine (gelatin).

Aji-no-moto The Japanese word for monosodium glutamate (MSG), which is widely used as a catalyst substance in cooking. For ease of reference, it is always referred to by its English name in this book. Obtainable from oriental stores and most supermarkets. It can safely be omitted from recipes if you prefer.

Bean curd Bean curd, called tofu in Japan, is made from soya beans and is an important ingredient in most oriental cuisines. Sold fresh, in shimmering, white 'cakes'. Store fresh bean curd in water in the refrigerator; keeps for two to three days. Also available canned. When canned bean curd is opened, treat as for fresh. For ease of reference, both English and Japanese names are given in this book. Obtainable from Chinese, Japanese and all other oriental stores.

Daikon A mild, long white radish very popular throughout Japan. Used both in cooking and as a garnish, and somewhat resembles the parsnip in appearance, although it is much paler in colour. Sometimes available from Chinese or Japanese stores. If unobtainable, small white turnips may be substituted.

Dashi The basic stock of all Japanese cooking (see recipe). It is now often made from an instant powder in Japan called dashi-no-moto. The powder can be obtained in Japanese supermarkets. If unavailable, chicken stock can be substituted.

Ginger Ginger is used extensively throughout the orient, and usually in its knobbly, root form rather than ground. To use fresh (green) ginger root, remove the brown skin and woody areas and chop the moist flesh. To store, either wrap tightly, unpeeled, in plastic film, or cover with dry sherry. Always keep in the refrigerator. Stored in this way it will keep for about six weeks. *In extremis* ground ginger can be substituted (although the taste is quite definitely not the same) – about $\frac{1}{2}$ teaspoon equals a 4cm./$1\frac{1}{2}$in. piece of fresh (green) ginger root. Ginger is available from all oriental stores and some specialty vegetable shops.

Ginko nuts (Also called ginnan in Japan) the kernels of the maidenhair tree. Used both as a flavouring and an ingredient in Japanese cooking. Available canned from Japanese stores. If it is unobtainable, omit from the recipe.

Ginseng Many drinks are made from the root of the ginseng plant. In Korea, the tea made from ginseng is very popular and many miraculous – and aphrodisiac – properties are attributed to it. Several liquors of varying strength are also made from the plant.

Hichimi togarashi A seven-flavour spice used as a garnish in Japanese cooking. It is darkish red in colour. Available from Japanese stores. If unobtainable, substitute paprika.

Kanpyo Dried gourd strips used as an ingredient in Japanese cooking. Available only from Japanese stores. No substitute.

Katsuobushi Katsuobushi are dried bonito (tuna fish) flakes, one of the basic ingredients in a proper dashi stock. Sold in flake form from Japanese general stores. There is no substitute.

Kombu A dried kelp, a sort of seaweed, sold in greyish-black ribbon blocks. Used as a flavouring in dashi and also to flavour vinegared rice (sushi). Available from Japanese or other oriental stores and health food shops.

Konnyaku Small, gelatinous white cakes, sold canned in Japanese or oriental stores. Often added to soups, chopped into bite-sized pieces. There is no substitute.

Mirin A sweet Japanese rice wine used only for cooking. If unobtainable sweet or medium sherry can be substituted. Available from Japanese stores.

Miso Miso is a fermented, dark grey paste made from cooked soya beans. Often added to dashi to make a thicker, more substantial stock for soups and dips. Miso is sold in plastic packs from Japanese stores or health food shops.

Noodles	Noodles of one type or another are very popular in Japanese cooking. There are four main types: *harusame* the equivalent of Chinese cellophane noodles, which are usually either soaked and added to recipes or deep-fried; *soba*, thin, green-brown noodles made from buckwheat flour; *somen*, fine white noodles, used in the same way as vermicelli – if they are unavailable, vermicelli can be used as a substitute; and *udon*, thicker noodles made from white flour – spaghetti makes an acceptable equivalent if they are unavailable.
Nori	Dried laver, an edible form of seaweed, is one of the most popular garnishes in Japanese cooking. Usually toasted until crisp, then crumbled over ingredients such as rice or noodles. It is available in blackish sheets from Japanese stores and some health food shops.
Sake	Japan's favourite rice wine, a dryish, greyish liquid that seems milder than it is. Used extensively in cooking, particularly in marinades and dipping sauces. Substitute dry sherry or dry white wine if unobtainable. Available usually from Japanese and other oriental stores and also better liquor stores.
Sesame seed	Used extensively as a flavouring in both Japanese and Korean cooking. In Japan it is usually toasted then pounded in a mortar until it releases its oil; in Korea it is roasted then ground and sprinkled over practically everything.
Shiitake	The Japanese form of dried mushrooms, a delicacy popular throughout the Orient. Available from Japanese or other oriental stores. If unavailable substitute Chinese dried mushrooms – and always treat in the same way, that is, soak in cold water for 30 minutes, drain and remove stalks before using. Do not substitute European dried mushrooms – the taste is completely different.
Shirataki	A type of transparent noodle made not from flour but from the starch of vegetable plants. Usually sold canned in Japanese stores. No substitute.
Soy sauce	Yet another product of the ubiquitous soya bean plant, and used by almost every cuisine in the Orient. In Japan, a lighter slightly less salty soy sauce (called shoyu) is used and if you are cooking Japanese food this version should be used if possible. Koreans use both the Chinese and Japanese versions, according to the dish being cooked.
Wakame	A type of dried seaweed. It is sold, dried, in ribbon strands in Japanese stores and some health food shops.
Wasabe	A green horseradish powder very popular as a garnish and as an ingredient in dipping sauces in Japan. Usually sold in tins and served mixed to a paste with cold water – see specific recipes for proportions. Sold in Japanese stores and some better supermarkets. If unavailable, substitute western horseradish or mustard paste.

INTRODUCTION Sharmini Tiruchelvam
TO SOUTH EAST ASIA

It has been said that all South-East Asian cooking is essentially peripheral to the cuisine of China. True – yet not quite true. The influence is certainly there: Singapore, Malaysia and Indonesia contain large immigrant Chinese populations which retain their traditional styles of cooking, undoubtedly influencing the cuisine of these countries, and both Vietnam and Burma became vassal states of China in the reign of the Emperor Chien-lung, with consequent effects on both culture and gastronomy. Despite this, however, the cuisines of Malaysia, Indonesia, Thailand and Burma (which together with those of Singapore, Vietnam, the Philippines and Cambodia are commonly and collectively called South-East Asian) remain more accurately and essentially based on the cuisine of India, on its methods and styles of cooking and types of dishes.

There are the hot spiced gravy dishes called *gulehs* or *kares* or curries, similar to the curries of South India, although usually much less spicy and hot. The custom in Indonesia, Burma and Thailand of having savoury-soupy accompaniments to some of their rice meals again resembles that of South India with its *rasams* and *mulligatawnies*. The *sambals* are very like the Indians' too: piquant hot mixtures, with chilli always present in some form or other, and in South-East Asia invariably combined with prawn or shrimp paste (*blachan*). As with the Indians, sambals are served both as appetizers and as an integral part of the main meal, and in South-East Asia the idea has been further refined to make *sambals goreng* dishes in which sambal sauces are combined with other ingredients (herbs, spices, sugar and thick coconut milk) and fried with meat, fish or vegetables.

The *rendangs* of the Malays are obviously derived from the great 'dry' curries of India although, again, made much less hot and marginally sweeter with the addition of ingredients such as jaggery (raw sugar) or a sweet fruit. The Malays also have a mild, thick-gravied meat dish which they call *korma*, which is patently one form of the Indians' classic range of the same name.

From the Chinese, though, comes one of the most popular forms of cooking: stir-frying in a wok. And, from them, too, the art of tossing together unusual assortments of fresh and dried meats, fresh, preserved and dried seafood, fresh and preserved vegetables, herbs, spices and flavourings, in apparently numberless computations of combi-

nations. The mixing of several kinds of meat and seafood within the same dish is so popular here that it is now widely regarded as a typically South-East Asian trait!

When a blander dish is absorbed from another cuisine – especially the Chinese – it is invariably adapted to the local taste by being 'hotted' up either by being combined with a spicy sauce, or by being accompanied by a hot or piquant dip. *Poppia*, that inspired Malaysian snack, is a perfect example: a version of the much simpler Chinese spring roll, it is made of diced ban quan (Chinese turnip), cooked shrimps, shredded crab and chicken, uncooked fresh bean sprouts, tiny cubes of fried bean curd, crisp-fried and cubed pork fat, dried prawns (shrimp), all wrapped up in fresh lettuce leaves, then in wafer-thin white pancakes, or fried crisp within a thin, light pastry. *Poppia* has two important points to it: first, the combination of fresh and dried versions of some of the same ingredients and, second, a smear of hot *blachan* (shrimp paste) within the pancake. This seems not only to give the whole dish a 'kick' but also to combine all the other mouth-watering flavours more successfully.

There are certain herbs, grasses, leaves, roots, fruits, seeds, nuts and dried preparations which are an essential part of the cooking and flavours of the region: lemon grass, daun pandan, laos, blachan, celery, cumin, coriander and coriander leaf (Chinese parsley), cloves, cardamoms, green ginger, fennel, curry leaves, sesame seed, sesame oil, limes and lemons, mustard seeds (whole or bruised but not powdered), whole nutmeg (grated freshly just before use), bean sprouts, black bean sauce, soy beans, soy sauce, bean curd, lotus seeds, water chestnuts, Chinese mushrooms, spring onion (scallions), tamarind, turmeric, peppers – green and red, dried squid, dried scallop cakes, dried prawns and shrimps, the list is exotic – and endless. Yet you can manage with only a few really indispensable ones, plus some inspired substitution! Which is how, in fact, many of the cuisines of the area were created.

All the lands of South-East Asia have access to the sea; all have therefore a great range of seafood at their disposal – the cooking of which they are all expert. Great attention is paid to what fish is in 'season'. What will cook best in what manner – What is best sautéed? . . . What steams or stir-fries

best? . . . What is best curried or devilled? – are all important questions. Mackerel does not steam well whereas it will sauté beautifully, sea bass and turbot are delicious steamed; pike poaches well; bream and red mullet both sauté and fry well. All are recognized and the most of them made. Fish-based soups and bouillons are popular especially in Burma, Thailand and Indonesia.

Like the Chinese, the South-East Asian cook pays very great attention to the quality and intrinsic properties of the ingredients; knowing what will combine most successfully with what is considered to be of paramount importance. Which leads to another very important aspect of South-East Asian cooking: it is not only the knowledge of these qualities but having the skill to choose the best raw materials that is important. It is, in fact, the starting point for much of the cooking. Many rules, handed down for generations by word of mouth within families, exist side by side with regional folklore.

Some foods are considered more healthy and 'cooling', others rich and/or 'heaty'. Like the Yin and Yang of the Chinese: 'heaty' and 'cooling' balancing opposites. One must learn how to combine them within a meal. Crabs, lobsters and oysters, for example, are heaty foods, as is garlic: they inflame the body and the passions, they say. White marrow (squash), lettuce, cucumber and milk are cooling. Pineapples and mangoes are heaty whereas limes and lemons are cooling. Yams and potatoes are heaty. Durian inflames; mangosteens

cool. It is always wise to follow a meal of the former group with a balancing amount of the latter. Many of the injunctions turn out to be surprisingly accurate. Drink milk or water out of the shell of the durian whose flesh you have eaten and you will not have any durian breath – a social disaster far worse than garlic breath. It is true! And . . . never buy crabs which have been caught in the waning season of the moon. The flesh is full and firm only when the moon is waxing, they say. Astonishingly, again, this too turns out to be true. The shells are a quarter or more filled with liquid and the flesh rather soft. But once the rules for the selection of the raw materials and the combination of the ingredients have been observed, along with the basic rules of health and hygiene, the rest is wide open to invention and innovation. In short, they are culinarily adventurous.

Derived then from the two great cuisines of the East – Indian and Chinese – influenced early by the trader Arabs and the Polynesians, linked together later still by invading foreigners from the West – the Portuguese, Dutch and English – South-East Asian cooking is not so much a great cuisine as it is a no-holds-barred amalgam of many cuisines.

There is no doubt that there is a strong regional similarity, especially between countries like Malaysia and Indonesia, Burma and Thailand. Indeed there is a great regional link, based on similar geography and climate – with access to the same food-rich terrain, oceans, seas and rivers. Common historical and ethnic bonds further bind them.

Despite all that, however, the cooking of each of the different countries is today quite distinct. Gourmets and experts on the cooking of the region can easily differentiate between the same dish cooked in the styles of two different countries: they can say, for example, if it is an Indonesian or Malaysian *rendang* merely by smelling it . . . So they say!

Malaysia and Singapore

There are four main groups of people in Malaysia and Singapore: the indigenous Malays, the immigrant Chinese, the once itinerant trader Indians and Sri Lankans, the former invader Europeans . . . . What is most important about the various groups is the fact that they all still keep to their own traditional styles of cooking, adding greatly to the local repertoire, even as they have adapted their own palates – religious taboos allowing in some instances – to appreciate a wide variety of other ethnic foods.

The Malays: Malaysian cooking is like that of their close relatives, the Indonesians, and has evolved most directly from the availability of foodstuffs locally, combined with the outside influence of the trader Arabs bringing in the spices of the Indians. Finally when the Indians themselves settled in their midst they were greatly influenced by that cuisine and from the names of their dishes alone one can trace the links (many of them shared with the Indonesians): *rendangs, gulehs, ajars, sambals, sambals goreng.*

Sate (or satay in Malaysia) is a good example of the development of the Malaysian (and Indonesian) cuisine. Undoubtedly it is descended from the trader Arabs' kebab, yet it has been developed into such a unique culinary item as to merit being classified as a classic dish in its own right. The Malaysian and Indonesian sate is made from sliver-thin pieces of beef, veal, lamb, poultry of any kind, livers, tripe (or even pork – this usually being cooked by the Chinese, pork being taboo to the Muslim Malay). These are first marinated in a sauce before being skewered and barbecued. Cooked correctly, sate should melt in the mouth. It is served straight off the fire on the skewers on which it was cooked, together with pieces of raw onions and cucumber cubes (thereby correctly balancing the overall dish) and a hot, cooked sate sauce, with a base of chillis and ground roasted peanuts (or peanut butter). It makes a marvellous first course to a meal.

The Chinese: In many of the South-East Asian cities, and especially in Singapore and Malaysia, there are whole streets of restaurants and mobile kitchens (stalls) which specialize in the cooking of any one of the separate regions or schools of Chinese cooking such as Peking (Shantung), Honan, Hunan, Fukien, Schezwan, Yang Chow, Hokien and, of course, Canton. In the final analysis, however, there are really three main types of Chinese cooking in South-East Asia: the *haute cuisine* of China as practised by the chefs in the restaurants; the provincial and regional home-cooking of China as made every day in the homes of the Chinese, and the Malaysian-Chinese cooking which has been evolving over the past century since the arrival of the immigrant Chinese coolie population within the Malay Archipelago.

All Malaysian-Chinese dishes have been adapted from the Chinese with a couple of exceptions such as pork or tripe sate taken from the Malays and dishes like *curry mee* taken from the Indians. Very popular dishes in this range too, are *mah mi, quay thiau* and *mi hoon* – which are made *goreng, rubus* or *soto* – i.e. fried, boiled or soupy.

Quay Thiau Goreng, for example, is a sort of *tagliatelle al vongole*, made with clams, eggs, flat noodles, bean sprouts, a soupçon of chilli powder, garlic, onion (optional), salt and soy sauce stir-fried in a wok. In a very grand version of this one you could use oysters! Perak, in North-Central Malaysia is supposed to make the best *quay thiau*. And one little man with a mobile stall, in Ipoh, called 'the Spider' makes it so well, with clams, that gourmets from all over the East, from princes to poor men, come to eat nightly at his stall.

Poppia has already been described. *Lobak* is a sort of *tempura*: soft-shelled baby crabs, crayfish, baby lobsters, giant prawns (shrimps) in their shell, squid, peppers and certain yams and a marvellous Chinese sausage are all dipped into the lightest of batters and crisp-fried, so that it is possible to eat the whole crab or prawn without having to spit out the shell. *Yong thou foo* is another delicacy, made with peppers, seeded red chillis, aubergines (egg-plants), marrows (squash), bitter gourds and bean curd cakes all stuffed with quenelles of pounded fresh fish or pork with onions, garlic and herbs and cooked for a very few minutes in simmering, delicate fish broth.

These Malaysian-Chinese dishes are made particularly well by the stall and mobile kitchen cooks. Throughout the whole of South-East Asia there is the phenomenon of the nocturnal cities and towns. Hundreds of thousands of mobile kitchens and stalls (each usually specializing in one or two dishes) mushroom even in the residential districts around the towns after sundown, and keep going until about midnight. Their expertise is hard to equal.

In Malaysia, especially in Malacca and Penang where the races intermarried more than on the mainland, there developed yet another strain of cooking primarily derived from the Chinese, but clearly and equally mixed with Indian and Malay cooking. Nowadays, it is called Straits Chinese or *nonya* cooking and there is great interest in it, especially in Singapore. The cuisine evolved when many of the Chinese men who came to these areas, well-off and ambitious traders who did not bring their own women, married the local Indian and Malay women (called *nonya* – hence the name of the cuisine). These men lived like princes and ate even better . . . for their foreign wives, wanting to please them, learned how to prepare their native dishes but invariably adapted them to their own tastes and local availability.

The Indians and Sri Lankans: As with the Chinese, there are as many different sects and groups of Indians and Sri Lankans here as there are to be found on their mainland – Punjabis, Bengalis, Gujeratis, Sindhis, Telugus, Nepalese, Pathans, Kashmiris, Goans, Tamils, Singhalese – and each continues to practise its own regional and classic cooking. But undoubtedly the greatest influence has been that of the South Indians, most specifically the Indian Tamils.

Indonesia
The cuisine of Indonesia is very similar to that of Malaysia, having basic ethnic, geographical, cultural, historical and religious links, and also having been influenced in turn by the Arabs, the Indians and the Chinese – each bringing their own culinary customs and religious taboos. More particularly, however, Indonesia's cuisine must be described as having been formed out of the cuisine of what was once Java and Sumatra.

The Javanese and Sumatrans: Javanese cuisine is based on the availability of local produce, the fruit of a fertile land tended by a fairly well populated and highly agricultural community. Everything is used very fresh and according to season, and the

dishes, although sometimes quite sophisticated, contain fewer Indian spices than Sumatra, which was more exposed to the Arab and Indian trader traffic. Instead, the Javanese use more sugar (which grows there), and much trasi (dried shrimp paste).

The Sumatrans, early exposed to Islamic traders, soon adapted their cuisine to the use of the imported spices: fennel, cumin, coriander, chilli, ginger, cardamoms, cinnamon, so that it was recognizably different from that of Java with its sweeter, trasi-flavoured dishes. They also use more chillis and ginger than the Javanese. In central Sumatra, where a very orthodox form of Islam is practised, meat and fish are prepared in a very austere way; in contrast to Central Java where there is a great light-heartedness – much more truly South-East Asian!

The Dutch: There is some confusion, especially in Western minds, about the influence of the Dutch on Indonesian cooking. It is believed that they *invented* Rijsttafel. Certainly the word is Dutch, (it means, literally translated, rice table). But it is not a dish but the description of a table set at once with about 30–40 dishes ranging from complex meat, fish and vegetable curries, sates, rendangs, soups, sambals, ajars, gado-gados and other accompaniments. In short it is a table holding practically all the various famous Indonesian and Indian dishes of that area, in quantities to enable everyone to have a bit of everything. The Dutch loved eating it! The basis is usually a great dish of exquisite, plain white boiled rice, although a saffron or turmeric flavoured rice is sometimes served. The average Indonesian meal consists of the classic combination of chicken, meat, fish, vegetable and egg dishes together with a savoury soup, various sambals, ajars, etc. There are usually about eight accompanying dishes to the basic rice of the meal.

Thailand
Although geographically closer to Malaysia, by some curious quirk Thai food is remarkably similar to that of Java! Like most Indonesians and unlike most Malays, they invariably serve a soup with their rice meals. And like the Javanese they use chillis, sugar, garlic, blachan and laos powder. Like the Indonesians, too, they decorate their food wonderously.

Thailand is a particularly excellent example of the dual heritage from India and China. For an average Thai meal will have, if rice based, a savoury soup eaten with the rice as the Southern Indians do, a curry or two and one or two obviously Chinese dishes only slightly modified to the South-East Asian taste.

The herb for which they have a passion is coriander leaf, and it is sprinkled liberally over almost every dish in the cuisine. They also use a great deal of crushed garlic and coriander root –

which is very much an acquired taste. *Nam pla* is a pungent fish sauce which is used greatly as a base in their cooking and *nam prik* is a hot fish sauce which is found on every Thai table – like soy sauce at a Chinese meal! It is used with everything except the sweet . . . .

Lahp Isan is a sort of Northern Thai spiced and savoury steak tartare. Java has Gado-Gado and Malaysia Rojak and so, too, in Thailand are *Yam Chomphu* a tart fruit salad, flavoured with fish sauce, tamarind or lemon-water, and sugar, *Yam Taong* and *Som Tom* the former with cooked shrimps, pork, crabmeat and dried shrimp with vegetables, the latter with mixed vegetables only. In Thailand, fish sauce replaces the Indonesian blachan-peanut-chilli sauce.

Burma

Once again the two parent cuisines are recognizable, but combined here in a typically Burmese way. In their daily life the Burmese have dishes which, like the Thais, clearly shows them to have a cuisine which is an amalgam of both the Indian and Chinese cuisines seafood and fish gravies dominate. Soups like *Hincho* with a fish gravy base, courgettes (zucchini) and cabbage and *Nga Hin*, again with a fish gravy base, fish, oil, sugar, tomatoes, onions and garlic are much loved. Each person usually has a bowl of soup with the rice-based meal. Mutton, especially, and beef are cooked with more spices than fish or poultry. Pork dishes are usually cooked Chinese-style. Shrimps fried with onions, garlic, ginger, chillis and a dash of sugar summarizes the South-East Asian cooking story here.

Vietnam and Cambodia

Vietnam and Cambodia have a cuisine which has been chiefly derived from the Chinese but greatly influenced by the presence of the French in their midst. Both have 'hot' dishes, which they call curries, but which owe more to Burma than to India, and which are served with noodles as often as with rice. Both have a passion for fish sauce – the Vietnamese version is heavier and saltier than anywhere else and is used not only in cooking but, diluted (called *nuoc cham*), as a garnish over almost everything!

The Philippines

The islands of the Philippines are rather an anomaly in South-East Asia, for here the influence is as much Spanish and American as Indian and Chinese, and both living and eating styles reflect this. The most popular stew, made with pork, or pork and chicken, is called *adobo*, and there is a version of that perennial Spanish favourite *arroz con pollo*. But the Chinese and Malay-Chinese influence *is* there, in a national snack called *lumpia* (a sort of spring roll), in

pancit molo (a sort of wonton soup) and a fondness for cooking in coconut milk.

Garnishes

South-East Asians have great grace and talent in garnishing their food, even the simplest daily meal. They use their natural materials – especially their fruit and vegetables – with considerable awareness of colour and texture. It is an art at which they all seem to be naturally adept: making lotuses out of onions, wild lilies out of carrots and chillis, crysanthemums out of papayas, roses from tomatoes, sea-anemones out of mangoes and melons, radish carnations, and Birds of Paradise out of pineapples and assortments of other fruits and vegetables, with an apparent ease as to make a sculptor swoon with envy.

There is one more quality common to all the countries of South-East Asia: a marvellous regional spirit. It pervades everything, not least their food. The ritual and enjoyable aspects of eating and serving food is very much to the taste and nature of the South-East Asian, the 'ritual' being of a Polynesian hedonistic sort rather than that of the courtly sophistication or religious traditions of the Chinese and Indians.

The very breaking open of crabs, lobsters or crayfish at the table; the breaking open and assessing of the first fruit of the seasons; the informality of using one's fingers; the creative delight of 'orchestrating' one's meal, dipping in at will, into the several flavours of the accompanying sauces and dips; the generous ceremonies of sharing and eating together, invariably informally and very relaxed, has a marvellous sensual sense of the sheer daily celebration of life . . . .

Since time immemorial the junk has plied the seas of the Orient, transporting everything from food to people. Even in modern times its popularity remains undiminished – the picture left shows a present day version entering Singapore harbour, its cargo of fish destined for the markets there.

SOUPS

SINIGANG

(Fish Soup)   (Philippines)

Metric/Imperial	American
400g./14oz. tin tomatoes	14oz. can tomatoes
2 onions, finely chopped	2 onions, finely chopped
1 large sweet potato, peeled and cut into cubes	1 large sweet potato, peeled and cut into cubes
225g./8oz. spinach, chopped	1⅓ cups chopped spinach
1 Tbs. tamarind pulp (optional)	1 Tbs. tamarind pulp (optional)
1.2l./2 pints water	5 cups water
salt and pepper	salt and pepper
½kg./1lb. firm white fish fillets, chopped	1lb. firm white fish fillets, chopped

Put the tomatoes and liquid, onions, vegetables and tamarind into a large saucepan. Pour over the water and seasoning to taste and bring to the boil. Reduce the heat to low and simmer for 15 minutes. Stir in the fish fillets and simmer for a further 15 to 20 minutes, or until the fish flakes easily. Serve at once.
Serves 6
Preparation and cooking time: 45 minutes

TOM YAM KUNG

(Shrimp and Lemon Soup)   (Thailand)

Metric/Imperial	American
1kg./2lb. prawn in the shell	2lb. shrimp in the shell
1.75l./3 pints water	1½ quarts water
2 tsp. chopped lemon grass or grated lemon rind	2 tsp. chopped lemon grass or grated lemon rind
¼ tsp. ground ginger	¼ tsp. ground ginger
3 lemon, lime or other citrus leaves (optional)	3 lemon, lime or other citrus leaves (optional)
2 dried whole chillis	2 dried whole chillis
1 Tbs. fish sauce	1 Tbs. fish sauce
2 Tbs. lemon juice	2 Tbs. lemon juice
1 red chilli, finely chopped	1 red chilli, finely chopped
3 spring onions, chopped	3 scallions, chopped
2 Tbs. chopped coriander leaves	2 Tbs. chopped coriander leaves

Shell and devein the prawns (shrimp) setting aside the meat. Put the shells and heads into a large saucepan and pour over the water. Stir in the lemon grass or rind, ginger, lemon or other leaves and whole chillis and bring to the boil. Reduce the heat to low and simmer the mixture for 10 minutes. Remove from the heat, strain the stock and set it aside.

Pour the stock into a second saucepan and return to the boil. Stir in the fish sauce and lemon juice, then stir in the prawns (shrimp). Cook over moderate heat for 5 minutes, or until they are cooked through. Stir in the chopped chilli, spring onions (scallions) and coriander leaves and remove from the heat.

Transfer the mixture to a warmed tureen and serve at once.

Serves 6-8
Preparation and cooking time: 40 minutes

KAENG CHUD SAKU

(Tapioca Soup)   (Thailand)

Metric/Imperial	American
1.2l./2 pints chicken stock	5 cups chicken stock
225g./8oz. minced pork	8oz. ground pork
½ tsp. salt	½ tsp. salt
125g./4oz. tapioca	⅔ cup tapioca
225g./8oz. crabmeat, shell and cartilage removed	8oz. crabmeat, shell and cartilage removed
1 small Chinese cabbage, shredded	1 small Chinese cabbage, shredded
1 Tbs. soya sauce	1 Tbs. soy sauce

Bring the chicken stock to the boil in a large saucepan. Add the pork and salt, stirring constantly to separate the meat. Reduce the heat to low and stir in the tapioca. Simmer for 20 minutes, or until the pork is cooked.

Flake the crabmeat and stir into the soup with the cabbage. Cover and simmer for 2 to 4 minutes, or until the crabmeat is heated through.

Stir in the soy sauce before serving.

Serves 6-8
Preparation and cooking time: 35 minutes

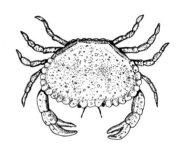

HINCHO

(Mixed Vegetable Soup)   (Burma)

The selection of vegetables given below is optional; any green vegetable, such as cauliflower, okra or cucumber could be added.

Metric/Imperial	American
1.2l./2 pints stock	5 cups stock
2 garlic cloves, crushed	2 garlic cloves, crushed
1 large onion, finely chopped	1 large onion, finely chopped
2 Tbs. dried prawns or 3 shelled fresh prawns	2 Tbs. dried shrimp or 3 shelled fresh shrimp
2 tsp. blachan (dried shrimp paste)	2 tsp. blachan (dried shrimp paste)
½ small Chinese cabbage, shredded	½ small Chinese cabbage, shredded
2 courgettes, thinly sliced	2 zucchini, thinly sliced
225g./8oz. pumpkin flesh, cubed	1⅓ cups cubed pumpkin flesh
pepper and salt	pepper and salt

Put the stock, garlic, onion, dried prawns or shrimp and blachan lnto a saucepan and bring to the boil. Add the remaining vegetables, adding those which take longest to cook first, and simmer until all are cooked through (about 5 minutes in all). Adjust seasoning and serve at once.

Serves 6-8
Preparation and cooking time: 20 minutes

Two traditional South-East
Asian favourites, Top:
Mah Mi (Singapore Soup
Noodles), a fabulous and
filling main dish soup;
and Below: Soto Ayam
from Indonesia, a spicy
curried chicken soup with
exotic garnishes.

MAH MI

(Singapore Soup Noodles)

Metric/Imperial	American
½kg./1lb. prawns, shelled and with the shells and heads reserved	1lb. shrimp, shelled and with the shells and heads reserved
salt and pepper	salt and pepper
3 Tbs. peanut oil	3 Tbs. peanut oil
3 garlic cloves, crushed	3 garlic cloves, crushed
4cm./1½in. piece of fresh root ginger, peeled and chopped	1½in. piece of fresh green ginger, peeled and chopped
225g./8oz. cooked pork, cut into strips	8oz. cooked pork, cut into strips
225g./8oz. bean sprouts	1 cup bean sprouts
125g./4oz. fine noodles or vermicelli	4oz. fine noodles or vermicelli
GARNISH	GARNISH
125g./4oz. tin crabmeat, shell and cartilage removed	4oz. can crabmeat, shell and cartilage removed
¼ cucumber, peeled and diced	¼ cucumber, peeled and diced
6 spring onions, chopped	6 scallions, chopped

First make the stock. Put the prawn or shrimp shells and heads into a saucepan and pour over about 1.2l./2 pints (5 cups) of water. Add salt and pepper to taste and bring to the boil. Reduce the heat to low and simmer the mixture for 30 minutes. Remove from the heat and strain the stock, reserving about 900ml./1½ pints (3½ cups). Set aside.

Heat the oil in a large saucepan. When it is very hot, add the garlic and ginger and stir-fry for 1 minute. Add the pork, prawns or shrimp and bean sprouts and stir-fry for 3 minutes. Pour over the reserved stock and bring to the boil. Stir in the noodles and cook the mixture for 5 minutes.

Transfer the mixture to a large serving bowl and garnish with the flaked crabmeat, cucumber and spring onions (scallions) before serving.
Serves 4-6
Preparation and cooking time: 1 hour

SOTO AYAM

(Chicken Soup)   (Indonesia)

Metric/Imperial	American
1 x 1½kg./3lb. chicken	1 x 3lb. chicken
1.75l./3 pints water	7½ cups water
salt and pepper	salt and pepper
2 medium onions, sliced	2 medium onions, sliced
3 Tbs. peanut oil	3 Tbs. peanut oil
2 garlic cloves, crushed	2 garlic cloves, crushed
4cm./1½in. piece of fresh root ginger, peeled and chopped	1½in. piece of fresh green ginger, peeled and chopped
2 red chillis, crumbled	2 red chillis, crumbled
1 tsp. blachan (dried shrimp paste)	1 tsp. blachan (dried shrimp paste)
1 tsp. turmeric	1 tsp. turmeric
2 tsp. ground coriander	2 tsp. ground coriander
½ tsp. grated nutmeg	½ tsp. grated nutmeg

GARNISH

125g./4oz. cooked vermicelli
4 Tbs. chopped spring onions
2 hard-boiled eggs, sliced

GARNISH

1 cup cooked vermicelli
4 Tbs. chopped scallions
2 hard-cooked eggs, sliced

Put the chicken into a large saucepan and pour over the water. Add salt and pepper to taste and one onion, and bring to the boil. Cover, reduce the heat to low and simmer the chicken for 1 hour, or until the chicken is cooked through. Remove from the heat. Transfer the chicken to a plate to cool and reserve the stock.

When the chicken is cool enough to handle, remove the skin and cut the meat into bite-sized pieces. Set aside.

Heat the oil in a large saucepan. When it is hot, add the remaining onion, the garlic, ginger, chillis and blachan and fry, stirring occasionally, until the onion is soft. Stir in the spices and fry for 1 minute. Pour over the stock and bring to the boil. Reduce the heat to low and simmer the soup for 15 minutes, skimming the surface occasionally.

Put the chicken meat and cooked vermicelli into a large tureen and pour over the stock. Add the spring onions (scallions) and egg slices before serving. Sometimes, dry fried chillis and sambal ulek are passed around in separate bowls to eat with the soup.

Serves 6-8
Preparation and cooking time: 1½ hours

MOHINGHA

(Fish Soup with Noodles)   (Burma)

Mohingha has often been described as the Burmese national dish — cooked and served on every conceivable occasion from family celebrations to roadside stalls. It is a meal in itself.

Metric/Imperial	American
½kg./1lb. whole fish, such as whiting, mackerel or herring	1lb. whole fish, such as whiting, mackerel or herring
600ml./1 pint water	2½ cups water
grated rind of 1 large lemon	grated rind of 1 large lemon
4 large onions, 2 finely chopped and 2 sliced	4 large onions, 2 finely chopped and 2 sliced
4 garlic cloves, crushed	4 garlic cloves, crushed
4cm./1½in. piece of fresh root ginger, peeled and chopped	1½in. piece of fresh green ginger, peeled and chopped
1 tsp. turmeric	1 tsp. turmeric
50ml./2fl.oz. sesame oil	¼ cup sesame oil
½ tsp. blachan (dried shrimp paste)	½ tsp. blachan (dried shrimp paste)
1 Tbs. fish sauce	1 Tbs. fish sauce
2 tsp. chick-pea flour	2 tsp. chick-pea flour
600ml./1 pint coconut milk	2½ cups coconut milk
¼ Chinese cabbage, shredded	¼ Chinese cabbage, shredded
350g./12oz. rice vermicelli	12oz. rice vermicelli
2 hard-boiled eggs, sliced	2 hard-cooked eggs, sliced
GARNISH	GARNISH
3 spring onions, chopped	3 scallions, chopped
2 Tbs. chopped coriander leaves	2 Tbs. chopped coriander leaves
1 lemon, cut into wedges	1 lemon, cut into wedges

Fillet the fish and put the heads, tails, skin and bones into a saucepan. Add the water and lemon rind and bring to the boil. Reduce the heat to low, cover the pan and simmer the stock for 15 minutes. Strain the liquid and set aside.

Meanwhile, put the chopped onions, garlic, ginger and turmeric into a blender and blend to a purée. Transfer to a small bowl. Heat the oil in a large saucepan. When it is hot, add the onion mixture and fry gently for 2 minutes, stirring constantly. Add the fish pieces and fry on both sides until they are lightly browned. Pour over the fish stock and bring to the boil.

Beat the blachan into the fish sauce, then stir in the flour. Stir the mixture into the mixture in the saucepan until it is thoroughly blended. Pour over the coconut milk and bring to the boil. Add the remaining onions and cabbage and reduce the heat to low. Cover the pan and simmer the soup for 15 minutes.

Meanwhile soak the rice vermicelli in warm water for 10 minutes or until it is cooked through. Drain and transfer to a warmed serving bowl.

Stir the egg slices into the fish soup, then transfer the mixture to a large, warmed tureen. Arrange the garnish ingredients in small, separate bowls.

To serve, spoon the vermicelli into individual serving bowls then pour over the fish soup. Garnish with spring onions (scallions), coriander leaves and lemon wedges to taste.

Serves 4
Preparation and cooking time: 2 hours

KAENG CHUD KAI HED

(Chicken and Mushroom Soup)   (Thailand)

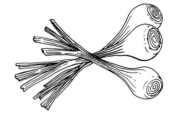

Metric/Imperial	American
1 x 2kg./4lb. chicken	1 x 4lb. chicken
1.2 l./2 pints chicken stock	5 cups chicken stock
1 tsp. salt	1 tsp. salt
6 spring onions, finely chopped	6 scallions, finely chopped
2 Tbs. vegetable oil	2 Tbs. vegetable oil
2 garlic cloves, crushed	2 garlic cloves, crushed
2 Tbs. chopped coriander leaves	2 Tbs. chopped coriander leaves
125g./4oz. bean sprouts	$\frac{1}{2}$ cup bean sprouts
1 Tbs. fish sauce	1 Tbs. fish sauce
4 dried mushrooms, soaked in cold water for 30 minutes, drained and finely chopped	4 dried mushrooms, soaked in cold water for 30 minutes, drained and finely chopped
1 small cucumber, peeled (skin reserved) and flesh chopped	1 small cucumber, peeled (skin reserved) and flesh chopped

Put the chicken in a large saucepan and pour over the stock. Add the salt and spring onions (scallions), cover and bring to the boil. Reduce the heat to low and simmer for 1¼ hours, or until the chicken is cooked through. Remove from the heat. Transfer the chicken to a plate and reserve the stock.

When the chicken is cool enough to handle, tear it into shreds with your fingers. Set aside.

Heat the oil in a large saucepan. When it is hot, add the garlic, coriander and bean sprouts and stir-fry for 2 minutes. Add the chicken pieces, fish sauce and mushrooms and stir-fry for 3 minutes. Add the reserved stock and bring to the boil. Reduce the heat to low and simmer for 3 minutes.

Transfer to a warmed tureen and float curls of cucumber skin on the surface. Serve with the chopped cucumber flesh.

Serves 4-6
Preparation and cooking time: 2½ hours

(See over) Thailand is the home of Kaeng Chud Kai Hed, a filling chicken and mushroom soup.

337

NOODLES & RICE

RICE NOODLES WITH SPICY BEEF

(Thailand)

Metric/Imperial	American
½kg./1lb. rice noodles	1lb. rice noodles
3 Tbs. peanut oil	3 Tbs. peanut oil
1 onion, thinly sliced	1 onion, thinly sliced
4cm./1½in. piece of fresh root ginger, peeled and chopped	1½in. piece of fresh green ginger, peeled and chopped
1 green chilli, chopped	1 green chilli, chopped
700g./1½lb. rump steak, cut into strips	1½lb. rump steak, cut into strips
1 Tbs. fish sauce	1 Tbs. fish sauce
125g./4oz. roasted peanuts, crushed	1 cup roasted peanuts, crushed

Cook the noodles in boiling salted water for 5 minutes. Drain and pour over cold water. Drain again. Transfer to a warmed serving dish and keep hot.

Heat the oil in a large frying-pan. When the oil is hot, add the onion, ginger, chilli and beef and stir-fry for 5 minutes. Add the fish sauce and remove the pan from the heat.

Spoon the mixture over the noodles and sprinkle over the peanuts before serving.

Serves 4-6
Preparation and cooking time: 15 minutes

PANCIT

(Fried Noodles)   (Philippines)

Pancit in Filipino means simply noodles – usually egg – which are served in a whole variety of delicious ways. The recipe given below is a fairly basic version and can be added to or subtracted from at will – for instance, cooked pork or fish fillets can be blended in pancit, and bean sprouts could be substituted for the cabbage suggested here.

MetricI/mperial	American
450g./1lb. egg noodles	1lb. egg noodles
½kg./1lb. shrimps, in the shell	1lb. shrimp, in the shell
300ml./10fl.oz. water	1¼ cups water
50g./2oz. lard	4 Tbs. lard
1 large onion, chopped	1 large onion, chopped
2 garlic cloves, crushed	2 garlic cloves, crushed
1 cooked chicken breast, skinned, boned and cut into strips	1 cooked chicken breast, skinned, boned and cut into strips
225g./8oz. cooked ham, cut into strips	8oz. cooked ham, cut into strips
5 leaves Chinese cabbage, shredded	5 leaves Chinese cabbage, shredded
¼ cucumber, chopped or sliced	¼ cucumber, chopped or sliced
2 Tbs. soya sauce	2 Tbs. soy sauce

Salt and pepper
3 spring onions, chopped

Salt and pepper
3 scallions, chopped

Cook the egg noodles in boiling, salted water for 5 minutes, or until they are just tender. Drain under cold running water and set aside.

Put the shrimps and water into a large saucepan and bring to the boil. Reduce the heat to low and simmer for 10 minutes. Remove from the heat and strain and reserve about 250ml./8fl.oz. (1 cup) of the cooking liquid. Shell and devein the shrimps and set them aside.

Melt half the lard in a large, deep frying-pan. Add the noodles and stir-fry for 3 minutes, or until they are evenly browned (cook them in batches if necessary). Using tongs or a slotted spoon, transfer the noodles to a plate and keep warm while you cook the meat and vegetables.

Melt the remaining lard in the frying-pan. Add the onion and garlic and fry, stirring occasionally, until the onion is soft. Add the chicken, ham, cabbage and cucumber and stir-fry for 3 minutes. Stir in the shrimps, the reserved cooking liquid, soy sauce and salt and pepper to taste. Bring the liquid to the boil. Return the noodles to the pan and stir-fry for a further 2 minutes, or until they are heated through.

Transfer the mixture to a warmed serving bowl and garnish with the spring onions (scallions) before serving.

Serves 6
Preparation and cooking time: 50 minutes

RICE NOODLES WITH PORK & PRAWNS OR SHRIMPS

(Thailand)

Metric/Imperial	American
½kg./1lb. rice noodles	1lb. rice noodles
4 Tbs. peanut oil	4 Tbs. peanut oil
350g./12oz. pork fillet, cut into strips	12oz. pork tenderloin, cut into strips
225g./8oz. prawns, shelled	8oz. shrimp, shelled
6 spring onions, chopped	6 scallions, chopped
1 garlic clove, crushed	1 garlic clove, crushed
6 dried mushrooms, soaked in cold water for 30 minutes, drained and sliced	6 dried mushrooms, soaked in cold water for 30 minutes, drained and sliced
½ tsp. sugar	½ tsp. sugar
2 Tbs. fish sauce	2 Tbs. fish sauce
1 Tbs. chopped coriander leaves	1 Tbs. chopped coriander leaves

Cook the noodles in boiling salted water for 5 minutes. Drain and pour over cold water. Drain again. Transfer to a warmed serving dish and keep hot.

Heat the oil in a large frying-pan. When it is hot, add the pork strips and stir-fry for 3 minutes. Add the prawns or shrimp and stir-fry for 3 minutes. Add the spring onions (scallions), garlic and mushrooms and stir-fry for 2 minutes. Stir in the remaining ingredients and remove the pan from the heat.

Spoon the mixture over the noodles and garnish with coriander leaves before serving.

Serves 4-6
Preparation and cooking time: 20 minutes

(See over) Rice noodles form the basis of many Oriental dishes and none is more delicious than this Thai version, Rice Noodles with Pork and Prawns or Shrimps.

341

BAHMI GORENG

(Indonesian Fried Noodles) (Indonesia)

Metric/Imperial	American
225g./8oz. fine egg noodles (vermicelli)	8oz. fine egg noodles (vermicelli)
4 Tbs. peanut oil	4 Tbs. peanut oil
1 onion, finely chopped	1 onion, finely chopped
2 garlic cloves, crushed	2 garlic cloves, crushed
2½cm./1in. piece of fresh root ginger, peeled and finely chopped	1in. piece of fresh green ginger, peeled and finely chopped
½ tsp. blachan (dried shrimp paste)	½ tsp. blachan (dried shrimp paste)
1 tsp. dried chillis or sambal ulek	1 tsp. dried chillis or sambal ulek
1 chicken breast, boned and cut into thin strips	1 chicken breast, skinned, boned and cut into thin strips
50g./2oz. frozen prawns, thawed	¼ cup frozen shrimp, thawed
1 large celery stalk, sliced	1 large celery stalk, sliced
2 Chinese or white cabbage leaves, shredded	2 Chinese or white cabbage leaves, shredded
2 Tbs. soya sauce	2 Tbs. soy sauce
GARNISH	GARNISH
1 Tbs. chopped peanuts	1 Tbs. chopped peanuts
2 spring onions, chopped	2 scallions, chopped

Cook the noodles in boiling salted water for 3 to 5 minutes, or until they are just tender. Drain and rinse under cold running water, then set aside.

Heat the oil in a large deep frying-pan. When it is hot, add the onion, garlic, ginger, blachan and sambal ulek and stir-fry for 3 minutes. Stir in the chicken and prawns (shrimp) and cook for a further 2 minutes. Add the celery and cabbage and stir-fry for 2 minutes. Stir in the noodles and cook for a further 2 to 3 minutes, or until they are heated through. Stir in the soy sauce.

Transfer the mixture to a large, warmed serving bowl and garnish with the chopped peanuts and spring onions (scallions) before serving.

Serves 3-4

Preparation and cooking time: 30 minutes

MIKROB

(Fried Crisp Noodles) (Thailand)

Metric/Imperial	American
vegetable oil for deep frying	vegetable oil for deep frying
½kg./1lb. rice vermicelli	1lb. rice vermicelli
50ml./2fl.oz. peanut oil	¼ cup peanut oil
4 spring onions, chopped	4 scallions, chopped
3 garlic cloves, crushed	3 garlic cloves, crushed
175g./6oz. pork fillet, cut into strips	6oz. pork tenderloin, cut into strips
1 chicken breast, skinned, boned and cut into strips	1 chicken breast, skinned, boned and cut into strips
125g./4oz. shelled prawns, chopped	4oz. shelled shrimp, chopped
1 bean curd cake, chopped	1 bean curd cake, chopped
225g./8oz. bean sprouts	1 cup bean sprouts
2 Tbs. sugar	2 Tbs. sugar
4 Tbs. vinegar	4 Tbs. vinegar

4 Tbs. fish sauce	4 Tbs. fish sauce
1 Tbs. lemon juice	1 Tbs. lemon juice
1 Tbs. grated orange rind	1 Tbs. grated orange rind
5 eggs, lightly beaten	5 eggs, lightly beaten
GARNISH	GARNISH
chopped coriander leaves	chopped coriander leaves
1 dried red chilli, crumbled	1 dried red chilli, crumbled

Fill a large deep-frying pan one-third full with the oil and heat it until it is hot. Carefully lower the vermicelli (straight from the packet, in batches), into the hot oil and fry until it is golden brown. Using a slotted spoon, remove from the oil and drain on kitchen towels. Keep hot while you cook the remaining vermicelli in the same way.

Heat the peanut oil in a deep frying-pan. When it is very hot, add the spring onions (scallions) and garlic and fry, stirring occasionally, until the spring onions (scallions) are soft. Add the meat, prawns (shrimp), bean curd and bean sprouts and stir-fry for 5 minutes. Add the sugar, vinegar, fish sauce, lemon juice and orange rind and mix well. Stir in the eggs and cook, stirring occasionally, until they have set.

Arrange the vermicelli in a warmed serving bowl. Pour over the meat mixture and garnish with the coriander leaves and chilli before serving.

Serves 6-8
Preparation and cooking time : 45 minutes

PHAT WUN SEN

(Fried Vermicelli)   (Thailand)

Metric/Imperial	American
350g./12oz. rice vermicelli	12oz. rice vermicelli
50ml./2fl.oz. peanut oil	¼ cup peanut oil
2 garlic cloves, crushed	2 garlic cloves, crushed
1 red chilli, chopped	1 red chilli, chopped
4 spring onions, chopped	4 scallions, chopped
1 pork chop, boned and cut into strips	1 pork chop, boned and cut into strips
125g./4oz. frozen prawns, thawed	4oz. frozen shrimp, thawed
8 dried mushrooms, soaked in cold water for 30 minutes, drained and sliced	8 dried mushrooms, soaked in cold water for 30 minutes, drained and sliced
2 carrots, thinly sliced	2 carrots, thinly sliced
1½ Tbs. fish sauce	1½ Tbs. fish sauce
1 Tbs. malt vinegar	1 Tbs. cider vinegar
1½ tsp. sugar	1½ tsp. sugar
salt and pepper	salt and pepper
2 Tbs. chopped coriander leaves	2 Tbs. chopped coriander leaves

Put the rice vermicelli into a large bowl and just cover with boiling water. Set aside to soak for 10 minutes, then drain thoroughly and set aside.

Meanwhile, heat the oil in a large saucepan. When it is hot, add the garlic, chilli and spring onions (scallions) and stir-fry for 2 minutes. Add the pork and stir-fry for a further 2 minutes. Add the prawns (shrimp), mushrooms and carrots and stir-fry for 1 minute. Add the fish sauce, vinegar, sugar and salt and pepper to taste and bring to the boil. Stir in the vermicelli and continue to stir-fry for a further 2 minutes, or until the mixture is throughly blended and the vermicelli heated through.

Transfer the mixture to a warmed serving dish and garnish with the coriander leaves before serving.

Serves 4-6

Preparation and cooking time: 1 hour

FRIED RICE

(Malaysia)

Metric/Imperial	American
350g./12oz. long-grain rice, soaked in cold water for 30 minutes and drained	2 cups long-grain rice, soaked in cold water for 30 minutes and drained
2 tsp. salt	2 tsp. salt
650ml./22fl.oz. water	2¾ cups water
50ml./2fl.oz. vegetable oil	¼ cup vegetable oil
2 medium onions, chopped	2 medium onions, chopped
2 red chillis, chopped	2 red chillis, chopped
½ tsp. blachan (dried shrimp paste)	½ tsp. blachan (dried shrimp paste)
1 garlic clove, crushed	1 garlic clove, crushed
2 tsp. ground coriander	2 tsp. ground coriander
175g./6oz. cooked shrimps, shelled	6oz. cooked shrimp, shelled
175g./6oz. cooked lamb or beef, sliced	6oz. cooked lamb or beef, sliced
2 tsp. soft brown sugar mixed with 1 Tbs. treacle and 2 Tbs. soya sauce	2 tsp. soft brown sugar, mixed with 1 Tbs. molasses and 2 Tbs. soy sauce
GARNISH	GARNISH
1 Tbs. butter	1 Tbs butter
2 eggs, lightly beaten	2 eggs, lightly beaten
¼ tsp. salt	¼ tsp. salt
2 Tbs. vegetable oil	2 Tbs. vegetable oil
2 red chillis, sliced	2 red chillis, sliced
2 onions, thinly sliced	2 onions, thinly sliced
½ cucumber, peeled and diced	½ cucumber, peeled and diced
6 spring onions, sliced	6 scallions, sliced

Put the rice, 1 teaspoon of salt and the water into a saucepan and bring to the boil. Reduce the heat to low, cover the pan and simmer for 15 to 20 minutes, or until the rice is tender and the water is absorbed.

Heat the oil in a large saucepan. When it is hot, add the onions and fry, stirring occasionally, until they are golden brown. Add the chillis, blachan, garlic and coriander and fry for 5 minutes, stirring constantly.

Stir in the shrimps and meat and fry for 1 to 2 minutes, or until they are well mixed with the spices. Stir in the rice, the soy sauce mixture and remaining salt. Reduce the heat to low and cook for 10 minutes, stirring occasionally.

Meanwhile, prepare the garnishes. Melt the butter in a small frying-pan. Add the eggs and salt and cook until the bottom is set and lightly browned. Turn the omelet over and fry for another 2 minutes. Remove from the heat and slide the omelet on to a plate. Cut into strips and set aside.

Wipe out the pan and heat the oil in it over moderately high heat. When it is hot, add the chillis and fry for 2 minutes, stirring constantly. Add the onions and fry, stirring occasionally, until they are golden brown. Remove from the heat and set aside.

When the rice mixture is ready, turn it out on to a warmed serving platter. Scatter the cucumber, spring onions (scallions), fried onions, chillis and the shredded omelet on top. Serve at once.

Serves 6

Preparation and cooking time: 1½ hours

NASI GORENG

(Indonesian Rice)   (Indonesia)

Metric/Imperial	American
350g./12oz. long-grain rice, soaked in cold water for 30 minutes and drained	2 cups long-grain rice, soaked in cold water for 30 minutes and drained
725ml./1¼ pints water	3 cups water
1 tsp. salt	1 tsp. salt
2 Tbs. vegetable oil	2 Tbs. vegetable oil
3 eggs, lightly beaten	3 eggs, lightly beaten
1 medium onion, finely chopped	1 medium onion, finely chopped
2 green chillis, finely chopped	2 green chillis, finely chopped
1 garlic clove, crushed	1 garlic clove, crushed
½kg./1lb. cooked chicken meat, cut into thin slices	1lb. cooked chicken meat, cut into thin slices
225g./8oz. prawns, shelled and chopped	8oz. shrimp, shelled and chopped
2 celery stalks, finely chopped	2 celery stalks, finely chopped
2 Tbs. soya sauce	2 Tbs. soy sauce

Put the rice into a large saucepan. Pour over the water and salt and bring to the boil. Reduce the heat to low, cover and simmer for 15 to 20 minutes, or until the rice is tender and the liquid absorbed. Set aside.

Heat half the oil in a small frying-pan. When it is hot, add the eggs and fry for 3 minutes on each side, or until they form an omelet. Slide the omelet on to a plate and cut into thin strips. Set aside.

Heat the remaining oil in a large frying-pan. When the oil is hot, add the onion, chillis and garlic and fry, stirring occasionally, until the onion is soft. Add the chicken, prawns or shrimp and celery and cook, stirring occasionally, until they are well mixed. Stir in the cooked rice, soy sauce and the omelet strips and cook for 3 to 5 minutes, or until all the ingredients are warmed through and well blended.

Transfer the mixture to a warmed serving bowl and serve at once.
Serves 6-7
Preparation and cooking time: 45 minutes

KAO PAD

(Thai Fried Rice)   (Thailand)

Metric/Imperial	American
4 Tbs. peanut oil	4 Tbs. peanut oil
1 large onion, chopped	1 large onion, chopped
1 red chilli, chopped	1 red chilli, chopped
225g./8oz. pork fillet, cut into strips	8oz. pork tenderloin, cut into strips
225g./8oz. frozen prawns	8oz. frozen shrimp
125g./4oz. crabmeat, shell and cartilage removed	4oz. crabmeat, shell and cartilage removed
3 eggs, lightly beaten	3 eggs, lightly beaten
2 Tbs. fish sauce	2 Tbs. fish sauce
350g./12oz. cooked long-grain rice	4 cups cooked long-grain rice
3 Tbs. tomato purée	3 Tbs. tomato paste
6 spring onions, chopped	6 scallions, chopped
2 Tbs. chopped coriander leaves	2 Tbs. chopped coriander leaves

Heat the oil in a large saucepan. When it is hot, add the onion and chilli and fry, stirring occasionally, until the onion is soft. Add the pork strips and stir-fry for 3 minutes. Add the prawns (shrimp) and crabmeat to the mixture and stir-fry for 2 minutes.

Break the eggs into the centre of the mixture and quickly stir until they are thoroughly combined. Stir in the fish sauce, cooked rice and tomato purèe (paste) and stir-fry for 5 minutes or until the rice is completely heated through and the mixture is blended.

Transfer the mixture to a large warmed serving bowl and garnish with the spring onions (scallions) and chopped coriander leaves.

Serve at once.

Serves 4-6

Preparation and cooking time: 50 minutes

Indonesian Liver and Rice is a satisfying one-dish meal, adapted from the traditional Indonesian Nasi Goreng.

INDONESIAN LIVER & RICE

Metric/Imperial	American
450g./1lb. long-grain rice, soaked in cold water for 30 minutes and drained	2⅔ cups long-grain rice, soaked in cold water for 30 minutes and drained
1.2l./2 pints water	5 cups water
1 tsp. salt	1 tsp. salt
3 Tbs. peanut oil	3 Tbs. peanut oil
3 eggs, lightly beaten	3 eggs, lightly beaten
4 spring onions, chopped	4 scallions, chopped
75g./3oz. mushrooms, sliced	¾ cup sliced mushrooms
1 tinned pimiento, drained and finely chopped	1 canned pimiento, drained and finely chopped
1 red chilli, chopped	1 red chilli, chopped
2 garlic cloves, crushed	2 garlic cloves, crushed
5cm./2in. piece of fresh root ginger, peeled and finely chopped	2in. piece of fresh green ginger, peeled and finely chopped
2 Tbs. soya sauce	2 Tbs. soy sauce
LIVER	LIVER
4 Tbs. soya sauce	4 Tbs. soy sauce
4 Tbs. beef stock	4 Tbs. beef stock
1 Tbs. wine vinegar	1 Tbs. wine vinegar
2 Tbs. water	2 Tbs. water
salt and pepper	salt and pepper
1 garlic clove, crushed	1 garlic clove, crushed
10cm./4in. piece of fresh root ginger, peeled and chopped	4in. piece of fresh green ginger, peeled and chopped
2 tsp. cornflour	2 tsp. cornstarch
1½kg./3lb. lambs liver, thinly sliced	3lb. lambs liver, thinly sliced
50ml./2fl.oz. peanut oil	¼ cup peanut oil
2 celery stalks, chopped	2 celery stalks, chopped
350g./12oz. bean sprouts	1½ cups bean sprouts

First prepare the liver. Combine the soy sauce, stock, vinegar, water, seasoning, garlic, half the ginger and cornflour (cornstarch) in a shallow bowl. Add the liver slices and set aside to marinate for 45 minutes, basting frequently.

Meanwhile, prepare the rice. Put the rice, water and salt into a large saucepan and bring to the boil. Cover, reduce the heat to low and simmer for 15 to 20 minutes, or until the rice is tender and the liquid absorbed. Remove from the heat and set aside.

Heat 1 tablespoon of the oil in a small frying-pan. When it is hot, add the eggs and fry on each side until they are set in a thin omelet. Slide the omelet on to a plate and cut into thin strips. Set aside.

Preheat the oven to very cool 130°C (Gas Mark ½, 250°F).

Heat the remaining oil in a large frying-pan. When it is hot, add the spring onions (scallions), mushrooms, pimiento, chilli, garlic and ginger and fry until the spring onions (scallions) are soft. Stir in the rice, soy sauce and omelet strips and fry for 3 minutes, stirring occasionally. Transfer to an ovenproof dish and keep hot in the oven while you cook the liver.

Heat the oil in a large frying-pan. When it is hot, add the remaining ginger and fry for 2 minutes. Increase the heat to moderately high and add the liver and marinade to the pan. Fry, stirring and turning occasionally, for 6 minutes. Stir in the remaining ingredients and fry for 3 minutes, or until the liver slices are cooked through.

Remove the dish from the oven and arrange the liver slices over the rice. Spoon over the sauce and vegetables and serve at once.

Serves 8
Preparation and cooking time: 1 hour

YELLOW RICE

(Indonesia)

Metric/Imperial	American
3 Tbs. vegetable oil	3 Tbs. vegetable oil
1 large onion, finely chopped	1 large onion, finely chopped
2 garlic cloves, crushed	2 garlic cloves, crushed
1 Tbs. turmeric	1 Tbs. turmeric
salt and pepper	salt and pepper
1 tsp. finely chopped lemon grass or grated lemon rind	1 tsp. finely chopped lemon grass or grated lemon rind
450g./1lb. long-grain rice, soaked in cold water for 30 minutes and drained	2⅔ cups long-grain rice, soaked in cold water for 30 minutes and drained
600ml./1 pint water	2½ cups water
300ml./10fl.oz. coconut milk	1¼ cups coconut milk
2 bay leaves	2 bay leaves
GARNISH	GARNISH
3 hard-boiled eggs, quartered	3 hard-cooked eggs, quartered
125g./4oz. roasted peanuts	⅔ cup roasted peanuts
2 bananas, sliced	2 bananas, sliced
coriander sprigs	coriander sprigs

Heat the oil in a large saucepan. When it is hot, add the onion and garlic and fry, stirring occasionally, until the onion is soft. Stir in the turmeric, seasoning to taste, lemon grass or rind and rice and fry for 3 minutes, stirring constantly. Pour over the water and coconut milk and bring to the boil. Reduce the heat to low, add the bay leaves and cover the pan. Simmer for 15 to 20 minutes, or until the rice is tender and the liquid absorbed. Discard the bay leaves.

Transfer the rice to a warmed serving dish, shaping it into a dome. Garnish with the eggs, peanuts, bananas and coriander and serve at once.
Serves 6
Preparation and cooking time: 35 minutes

INDONESIAN SPICED RICE

Metric/Imperial	American
50g./2oz. tamarind	¼ cup tamarind
250ml./8fl.oz. boiling water	1 cup boiling water
350g./12oz. long-grain rice, soaked in cold water for 30 minutes and drained	2 cups long-grain rice, soaked in cold water for 30 minutes and drained
1 tsp. salt	1 tsp. salt
2 Tbs. dark treacle	2 Tbs. molasses
1 tsp. ground cumin	1 tsp. ground cumin
1 Tbs. soya sauce	1 Tbs. soy sauce
1 Tbs. ground coriander	1 Tbs. ground coriander
1 tsp. hot chilli powder	1 tsp. hot chilli powder
½ medium coconut, grated	½ medium coconut, grated
4 Tbs. vegetable oil	4 Tbs. vegetable oil
1 medium onion, thinly sliced	1 medium onion, thinly sliced
125g./4oz. chopped peanuts	⅔ cup chopped peanuts
450ml./15fl.oz. boiling chicken stock	2 cups boiling chicken stock

Put the tamarind pulp into a bowl and pour over the water. Set aside to cool. Pour the contents of the bowl through a strainer into a saucepan, pressing as much pulp through as possible.

Half fill a large saucepan with water and bring to the boil. Add the rice and salt and boil briskly for 2 minutes. Drain, discard the cooking liquid and set the rice aside.

Stir the treacle (molasses), cumin, soy sauce, coriander and chilli powder into the tamarind liquid. Bring to the boil, then cook for 5 to 10 minutes, stirring occasionally, or until the mixture thickens slightly. Stir in the rice and grated coconut, remove from the heat and keep hot.

Heat the oil in a large saucepan. When it is hot, add the onion and fry, stirring occasionally, for 3 minutes. Add the peanuts and fry for 5 minutes, or until both they and the onions are browned. Stir in the rice mixture and cook for a further 2 minutes. Pour over the stock, cover and reduce the heat to low. Simmer for 10 to 15 minutes, or until the rice is tender and the liquid absorbed.

Transfer to a warmed serving bowl and serve at once.

Serves 4-6
Preparation and cooking time: 1¼ hours

FRIED RICE WITH MEATS

In Vietnam, the rice for this dish is traditionally 'roasted' in an earthenware pot. However, the method suggested below is somewhat easier for less experienced rice cooks to follow and produces authentic – and excellent – results.

Metric/Imperial	American
75ml./3fl. oz. peanut oil	6 Tbs. peanut oil
350g./12oz. long- or medium-grain rice soaked in cold water for 30 minutes and drained	2 cups long- or medium-grain rice, soaked in cold water for 30 minutes and drained
600ml./1 pint boiling water	2½ cups boiling water
4cm./1½in. piece of fresh root ginger, peeled and chopped	1½in. piece of fresh green ginger, peeled and chopped
1 garlic clove, crushed	1 garlic clove, crushed
4 spring onions, chopped	4 scallions, chopped
1 chicken breast, skinned, boned and cut into thin strips	1 chicken breast, skinned, boned and cut into thin strips
125g./4oz. lean pork meat, cut into thin strips	4 oz. lean pork meat, cut into thin strips
8 dried mushrooms, soaked in cold water for 30 minutes, drained and chopped	8 dried mushrooms, soaked in cold water for 30 minutes, drained and chopped
1 Tbs. fish sauce	1 Tbs. fish sauce
2 eggs	2 eggs
1 Tbs. chopped coriander leaves	1 Tbs. chopped coriander leaves

Heat half the oil in a large saucepan. When it is hot, add the rice and stir-fry for 2 minutes, or until it becomes opaque. Reduce the heat to very low and simmer the rice gently for a further 10 minutes, stirring occasionally. Pour over the water and return to the boil. Reduce the heat to low, cover the pan and simmer the rice for 10 to 15 minutes, or until it is tender and the liquid absorbed.

Meanwhile, heat the remaining oil in a large, deep frying-pan. When it is hot, add the ginger, garlic and about three-quarters of the spring onions (scallions) and stir-fry for 2 minutes. Add the chicken and pork meat and continue to stir-fry for 4 minutes, or until the meat is cooked through. Add the mushrooms and fish sauce and stir-fry for 2 minutes. Remove the pan from the heat.

When all the liquid has been absorbed from the rice, make a well in the centre and carefully pour in the chicken and pork mixture. Break the eggs into the centre of the chicken and pork mixture and stir-fry briskly into the meat, then the rice until the eggs are 'cooked'.

Transfer the mixture to a warmed serving bowl or platter and garnish with the remaining spring onion (scallion) and chopped coriander leaves before serving.
Serves 4
Preparation and cooking time: 1 hour 10 minutes

NASI KUNING LENGKAP

(Festive Rice)   (Indonesia)

Metric/Imperial	American
2 Tbs. peanut oil	2 Tbs. peanut oil
1 large onion, chopped	1 large onion, chopped
2 garlic cloves, crushed	2 garlic cloves, crushed
1 tsp. chopped lemon grass or grated lemon rind	1 tsp. chopped lemon grass or grated lemon rind
1 tsp. turmeric	1 tsp. turmeric
½ tsp. laos powder	½ tsp. laos powder
3 curry or bay leaves	3 curry or bay leaves
1 tsp. salt	1 tsp. salt
450g./1lb. long-grain rice, soaked in cold water for 30 minutes and drained	2⅔ cups long-grain rice, soaked in cold water for 30 minutes and drained
1.2l./2 pints coconut milk	5 cups coconut milk
GARNISH	GARNISH
1 Tbs. vegetable oil	1 Tbs. vegetable oil
2 small eggs, beaten	2 small eggs, beaten
4 spring onions, chopped	4 scallions, chopped
2 red chillis, quartered	2 red chillis, quartered
2 green chillis, quartered	2 green chillis, quartered
2 hard-boiled eggs, sliced	2 hard-cooked eggs, sliced
⅓ cucumber, sliced or cut into 2½cm./ 1in. lengths	⅓ cucumber, sliced or cut into 1in. lengths

Heat the peanut oil in a large saucepan. When it is hot, add the onion and garlic and fry, stirring occasionally, until the onion is soft. Stir in the lemon grass or rind, turmeric, laos powder, curry or bay leaves and salt. Add the rice and stir-fry for 2 to 3 minutes, or until it becomes opaque. Pour over the coconut milk and bring to the boil. Reduce the heat to low, cover the pan and simmer the mixture for 20 to 25 minutes, or until the rice is cooked and tender and the liquid absorbed.

Meanwhile, make the garnish. Heat the vegetable oil in a small frying-pan. When it is hot, add the eggs and cook until the bottom is set and lightly browned. Turn the omelet over and cook for another 2 minutes. Remove from the heat and slide the omelet onto a plate. Cut into strips and set aside.

When the rice is cooked, transfer to a large serving dish. Using greaseproof or waxed paper, carefully pat the rice into a conical shape (if you have a cone-shaped strainer, you can put the rice into this, then carefully unmould it on to the dish). Put the chillis in rows up and down the shaped rice and scatter the omelet strips over the top. Arrange the hard-boiled (hard-cooked) egg slices and cucumbers (plus any of the other garnishes suggested) around the base of the rice.
Serve at once.
Serves 6
Preparation and cooking time: 1¼ hours

BEEF

STIR-FRIED BEEF

(Malaysia)

Metric/Imperial	American
3 Tbs. dark soya sauce	3 Tbs. dark soy sauce
2 garlic cloves, crushed	2 garlic cloves, crushed
2 tsp. cornflour	2 tsp. cornstarch
1 tsp. sugar	1 tsp. sugar
700g./1½lb. rump steak, cut into strips	1½lb. rump steak, cut into strips
4 Tbs. vegetable oil	4 Tbs. vegetable oil
7½cm./3in. piece of fresh root ginger, peeled and chopped	3in. piece of fresh green ginger, peeled and chopped
225g./8oz. bean sprouts	1 cup bean sprouts

Combine the soy sauce, garlic, cornflour (cornstarch) and sugar in a shallow bowl. Add the beef strips and mix well. Cover and set aside for 30 minutes, stirring occasionally.

Heat the oil in a large frying-pan. When it is hot, add the ginger and stir-fry for 3 minutes. Add the beef mixture and stir-fry for 5 minutes. Stir in the bean sprouts and stir-fry for a further 4 minutes.

Spoon into a warmed bowl and serve at once.

Serves 4-6
Preparation and cooking time : 50 minutes

MORCON

(Beef Roll with Tomato Sauce)   (Philippines)

Metric/Imperial	American
1½kg./3lb. beef skirt, cut crosswise into 2 or 3 pieces and flattened by beating to ½cm./¼in. thick	3lb. beef flank, cut crosswise into 2 or 3 pieces and flattened by beating to ¼in. thick
½ tsp. salt	½ tsp. salt
¼ tsp. pepper	¼ tsp. pepper
1 Tbs. lemon juice	1 Tbs. lemon juice
1 garlic clove, crushed	1 garlic clove, crushed
4 cooked ham slices	4 cooked ham slices
4 hard-boiled eggs, sliced	4 hard-cooked eggs, sliced
125g./4oz. Cheddar cheese, thinly sliced	4oz. Cheddar cheese, thinly sliced
225g./8oz. green olives, stoned and chopped	2 cups green olives, pitted and chopped
75ml./3fl.oz. vegetable oil	⅓ cup vegetable oil
25g./1oz. butter	2 Tbs. butter
½kg./1lb. tomatoes, blanched, peeled and chopped	1lb. tomatoes, blanched, peeled and chopped
1 Tbs. soya sauce	1 Tbs. soy sauce
125ml./4fl.oz. water	½ cup water
25g./1oz. beurre manié	2 Tbs. beurre manié

Put the beef pieces on a flat surface, overlapping to make a large oblong. Pound the overlapping edges together to seal. Sprinkle over the salt, pepper, lemon juice and garlic.

Arrange the ham slices over the beef, then the egg slices, in lines. Top with the cheese. Sprinkle over the olives and a third of the oil. Roll up Swiss (jelly) roll fashion and secure with string at intervals to keep the shape.

Melt the butter with the remaining oil in a large saucepan. Add the meat roll and brown, turning from time to time, for 10 minutes. Reduce the heat to low and add the tomatoes, soy sauce and water and bring to the boil. Cover and simmer for 45 minutes to 1 hour, or until the meat is cooked through.

Remove the roll to a carving board and discard the string. Cut into 2½cm./1in. slices and arrange on a heated serving dish. Keep warm.

Bring the pan juices to the boil and add the beurre manié, stirring constantly until it has dissolved. Cook for 3 to 5 minutes, or until the sauce has thickened. Pour over the meat before serving.

Serves 6
Preparation and cooking time: 1¾ hours

Top: Morcon (beef roll with tomato sauce), is a popular Filipino dish, where the Spanish influence is clearly discernible. Below: Malaysia is the home of Rendang, a spicy beef stew which is adapted from an Indian curry. If you prefer your curries to be less than lethal, you can adjust the amount of chilli powder used in a recipe, or seed fresh chillis – the heat is in the seeds rather than the pods.

RENDANG

(Spicy Beef)   (Malaysia)

Metric/Imperial	American
1kg./2lb. topside of beef, cut into cubes	2lb. top round of beef, cut into cubes
2 garlic cloves, crushed	2 garlic cloves, crushed
2½cm./1in. piece of fresh root ginger, peeled and chopped	1in. piece of fresh green ginger, peeled and chopped
1 green chilli, chopped	1 green chilli, chopped
1 tsp. salt	1 tsp. salt
2 tsp. hot chilli powder	2 tsp. hot chilli powder
1 Tbs. ground coriander	1 Tbs. ground coriander
1 tsp. ground cumin	1 tsp. ground cumin
1 tsp. turmeric	1 tsp. turmeric
1 tsp. sugar	1 tsp. sugar
2 medium onions, chopped	2 medium onions, chopped
1 stalk lemon grass or 1 x 5cm./2in. piece finely pared lemon rind	1 stalk lemon grass or 1 x 2in. piece of finely pared lemon rind
juice of ½ lemon	juice of ½ lemon
600ml./1 pint thick coconut milk	2½ cups thick coconut milk

Put the beef cubes in a large bowl. Mix the garlic, ginger, chilli and salt together and rub the mixture into the cubes. Set aside for 30 minutes.

Combine the chilli powder, coriander, cumin, turmeric, sugar, onions, lemon grass or rind, lemon juice and coconut milk in a saucepan and bring to the boil. Add the beef cubes and bring to the boil again, stirring constantly. Reduce the heat to moderately low and cook uncovered, for 1 to 1¼ hours, or until the beef is cooked through and tender. Reduce the heat to low and cook, stirring constantly, until the meat is golden brown and all the liquid has evaporated.

Remove from the heat and transfer the meat to a warmed serving dish. Serve at once.

Serves 4-6
Preparation and cooking time: 2¼ hours.
Note: great care must be taken during the last stage of cooking. The heat must be carefully adjusted and the ingredients stirred constantly or else the meat will burn and the dish will be ruined.

Bun Bo could be described as the Vietnamese national dish – a platter of vermicelli, one of succulent meat garnished with crushed peanuts, and a third containing refreshing salad. And, of course, always on the Vietnamese table is Nuoc Cham, a dipping sauce made from fish sauce. It is used as a condiment in much the same way as ketchup is used in the West.

BUN BO

(Stir-fried Beef with Noodles) (Vietnam)

Metric/Imperial	American
½kg./1lb. rice vermicelli	1lb. rice vermicelli
50ml./2fl.oz. peanut oil	¼ cup peanut oil
1kg./2lb. rump steak, cut into strips	2lb. rump steak, cut into strips
2 onions, chopped	2 onions, chopped
1 Tbs. fish sauce	1 Tbs. fish sauce
125g./4oz. roasted peanuts, crushed	⅔ cup roasted peanuts, crushed
GARNISH	GARNISH
1 small crisp lettuce, shredded	1 small crisp lettuce, shredded
½ small cucumber, chopped	½ small cucumber, chopped
3 spring onions (green part only), chopped	3 scallions (green part only), chopped
1 serving nuoc cham (page 412)	1 serving nuoc cham (page 412)

Cook the vermicelli in boiling salted water for 5 minutes. Drain, refresh under cold water, then keep hot while you cook the meat.

Heat the oil in a large frying-pan. When it is hot, add the meat and onions and stir-fry for 5 minutes. Stir in the fish sauce and stir-fry for a further 1 minute.

To serve, assemble the salad ingredients on one platter, the vermicelli on another and the meat on a third. Sprinkle the meat mixture with the crushed peanuts and serve the dish with the fish sauce.

Serves 6-8
Preparation and cooking time: 35 minutes

JAVANESE CURRY

Metric/Imperial	American
1 tsp. cumin seeds	1 tsp. cumin seeds
1 Tbs. coriander seeds	1 Tbs. coriander seeds
2 Tbs. blanched almonds	2 Tbs. blanched almonds
2 onions, coarsely chopped	2 onions, coarsely chopped
3 red or green chillis	3 red or green chillis
4cm./1½in. piece of fresh root ginger, peeled	1½in. piece of fresh green ginger, peeled
3 garlic cloves	3 garlic cloves
½ tsp. blachan (dried shrimp paste)	½ tsp. blachan (dried shrimp paste)
50ml./2fl.oz. vegetable oil	¼ cup vegetable oil
1kg./2lb. stewing steak, cubed	2lb. chuck steak, cubed
300ml./10fl.oz. water	1¼ cups water
1 tsp. salt	1 tsp. salt
½ tsp. laos powder (optional)	½ tsp. laos powder (optional)
1 tsp. chopped lemon grass or grated lemon rind	1 tsp. chopped lemon grass or grated lemon rind
25g./1oz. tamarind	2 Tbs. tamarind
125ml./4fl.oz. boiling water	½ cup boiling water
225g./8oz. green cabbage, shredded	8oz. green cabbage, shredded
8 spring onions, cut into lengths	8 scallions, cut into lengths
175ml./6fl.oz. thick coconut milk	¾ cup thick coconut milk

Put the cumin, coriander and almonds in a blender with the onions, chillis, ginger,

garlic and blachan. Blend to a paste, adding enough water to prevent the blades from sticking.

Heat the oil in a large saucepan. When it is hot, add the spice paste and fry for 5 minutes, or until it comes away from the sides of the pan. Add the beef cubes and fry until they are evenly browned. Pour in the water and stir in the salt, laos, and lemon grass and bring to the boil. Reduce the heat to low, cover and simmer for 2 to 2½ hours, or until the beef is cooked through and tender.

Meanwhile, put the tamarind into a bowl and pour over the water. Set aside until it is cool. Pour the contents of the bowl through a strainer into a bowl, pressing as much of the pulp through as possible.

Add the shredded cabbage, spring onions (scallions), coconut milk and tamarind liquid to the curry and bring to the boil again. Stir and allow to boil for 2 minutes.

Remove from the heat and transfer to a warmed serving dish. Serve at once.
Serves 4-6
Preparation and cooking time: 2½ hours

Javanese Curry is hot and very spicy. Serve with cooling raitas and sambals and plain rice for the best effect.

BEEF SATE

(Indonesia)

Metric/Imperial	American
1 Tbs. coriander seeds	1 Tbs. coriander seeds
2 garlic cloves	2 garlic cloves
2 green chillis	2 green chillis
1 tsp. turmeric	1 tsp. turmeric
2½cm./1in. piece of fresh root ginger, peeled	1in. piece of fresh green ginger, peeled
2 medium onions, chopped	2 medium onions, chopped
2 Tbs. lemon juice	2 Tbs. lemon juice
1 Tbs. soya sauce	1 Tbs. soy sauce
4 Tbs. peanut oil	4 Tbs. peanut oil
700g./1½lb. rump steak, cubed	1½lb. rump steak, cubed
250ml./8fl.oz. thick coconut milk	1 cup thick coconut milk
125ml./4fl.oz. water	½ cup water
1 curry or bay leaf	1 curry or bay leaf

Put the coriander, garlic, chillis, turmeric, ginger, onions, lemon juice and soy sauce into a blender and blend to a smooth purée. Alternatively, pound the ingredients in a mortar with a pestle until they are smooth.

Heat the oil in a large saucepan. When it is hot, add the spice paste and fry for 5 minutes, stirring constantly. Add the meat cubes, and remaining ingredients and bring to the boil. Reduce the heat to low and simmer for 40 to 45 minutes, or until the meat is cooked through and the sauce is very thick. Set aside until the meat is cool enough to handle, then transfer the meat to a plate. Remove the curry or bay leaf and keep the sauce warm.

Preheat the grill (broiler) to high. Thread the cubes on to skewers and arrange on the rack of the grill (broiler). Grill (broil) the meat for 5 minutes on each side, or until it is golden brown, basting frequently with the sauce.

Pile the skewers on to a warmed serving platter and serve with the remaining sauce.

Serves 6
Preparation and cooking time: 1¼ hours

SATE MANIS

(Sweet Sate)   (Indonesia)

Metric/Imperial	American
1½ Tbs. jaggery or soft brown sugar	1½ Tbs. jaggery or soft brown sugar
3 Tbs. soya sauce	3 Tbs. soy sauce
3 Tbs. water	3 Tbs. water
2 tsp. lemon juice	2 tsp. lemon juice
2 garlic cloves, crushed	2 garlic cloves, crushed
2 red or green chillis, seeded and chopped	2 red or green chillis, seeded and chopped
salt and pepper	salt and pepper
700g./1½lb. rump steak, cut into 2½cm./1in. cubes	1½lb. rump steak, cut into 1in. cubes
1 Tbs. peanut oil	1 Tbs. peanut oil

SAUCE	SAUCE
1 Tbs. peanut oil	1 Tbs. peanut oil
2 garlic cloves, crushed	2 garlic cloves, crushed
1½ tsp. dried chillis or sambal ulek	1½ tsp. dried chillis or sambal ulek
1 tsp. blachan (dried shrimp paste)	1 tsp. blachan (dried shrimp paste)
¼ tsp. laos powder (optional)	¼ tsp. laos powder (optional)
½ tsp. jaggery or soft brown sugar	½ tsp. jaggery or soft brown sugar
5 Tbs. peanut butter	5 Tbs. peanut butter
350ml./12fl. oz. coconut milk or water	1½ cups coconut milk or water
2 Tbs. lemon juice	2 Tbs. lemon juice

Put the jaggery or brown sugar, soy sauce, water and lemon juice into a large shallow dish. Stir in the garlic and chilli and add salt and pepper to taste. Arrange the beef cubes in the mixture and baste well. Set aside at room temperature for 4 hours, basting occasionally. Remove the cubes from the marinade mixture and pat dry with kitchen towels. Discard the marinade.

Preheat the grill (broiler) to moderately high. Thread the beef cubes on to skewers and arrange the skewers on the rack of the grill (broiler) and grill (broil) for 15 to 20 minutes, turning and basting occasionally with the tablespoon of peanut oil, or until the beef is cooked through and tender.

Meanwhile, to make the sauce, heat the oil in a frying-pan. When it is hot, add the garlic and sambal ulek and stir-fry for 1 minute. Stir in the blachan, laos powder and jaggery or brown sugar, until the sugar has dissolved. Add the peanut butter and stir until it becomes smooth. Gradually add the coconut milk or water, stirring constantly and bring to the boil. Remove the pan from the heat. (The sauce should be of a thick pouring consistency so thin down if necessary with more coconut milk or water).

To serve, arrange the beef, on skewers, across a serving dish and spoon a little of the sauce on top. Pour the remaining sauce into a warmed sauceboat and serve it with the sate.

Serves 4-6
Preparation and cooking time : 4½ hours

REMPAH

(Beef and Coconut Patties)   (Indonesia)

Rempah are a sort of Eastern hamburger and are just as delicious to eat and as easy to make as their Western equivalent! They are usually eaten as a snack or hors d'oeuvre and the servings below reflect this. However, they would make an excellent main dish served with a rice or noodle dish and some vegetables – but in this case make double quantities to serve 6-8.

Metric/Imperial	American
125g./4oz. desiccated coconut	1 cup shredded coconut
225g./8oz. minced beef	8oz. ground beef
1 garlic clove, crushed	1 garlic clove, crushed
¼ tsp. blachan (dried shrimp paste) (optional)	¼ tsp. blachan (dried shrimp paste) (optional)
1 tsp. ground coriander	1 tsp. ground coriander
½ tsp. ground cumin	½ tsp. ground cumin
¼ tsp. laos powder or ground ginger	¼ tsp. laos powder or ground ginger
1 egg, lightly beaten	1 egg, lightly beaten
50g./2oz. cornflour	½ cup cornstarch
125ml./4fl.oz. peanut oil	½ cup peanut oil

Put the coconut into a bowl and moisten with about 4 tablespoons of boiling water. Then stir in all the remaining ingredients, except the cornflour (cornstarch) and oil and beat until they are smooth and well blended.

Using your hands, shape the mixture into about 12 small patty shapes. Dip each shape into the cornflour (cornstarch), shaking off any excess.

Heat about half the oil in a large frying-pan. When it is very hot, add half the patties and fry for about 5 minutes on each side, or until they are cooked through and golden. Remove from the heat and drain on kitchen towels. Keep the rempah hot while you cook the remaining batch of patties in the same way.

Serves 6-8

Preparation and cooking time: 40 minutes

KAENG MASAMAN

(Mussulman Curry) (Thailand)

Metric/Imperial	American
1kg./2lb. braising steak, cubed	2lb. chuck steak, cubed
900ml./1½ pints thick coconut milk	3¾ cups thick coconut milk
125g./4oz. roasted peanuts	⅔ cup roasted peanuts
1 Tbs. fish sauce (optional)	1 Tbs. fish sauce (optional)
25g./1oz. tamarind	2 Tbs. tamarind
50ml./2fl.oz. boiling water	¼ cup boiling water
2 Tbs. lime or lemon juice	2 Tbs. lime or lemon juice
2 tsp. soft brown sugar	2 tsp. soft brown sugar
CURRY PASTE	CURRY PASTE
1 Tbs. hot chilli powder	1 Tbs. hot chilli powder
2 Tbs. ground coriander	2 Tbs. ground coriander
2 tsp. ground cumin	2 tsp. ground cumin
½ tsp. ground fennel	½ tsp. ground fennel
1 tsp. laos powder	1 tsp. laos powder
1 tsp. ground ginger	1 tsp. ground ginger
½ tsp. ground cardamom	½ tsp. ground cardamom
½ tsp. ground cinnamon	½ tsp. ground cinnamon
½ tsp. ground cloves	½ tsp. ground cloves
2 tsp. chopped lemon grass or grated lemon rind	2 tsp. chopped lemon grass or grated lemon rind
3 Tbs. peanut oil	3 Tbs. peanut oil
4 garlic cloves, crushed	4 garlic cloves, crushed
1 large onion, chopped	1 large onion, chopped
½ tsp. blachan (dried shrimp paste)	½ tsp. blachan (dried shrimp paste)

To make the curry paste, combine the chilli powder, coriander, cumin, fennel, laos, ginger, cardamom, cinnamon and cloves. Stir in the lemon grass or rind. Heat the oil in a small frying-pan. When it is hot, add the garlic, onion and blachan and fry, stirring occasionally, until the onion is soft. Remove from the heat and set aside to cool. When the mixture has cooled a little, put it into a blender and blend to a purée. Stir the purée into the ground spice mixture until all the ingredients are well blended.

Put the beef and coconut milk into a saucepan and bring to the boil. Add the peanuts and fish sauce and reduce the heat to low. Simmer the mixture, uncovered, for 2 hours, or until the beef is cooked through and tender. Using a slotted spoon, transfer the meat to a plate.

Set the pan with the cooking liquid over high heat and bring to the boil. Continue to boil rapidly until the gravy has reduced by about one-third.

A mini-Rijsttafel with a
marvellous taste! Left:
Semur Banka, a superb
Malay-Chinese beef stew
in soy sauce; Centre:
Chicken Sate with its spicy
peanut sauce (almost the
Indonesian national dish);
and Right: Baked
Bananas, one of the very
best of the rijsttafel
accompaniments.

Meanwhile, put the tamarind into a bowl and pour over the water. Set aside until it is cool. Pour the contents of the bowl through a strainer into a bowl, pressing as much of the pulp through as possible. Set aside.

Stir the curry paste into the pan containing the gravy, then return the beef cubes to the pan. Simmer for 5 minutes, basting the beef thoroughly in the liquid. Stir in the tamarind water, lime or lemon juice and brown sugar and heat until just below boiling.

Serve at once.

Serves 4-6

Preparation and cooking time: $2\frac{1}{2}$ hours

SEMUR BANKA

(Beef in Soy Sauce)   (Indonesia)

Metric/Imperial	American
25g./1oz. tamarind	2 Tbs. tamarind
125ml./4fl.oz. boiling water	$\frac{1}{2}$ cup boiling water
50ml/2fl.oz. groundnut oil	$\frac{1}{4}$ cup groundnut oil
2 medium onions, thinly sliced	2 medium onions, thinly sliced
3 garlic cloves, crushed	3 garlic cloves, crushed
4cm./1$\frac{1}{2}$in. piece of fresh root ginger, peeled and finely chopped	1$\frac{1}{2}$in. piece of fresh green ginger, peeled and finely chopped
3 cloves, crushed	3 cloves, crushed
$\frac{1}{4}$ tsp. grated nutmeg or garam masala	$\frac{1}{4}$ tsp. grated nutmeg or garam masala
$\frac{1}{4}$ tsp. black pepper	$\frac{1}{4}$ tsp. black pepper
1kg./2lb. stewing or braising steak, cut into 4cm./1$\frac{1}{2}$in. pieces	2lb. chuck steak, cut into 1$\frac{1}{2}$in. pieces
1 tsp. salt	1 tsp. salt
2 tsp. soft brown sugar mixed with 1 Tbs. treacle and 2 Tbs. dark soy sauce	2 tsp. soft brown sugar mixed with 1 Tbs. molasses and 2 Tbs. dark soy sauce
150ml./5fl.oz. water	$\frac{2}{3}$ cup water

Put the tamarind into a bowl and pour over the water. Set aside until it is cool. Pour the contents of the bowl through a strainer into a bowl, pressing as much of the pulp through as possible. Set aside the liquid.

Heat the oil in a large deep frying-pan. When it is hot, add the onions and fry, stirring occasionally, until they are soft. Add the garlic, ginger, spices and pepper and fry for 3 minutes, stirring frequently. Add the meat and increase the heat to moderately high. Cook the meat, turning from time to time, until it is deeply and evenly browned.

Stir in the remaining ingredients, including the reserved tamarind, and bring to the boil. Reduce the heat to low, cover the pan and simmer for 2 to 2$\frac{1}{2}$ hours, or until the meat is cooked through and tender and the sauce is thick and rather rich in texture.

Remove from the heat, transfer the mixture to a large, warmed serving platter and serve at once.

Serves 6

Preparation and cooking time: 3 hours

CURRY PUFFS

(Malaysia)

Metric/Imperial	American
350g./12oz. puff pastry	2 cups puff pastry
FILLING	FILLING
2 Tbs. vegetable oil	2 Tbs. vegetable oil
1 onion, finely chopped	1 onion, finely chopped
1cm./½in. piece of fresh root ginger, peeled and chopped	2in. piece of fresh green ginger, peeled and chopped
1 garlic clove, crushed	1 garlic clove, crushed
2 red or green chillis, finely chopped	2 red or green chillis, finely chopped
1 tsp. hot chilli powder	1 tsp. hot chilli powder
½ tsp. turmeric	½ tsp. turmeric
½ tsp. ground coriander	½ tsp. ground coriander
½ tsp. salt	½ tsp. salt
225g./8oz. minced beef	8oz. ground beef
1 tomato, blanched, peeled and chopped	1 tomato, blanched, peeled and chopped
3 Tbs. frozen cooked peas	3 Tbs. frozen cooked peas
2 Tbs. lime or lemon juice	2 Tbs. lime or lemon juice

Heat the oil in a frying-pan. When it is hot, add the onion, ginger, garlic and chillis and fry, stirring occasionally, until the onion is soft. Stir in the spices and salt and fry for 3 minutes, stirring constantly. Add the beef and fry for 5 minutes, or until it loses its pinkness. Add the remaining filling ingredients and cook for 5 minutes. Set aside. Preheat the oven to fairly hot 190°C (Gas Mark 5, 375°F).

Roll the dough out to a circle about ¼cm./⅛in. thick. Using a 10cm./4in. pastry cutter, cut it into circles.

Place about 2 teaspoonfuls of the filling mixture slightly to the side of each circle and dampen the edges with water. Fold over one-half of the circle to make a semi-circle and press the edges to seal.

Put the semi-circles on a baking sheet and bake for 30 to 35 minutes, or until they are golden brown. Serve warm.

Makes 20 puffs
Preparation and cooking time: 1 hour

BO XAO MANG

(Beef with Bamboo Shoot)   (Vietnam)

Metric/Imperial	American
50ml./2fl.oz. peanut oil	¼ cup peanut oil
½kg./1lb. rump steak, cut into thin strips	1lb. rump steak, cut into thin strips
400g./14oz. tin bamboo shoot, drained and cut into strips about the same size as the meat	14oz. can bamboo shoot, drained and cut into strips about the same size as the meat
4 spring onions, chopped	4 scallions, chopped
1 garlic clove, crushed	1 garlic clove, crushed
1 Tbs. fish sauce	1 Tbs. fish sauce
salt and pepper	salt and pepper
2 Tbs. roasted sesame seeds, crushed	2 Tbs. roasted sesame seeds, crushed

Heat half the oil in a large, deep frying-pan. When it is very hot, add the beef strips and stir-fry for 2 minutes, or until they just lose their pinkness. Using a slotted spoon, transfer them to a plate and keep warm.

Add the remaining oil to the frying-pan. When it is hot, add the bamboo shoot, spring onions (scallions) and garlic to the pan and stir-fry for 3 minutes. Add the fish sauce and salt and pepper to taste, stirring until they are well blended.

Return the beef to the pan and stir in the sesame seeds. Continue to stir-fry for a further 1 minute, or until they are heated through.

Transfer the mixture to a warmed serving dish and serve at once.

Serves 4

Preparation and cooking time: 30 minutes

RENDANG DAGING

(Fried Beef Curry)   (Indonesia)

Metric/Imperial	American
1 large onion, chopped	1 large onion, chopped
3 garlic cloves, crushed	3 garlic cloves, crushed
4cm./1½in. piece of fresh root ginger, peeled and chopped	1½in. piece of fresh green ginger, peeled and chopped
450ml./15fl. oz. thick coconut milk	2 cups thick coconut milk
1½ tsp. hot chilli powder	1½ tsp. hot chilli powder
1 tsp. turmeric	1 tsp. turmeric
2 tsp. ground coriander	2 tsp. ground coriander
1 tsp. ground cumin	1 tsp. ground cumin
½ tsp. laos powder	½ tsp. laos powder
50ml./2fl. oz. vegetable oil	¼ cup vegetable oil
1kg./2lb. braising steak, cut into strips or small cubes	2lb. chuck steak, cut into strips or small cubes
2 Tbs. desiccated coconut, roasted	2 Tbs. shredded coconut, roasted
½ tsp. chopped lemon grass or grated lemon rind	½ tsp. chopped lemon grass or grated lemon rind
25g./1oz. tamarind	2 Tbs. tamarind
125ml./4fl. oz. boiling water	½ cup boiling water
1 tsp. soft brown sugar	1 tsp. soft brown sugar

Put the onion, garlic and ginger into a blender with about 50ml./2fl.oz. (¼ cup) of coconut milk and blend to a smooth, thick paste. Stir in the ground chilli powder, turmeric, coriander, cumin and laos powder until the mixture is thoroughly blended. Set aside.

Heat the oil in a large saucepan. When it is hot, add the beef pieces and fry, stirring occasionally, until they are browned. Add the coconut mixture and fry for 3 minutes, stirring constantly. Add a spoonful or two of water if the mixture becomes too dry. Stir in the desiccated (shredded) coconut and lemon grass or rind then pour over the remaining coconut milk. Bring to the boil. Reduce the heat to low, cover the pan and simmer the mixture for 1½ hours, stirring occasionally.

Meanwhile, put the tamarind into a bowl and pour over the boiling water. Set aside until it is cool. Put the contents of the bowl through a strainer into the saucepan, pressing as much of the pulp through as possible.

Stir the tamarind liquid and brown sugar into the meat mixture until it is well blended. Re-cover and continue to simmer for a further 30 minutes, or until the meat is cooked through and tender.

Transfer the mixture to a warmed serving bowl and serve at once.

Serves 4-6

Preparation and cooking time: 2¾ hours

LAMB

SAMBAI GORENG ATI

(Spiced Liver)   (Indonesia)

The best type of liver to use in this recipe is probably calf's liver but lamb's liver or chicken livers could be substituted with very little loss of taste. Don't use pig or ox liver, however; they are rather tough and require longer, slower cooking.

Metric/Imperial	American
1 onion, chopped	1 onion, chopped
1 garlic clove, crushed	1 garlic clove, crushed
2 tsp. chopped dried chillis or sambal ulek	2 tsp. chopped dried chillis or sambal ulek
½ tsp. blachan (dried shrimp paste)	½ tsp. blachan (dried shrimp paste)
1 tsp. laos powder	1 tsp. laos powder
1 tsp. chopped lemon grass or grated lemon rind	1 tsp. chopped lemon grass or grated lemon rind
3 Tbs. peanut oil	3 Tbs. peanut oil
½kg./1lb. liver, cut into strips	1lb. liver, cut into strips
2 tsp. soft brown sugar	2 tsp. soft brown sugar
175ml./6fl.oz. thick coconut milk	¾ cup thick coconut milk

Put the onion, garlic, chillis or sambal ulek and blachan into a blender and blend to a smooth purée. Stir the laos powder and lemon grass or rind into the mixture.

Heat the oil in a large frying-pan. When it is hot, add the spice mixture and stir-fry for 3 minutes. Add the liver strips and stir-fry for 3 minutes, or until they lose their pinkness. Stir in the sugar and coconut milk and bring to the boil. Reduce the heat to low and simmer the mixture for 5 minutes, or until the liver is cooked through and tender and the liquid has thickened slightly.

Transfer the mixture to a warmed serving dish and serve at once.
Serves 4
Preparation and cooking time: 30 minutes

GULEH KAMBLING

(Lamb Curry)   (Indonesia)

Metric/Imperial	American
5cm./2in. piece of fresh root ginger, peeled and chopped	2in. piece of fresh green ginger, peeled and chopped
2 garlic cloves, crushed	2 garlic cloves, crushed
5 green chillis, chopped	5 green chillis, chopped
1 tsp. ground lemon grass or finely grated lemon rind	1 tsp. ground lemon grass or finely grated lemon rind
½ tsp. laos powder	½ tsp. laos powder
2 tsp. turmeric	2 tsp. turmeric
2 tsp. salt	2 tsp. salt
50g./2oz. ground almonds	⅓ cup ground almonds

7 Tbs. vegetable oil	7 Tbs. vegetable oil
2 medium onions, chopped	2 medium onions, chopped
1¼kg./2½lb. boned leg of lamb, cubed	2½lb. boned leg of lamb, cubed
225g./8oz. tomatoes, blanched, peeled and chopped	8oz. tomatoes, blanched, peeled and chopped
300ml./10fl.oz. coconut milk	1¼ cups coconut milk
1 small onion, sliced	1 small onion, sliced
6 cloves, lightly crushed	6 cloves, lightly crushed
1 Tbs. crushed coriander seeds	1 Tbs. crushed coriander seeds
1 tsp. crushed cumin seeds	1 tsp. crushed cumin seeds

Another delicious lamb curry from Indonesia, Guleh Kambling is also sometimes served as part of a rijsttafel. However, it also makes an excellent Western-style meal served with rice, salad and chutneys.

Combine the ginger, garlic, chillis, lemon grass or rind, laos, turmeric, salt and ground almonds with 1 tablespoon of oil and 1 tablespoon of water to make a paste. Add more water if necessary. Set aside.

Heat 50ml./2fl.oz. (¼ cup) of the oil in a large saucepan. When it is hot, add the chopped onions and fry, stirring occasionally, until they are golden brown. Add the spice paste and fry for 5 minutes, stirring frequently. Add the lamb cubes and fry for 15 to 20 minutes, or until they have completely lost their pinkness and are thoroughly coated with the spice mixture.

Stir in the tomatoes and cook for 1 minute. Add the milk and bring to the boil. Reduce the heat to low, cover and simmer the curry for 1 hour, or until the meat is cooked through and tender and the gravy is thick.

Meanwhile, heat the remaining oil in a small frying-pan. When it is hot, add the sliced onion and spices and fry, stirring frequently, until the onion is golden brown. Ten minutes before the end of the cooking time, stir the onion and spice mixture into the lamb.

Transfer the mixture to a warmed serving dish and serve at once.
Serves 8
Preparation and cooking time: 2 hours

MURTABA

(Savoury Lamb Crêpes)   (Singapore)

Metric/Imperial	American
350g./12oz. wholewheat flour	3 cups wholewheat flour
½ tsp. salt	½ tsp. salt
250ml./8fl.oz. lukewarm water	1 cup lukewarm water
50g./2oz. ghee or clarified butter	4 Tbs. ghee or clarified butter
FILLING	FILLING
3 Tbs. vegetable oil	3 Tbs. vegetable oil
1 onion, finely chopped	1 onion, finely chopped
1 garlic clove, crushed	1 garlic clove, crushed
2 green chillis, chopped	2 green chillis, chopped
350g./12oz. minced lamb	12oz. ground lamb
1 tomato, blanched, peeled and chopped	1 tomato, blanched, peeled and chopped
3 Tbs. cooked green peas	3 Tbs. cooked green peas
salt and pepper	salt and pepper
1 tsp. garam masala	1 tsp. garam masala
1 egg, beaten	1 egg, beaten

First make the dough. Put the flour and salt into a bowl and make a well in the centre. Pour in the water and beat briskly until a stiff dough is formed. Cover the bowl and set the dough aside for 1 hour.

Meanwhile, make the filling. Heat the oil in a medium frying-pan. When it is hot, add the onion, garlic and chillis and fry until the onion is soft, stirring occasionally. Stir in the lamb and continue to fry the mixture until the meat loses its pinkness. Stir in the tomato, peas and salt and pepper to taste and cook for a further 3 minutes. Reduce the heat to low and simmer the mixture for 10 minutes. Sprinkle over the garam masala, remove from the heat and keep warm.

Remove the dough from the bowl and knead the dough gently. On a slightly oiled board, divide the mixture into balls, then gently press each ball out into a very thin crêpe (as thin as possible without tearing the dough – it should resemble strudel pastry).

Melt a little ghee in a frying-pan or griddle and gently ease in one of the crêpes. Carefully brush a little beaten egg over the exposed side of the crêpe and spoon over some filling. Fold over the sides of the crêpe so that the filling is completely enclosed and fry for 1 minute. Carefully turn over the crêpe and cook for a further 1 minute, then remove from the pan. Cook the other crêpes in the same way, then serve hot.

Serves 6-8 (as a snack or hors d'oeuvre)
Preparation and cooking time: 1¾ hours

LAMB SATE

(Indonesia)

Metric/Imperial	American
3 garlic cloves, crushed	3 garlic cloves, crushed
4 Tbs. soya sauce	4 Tbs. soy sauce
1 Tbs. soft brown sugar	1 Tbs. soft brown sugar
1 small onion, grated	1 small onion, grated
1 Tbs. lemon juice	1 Tbs. lemon juice
½ tsp. salt	½ tsp. salt
1kg./2lb./boned lean lamb, cubed	2lb. boned lean lamb, cubed
SAUCE	SAUCE
150ml./5fl.oz. soya sauce	⅔ cup soy sauce
1 tsp. ground coriander	1 tsp. ground coriander
1 garlic clove, crushed	1 garlic clove, crushed
1 green or red chilli, crumbled	1 green or red chilli, crumbled
3 Tbs. soft brown sugar	3 Tbs. soft brown sugar
2 Tbs. dark treacle	2 Tbs. molasses
1 Tbs. lemon juice	1 Tbs. lemon juice

Sates come in all shapes and forms in Indonesia and can be made from almost any ingredient. While Lamb Sate is more unusual than pork, chicken or beef, it is equally delicious. And in this case the accompanying sauce has a soy sauce base instead of peanuts. Sates are perfect for summer barbecues.

Mix the garlic, soy sauce, sugar, onion, lemon juice and salt in a small bowl. Add the meat cubes and set aside to marinate for 1 hour, basting occasionally.

Meanwhile, combine all the sauce ingredients in a medium saucepan. Set over moderate heat and bring to the boil, stirring constantly. Reduce the heat to low and simmer for 5 minutes. Remove from the heat and keep warm while you cook the sate.

Preheat the grill (broiler) to high. Thread the cubes on to skewers and arrange on the rack of the grill (broiler). Grill (broil) for 8 minutes, turn and grill (broil) for a further 6 minutes or until the meat is cooked through.

Pile the skewers on to a warmed serving platter. Pour the sauce into a small bowl and serve at once, with the kebabs.

Serves 8
Preparation and cooking time: 1½ hours

PORK

THIT KHO

(Pork Stew)   (Vietnam)

This is a northern Vietnamese dish, often served during the New Year festival. Belly or bacon of pork is probably the cut the Vietnamese would use but if you prefer leaner meat use blade or even leg.

Metric/Imperial	American
3 Tbs. peanut oil	3 Tbs. peanut oil
2 Tbs. sugar	2 Tbs. sugar
1kg./2lb. pork meat (with fat), cut into cubes	2lb. pork meat (with fat), cut into cubes
3 Tbs. fish sauce	3 Tbs. fish sauce
1 Tbs. soya sauce	1 Tbs. soy sauce
6 spring onions, chopped	6 scallions, chopped
3 hard-boiled eggs	3 hard-cooked eggs

Heat the oil in a large saucepan. When it is hot, stir in the sugar and cook until it browns slightly. Add the pork cubes and cook, basting with the sugar mixture, until they are browned. Add the fish sauce and soy sauce, and stir-fry for 1 minute. Pour over enough cold water just to cover and bring to the boil. Reduce the heat to low and simmer, uncovered, for 2 to 2½ hours, or until the liquid has reduced by about half, and the meat is very tender.

Add the spring onions (scallions) and sliced eggs and simmer for 5 minutes before serving.

Serves 6
Preparation and cooking time: 2¼ hours

VIETNAMESE PORK LOAF

Metric/Imperial	American
½kg./1lb. minced pork	1lb. ground pork
8 dried mushrooms, soaked in cold water for 30 minutes, drained, stalks removed and chopped	8 dried mushrooms, soaked in cold water for 30 minutes, drained, stalks removed and chopped
4 spring onions, chopped	4 scallions, chopped
3 eggs, beaten	3 eggs, beaten
2 tsp. fish sauce	2 tsp. fish sauce
salt and black pepper	salt and black pepper

Put all the ingredients into a bowl and mix well. Arrange the mixture in a small, greased loaf pan and cover with a double thickness of foil. Place in the top of a steamer or in a large pan one-third full of boiling water. Steam for 1 hour.

Remove the pan from the heat and unwrap the loaf. Leave the loaf in the pan for 10 minutes, then transfer to a chopping board. Cut into thin slices and serve with salad.

Serves 4
Preparation and cooking time: 1½ hours

MAH HO

(Galloping Horses)   (Thailand)

This exotically named dish is a typically Thai mixture of the sweet and savoury – savoury minced (ground) pork served on slices or rounds of sweet fruit. Pineapple is the fruit suggested here but more exotic oriental fruit such as rambutans could also be used. Mah ho is usually served as an hors d'oeuvre.

Metric/Imperial	American
2 Tbs. peanut oil	2 Tbs. peanut oil
1 garlic clove, crushed	1 garlic clove, crushed
1 small onion, finely chopped	1 small onion, finely chopped
350g./12oz. minced pork	12oz. ground pork
3 Tbs. roasted peanuts, ground	3 Tbs. roasted peanuts, ground
3 Tbs. jaggery or brown sugar	3 Tbs. jaggery or brown sugar
salt and pepper	salt and pepper
1 fresh pineapple, peeled, cored and cut into rounds	1 fresh pineapple, peeled, cored and cut into rounds
1 dried red chilli, crumbled	1 dried red chilli, crumbled
2 Tbs. chopped coriander leaves	2 Tbs. chopped coriander leaves

Heat the oil in a large frying-pan. When it is hot, add the garlic and onion and fry, stirring occasionally, until the onion is soft. Stir in the minced (ground) pork and fry until it loses its pinkness. Add the roasted peanuts, jaggery or sugar and seasoning to taste. Reduce the heat to low and simmer the mixture for 10 to 15 minutes, or until the pork is cooked through and the mixture is thick and dryish. Remove from the heat.

Arrange the pineapple rounds on a large serving platter. Carefully spoon the mixture over the rounds, doming it up slightly in the middle. Garnish with crumbled red chilli and the coriander leaves. Serve at once.

Serves 8-10
Preparation and cooking time: 35 minutes

PO CHERO

(Mixed Meat and Chick-Pea Ragout)   (Philippines)

Metric/Imperial	American
4 chicken pieces, cut into large bite-sized pieces	4 chicken pieces, cut into large bite-sized pieces
½kg./1lb. pork fillet, cut into large cubes	1lb. pork tenderloin, cut into large cubes
3 hot sausages, halved	3 hot sausages, halved
2 medium onions, sliced	2 medium onions, sliced
salt and pepper	salt and pepper
50ml./2fl.oz. vegetable oil	¼ cup vegetable oil
3 spring onions, chopped	3 scallions, chopped
3 garlic cloves, crushed	3 garlic cloves, crushed
2 sweet potatoes, cubed	2 sweet potatoes, cubed
½ white cabbage, shredded	½ white cabbage, shredded
400g./14oz. tin chick-peas, drained	14oz. can chick-peas, drained
1 Tbs. sugar	1 Tbs. sugar
2 Tbs. tomato purée	2 Tbs. tomato paste

Put the chicken pieces, pork, sausages, onions and salt and pepper to taste in a large saucepan. Just cover with water and bring to the boil. Cover the pan, reduce the heat to low and simmer for 50 minutes to 1¼ hours, or until the meat is cooked through. Remove from the heat, transfer the meat to a plate and strain and reserve 300ml./10fl.oz. (1¼ cups) of the cooking liquid.

Heat the oil in a large, deep frying-pan. When it is hot, add the spring onions (scallions) and garlic and fry for 3 minutes. Pour over the strained liquid and bring to the boil. Add the sweet potato cubes, reduce the heat to low and simmer for 30 minutes. Stir in the meat pieces, cabbage, chick-peas, sugar and tomato purée (paste), and bring to the boil. Reduce the heat to low, cover and simmer for 10 minutes, or until the cabbage is just cooked through and all the meats are tender.

Adjust the seasoning and serve at once.

Serves 8
Preparation and cooking time: 2¼ hours

SWEET & SOUR SPARERIBS

(Singapore)

Metric/Imperial	American
1½kg./3lb. American-style spareribs, cut into 2in. pieces	3lb. spareribs, cut into 2-rib serving pieces
2 garlic cloves, crushed	2 garlic cloves, crushed
3 Tbs. peanut oil	3 Tbs. peanut oil
5cm./2in. piece of fresh root ginger, peeled and chopped	2in. piece of fresh green ginger, peeled and chopped
1 large green pepper, pith and seeds removed and sliced	1 large green pepper, pith and seeds removed and sliced
1 large red pepper, pith and seeds removed and sliced	1 large red pepper, pith and seeds removed and sliced
175g./6oz. tin pineapple chunks, juice reserved	6oz. can pineapple chunks, juice reserved
1½ Tbs. wine vinegar	1½ Tbs. wine vinegar
1½ Tbs. soya sauce	1½ Tbs. soy sauce
1 Tbs. soft brown sugar	1 Tbs. soft brown sugar
1 Tbs. cornflour, mixed to a paste with 2 Tbs. water	1 Tbs. cornstarch, mixed to a paste with 2 Tbs. water

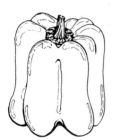

Preheat the oven to hot 220°C (Gas Mark 7, 425°F). Rub the spareribs with half the garlic and arrange them in a roasting pan. Roast for 30 minutes.

Meanwhile, heat the oil in a large frying-pan. When it is hot, add the remaining garlic and ginger and cook for 1 minute. Add the peppers and fry for 5 minutes, stirring occasionally. Stir in the pineapple chunks and fry for 3 minutes. Add the reserved pineapple juice, vinegar, soy sauce and sugar and bring to the boil.

Reduce the oven temperature to moderate 180°C (Gas Mark 4, 350°F).

Remove the ribs from the oven and pour off the fat. Stir in the pineapple mixture, basting the ribs thoroughly, and return the pan to the oven. Cook for 1 hour, basting occasionally, or until the ribs are golden brown and crisp. Remove from the oven and transfer the ribs to a serving plate.

Put the roasting pan over low heat and stir in the cornflour (cornstarch) mixture. Bring to the boil, stirring constantly, then cook until the sauce has thickened slightly and become translucent.

Pour the sauce over the ribs and serve at once.

Serves 6-8
Preparation and cooking time: 1¾ hours

PORK ADOBO

(The Philippines)

Metric/Imperial	American
1½kg./3lb. pork chops or fillet, cut into large cubes	3lb. pork chops or tenderloin, cut into large cubes
8 garlic cloves, crushed	8 garlic cloves, crushed
250ml./8fl.oz. wine vinegar	1 cup wine vinegar
350ml./12fl.oz. water	1½ cups water
2 tsp. soya sauce	2 tsp. soy sauce
black pepper	black pepper
4 Tbs. vegetable oil	4 Tbs. vegetable oil

Put all the ingredients except the oil into a large saucepan and bring to the boil. Cover, reduce the heat to low and simmer gently for 1¼ to 1½ hours, or until the pork is tender. Remove the pork from the pan and set aside. Boil the liquid rapidly until it has reduced by half. Remove from the heat and keep hot.

Meanwhile, heat the oil in a large frying-pan. When it is very hot, add the pork pieces and fry them until they are evenly browned. Transfer them to a serving bowl. Strain over the cooking liquid and serve at once.

Serves 6
Preparation and cooking time: 2 hours

BARBECUED SPARERIBS

(Singapore)

Metric/Imperial	American
1½kg./3lb. American-style spareribs, cut into 2in. pieces	3lb. spareribs, cut into 2-rib serving pieces
salt and pepper	salt and pepper
3 Tbs. soya sauce	3 Tbs. soy sauce
2 Tbs. clear honey	2 Tbs. clear honey
2 tsp. brown sugar	2 tsp. brown sugar
3 Tbs. hoi sin sauce	3 Tbs. hoi sin sauce
2 Tbs. wine vinegar	2 Tbs. wine vinegar
1 Tbs. dry sherry	1 Tbs. dry sherry
1 small onion, chopped	1 small onion, chopped
3 Tbs. chicken stock	3 Tbs. chicken stock
½ tsp. 5-spice powder	½ tsp. 5-spice powder
400g./14oz. tin Chinese plum sauce	14oz. can Chinese plum sauce

Rub the spareribs all over with salt and pepper and arrange them in a shallow dish. Mix all the remaining ingredients, except the plum sauce, together, and pour over the spareribs, basting them well. Set aside to marinate at room temperature for 1 hour, basting occasionally.

Preheat the oven to hot 220°C (Gas Mark 7, 425°F). Remove the spareribs from the liquid and pat dry on kitchen towels. Reserve the marinating liquid. Arrange the ribs in a roasting pan and put into the oven for 30 minutes. Remove from the oven and pour off the fat. Stir in the marinating liquid, basting the ribs thoroughly and return the pan to the oven. Reduce the oven temperature to moderate 180°C (Gas Mark 4, 350°F) and roast the ribs for 1 hour, basting occasionally, or until they are golden brown and crisp. Remove from the oven, and transfer to a serving plate. Strain the cooking liquid and warm it with the plum sauce gently over low heat, stirring occasionally. Pour over the ribs and baste gently until they are thoroughly mixed. Serve at once.

Serves 6-8
Preparation and cooking time: 2½ hours

WETHA HIN LAY

(Pork Curry with Mango)   (Burma)

Metric/Imperial	American
2 medium onions, chopped	2 medium onions, chopped
3 garlic cloves, crushed	3 garlic cloves, crushed
4cm./1½in. piece of fresh root ginger, peeled and chopped	1½in. piece of fresh green ginger, peeled and chopped
1 tsp. ground chilli powder	1 tsp. ground chilli powder
1 tsp. turmeric	1 tsp. turmeric
50ml./2fl. oz. sesame oil	¼ cup sesame oil
1kg./2lb. lean pork, cubed	2 lb. lean pork, cubed
1 Tbs. tamarind	1 Tbs. tamarind
50ml./2fl. oz. boiling water	¼ cup boiling water
1 Tbs. lemon juice	1 Tbs. lemon juice
2 Tbs. mango pickle	2 Tbs. mango pickle
GARNISH	GARNISH
1 fresh mango, stoned and sliced	1 fresh mango, pitted and sliced
2 Tbs. chopped coriander leaves	2 Tbs. chopped coriander leaves

Put the onions, garlic and ginger into a blender and blend to a smooth purée. Stir the chilli powder and turmeric into the spice mixture.

Heat the oil in a large saucepan. When it is hot, add the spice mixture and stir-fry over low heat for 5 minutes. Add the pork cubes and continue to fry until they are evenly browned. Reduce the heat to low and cover the pan. Simmer the pork for 30 minutes.

Meanwhile, put the tamarind into a bowl and pour over the boiling water. Set aside until it is cool. Put the contents of the bowl through a strainer into a second bowl, pressing as much of the pulp through as possible.

Stir the tamarind liquid, lemon juice and mango pickle into the saucepan, re-cover and continue to simmer the mixture for a further 1 hour, or until the pork is cooked through and tender.

Transfer the mixture to a warmed serving dish and garnish with the mango slices and coriander leaves before serving.

Serves 6
Preparation and cooking time: 1¾ hours

WETHANI

(Golden Pork)   (Burma)
The amounts of garlic and ginger are not a mistake – they reflect Burmese taste and are also supposed to 'preserve' the pork!

Metric/Imperial	American
3 onions, finely chopped	3 onions, finely chopped
12 garlic cloves, crushed	12 garlic cloves, crushed
175g./6oz. fresh root ginger, peeled and chopped	1 cup fresh green ginger, peeled and chopped
1½kg./3lb. lean pork, cubed	3lb. lean pork, cubed
salt	salt
2 Tbs. vinegar	2 Tbs. vinegar
50ml./2fl.oz. vegetable oil	¼ cup vegetable oil
1 tsp. hot chilli powder	1 tsp. hot chilli powder

Put the onions, garlic and ginger into a blender and blend to a paste. Put the paste into a strainer or cheesecloth and squeeze gently over a bowl to extract as much juice as possible.

Put the liquid into a large saucepan with the pork, salt, vinegar, oil and chilli powder and bring to the boil. Cover, reduce the heat to low and simmer the pork for 2 hours, or until it is very tender. (You may have to add a tablespoon or two of water during the cooking period if the mixture becomes too dry.) The dish should be 'golden' at the end of cooking, as the translation of its name suggests.
Serves 8
Preparation and cooking time: 2¼ hours

PORK SATE

(Indonesia)

Metric/Imperial	American
½kg./1lb. pork fillet, cut into small cubes	1lb. pork tenderloin, cut into small cubes
MARINADE	MARINADE
3 Tbs. dark soya sauce	3 Tbs. dark soy sauce
2 dried red chillis, crumbled or 1 tsp. sambal ulek	2 dried red chillis, crumbled or 1 tsp. sambal ulek
2 garlic cloves, crushed	2 garlic cloves, crushed
1 Tbs. water	1 Tbs. water
½ tsp. laos powder	½ tsp. laos powder
SAUCE	SAUCE
1 small onion, chopped	1 small onion, chopped
2 garlic cloves, crushed	2 garlic cloves, crushed
2 dried red chillis, crumbled or 1 tsp. sambal ulek	2 dried red chillis, crumbled or 1 tsp. sambal ulek
1 tsp. blachan (dried shrimp paste)	1 tsp. blachan (dried shrimp paste)
1 tsp. chopped lemon grass or grated lemon rind	1 tsp. chopped lemon grass or grated lemon rind
2 tsp. soft brown sugar	2 tsp. soft brown sugar
3 Tbs. peanut oil	3 Tbs. peanut oil
1 Tbs. soya sauce	1 Tbs. soy sauce
2 tsp. lemon juice	2 tsp. lemon juice
4 Tbs. peanut butter	4 Tbs. peanut butter
250ml./8fl.oz. coconut milk	1 cup coconut milk

Combine all the marinade ingredients in a shallow bowl. Add the pork pieces and marinate for 30 minutes, basting occasionally. Thread the pork on to skewers and reserve the marinade.

Preheat the grill (broiler) to moderately high. Arrange the skewers on the rack of the grill (broiler) and grill (broil) for 20 minutes, turning and basting occasionally with the marinade, or until the pork is cooked through.

To make the sauce, combine the onion, garlic, chillis, blachan, lemon grass and sugar in a blender. Heat the oil in a saucepan. When it is hot, add the spice paste and fry for 2 minutes, stirring constantly. Add all the remaining ingredients and combine thoroughly. Bring to the boil. Remove from the heat.

To serve, pour the sauce into a shallow serving bowl and arrange the skewers across.

Serves 4
Preparation and cooking time: 1 hour

MARINATED PORK CHOPS

(Malaysia)

Metric/Imperial	American
2 garlic cloves, crushed	2 garlic cloves, crushed
1 Tbs. crushed coriander seeds	1 Tbs. crushed coriander seeds
8 crushed peppercorns	8 crushed peppercorns
3 Tbs. soya sauce	3 Tbs. soy sauce
1 tsp. soft brown sugar	1 tsp. soft brown sugar
4 loin pork chops	4 loin pork chops

Mix all the ingredients except the chops together in a shallow dish. Put in the chops and coat well. Cover and set aside for 30 minutes, basting the chops occasionally.

Preheat the grill (broiler) to moderately high. Transfer the chops to the rack of the grill (broiler) and reserve the marinade. Grill (broil) the chops for 2 minutes. Reduce the heat to moderate and grill (broil) for 8 to 10 minutes on each side, basting occasionally with the marinating liquid.

Serve at once.

Serves 4
Preparation and cooking time: 1 hour

Easy to make – and even easier to eat – are Marinated Pork Chops, a satisfying dish from Malaysia. Serve with bean sprouts or perhaps mashed potatoes for a filling meal.

378

CHICKEN

HOT & SOUR CHICKEN, PENANG STYLE

(Malaysia)

Metric/Imperial	American
4 Tbs. vegetable oil	4 Tbs. vegetable oil
3 medium onions, finely chopped	3 medium onions, finely chopped
2 garlic cloves, crushed	2 garlic cloves, crushed
2 red or green chillis, finely chopped	2 red or green chillis, finely chopped
1 Tbs. soft brown sugar	1 Tbs. soft brown sugar
8 chicken pieces	8 chicken pieces
3 Tbs. dark soya sauce	3 Tbs. dark soy sauce
3 Tbs. wine vinegar	3 Tbs. wine vinegar
2 Tbs. water	2 Tbs. water
$\frac{1}{2}$ tsp. salt	$\frac{1}{2}$ tsp. salt

Heat the oil in a deep frying-pan. When it is hot, add the onions, garlic and chillis and fry for 5 minutes, stirring occasionally. Stir in the sugar and fry until the onions are golden brown.

Add the chicken pieces and fry for 8 minutes, turning frequently, or until they are deeply browned. Stir in the remaining ingredients and bring to the boil. Cover, reduce the heat to low and simmer for 15 minutes. Uncover the pan, increase the heat to moderate and cook the chicken for 25 to 30 minutes, or until it is cooked through.

Serve at once.
Serves 8
Preparation and cooking time: 1 hour

SOY SAUCE CHICKEN

(Indonesia)

Metric/Imperial	American
1 tsp. salt	1 tsp. salt
3 Tbs. wine vinegar	3 Tbs. wine vinegar
1 Tbs. soft brown sugar	1 Tbs. soft brown sugar
1 x 1½kg./3lb. chicken, cut into 12 serving pieces	1 x 3lb. chicken, cut into 12 serving pieces
2 Tbs. peanut or coconut oil	2 Tbs. peanut or coconut oil
SAUCE	SAUCE
1 onion, finely chopped	1 onion, finely chopped
1 green chilli, seeded and finely chopped	1 green chilli, seeded and finely chopped
2 garlic cloves	2 garlic cloves
250ml./8fl.oz. water	1 cup water
1 Tbs. wine vinegar	1 Tbs. wine vinegar
2 Tbs. soya sauce	2 Tbs. soy sauce
1 Tbs. sugar	1 Tbs. sugar
4 medium tomatoes, blanched, peeled, seeded and chopped	4 medium tomatoes, blanched, peeled, seeded and chopped

Combine the salt, vinegar and sugar in a bowl. Toss the chicken pieces in the mixture and set aside for 30 minutes.

Meanwhile, prepare the sauce. Put all the ingredients, except the tomatoes, in a blender and blend until smooth. Pour into a large saucepan and set aside.

Heat the oil in a large frying-pan. When it is hot, add the chicken pieces and fry until they are golden brown all over. Using tongs, transfer to kitchen towels to drain.

Set the pan containing the sauce over moderate heat and bring to the boil. Add the chicken pieces and tomatoes and reduce the heat to low. Cover and simmer for 20 to 25 minutes, or until the chicken is cooked through. Uncover and simmer for a further 10 minutes, or until about a third of the liquid has evaporated.

Transfer the mixture to a warmed serving dish and serve at once.

Serves 6
Preparation and cooking time: 1½ hours

OPAR AYAM

(Chicken in Coconut Gravy)   (Indonesia)

Metric/Imperial	American
3 garlic cloves, crushed	3 garlic cloves, crushed
5cm./2in. piece of fresh root ginger, peeled and chopped	2in. piece of fresh green ginger, peeled and chopped
2 red chillis, chopped	2 red chillis, chopped
3 candle or brazil nuts, chopped	3 candle or brazil nuts, chopped
1 Tbs. ground coriander	1 Tbs. ground coriander
1 tsp. ground cumin	1 tsp. ground cumin
½ tsp. ground fennel	½ tsp. ground fennel
½ tsp. laos powder	½ tsp. laos powder
5 Tbs. peanut oil	5 Tbs. peanut oil
2 medium onions, sliced	2 medium onions, sliced
1 x 2kg./4lb. chicken, cut into serving pieces	1 x 4lb. chicken, cut into serving pieces
1 tsp. chopped lemon grass or grated lemon rind	1 tsp. chopped lemon grass or grated lemon rind
600ml./1 pint thick coconut milk	2½ cups thick coconut milk
2 curry leaves (optional)	2 curry leaves (optional)
1 tsp. sugar	1 tsp. sugar

Put the garlic, ginger, chillis and nuts into a blender and blend to a paste. Transfer to a mixing bowl and stir in the coriander, cumin, fennel and laos powder until they are well mixed. Add about 1 tablespoon of the peanut oil, or a little more if necessary, to blend the mixture to a smooth, thick paste and set aside.

Heat the remaining oil in a large, deep frying-pan. When it is hot, add the onions and fry, stirring occasionally, until they are soft. Add the spice paste and stir-fry for 2 minutes. Add the chicken pieces and baste with the spice mixture until they are thoroughly coated. Stir in the lemon grass or rind and half the coconut milk, and bring to the boil. Reduce the heat to low, cover the pan and simmer for 30 minutes.

Stir in the curry leaves and sugar, then pour over the remaining coconut milk and bring to the boil. Reduce the heat to low and simmer the mixture, uncovered, for 20 to 30 minutes, or until the chicken pieces are cooked through and tender.

Serve at once.

Serves 4–6
Preparation and cooking time: 1¼ hours

TIMOLA

(Chicken Stew)   (The Philippines)

Pawpaw or papaya can be difficult to find in the West; if this is so, mango or guava can be substituted.

Metric/Imperial	American
50g./2oz. vegetable fat	4 Tbs. vegetable fat
1 medium onion, sliced	1 medium onion, sliced
2 garlic cloves, crushed	2 garlic cloves, crushed
4cm./1½in. piece of fresh root ginger, peeled and chopped	1½in. piece of fresh green ginger, peeled and chopped
1 x 1½kg./3lb. chicken, cut into serving pieces	1 x 3lb. chicken, cut into serving pieces
300ml./10fl.oz. water	1¼ cups water
1 pawpaw, peeled and finely chopped	1 pawpaw, peeled and finely chopped
225g./8oz. spinach leaves, chopped	1⅓ cups chopped spinach leaves

Melt the fat in a large saucepan. Add the onion, garlic and ginger and fry, stirring occasionally, until the onion is soft. Add the chicken pieces and fry gently until they are browned all over. Pour over the water and bring to the boil. Reduce the heat to low, cover the pan and simmer for 45 minutes to 1 hour, or until the chicken is cooked through and tender.

Stir in the pawpaw and spinach and cook for a further 10 minutes. Serve at once.
Serves 4
Preparation and cooking time: 1½ hours

SATAY AYAM

(Chicken Sate)   (Indonesia)

Metric/Imperial	American
2 Tbs. soft brown sugar	2 Tbs. soft brown sugar
50ml./2fl.oz. dark treacle	¼ cup molasses
125ml./4fl.oz. dark soy sauce	½ cup dark soy sauce
2 garlic cloves, crushed	2 garlic cloves, crushed
juice of ½ lemon	juice of ½ lemon
2 Tbs. groundnut oil	2 Tbs. groundnut oil
3 chicken breasts	3 chicken breasts
SAUCE	SAUCE
225g./8oz. unsalted peanuts, shelled	1⅓ cups unsalted peanuts, shelled
2 red chillis or 1 tsp. sambal ulek	2 red chillis or 1 tsp. sambal ulek
3 garlic cloves	3 garlic cloves
1 tsp. salt	1 tsp. salt
1 onion, coarsely chopped	1 onion, coarsely chopped
50ml./2fl.oz. groundnut oil	¼ cup groundnut oil
75-125ml./3-4fl.oz. water	⅓-½ cup water
1 Tbs. soft brown sugar mixed with 2 Tbs. dark soy sauce	1 Tbs. soft brown sugar mixed with 2 Tbs. dark soy sauce
1-2 Tbs. lemon juice	1-2 Tbs. lemon juice

Mix the sugar, treacle (molasses) and soy sauce together in a small bowl. Stir in the garlic, lemon juice and oil and set aside.

Skin and bone the chicken breasts, then cut the meat into 1½cm./¾in. cubes. Thread the cubes on to skewers and arrange the skewers in a shallow dish. Pour over the soy sauce mixture and set aside to marinate at room temperature for 1 hour, basting occasionally. Turn the skewers in the marinade from time to time.

Preheat the grill (broiler) to high.

To make the sauce, put the peanuts in the grill (broiler) pan and grill (broil) them for 2 to 3 minutes, turning occasionally. Remove from the heat and gently rub them between your hands to remove the skins. Put the peanuts in a grinder or blender with the chillis or sambal ulek, garlic, salt, onion and 2 tablespoons of the groundnut oil. Blend to a thick paste, adding enough of the water to prevent the blender from sticking. Remove the paste from the blender, put in a bowl and set aside.

Heat the remaining oil in a saucepan. When it is hot, add the nut paste. Reduce the heat to moderately low and fry the paste for 3 minutes, stirring constantly. Stir in the remaining water and simmer gently for 5 minutes, or until it is thick and smooth. Remove from the heat and stir in the soy sauce mixture and lemon juice. Taste and add more salt and lemon if necessary. Keep hot while you cook the chicken.

Arrange the skewers on the rack of the grill (broiler). Grill (broil) the chicken for 5 minutes, turning occasionally, or until the cubes are cooked through and tender.

Remove from the heat and arrange the skewers on a warmed serving platter, or across a serving bowl. Serve at once, with the sauce.

Serves 4-6
Preparation and cooking time: 1½ hours

MANGO CHICKEN

(Malaysia)

Metric/Imperial	American
1 x 2kg./4lb. chicken, cut into serving pieces	1 x 4lb. chicken, cut into serving pieces
salt and pepper	salt and pepper
3 Tbs. peanut oil	3 Tbs. peanut oil
1 large onion, thinly sliced	1 large onion, thinly sliced
1 mango, peeled, stoned and sliced	1 mango, peeled, pitted and sliced
1 tsp. chopped lemon grass or grated lemon rind	1 tsp. chopped lemon grass or grated lemon rind
¼ tsp. ground coriander	¼ tsp. ground coriander
¼ tsp. ground cinnamon	¼ tsp. ground cinnamon
250ml./8fl.oz. chicken stock	1 cup chicken stock
250ml./8fl.oz. single cream	1 cup light cream
2 tsp. flour, mixed to a paste with 1 Tbs. lemon juice and 1 Tbs. water	2 tsp. flour, mixed to a paste with 1 Tbs. lemon juice and 1 Tbs. water

Preheat the oven to fairly hot 190°C (Gas Mark 5, 375°F).

Rub the chicken pieces all over with the salt and pepper, then set aside.

Heat the oil in a large frying-pan. When it is hot, add the chicken pieces and fry, stirring occasionally, until they are evenly browned. Using a slotted spoon, transfer

the chicken pieces to a flameproof casserole. Set aside.

Add the onion to the frying-pan and fry until it is soft. Using the slotted spoon, transfer the onion to the casserole.

Add the mango slices to the frying-pan and fry, turning once, for 4 minutes. Stir in the lemon grass or rind, coriander, cinnamon and stock to the pan and bring to the boil, stirring constantly. Pour over the chicken and onion mixture in the casserole.

Cover the casserole and put into the oven. Bake for 1¼ hours, or until the chicken is cooked through and tender. Remove from the oven and, using tongs or a slotted spoon, transfer the chicken pieces to a warmed serving dish. Keep hot while you finish the sauce.

Bring the casserole liquid to the boil. Reduce the heat to low and stir in the cream and flour mixture. Cook the sauce, stirring constantly, until it is hot but not boiling and has thickened.

Remove the casserole from the heat and pour the sauce over the chicken pieces. Serve at once.

Serves 4
Preparation and cooking time: 2 hours

This dish combines two favourite South-East Asian foods: mangoes and chicken. Mango Chicken is smooth, rich and spicy, without being hot.

AYAM BALI

(Balinese Fried Chicken)   (Indonesia)

Metric/Imperial	American
1 medium onion, chopped	1 medium onion, chopped
2 garlic cloves, crushed	2 garlic cloves, crushed
2½cm./1in. piece of fresh root ginger, peeled and chopped	1in. piece of fresh root ginger, peeled and chopped
2 red chillis, chopped	2 red chillis, chopped
4 candle or brazil nuts, chopped	4 candle or brazil nuts, chopped
250ml./8fl.oz. coconut milk or water	1 cup coconut milk or water
50ml./2fl.oz. peanut oil	¼ cup peanut oil
4 large chicken pieces	4 large chicken pieces
1 Tbs. soya sauce	1 Tbs. soy sauce
1 tsp. soft brown sugar	1 tsp. soft brown sugar
1 tsp. wine vinegar	1 tsp. wine vinegar

Put the onion, garlic, ginger, chillis and nuts into a blender with 2 tablespoons of the coconut milk or water and blend to a smooth purée.

Heat the oil in a large, deep frying-pan. When it is hot, add the chicken pieces and fry for 8 to 10 minutes, or until they are evenly browned. Using tongs or a slotted spoon, transfer the chicken pieces to a plate and keep hot.

Add the purée mixture to the frying-pan and stir-fry for 5 minutes. Stir in the remaining coconut milk or water, the soy sauce, sugar and vinegar and bring to the boil. Add the chicken pieces to the pan and baste them thoroughly with the liquid. Reduce the heat to low and simmer the chicken, uncovered, for 30 to 40 minutes, or until the pieces are cooked through and tender.

Transfer the mixture to a warmed serving dish and serve at once.
Serves 4
Preparation and cooking time: 1¼ hours

KAUKSWE-HIN

(Curried Chicken with Noodles)   (Burma)

Metric/Imperial	American
½ tsp. hot chilli powder	½ tsp. hot chilli powder
1 tsp. turmeric	1 tsp. turmeric
½ tsp. ground cumin	½ tsp. ground cumin
3 Tbs. sesame oil	3 Tbs. sesame oil
4 garlic cloves, crushed	4 garlic cloves, crushed
2½cm./1in. piece of fresh root ginger, peeled and chopped	1in. piece of fresh green ginger, peeled and chopped
4 onions, chopped	4 onions, chopped
½ tsp. chopped lemon grass or grated lemon rind	½ tsp. chopped lemon grass or grated lemon rind
1 x 2kg./4lb. chicken, cut into serving pieces	1 x 4lb. chicken, cut into serving pieces
450ml./15fl.oz. thin coconut milk	2 cups thin coconut milk
300ml./10fl.oz. thick coconut milk	1¼ cups thick coconut milk
salt	salt
½ tsp. lime or lemon juice	½ tsp. lime or lemon juice
½ kg./1lb. fine noodles or vermicelli	1lb. fine noodles or vermicelli

Kaukswe-Hin, a delectable mixture of chicken curry and noodles topped by a variety of garnishes, is almost the Burmese national dish. It is served here with Than That, a popular cucumber pickle.

GARNISH	GARNISH
4 spring onions, chopped	4 scallions, chopped
2 Tbs. chopped coriander leaves	2 Tbs. chopped coriander leaves
6 lemon wedges	6 lemon wedges
3 hard-boiled eggs, chopped	3 hard-cooked eggs, chopped

Mix together the chilli powder, turmeric and cumin and set aside.

Heat the oil in a large saucepan. When it is hot, add the garlic, ginger and onions and fry, stirring occasionally, until the onions are soft. Stir in the spice mixture and fry for 1 minute, stirring constantly. Add the chicken pieces and fry until they are lightly browned all over. Pour over the thin coconut milk and bring to the boil. Reduce the heat to low and simmer the mixture, uncovered, for 1 to $1\frac{1}{4}$ hours, or until the chicken pieces are tender. Stir in the thick coconut milk, salt and lime or lemon juice. Simmer for 5 minutes.

Meanwhile, cook the noodles in boiling salted water for 5 minutes. Drain and keep them hot. Arrange the garnishes in separate, small bowls.

To serve, put the chicken curry in one large serving bowl, and divide the noodles among individual bowls. Each diner should ladle the chicken and gravy over the noodles and sprinkle over the garnishes as required.

Serves 4-6
Preparation and cooking time: 2 hours

AJAM GORENG

(Spicy Fried Chicken)   (Indonesia)

Metric/Imperial	American
1 x 1½kg./3lb. chicken, cut into 12 or 15 pieces	1 x 3lb. chicken, cut into 12 or 15 pieces
25g./1oz. tamarind	1oz. tamarind
125ml./4fl. oz. boiling water	½ cup boiling water
2 garlic cloves, crushed	2 garlic cloves, crushed
2 tsp. ground coriander	2 tsp. ground coriander
1 tsp. ground ginger	1 tsp. ground ginger
1 Tbs. wine vinegar or lemon juice	1 Tbs. wine vinegar or lemon juice
1 tsp. soft brown sugar	1 tsp. soft brown sugar
50g./2oz. flour	½ cup flour
vegetable oil for deep-frying	vegetable oil for deep-frying

Put the chicken pieces into a large, shallow dish and set aside.

Put the tamarind into a bowl and pour over the boiling water. Set aside until it is cool. Put the contents of the bowl through a strainer into the dish containing the chicken, pressing as much of the pulp through as possible.

Combine all the remaining ingredients, except the flour and oil, beating until they are thoroughly combined. Stir them into the dish containing the chicken until the mixture is blended and all the pieces are well coated. Put into the refrigerator to marinate for at least 8 hours, or overnight. Remove from the dish.

Fill a large deep-frying pan about one-third full with oil and heat until it is very hot. Dip the chicken pieces into the flour, shaking off any excess flour. Carefully lower the pieces into the oil, a few at a time, and deep-fry for 5 to 8 minutes, or until they are cooked through and golden brown. Remove from the oil and drain on kitchen towels. Serve hot.

Serves 4
Preparation and cooking time: $8\frac{1}{2}$ hours

FRIED CHICKEN WITH MUSHROOMS

(Cambodia)

Metric/Imperial	American
50ml./2fl.oz. peanut oil	¼ cup peanut oil
3 garlic cloves, crushed	3 garlic cloves, crushed
5cm./2in. piece of fresh root ginger, peeled and chopped	2in. piece of fresh green ginger, peeled and chopped
1 x 1½kg./3lb. chicken, cut into small pieces	1 x 3lb. chicken, cut into small pieces
8 dried Chinese mushrooms, soaked in cold water for 30 minutes, drained, stalks removed and sliced	8 dried Chinese mushrooms, soaked in cold water for 30 minutes, drained, stalks removed and sliced
1 Tbs. sugar	1 Tbs. sugar
2 Tbs. vinegar	2 Tbs. vinegar
2 Tbs. fish sauce	2 Tbs. fish sauce
175ml./6fl.oz. water	¾ cup water
1 Tbs. chopped coriander leaves	1 Tbs. chopped coriander leaves

Heat the oil in a large saucepan. When it is hot, add the garlic and ginger and stir-fry for 2 minutes. Add the chicken and cook for 8 to 10 minutes, stirring occasionally. Stir in all the remaining ingredients, except the coriander, and stir-fry for 10 minutes, or until the chicken is cooked through.

Transfer the mixture to a warmed serving bowl and garnish with the coriander before serving.

Serves 4
Preparation and cooking time: 50 minutes

KAI TOM KHA

(Chicken with Laos Powder)   (Thailand)

Metric/Imperial	American
1 x 2kg./4lb. chicken, cut into serving pieces	1 x 4lb. chicken, cut into serving pieces
450ml./15fl.oz. thin coconut milk	2 cups thin coconut milk
4 tsp. laos powder	4 tsp. laos powder
2 tsp. chopped lemon grass or grated lemon rind	2 tsp. chopped lemon grass or grated lemon rind
1 green chilli, finely chopped	1 green chilli, finely chopped
250ml./8fl.oz. thick coconut milk	1 cup thick coconut milk
1 tsp. fish sauce	1 tsp. fish sauce
1 Tbs. lemon juice	1 Tbs. lemon juice
2 Tbs. chopped coriander leaves	2 Tbs. chopped coriander leaves

Put the chicken pieces into a large saucepan and pour over the thin coconut milk. Stir in the laos powder, chopped lemon grass or lemon rind and chilli and bring to the boil. Cover the pan, reduce the heat to low and simmer the mixture gently for 30 minutes. Uncover and continue to simmer for a further 15 to 20 minutes, or until the chicken pieces are cooked through and tender.

Pour over the thick coconut milk and bring to the boil. Reduce the heat to low and simmer for 5 minutes. Stir in the fish sauce and lemon juice.

Transfer the mixture to a warmed serving bowl and garnish with the chopped coriander leaves before serving.

Serves 4-6
Preparation and cooking time: 1¼ hours

GRILLED (BROILED) CHICKEN

(Malaysia)

Metric/Imperial	American
25 blanched almonds,	25 blanched almonds
2 green chillis	2 green chillis
3 garlic cloves	3 garlic cloves
1 tsp. chopped lemon grass or grated lemon rind	1 tsp. chopped lemon grass or grated lemon rind
2 tsp. turmeric	2 tsp. turmeric
1 Tbs. coriander seeds	1 Tbs. coriander seeds
½ tsp. hot chilli powder	½ tsp. hot chilli powder
1 tsp. sugar	1 tsp. sugar
½ tsp. laos powder	½ tsp. laos powder
½ tsp. salt	½ tsp. salt
juice of 1 lemon	juice of 1 lemon
3 Tbs. vegetable oil	3 Tbs. vegetable oil
300ml./10fl.oz. coconut milk	1¼ cups coconut milk
1 x 2kg./4lb. chicken, cut into quarters	1 x 4lb. chicken, cut into quarters

Put the almonds, spices, salt and lemon juice into a blender and blend, adding a spoonful or two of water, until the mixture becomes a thick paste. Scrape into a cup and set aside.

Heat the oil in a large saucepan. When it is hot, add the spice paste and fry for 5 minutes, stirring constantly. Stir in the coconut milk and chicken pieces and bring to the boil. Cover, reduce the heat to low and simmer for 40 minutes, or until the chicken is just cooked and the liquid is thick and nearly all evaporated. Cook uncovered for the last 10 minutes.

Preheat the grill (broiler) to high. Put the chicken pieces on the rack in the grill (broiler) and grill (broil) for 3 to 4 minutes on each side, or until they are golden brown, basting occasionally with the reserved cooking liquid.

Serve at once.

Serves 6
Preparation and cooking time: 1 hour

KAPITAN CURRY

(Singapore)

Metric/Imperial	American
4 Tbs. vegetable oil	4 Tbs. vegetable oil
2 medium onions, finely chopped	2 medium onions, finely chopped
3 garlic cloves, crushed	3 garlic cloves, crushed

4cm./1½in. piece of fresh root ginger, peeled and chopped	1½in. piece of fresh green ginger, peeled and chopped
6 green chillis, 2 finely chopped and 4 whole	6 green chillis, 2 finely chopped and 4 whole
2 Tbs. ground coriander	2 Tbs. ground coriander
2 tsp. ground cumin	2 tsp. ground cumin
1 whole star anise, crushed	1 whole star anise, crushed
1 tsp. turmeric	1 tsp. turmeric
½ tsp. grated nutmeg	½ tsp. grated nutmeg
½ tsp. ground cinnamon	½ tsp. ground cinnamon
½ tsp. ground cardamom	½ tsp. ground cardamom
8 chicken pieces	8 chicken pieces
600ml./1 pint coconut milk	2½ cups coconut milk
1 tsp. salt	1 tsp. salt

Heat the oil in a large saucepan. When it is hot, add the onions, garlic, ginger and chopped chillis and fry, stirring occasionally, until the onions are golden brown. Stir in the spices and fry for 5 minutes, stirring constantly. If the mixture becomes too dry, add a spoonful or two of water. Add the chicken pieces and turn over in the spice mixture. Fry for 5 minutes, turning occasionally.

Pour over the coconut milk and add the salt and whole chillis. Cover, reduce the heat to low and simmer the curry for 45 minutes to 1 hour, or until the chicken is cooked through.

Transfer the chicken pieces to a serving bowl and pour over the sauce. Serve at once.

Serves 8
Preparation and cooking time: 1¼ hours

Kapitan Curry from Singapore is a delightful chicken dish with a coconut-flavoured gravy. Serve with rice and a variety of chutneys for a superb meal.

PAPER WRAPPED CHICKEN

(Singapore)

This dish reflects the very strong Chinese influence still present in Singapore and Malay food – it is, in fact, a standard dish in many ethnic Chinese restaurants as well as Singapore and Malaysian ones. In the Far East the chicken pieces would undoubtedly be deep-fried in rice paper, which is edible, and these can be obtained from Chinese general stores. However, if they are not available, greaseproof or waxed paper can be used instead.

Metric/Imperial	American
2 large chicken breasts, skinned, boned and cut into bite-sized pieces	2 large chicken breasts, skinned, boned and cut into bite-sized pieces
rice or greaseproof paper	rice or waxed paper
8 dried mushrooms, soaked in cold water for 30 minutes, drained and chopped	8 dried mushrooms, soaked in cold water for 30 minutes, drained and chopped
4 spring onions, chopped	4 scallions, chopped
4cm./1½in. piece of fresh root ginger, peeled and thinly sliced	1½in. piece of fresh green ginger, peeled and thinly sliced
3 Tbs. frozen green peas, thawed	3 Tbs. frozen green peas, thawed
vegetable oil for deep-frying	vegetable oil for deep-frying
MARINADE	MARINADE
1½ Tbs. oyster sauce	1½ Tbs. oyster sauce
1 Tbs. sesame oil	1 Tbs. sesame oil
1 Tbs. rice wine or sherry	1 Tbs. rice wine or sherry
½ tsp. sugar	½ tsp. sugar
¼ tsp. ground ginger	¼ tsp. ground ginger

First, make the marinade. Put all the ingredients into a shallow bowl and mix until they are thoroughly blended. Add the chicken pieces to the bowl and stir them gently until they are thoroughly basted. Set aside at room temperature for 1 hour, turning and basting from time to time.

Cut the paper into squares about 15cm./6in. in diameter. Arrange a little of the filling just off centre (see the sketch below) and carefully add a little mushroom, spring onion (scallion), ginger and peas to the filling. Fold up the paper, as explained in the sketch so that the filling is completely enclosed, envelope fashion.

Fill a large deep-frying pan about one-third full with vegetable oil and heat until it is hot. Carefully lower the 'packets' into the oil, two or three at a time, and fry for 3 to 5 minutes, turning occasionally. Remove from the oil and drain on kitchen towels.

To serve, if using rice paper serve the packets to be eaten, paper and all; if using greaseproof or waxed paper, open the packets on individual serving plates and serve at once.

Serves 4

Preparation and cooking time: 1¾ hours

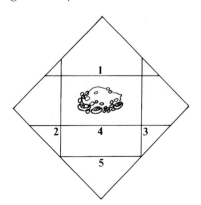

DUCK

GREEN DUCK CURRY

(Thailand)

This dish can be made with either duck or chicken; the 'green' part of the title comes from the greenish tinge of the curry paste, which is effected by using green rather than red chillis and coriander leaves. The root of the coriander plant is traditionally used in Thailand as an ingredient in this curry paste but since it is virtually unobtainable in the West, the leaf has been substituted.

Metric/Imperial	American
300ml./10fl.oz. thin coconut milk	1¼ cups thin coconut milk
1 x 3kg./6lb. duck, cut into 8-10 serving pieces	1 x 6lb. duck, cut into 8-10 serving pieces
1 Tbs. fish sauce	1 Tbs. fish sauce
2 Tbs. chopped coriander leaves	2 Tbs. chopped coriander leaves
300ml./10fl.oz. thick coconut milk	1¼ cups thick coconut milk
CURRY PASTE	CURRY PASTE
3 spring onions, green part included, chopped	3 scallions, green part included, chopped
2 garlic cloves, crushed	2 garlic cloves, crushed
3 green chillis, chopped	3 green chillis, chopped
2 tsp. grated lime rind	2 tsp. grated lime rind
1 Tbs. chopped coriander leaves	1 Tbs. chopped coriander leaves
1 tsp. chopped lemon grass or grated lemon rind	1 tsp. chopped lemon grass or grated lemon rind
2 tsp. ground coriander	2 tsp. ground coriander
1 tsp. ground cumin	1 tsp. ground cumin
1 tsp. laos powder	1 tsp. laos powder
salt and pepper	salt and pepper
1 tsp. blachan (dried shrimp paste)	1 tsp. blachan (dried shrimp paste)
½ tsp. turmeric	½ tsp. turmeric

To make the curry paste, put the spring onions (scallions), garlic, chillis, lime rind, coriander leaves and lemon grass or rind into a blender with a little of the thin coconut milk. Blend to a very thick purée. Transfer the purée to a bowl and stir in the remaining curry paste ingredients until all the ingredients are well blended.

Put the remaining thin coconut milk into a large saucepan and bring to the boil. Add the duck pieces and return the mixture to the boil. Reduce the heat to low and simmer for 1 to 1¼ hours, or until the duck is cooked through and tender.

Pour about half of the liquid in the pan with the duck into a second large saucepan and bring to the boil. Stir in the curry paste and fry, stirring frequently, over high heat until the milk has almost evaporated. Reduce the heat to moderate and continue frying the mixture for 3 minutes in the oily milk residue, stirring constantly. Gradually stir in the remaining coconut milk from the pan containing the duck and cook the mixture until it is thick and the oil begins to separate from the liquid.

Add the cooked duck pieces, fish sauce, half the chopped coriander and the thick coconut milk. Bring to the boil and reduce the heat to moderately low. Cook the mixture for 5 minutes, or until the liquid has thickened. Stir in the remaining coriander leaves and simmer for 5 minutes.

Serve at once.

Serves 4–6
Preparation and cooking time: 2 hours

MALAYSIAN DUCK

Metric/Imperial	American
1 Tbs. ground coriander	1 Tbs. ground coriander
2 tsp. ground fenugreek	2 tsp. ground fenugreek
2 tsp. ground cumin	2 tsp. ground cumin
1 tsp. turmeric	1 tsp. turmeric
1 tsp. ground cinnamon	1 tsp. ground cinnamon
½ tsp. ground cardamom	½ tsp. ground cardamom
¼ tsp. grated nutmeg	¼ tsp. grated nutmeg
1 tsp. mild chilli powder	1 tsp. mild chilli powder
salt and pepper	salt and pepper
juice of 1 lemon	juice of 1 lemon
1cm./½in. piece of fresh root ginger, peeled and chopped	½in. piece of fresh green ginger, peeled and chopped
2 small onions, minced	2 small onions, ground
2 garlic cloves, crushed	2 garlic cloves, crushed
125g./4oz. desiccated coconut, soaked in 175ml./6fl.oz. boiling water	½ cup shredded coconut, soaked in ¾ cup boiling water
1 x 2½kg./5lb. duck, split through the breast bone, ribs broken at the backbone and wings and legs tied together	1 x 5lb. duck, split through the breast bone, ribs broken at the backbone and wings and legs tied together

Preheat the oven to fairly hot 190°C (Gas Mark 5, 375°F).

Mix all the spices together in a bowl and add seasoning, lemon juice, ginger, onions, garlic and coconut milk to form a thick paste. Spread the paste over the duck.

Put the duck on a rack in a roasting pan and roast for 1½ hours, basting every 15 minutes or so. Halfway through roasting, turn the duck over. When it is cooked through, baste once more then remove from the oven.

Serve at once.

Serves 4–6
Preparation and cooking time: 1¾ hours

Barbecuing is a very popular method of cooking in Malaysia, and this simple but delicious Malaysian Duck demonstrates why. The duck is first marinated in a spicy coconut paste, then barbecued to crisp perfection.

FISH

IKAN BANDENG

(Baked Spiced Fish)   (Indonesia)

Bandeng is a type of sole, found around the coast of Indonesia. Any type of fish can be substituted however – grey mullet, red snapper, even a large whiting.

Metric/Imperial	American
2 Tbs. vegetable oil	2 Tbs. vegetable oil
1 x 1½kg./3lb. fish, cleaned and gutted	1 x 3lb fish, cleaned and gutted
3 garlic cloves, crushed	3 garlic cloves, crushed
7½cm./3in. piece of fresh root ginger, peeled and minced	3in. piece of fresh green ginger, peeled and minced
3 Tbs. soya sauce	3 Tbs. soy sauce
1½ Tbs. lemon juice	1½ Tbs. lemon juice
3 tsp. dried chillis or sambal ulek	3 tsp. dried chillis or sambal ulek
GARNISH	GARNISH
2 lemons, cut into wedges	2 lemons, cut into wedges
3 Tbs. chopped coriander leaves	3 Tbs. chopped coriander leaves

Preheat the oven to fairly hot 190°C (Gas Mark 5, 375°F).

Make some deep gashes across the fish with a sharp knife. Pour the oil into a roasting pan, then transfer the fish to the pan.

Beat the garlic, ginger, soy sauce, lemon juice and sambal ulek together until they are well blended, then pour over the fish, rubbing the mixture into the flesh and gashes.

Cover with foil then put the roasting pan into the oven. Bake the fish for 25 to 30 minutes, or until the flesh flakes easily.

Remove from the oven and serve at once, garnished with lemon wedges and coriander leaves.

Serves 4-6
Preparation and cooking time: 40 minutes

VIETNAMESE FRIED FISH

Metric/Imperial	American
4 Tbs. cornflour	4 Tbs. cornstarch
salt and pepper	salt and pepper
4 small bream, cleaned and with the eyes removed	4 small porgy, cleaned and with the eyes removed
50ml./2fl.oz. peanut oil	¼ cup peanut oil
nuoc cham (page 412)	nuoc cham (page 412)

Mix the cornflour (cornstarch) with salt and pepper to taste and use to coat the fish lightly. Heat the oil in a large frying-pan. When it is hot, add the fish and fry for 10 to 12 minutes, or until the flesh flakes.

Serve at once, with nuoc cham.

Serves 4
Preparation and cooking time: 15 minutes

Fish with Pineapple and
Ginger comes from
Malaysia, where fish such
as mullet or snapper would
be used in its cooking. But
the combination is a
delicious one with any
firm-fleshed white fish.

FISH FILLETS WITH PINEAPPLE AND GINGER

(Malaysia)

Metric/Imperial	American
2 tsp. turmeric	2 tsp. turmeric
1½ tsp. salt	1½ tsp. salt
700g./1½lb. fish fillets, cut into bite-sized pieces	1½lb. fish fillets, cut into bite-sized pieces
3 Tbs. vegetable oil	3 Tbs. vegetable oil
2 onions, finely chopped	2 onions, finely chopped
4cm./1½in. piece of fresh root ginger, peeled and chopped	1½in. piece of fresh green ginger, peeled and chopped
2 chillis, finely chopped	2 chillis, finely chopped
1 tsp. blachan (dried shrimp paste)	1 tsp. blachan (dried shrimp paste)
1 tsp. ground lemon grass or finely grated lemon rind	1 tsp. ground lemon grass or finely grated lemon rind
1 tsp. sugar	1 tsp. sugar
4 tomatoes, blanched, peeled and chopped	4 tomatoes, blanched, peeled and chopped
1 small pineapple, peeled, cored and cut into chunks	1 small pineapple, peeled, cored and cut into chunks

Mix half the turmeric with 1 teaspoon of salt, then rub over the fish pieces.

Heat the oil in a large frying-pan. When it is hot, add the fish pieces and fry for 2 minutes on each side. Remove the fish to a plate. If necessary, add more oil to the pan to cover the bottom. Add the onions and fry, stirring occasionally, until they are golden brown. Add the ginger, chillis, blachan, lemon grass or rind and remaining turmeric and fry over low heat for 5 minutes, stirring constantly. Stir in the sugar, tomatoes and remaining salt, the pineapple and fish pieces. Cover and simmer for 20 to 25 minutes, or until the fish flakes easily. Serve at once.
Serves 6–8
Preparation and cooking time: 50 minutes

OTAK-OTAK

(Steamed Fish Parcels)   (Malaysia)

In Malaysia banana leaves are used as wrappers for this dish, but foil or any other heatproof wrapping makes a good Western substitute.

Metric/Imperial	American
700g./1½lb. cod or other white fish fillets, skinned and cut into strips	1½lb. cod or other white fish fillets, skinned and cut into strips
SAUCE	SAUCE
2 garlic cloves, crushed	2 garlic cloves, crushed
4 green chillis, finely chopped	4 green chillis, finely chopped
½ tsp. chopped lemon grass or grated lemon rind	½ tsp. chopped lemon grass or grated lemon rind
1 tsp. turmeric	1 tsp. turmeric
salt and pepper	salt and pepper
4 Tbs. desiccated coconut	4 Tbs. shredded coconut
250ml./8fl.oz. thick coconut milk	1 cup thick coconut milk

Pound all the sauce ingredients, except the coconut milk, together until they form a smooth paste. Put the milk into a saucepan and heat until it is hot but not boiling. Remove the pan from the heat and stir in the paste mixture.

Cut out four medium squares of foil. Spread some of the coconut mixture over the bottom of each one, then divide the fish between them. Cover with the remaining coconut mixture. Fold the foil into neat parcels, to enclose the filling completely.

Place the parcels in the top of a double boiler or in a heatproof plate set over a pan of boiling water. Cover and steam for 30 minutes.

Serve straight from the wrapping.

Serves 4
Preparation and cooking time : 45 minutes

IKAN ACHAR

(Vinegar Fish)   (Malaysia)

Metric/Imperial	American
1 onion, chopped	1 onion, chopped
1 garlic clove, crushed	1 garlic clove, crushed
2½cm./1in. piece of fresh root ginger, peeled and chopped	1in. piece of fresh green ginger, peeled and chopped
4 candle or brazil nuts, chopped	4 candle or brazil nuts, chopped
1 tsp. chopped dried red chillis or sambal ulek	1 tsp. chopped dried red chillis or sambal ulek
125ml./4fl.oz. water	½ cup water
50ml./2fl.oz. peanut oil	¼ cup peanut oil
2 Tbs. wine vinegar	2 Tbs. wine vinegar
½ tsp. soft brown sugar	½ tsp. soft brown sugar
½kg./1lb. fish fillets, skinned	1lb. fish fillets, skinned

Put the onion, garlic, ginger, candle or brazil nuts, chillis or sambal ulek into a blender with about 3 tablespoons of the water. Blend to a smooth purée.

Heat the oil in a large frying-pan. When it is hot, add the purée mixture and stir-fry for 3 minutes. Pour over the remaining water, the vinegar and stir in the sugar. Bring to the boil, then reduce the heat to low.

Arrange the fish fillets in the pan and spoon over the sauce to baste them completely. Cover the pan and simmer the fish for 10 to 15 minutes, or until the flesh flakes easily.

Transfer the mixture to a warmed serving dish and serve at once.

Serves 4
Preparation and cooking time : 35 minutes

SAMBAL GORENG SOTONG

(Squid Sambal)   (Malaysia)

Metric/Imperial	American
25g./1oz. tamarind	2 Tbs. tamarind
125ml./4fl.oz. boiling water	½ cup boiling water
4 whole almonds	4 whole almonds
4 dried red chillis, chopped	4 dried red chillis, chopped

2 garlic cloves, crushed
1 small onion, chopped
½ tsp. blachan (dried shrimp paste)
1½ Tbs. peanut oil
½ tsp. chopped lemon grass or
   grated lemon rind
2 tsp. jaggery or soft brown sugar
2 tsp. paprika
4 large squid, cleaned, gutted and
   sliced crosswise

2 garlic cloves, crushed
1 small onion, chopped
½ tsp. blachan (dried shrimp paste)
1½ Tbs. peanut oil
½ tsp. chopped lemon grass or
   grated lemon rind
2 tsp. jaggery or soft brown sugar
2 tsp. paprika
4 large squid, cleaned, gutted and
   sliced crosswise

Put the tamarind into a bowl and pour over the boiling water. Set aside until it is cool. Pour the contents of the bowl through a strainer into a second bowl, pressing as much of the pulp through as possible. Set aside.

Meanwhile, put the almonds, chillis, garlic, onion, blachan and about 1 tablespoon of oil into a blender and blend to a smooth purée.

Heat the remaining oil in a large, deep frying-pan. When it is hot, add the almond mixture and lemon grass or rind and stir-fry for 2 minutes. Add the tamarind water, sugar and paprika and continue to cook for 3 minutes, stirring constantly. Add the squid and cook for 10 to 15 minutes, stirring occasionally, or until the squid is cooked through and tender.

Transfer the mixture to a warmed serving dish and serve at once.
Serves 4-6
Preparation and cooking time: 45 minutes

PLA NUM

(Fish in Red Sauce)   (Thailand)

Metric/Imperial	American
700g./1½lb. fish	1½lb. fish
50ml./2fl. oz. peanut oil	¼ cup peanut oil
1 large onion, chopped	1 large onion, chopped
2 garlic cloves, crushed	2 garlic cloves, crushed
1 red chilli, chopped	1 red chilli, chopped
2 large tomatoes, blanched, peeled and chopped	2 large tomatoes, blanched, peeled and chopped
2 Tbs. tomato purée	2 Tbs. tomato paste
4 Tbs. water	4 Tbs. water
2 Tbs. wine vinegar	2 Tbs. wine vinegar
salt and pepper	salt and pepper
2 Tbs. chopped coriander leaves	2 Tbs. chopped coriander leaves

Clean and cut the fish if you are using a whole one; skin if you are using fillets.

Heat the oil in a large deep frying-pan. When it is hot, add the onion, garlic and chilli and stir-fry for 3 minutes. Add the tomatoes and cook gently until they have pulped. Stir in the tomato purée (paste), water and vinegar, and season to taste. Bring the mixture to the boil, then reduce the heat to low. Simmer, covered, for 10 minutes.

Arrange the fish in the sauce, basting thoroughly. Re-cover the pan and simmer the fish for 10 to 20 minutes, or until the flesh flakes easily. Just before serving, stir in about half of the coriander leaves.

Transfer the mixture to a warmed serving dish and garnish with the remaining coriander leaves before serving.
Serves 4-6
Preparation and cooking time: 1 hour

*Spiced Plaice (Flounder)
The combination of
Chinese and Malay
expertise is demonstrated
beautifully in Spiced
Plaice (Flounder) – fish
marinated in a mixture of
soy sauce, sugar and chilli
powder and
then barbecued.*

SPICED PLAICE (FLOUNDER)

(Malaysia)

Metric/Imperial	American
125ml./4fl.oz. dark soy sauce	½ cup dark soy sauce
2 Tbs. soft brown sugar	2 Tbs. soft brown sugar
1 tsp. hot chilli powder	1 tsp. hot chilli powder
2 garlic cloves, crushed	2 garlic cloves, crushed
4 plaice, cleaned, gutted and prepared for cooking	4 flounder, cleaned, gutted and prepared for cooking
25g./1oz. butter	2 Tbs. butter
juice of 1 lemon	juice of 1 lemon

Combine the soy sauce, sugar, chilli powder and garlic together. Put the fish in a shallow dish and pour over the soy sauce mixture. Cover and set aside for 1 hour, basting occasionally.

Preheat the grill (broiler) to high.

Arrange the fish on the rack of the grill (broiler) and grill (broil) the fish, turning them once, for 8 to 10 minutes, or until the flesh flakes easily, basting occasionally with the marinade.

Melt the butter in a small saucepan. Stir in the lemon juice and remove from the heat. Carefully transfer the fish to individual plates and discard the remaining marinade.

Pour the melted butter mixture over the fish and serve at once.

Serves 4

Preparation and cooking time: 1¼ hours

IKAN GORENG

(Fried Fish in Lime Juice)   (Indonesia)

Ikan Goreng (Fried Fish in Lime Juice) comes from Indonesia and is made here with mackerel. The rich yellow colour is produced by rubbing turmeric over the marinated fish.

Metric/Imperial	American
300ml./10fl.oz. lime juice	1¼ cups lime juice
50ml./2fl.oz. wine vinegar	¼ cup wine vinegar
1 tsp. salt	1 tsp. salt
6 black peppercorns	6 black peppercorns
2 1k x g./2lb. mackerel, filleted	2 x 2lb. mackerel, filleted
1 tsp. turmeric	1 tsp. turmeric
4 Tbs. peanut oil	4 Tbs. peanut oil

Combine the lime juice, vinegar, ½ teaspoon of salt and the peppercorns together in a large, shallow dish. Place the fish in the dish and baste well. Set aside for 1 hour, basting occasionally. Remove from the marinade and dry on kitchen towels. Remove and discard the peppercorns from the marinade and reserve about 50ml./2 fl. oz. (¼ cup).

Rub the fish all over with the remaining salt and the turmeric.

Heat the oil in a large frying-pan. When it is hot, add the fish fillets and fry for 5 minutes on each side, or until they flake easily. Remove from the pan and drain on kitchen towels. Transfer to a warmed serving dish.

Pour over the reserved marinade and serve at once.

Serves 4

Preparation and cooking time: 1½ hours

TAMARIND FISH

Metric/Imperial	American
25g./1oz. tamarind	2 Tbs. tamarind
125ml./4fl.oz. boiling water	½ cup boiling water
4 medium red mullets, cleaned and with the eyes removed	4 medium red mullets, cleaned and with the eyes removed
50ml./2fl.oz. peanut oil	¼ cup peanut oil
4 red chillis, seeded	4 red chillis, seeded
1 medium onion, quartered	1 medium onion, quartered
2 garlic cloves	2 garlic cloves
1cm./½in. piece of fresh root ginger, peeled and sliced	½ piece of fresh green ginger, peeled and sliced
175ml./6fl.oz. water	¾ cup water
1 tsp. soya sauce	1 tsp. soy sauce
½ tsp. salt	½ tsp. salt

Put the tamarind into a bowl and pour over the water. Set aside until it is cool. Pour the contents of the bowl through a strainer into a bowl, pressing as much of the pulp through as possible. Rub the fish all over with the tamarind pulp and set aside.

Heat the oil in a large frying-pan. When it is hot, add the fish and cook for 7 minutes on each side.

Meanwhile, put the chillis, onion, garlic, ginger and 50ml./2fl.oz. (¼ cup) of water in a blender and blend to a smooth purée. Transfer the mixture to a small bowl and set aside.

Remove the fish from the pan and keep them hot. Add the spice purée to the pan and cook for 2 minutes, stirring constantly. Stir in the soy sauce, salt and remaining water and bring to the boil, stirring constantly. Reduce the heat to moderately low and return the fish to the pan, basting with the pan mixture.

Transfer the fish to a warmed serving dish and pour the sauce into a warmed sauceboat. Serve at once, with the fish.

Serves 4
Preparation and cooking time: 1 hour

IKAN BALI

(Balinese Sweet and Sour Fish)   (Indonesia)

The fish in this dish can be as you prefer – whole (but with the head and tail removed), in fillets, or in steaks. Slightly oily fish would be best – mackerel, mullet, or halibut steaks if you are feeling rich!

Metric/Imperial	American
1 Tbs. tamarind	1 Tbs. tamarind
50ml./2fl.oz. boiling water	¼ cup boiling water
3 Tbs. peanut oil	3 Tbs. peanut oil
1 large onion, finely chopped	1 large onion, finely chopped
2 garlic cloves, crushed	2 garlic cloves, crushed
4cm./1½in. piece of fresh root ginger, peeled and chopped	1½in. piece of fresh green ginger, peeled and chopped
1 tsp. chopped lemon grass or grated lemon rind	1 tsp. chopped lemon grass or grated lemon rind

Metric/Imperial	American
½ tsp. laos powder (optional)	½ tsp. laos powder (optional)
1 tsp. dried red chillis or sambal ulek	1 tsp. dried red chillis or sambal ulek
1½ Tbs. soya sauce	1 Tbs. soy sauce
1½ Tbs. lemon juice	1½ Tbs. lemon juice
1 Tbs. soft brown sugar	1 Tbs. soft brown sugar
vegetable oil for deep-frying	vegetable oil for deep-frying
700g./1½lb. fish	1½lb. fish
50g./2oz. cornflour	½ cup cornstarch

Put the tamarind into a bowl and pour over the boiling water. Set aside until it is cool. Pour the contents of the bowl through a strainer into a second bowl, pressing as much of the pulp through as possible. Set aside.

Heat the peanut oil in a small saucepan. When it is hot, add the onion, garlic and ginger and stir-fry for 3 minutes. Stir in the lemon grass or rind, laos powder and chillis or sambal ulek and continue to stir-fry for a further 2 minutes. Add the soy sauce, lemon juice, sugar and tamarind liquid and cook, stirring constantly until the sugar has dissolved. Remove the pan from the heat and set aside. Keep hot.

Fill a large deep-frying pan about one-third full with vegetable oil and heat until the oil is hot. Gently coat the fish in the cornflour, shaking off any excess, then carefully lower into the oil. Cook for 3 to 8 minutes (depending on the type of fish and cut used), or until crisp and golden brown. Remove the fish from the oil and drain on kitchen towels.

Return the saucepan containing the sauce to low heat and heat gently until it is hot. Arrange the fish on a warmed serving dish and spoon over the sauce. Serve at once.

Serves 4-6
Preparation and cooking time: 30 minutes

GULEH IKAN

(Fish Curry) (Malaysia)

Metric/Imperial	American
1 large onion, chopped	1 large onion, chopped
1 garlic clove	1 garlic clove
2½cm./1in. piece of fresh root ginger, peeled and chopped	1in. piece of fresh green ginger, peeled and chopped
2 chillis, chopped	2 chillis, chopped
250ml./8fl.oz. thin coconut milk	1 cup thin coconut milk
1 Tbs. ground coriander	1 Tbs. ground coriander
½ tsp. ground cumin	½ tsp. ground cumin
½ tsp. turmeric	½ tsp. turmeric
½ tsp. ground fennel	½ tsp. ground fennel
1 tsp. chopped lemon grass or grated lemon rind	1 tsp. chopped lemon grass or grated lemon rind
125ml./4fl.oz. thick coconut milk	½ cup thick coconut milk
1 Tbs. tamarind	1 Tbs. tamarind
50ml./2fl.oz. boiling water	¼ cup boiling water
½kg./1lb. firm white fish steaks (cod, grey mullet, etc.), chopped	1lb. firm white fish steaks (cod, grey mullet, etc.), chopped

Put the onion, garlic, ginger and chillis into a blender and blend to a purée (add a spoonful or two of thin coconut milk if the mixture is too dry). Transfer the mixture to a saucepan and stir in half the thin coconut milk and the spices and lemon grass or rind.

Set the saucepan over moderate heat and add the remaining thin coconut milk and the thick coconut milk. Bring to the boil, reduce the heat to low and simmer for 15 minutes.

Meanwhile, put the tamarind into a bowl and pour over the boiling water. Set aside until it is cool. Pour the contents of the bowl through a strainer into the saucepan, pressing as much of the pulp through as possible.

Stir in the fish pieces and bring to the boil again. Reduce the heat to low and simmer for 10 to 15 minutes, or until the flesh flakes easily. Serve at once.

Serves 3–4
Preparation and cooking time: 50 minutes

PLA PRIO WAN

(Fried Fish with Piquant Sauce)   (Thailand)

Any whole fish suitable for frying can be used in this dish; sea bream is probably the best but red snapper and jewfish could also be used.

Metric/Imperial	American
1 x 1kg./2lb. whole fish, cleaned, gutted and with the head still on	1 x 2lb. whole fish, cleaned, gutted and with the head still on
25g./1oz. cornflour	¼ cup cornstarch
vegetable oil for deep-frying	vegetable oil for deep-frying
1 Tbs. chopped coriander leaves	1 Tbs. chopped coriander leaves
PIQUANT SAUCE	PIQUANT SAUCE
1 Tbs. peanut oil	1 Tbs. peanut oil
10cm./4in. piece of fresh root ginger, peeled and finely chopped	4in. piece of fresh green ginger, peeled and finely chopped
1 garlic clove, crushed	1 garlic clove, crushed
1 red chilli, seeded and chopped	1 red chilli, seeded and chopped
4 Tbs. wine vinegar	4 Tbs. wine vinegar
4 Tbs. soft brown sugar	4 Tbs. soft brown sugar
125ml./4fl.oz. water	½ cup water
3 spring onions, green part included, finely chopped	3 scallions, green part included, finely chopped
1 Tbs. soya sauce	1 Tbs. soy sauce
1 Tbs. cornflour, mixed to a paste with 1 Tbs. water	1 Tbs. cornstarch, mixed to a paste with 1 Tbs. water

Rub the fish, inside and out, with salt, then wash and dry on kitchen towels. Make four or five deep incisions on each side of the fish, almost to the centre bone. Coat the fish in the cornflour (cornstarch) shaking off any excess.

Fill a large deep-frying pan one-third full with oil and heat it until it is very hot. Carefully lower the fish into the pan and deep-fry it for 5 minutes, or until it is golden brown and crisp. Remove the fish from the oil and drain on kitchen towels. Keep hot while you make the sauce.

Heat the oil in a deep frying-pan. When it is hot, add the ginger and garlic and stir-fry for 2 minutes. Stir in all the remaining sauce ingredients, except the cornflour (cornstarch) and bring to the boil, stirring constantly. Reduce the heat to moderately low and cook for 3 minutes. Stir in the cornflour (cornstarch) mixture and continue to cook the sauce until it thickens and becomes translucent.

Arrange the fish on a warmed serving dish and pour over the sauce. Garnish with the coriander and serve at once.

Serves 4–6
Preparation and cooking time: 35 minutes

SHELL FOOD

PRAWNS IN CHILLI SAUCE

(Singapore)

Metric/Imperial	American
4 Tbs. peanut oil	4 Tbs. peanut oil
½kg./1lb. shelled prawns	1lb. shelled shrimp
1 garlic clove, crushed	1 garlic clove, crushed
4cm./1½in. piece of fresh root ginger, peeled and chopped	1½in. piece of fresh green ginger, peeled and chopped
2 red chillis, chopped	2 red chillis, chopped
1 green pepper, pith and seeds removed and cut into strips	1 green pepper, pith and seeds removed and cut into strips
1 Tbs. Chinese chilli sauce	1 Tbs. Chinese chilli sauce
1 Tbs. tomato purée	1 Tbs. tomato paste
salt and pepper	salt and pepper
2 spring onions, chopped	2 scallions, chopped

Heat the oil in a large, deep frying-pan. When it is hot, add the prawns (shrimp) and stir-fry for 5 minutes, or until they are cooked. Using a slotted spoon, transfer the prawns (shrimp) to a plate. Keep hot.

Add the garlic, ginger, chillis and pepper to the pan and stir-fry for 3 minutes. Stir in the chilli sauce, tomato purée (paste) and seasoning to taste and stir-fry for a further 2 minutes. Return the prawns (shrimp) to the pan and stir-fry for 1 minute, or until they are well blended with the sauce.

Transfer to a warmed serving bowl and sprinkle over the spring onions (scallions). Serve at once.

Serves 4–6
Preparation and cooking time : 25 minutes

CHILLI CRAB

(Singapore)

Metric/Imperial	American
vegetable oil for deep-frying	vegetable oil for deep-frying
3 medium crabs, claws cracked and chopped through the shell into pieces	3 medium crabs, claws cracked and chopped through the shell into pieces
3 red chillis, chopped	3 red chillis, chopped
1cm./½in. piece of fresh root ginger, peeled and chopped	½in. piece of fresh green ginger, peeled and chopped
2 garlic cloves, crushed	2 garlic cloves, crushed
2 tsp. sugar	2 tsp. sugar
salt and pepper	salt and pepper
250ml./8fl.oz. chicken stock	1 cup chicken stock
2 tsp. cornflour, mixed to a paste with 2 tsp. water	2 tsp. cornstarch, mixed to a paste with 2 tsp. water
1 egg, lightly beaten	1 egg, lightly beaten
1 tsp. vinegar	1 tsp. vinegar
2 Tbs. tomato purée	2 Tbs. tomato paste

Fill a large deep-frying pan one-third full with oil and heat it until it is very hot. Carefully lower the crab pieces, a few at a time, into the oil and deep-fry for 1 minute. Using tongs or a slotted spoon, remove the pieces from the oil and drain on kitchen towels.

Reserve 3 tablespoons of the oil from the pan and pour it into a deep frying-pan. When it is hot, add the chillis, ginger and garlic. Fry, stirring occasionally, for 3 minutes. Return the crab pieces to the pan and add sugar, salt and pepper to taste, and stock. Bring to the boil, reduce the heat to low and cover the pan. Simmer for 15 minutes, or until the crab pieces are cooked through. Stir in the cornflour (cornstarch) mixture and cook until the liquid thickens and becomes translucent.

Stir in all of the remaining ingredients and cook gently for 2 to 3 minutes, or until the egg 'sets'.

Transfer the mixture to a large warmed serving bowl or deep serving platter and serve at once.

Serves 4
Preparation and cooking time: 1 hour

KARI BONGKONG LASAK

(Curried Shrimps and Cucumbers)   (Cambodia)

Metric/Imperial	American
2 garlic cloves, crushed	2 garlic cloves, crushed
2 spring onions, chopped	2 scallions, chopped
4cm./1½in. piece of fresh root ginger, peeled and chopped	1½in. piece of fresh green ginger, peeled and chopped
1 tsp. ground fennel	1 tsp. ground fennel
2 tsp. ground coriander	2 tsp. ground coriander
½ tsp. turmeric	½ tsp. turmeric
2 tsp. hot chilli powder	2 tsp. hot chilli powder
4 Tbs. peanut oil	4 Tbs. peanut oil
½kg./1lb. shelled prawns	1lb. shelled shrimp
450ml./15fl.oz. coconut milk	2 cups coconut milk
1 cucumber, quartered lengthways, seeds removed and cut into thick slices	1 cucumber, quartered lengthways, seeds removed and cut into thick slices
2 tsp. chopped lemon grass or grated lemon rind	2 tsp. chopped lemon grass or grated lemon rind
juice of 1 lemon	juice of 1 lemon
1 tsp. sugar	1 tsp. sugar
1 Tbs. fish sauce	1 Tbs. fish sauce

Put the garlic, spring onions (scallions) and ginger into a blender and blend to a purée. Scrape the mixture from the blender and transfer to a mixing bowl. Stir in the ground spices.

Heat the oil in a deep frying-pan. When it is hot, add the spice purée and stir-fry for 3 minutes. Add the prawns or shrimp and stir-fry for 5 minutes. Stir in the coconut milk and bring to the boil. Reduce the heat to low, add the cucumber and remaining ingredients and simmer gently for 5 minutes, or until the cucumber is translucent.

Serve at once.
Serves 6
Preparation and cooking time: 25 minutes

The cuisine of Cambodia tends to be overshadowed by its neigbours Vietnam and Thailand, but it has many unique features of its own. One of the most popular dishes is Kari Bongkong Lasak, a refreshing mixture of curried shrimps and cucumbers cooked in coconut milk flavoured with lemon.

TOM VO VIEN

(Shrimp Cakes)   (Vietnam)

Metric/Imperial	American
½kg./1lb. shelled prawns	1lb. shelled shrimp
1 Tbs. fish sauce	1 Tbs. fish sauce
½ tsp. sugar	½ tsp. sugar
2 spring onions, chopped	2 scallions, chopped
3 Tbs. chopped coriander leaves	3 Tbs. chopped coriander leaves
salt and pepper	salt and pepper
125ml./4fl.oz. peanut oil	½ cup peanut oil

Put the prawns or shrimp, fish sauce, sugar, spring onions (scallions), half the coriander leaves and seasoning into a blender and blend to a smooth paste. Shape into little cakes with floured hands and chill in the refrigerator for 15 minutes.

Cover the bottom of a frying-pan with half the oil. When it is hot, add about half the cakes and fry for 5 minutes on each side, or until they are golden and cooked through. Cook the remaining cakes in the same way. Drain on kitchen towels and serve hot, with nuoc cham (page 412).
Serves 4-6
Preparation and cooking time: 30 minutes

GULEH UDANG DENGAN LABU KUNING

(Prawn [Shrimp] and Marrow [Squash] Curry)   (Malaysia)

If you prefer, courgettes (zucchini) can be used instead of marrow (squash) in this recipe. If you do use them, do not peel – the green skin will make the dish look particularly attractive.

Metric/Imperial	American
1 large onion, chopped	1 large onion, chopped
2 red chillis, chopped	2 red chillis, chopped
1 tsp. chopped lemon grass or grated lemon rind	1 tsp. chopped lemon grass or grated lemon rind
1 tsp. turmeric	1 tsp. turmeric
¼ tsp. laos powder (optional)	¼ tsp. laos powder (optional)
½ tsp. dried basil	½ tsp. dried basil
250ml./8fl.oz. water	1 cup water
1 tsp. lemon juice	1 tsp. lemon juice
350g./12oz. marrow, peeled and cut into cubes	2 cups peeled and cubed winter squash
½kg./1lb. peeled prawns	1lb. peeled shrimp
175ml./6fl.oz. thick coconut milk	¾ cup thick coconut milk

Put the onion and chillis into a blender and blend to a smooth purée. Transfer the purée to a saucepan, then stir in the lemon grass or rind, turmeric, laos powder and basil until they are thoroughly blended. Gradually stir in the water and lemon juice.

Set the saucepan over moderately low heat and cook the mixture until it comes to the boil, stirring constantly. Reduce the heat to low and add the marrow (squash) cubes. Cook the mixture gently for 5 minutes, or until the cubes are half cooked. Add the prawns (shrimp) and coconut milk and continue to cook gently for a further 5 minutes, or until the prawns (shrimp) are cooked through and tender.

Transfer the mixture to a warmed serving bowl or large serving platter and serve at once.

Serves 4
Preparation and cooking time: 20 minutes

UKOY

(Shrimp and Sweet Potato Cakes)   (Philippines)

Metric/Imperial	American
10 medium shrimps, in the shell	10 medium shrimp, in the shell
300ml./10fl.oz. water	1¼ cups water
125g./4oz. plain flour	1 cup all-purpose flour
125g./4oz. cornflour	1 cup cornstarch
1 tsp. salt	1 tsp. salt
1 large egg, beaten	1 large egg, beaten
2 sweet potatoes, peeled	2 sweet potatoes, peeled
4 spring onions, chopped	4 scallions, chopped
salt and pepper	salt and pepper
vegetable oil for deep-frying	vegetable oil for deep-frying
DIPPING SAUCE	DIPPING SAUCE
2 garlic cloves, crushed	2 garlic cloves, crushed
1 tsp. salt	1 tsp. salt
125ml./4fl.oz. malt vinegar	½ cup cider vinegar

First make the dipping sauce. Stir the garlic and salt into the vinegar until all the ingredients are thoroughly combined. Set aside.

Put the shrimps and water into a small saucepan and bring to the boil. Cook for about 5 minutes, or until the shrimps are cooked through. Remove from the heat and transfer the shrimps to a plate. Strain the cooking liquid and reserve it. Remove the shells and veins from the shrimps.

Put the flour, cornflour (cornstarch) and salt into a mixing bowl. Gradually beat in the egg, then the reserved shrimp liquid until the mixture resembles a slightly thick pancake batter. Grate the sweet potatoes into the mixture, then stir until it is completely blended. Beat in the spring onions (scallions) and seasoning to taste.

Fill a large deep-frying pan about one-third full with oil and heat until it is hot. Carefully slide about a heaped tablespoonful of the batter mixture into the oil and arrange a shrimp in the centre. Cook the cakes in this way, two or three at a time, pressing down lightly on them with a slotted spoon and spooning oil over occasionally. Cook for about 3 minutes, then carefully turn over and cook for a further 3 minutes, or until the cakes are crisp and golden brown. Remove from the oil and drain on kitchen towels.

Serve at once, with the dipping sauce.

Makes 10 cakes
Preparation and cooking time: 50 minutes

Cabbage with Shrimps, Penang-Style is a brilliant example of the Oriental ability to make a very little go a long way. Here an ordinary white cabbage is transformed by the addition of ginger and a few shrimps. The result can either be a vegetable accompaniment dish, or a light meal on its own. Or, best of all, it can be served in the Oriental way, as one of several dishes arranged all at once on the table.

CABBAGE WITH SHRIMP

(Malaysia)

Metric/Imperial	American
3 Tbs. vegetable oil	3 Tbs. vegetable oil
225g./8oz. prawns, shelled	8oz. shrimp, shelled
2 medium onions, sliced	2 medium onions, sliced
4cm./1½in. piece of fresh root ginger, peeled and shredded	1½in. piece of fresh green ginger, peeled and shredded
2 red chillis, finely chopped	2 red chillis, finely chopped
1 medium white cabbage, shredded	1 medium white cabbage, shredded
1 tsp. salt	1 tsp. salt
1cm./½in. slice of creamed coconut, dissolved in 1½ Tbs. boiling water	½in. slice of creamed coconut, dissolved in 1½ Tbs. boiling water

Heat the oil in a large frying-pan. When it is hot, add the prawns or shrimp and fry for 3 to 5 minutes, or until they are pink and firm. Transfer to a plate and keep hot.

Add the onions, ginger and chillis to the pan and fry, stirring occasionally, until the onions are soft. Stir in the cabbage and stir-fry for 2 minutes. Stir in the salt and coconut mixture and cook for 5 minutes, stirring frequently. Stir in the prawns or shrimp. Serve at once.

Serves 6
Preparation and cooking time: 30 minutes

SAMBAL I

(Potato Sambal)   (Indonesia)

Metric/Imperial	American
225g./8oz. potatoes, boiled in their skins, peeled and coarsely mashed	8oz. potatoes, boiled in their skins, peeled and coarsely mashed
4 spring onions, finely chopped	4 scallions, finely chopped
2 green chillis, finely chopped	2 green chillis, finely chopped
½ tsp. salt	½ tsp. salt
1 Tbs. lemon juice	1 Tbs. lemon juice
2 Tbs. thick coconut milk	2 Tbs. thick coconut milk
1 Tbs. chopped coriander leaves	1 Tbs. chopped coriander leaves

Combine all the ingredients, except the coriander, in a shallow serving bowl. Taste the mixture and add more salt or lemon juice if necessary. Sprinkle over the coriander.

Chill in the refrigerator until ready to use.

Serves 3–4
Preparation and cooking time: 25 minutes

SAMBAL II

(Chicken Liver Sambal)   (Indonesia)

Metric/Imperial	American
3 Tbs. vegetable oil	3 Tbs. vegetable oil
2 medium onions, very finely chopped	2 medium onions, very finely chopped
2 garlic cloves, crushed	2 garlic cloves, crushed
700g./1½lb. chicken livers, cleaned and halved	1½lb. chicken livers, cleaned and halved
2-4 red chillis, finely chopped	2-4 red chillis, finely chopped
1 tsp. chopped lemon grass or grated lemon rind	1 tsp. chopped lemon grass or grated lemon rind
½ tsp. laos powder	½ tsp. laos powder
1 tsp. sugar	1 tsp. sugar
1 tsp. salt	1 tsp. salt
2 curry leaves (optional)	2 curry leaves (optional)
350ml./12fl.oz. thick coconut milk	1½ cups thick coconut milk

Heat the oil in a large saucepan. When it is hot, add the onions and garlic and fry, stirring occasionally, until the onions are golden brown. Add the chicken livers and fry until they lose their pinkness. Stir in all the remaining ingredients and bring to the boil, stirring occasionally. Reduce the heat to low and simmer for 20 minutes, or until the sauce is thick.

Spoon the sambal into a warmed serving dish and serve at once.

Serves 4–6
Preparation and cooking time: 35 minutes

SAMBAL GORENG TELUR

(Egg and Chilli Sambal)   (Indonesia)

Metric/Imperial	American
4 eggs	4 eggs
1 large onion, chopped	1 large onion, chopped
2 garlic cloves	2 garlic cloves
1 Tbs. dried chillis or sambal ulek	1 Tbs. dried chillis or sambal ulek
3 Tbs. peanut oil	3 Tbs. peanut oil
½ tsp. blachan (dried shrimp paste)	½ tsp. blachan (dried shrimp paste)
1 tsp. sugar	1 tsp. sugar
½ tsp. laos powder	½ tsp. laos powder
½ tsp. chopped lemon grass or grated lemon rind	½ tsp. chopped lemon grass or grated lemon rind
250ml./8fl.oz. coconut milk	1 cup coconut milk

Hard-boil the eggs, then shell and halve them. Set them aside. Put the onion, garlic and chillis into a blender and blend to a rough purée.

Heat the oil in a large, shallow saucepan. When it is hot, add the onion puree and fry, stirring frequently, for 2 minutes. Stir in the remaining ingredients and bring to the boil, stirring constantly. Reduce the heat to very low and carefully add the egg halves. Simmer gently until the mixture thickens slightly.

Serve at once.

Serves 6–8
Preparation and cooking time: 20 minutes

THAN THAT

(Cucumber Pickle) (Burma)

Metric/Imperial	American
2 cucumbers, peeled and cut in half lengthways	2 cucumbers, peeled and cut in half lengthways
50ml./2fl.oz. vinegar	¼ cup vinegar
250ml./8fl.oz. water	1 cup water
Pepper and salt	Pepper and salt
75ml./3fl.oz. sesame oil	⅓ cup sesame oil
1 large onion, finely chopped	1 large onion, finely chopped
6 large garlic cloves, crushed	6 large garlic cloves, crushed
2 Tbs. sesame seeds	2 Tbs. sesame seeds

Remove the seeds from the cucumbers and cut into strips. Put into a saucepan and add all the vinegar except 1 tablespoon, the water and seasoning and bring to the boil. Reduce the heat to low and simmer for 5 minutes, or until the strips are translucent. Drain and transfer the strips to a shallow serving bowl to cool to room temperature.

Heat the oil in a frying-pan. When it is hot, add the onion and garlic and fry gently for 5 minutes, or until they are lightly browned. Transfer to a plate. Add the sesame seeds to the pan and fry gently until they are lightly toasted. Tip the sesame seeds and oil into the onion and garlic, add the reserved vinegar and mix. When the cucumber strips are cool, pour over the sesame oil mixture and toss gently. Serve at once.
Serves 6–8
Preparation and cooking time: 1 hour

ROJAK

(Mixed Salad) (Malaysia)

Metric/Imperial	American
½ cucumber, diced	½ cucumber, diced
½ small pineapple, peeled, cored and diced	½ small pineapple, peeled, cored and diced
1 green mango, peeled, stoned and diced	1 green mango, peeled, pitted and diced
2 dried red chillis, crumbled	2 dried red chillis, crumbled
DRESSING	DRESSING
2 tsp. dried chillis or sambal ulek	2 tsp. dried chillis or sambal ulek
½ tsp. blachan (dried shrimp paste)	½ tsp. blachan (dried shrimp paste)
1 Tbs. sugar	1 Tbs. sugar
1 Tbs. vinegar	1 Tbs. vinegar
1 Tbs. lemon juice	1 Tbs. lemon juice

Put the cucumber, pineapple and mango in a shallow bowl. Combine all the dressing ingredients in a blender, then pour over the salad. Toss gently, then scatter over the crumbled chillis.

Set aside at room temperature for 10 minutes before serving.
Serves 6
Preparation and cooking time: 15 minutes

GADO-GADO

(Indonesia)

Metric/Imperial	American
½ small white cabbage, shredded	½ small white cabbage, shredded
225g./8oz. French beans	1⅓ cups green beans
125g./4oz. bean sprouts	½ cup bean sprouts
¼ small cucumber, chopped	¼ small cucumber, chopped
2 potatoes	2 potatoes
2 hard-boiled eggs, sliced	2 hard-boiled eggs, sliced
PEANUT SAUCE	PEANUT SAUCE
2 Tbs. peanut oil	2 Tbs. peanut oil
2 garlic cloves, crushed	2 garlic cloves, crushed
2 red chillis, crumbled	2 red chillis, crumbled
1 tsp. blachan (dried shrimp paste)	1 tsp. blachan (dried shrimp paste)
½ tsp. laos powder	½ tsp. laos powder
1 tsp. soft brown sugar	1 tsp. soft brown sugar
4 Tbs. peanut butter	4 Tbs. peanut butter
250ml./8fl.oz. coconut milk	1 cup coconut milk
2 tsp. lemon juice or vinegar	2 tsp. lemon juice or vinegar
GARNISH	GARNISH
prawn crackers	shrimp crackers
2 Tbs. chopped spring onions	2 Tbs. chopped scallions

Cook all of the vegetables lightly but separately. Drain and arrange in layers on a serving platter. Set aside until cold.

To make the sauce, heat the oil in a small saucepan. When it is hot, add the garlic and chillis and stir-fry for 3 minutes. Stir in the blachan, laos and sugar and cook until they have dissolved. Stir in the peanut butter and coconut milk and blend thoroughly. Bring to the boil. Remove from the heat and stir in the lemon juice or vinegar.

Pour the sauce over the top of the vegetables and garnish with the crackers and chopped spring onions (scallions).
Serves 6
Preparation and cooking time: 40 minutes

NUOC CHAM

(Prepared Fish Sauce)   (Vietnam)

Metric/Imperial	American
4 Tbs. fish sauce	4 Tbs. fish sauce
2 garlic cloves, crushed	2 garlic cloves, crushed
juice of 1 lemon (use a little flesh as well)	juice of 1 lemon (use a little flesh as well)
½ dried chilli, crumbled (optional)	½ dried chilli, crumbled (optional)
1 tsp. sugar	1 tsp. sugar
2 Tbs. water	2 Tbs. water

Mix all the ingredients, except the water, together and beat well. Add the water and stir well. If you prefer the sauce less strong, dilute it with more water to taste.
Makes 1 table serving
Preparation time: 5 minutes

YAHM CHOMPU

(Savoury Fruit Salad)   (Thailand)

Metric/Imperial	American
1 large tart apple, diced	1 large tart apple, diced
1 small pineapple, peeled, sliced then diced	1 small pineapple, peeled, sliced then diced
225g./8oz. lean cooked pork, diced	1⅓ cups diced lean cooked pork
125g./4oz. prawns, shelled	4oz. shrimps, shelled
2 Tbs. chopped spring onions	2 Tbs. chopped scallions
1 cos lettuce, shredded	1 romaine lettuce, shredded
DRESSING	DRESSING
6 Tbs. olive oil	6 Tbs. olive oil
juice of 1 lemon	juice of 1 lemon
2 Tbs. soya sauce	2 Tbs. soy sauce
1 Tbs. soft brown sugar	1 Tbs. soft brown sugar

To make the dressing, combine all the ingredients in a small bowl and set aside.

Put the fruit, pork, prawns or shrimp and spring onions (scallions) in a large bowl. Pour over the dressing and mix well.

Arrange the lettuce around the edges of a dish and pile the salad into the centre. Serve at once.

Serves 6
Preparation time: 10 minutes

Fruit is often served as a salad, or is included in salads in South-East Asia, and Yahm Chompu from from Thailand is no exception. This particular version is made more substantial by the addition of pork and shrimps.

CHA GIO

(Vietnamese Spring Rolls)

In Vietnam, these rolls are wrapped in special rice paper called banh-da and then deep-fried; spring roll wrappers, however, are a good substitute. If you prefer, minced (ground) pork or shrimp may be substituted for the crab.

Metric/Imperial	American
225g./8oz. crabmeat, shell and cartilage removed and flaked	8oz. crabmeat, shell and cartilage removed and flaked
1 small onion, finely chopped	1 small onion, finely chopped
1 carrot, grated	1 carrot, grated
50g./2oz. bean sprouts	¼ cup bean sprouts
1 egg	1 egg
10 spring roll wrappers	10 spring roll wrappers
vegetable oil for deep-frying	vegetable oil for deep-frying

Put the crabmeat, onion, carrot, bean sprouts, and egg in a bowl and combine thoroughly. Put about 2 tablespoons of the filling in the centre of one spring roll wrapper and carefully roll up diagonally to make a neat parcel, making sure that the filling is completely enclosed.

Fill a large deep-frying pan one-third full of oil and heat it until it is very hot. Carefully lower the rolls (on a spatula or slotted spoon), a few at a time, into the oil and fry until they are golden brown and crisp. Remove from the oil and drain on kitchen towels. Serve hot with nuoc cham (see recipe on page 412)
Serves 8
Preparation and cooking time: 20 minutes

MASAK LEMAK

(Cabbage Curry)   (Malaysia)

Metric/Imperial	American
1 onion, sliced	1 onion, sliced
2 red chillis, chopped	2 red chillis, chopped
½ tsp. blachan (dried shrimp paste)	½ tsp. blachan (dried shrimp paste)
1 tsp. turmeric	1 tsp. turmeric
250ml./8fl.oz. thin coconut milk	1 cup thin coconut milk
1 potato, cut into large cubes	1 potato, cut into large cubes
1 small white cabbage, shredded	1 small white cabbage, shredded
125ml./4fl.oz. thick coconut milk	½ cup thick coconut milk

Put the onion, chillis, blachan, turmeric and thin coconut milk into a saucepan. Bring to the boil. Reduce the heat to moderately low and add the potato pieces. Cook for 10 minutes, or until the potato is half-cooked. Stir in the cabbage and cook for 5 minutes. Pour over the remaining thick coconut milk and bring to the boil, stirring constantly.

Serve at once.
Serves 4
Preparation and cooking time: 30 minutes

URAP

(Mixed Vegetables with Coconut)   (Indonesia)

Metric/Imperial	American
2 celery stalks, cut into 2½cm./1in. lengths	2 celery stalks, cut into 1in. lengths
225g./8oz. bean sprouts	1 cup bean sprouts
225g./8oz. French beans, cut into 2½cm./1in. lengths	1⅓ cups green beans, cut into 1in. lengths
125g./4oz. Chinese cabbage, shredded	1 cup shredded Chinese cabbage
½ fresh coconut, grated	½ fresh coconut, grated
2 spring onions, finely chopped	2 scallions, finely chopped
1 tsp. sambal ulek or 2 dried red chillis, crumbled	1 tsp. sambal ulek or 2 dried red chillis, crumbled
½ tsp. blachan (dried shrimp paste)	½ tsp. blachan (dried shrimp paste)
1 Tbs. lemon juice	1 Tbs. lemon juice

Steam or boil the vegetables, separately, until they are just cooked through. Set aside and keep hot.

Combine all the remaining ingredients in a mixing bowl until they are well blended. Stir into the vegetables until all the vegetable pieces are coated.

Serve at once, either as a vegetable dish or as an accompaniment.

Serves 6
Preparation and cooking time: 15 minutes

SERUNDENG

(Coconut and Peanut Garnish)   (Indonesia)

Metric/Imperial	American
1 Tbs. peanut oil	1 Tbs. peanut oil
1 small onion, chopped	1 small onion, chopped
1 garlic clove, crushed	1 garlic clove, crushed
1 tsp. blachan (dried shrimp paste)	1 tsp. blachan (dried shrimp paste)
1 Tbs. ground coriander	1 Tbs. ground coriander
2 Tbs. sugar	2 Tbs. sugar
1 tsp. salt	1 tsp. salt
125g./4oz. coconut, freshly grated	1 cup freshly grated coconut
225g./8oz. shelled salted peanuts	1⅓ cups shelled salted peanuts

Heat the oil in a saucepan. When it is hot, add the onion and garlic and fry, stirring occasionally, until the onion is soft. Stir in the blachan and cook for 5 minutes, stirring frequently. Reduce the heat to low. Stir in the coriander, sugar, salt and coconut and fry, stirring constantly, until the coconut is golden brown. Stir in the salted peanuts and mix until the ingredients are thoroughly blended.

Remove from the heat. Set aside to cool completely, then transfer the serundeng to a storage jar. Store in a cool, dry place until you are ready to use.

Serves 6–8
Preparation and cooking time: 25 minutes

Kachang Bendi Goreng is a Malaysian dish of fried mixed green vegetables with shrimps. It can be served as part of an Oriental meal, as a fairly substantial vegetable accompaniment, or even as a light snack dish on its own.

KACHANG BENDI GORENG

(Fried Mixed Green Vegetables with Shrimps) (Malaysia)

Metric/Imperial	American
3 Tbs. peanut oil	3 Tbs. peanut oil
2 onions, finely chopped	2 onions, finely chopped
1 garlic clove, crushed	1 garlic clove, crushed
2 green chillis, finely chopped	2 green chillis, finely chopped
4cm./1½in. piece of fresh root ginger, peeled and chopped	1½in. piece of fresh green ginger, peeled and chopped
1 Tbs. ground almonds	1 Tbs. ground almonds
2 Tbs. soya sauce	2 Tbs. soy sauce
½ tsp. black pepper	½ tsp. black pepper
350g./12oz. prawns, shelled	12 oz. shrimp, shelled
1 green pepper, pith and seeds removed and sliced	1 green pepper, pith and seeds removed and sliced
175g./6oz. French beans	1 cup green beans
2 courgettes, sliced	2 zucchini, sliced

Heat the oil in a large frying-pan. When it is hot, add the onions, garlic, chillis and ginger and fry, stirring occasionally, until the onions are golden brown. Stir in the ground almonds, soy sauce and pepper and cook for 2 minutes. Add the prawns or shrimp and stir-fry for 3 minutes. Add the vegetables. Reduce the heat to low and simmer the mixture for 10 minutes, or until the vegetables are cooked through.

Serve at once.

Serves 6–8
Preparation and cooking time: 30 minutes

SAJUR LODEH

(Mixed Vegetables Cooked with Coconut)   (Indonesia)

Almost any vegetable can be used in this soupy dish although, traditionally, there would be a mixture of at least three or four different types. Chinese or white cabbage, courgettes (zucchini) or pumpkin, French (green) beans, bamboo shoots, aubergine (eggplant), onion or even leeks, would all be successful.

Metric/Imperial	American
1 medium onion, chopped	1 medium onion, chopped
2 garlic cloves, crushed	2 garlic cloves, crushed
1½ tsp. dried chillis or sambal ulek	1½ tsp. dried chillis or sambal ulek
1 tsp. blachan (dried shrimp paste)	1 tsp. blachan (dried shrimp paste)
½ tsp. laos powder	½ tsp. laos powder
3 Tbs. peanut oil	3 Tbs. peanut oil
700g./1½lb. mixed vegetables, cut into bite-sized pieces	1½lb. mixed vegetables, cut into bite-sized pieces
1 large tomato, blanched, peeled and chopped	1 large tomato, blanched, peeled and chopped
725ml./1¼ pints coconut milk	3 cups coconut milk
1 tsp. soft brown sugar	1 tsp. soft brown sugar
1 Tbs. peanut butter (optional)	1 Tbs. peanut butter (optional)

Put the onion, garlic, sambal ulek and blachan into a mortar and pound to a paste with a pestle. Alternatively, purée in a blender. Stir in the laos powder.

Heat the oil in a large saucepan. When it is very hot, add the spice paste and stir-fry for 2 minutes. Add the tomato and stir-fry for 3 minutes, or until it has pulped. Gradually stir in the coconut milk and bring to the boil. Add the veget-

ables to the pan, in the order in which they should be cooked (longest cooking vegetable first). Reduce the heat to moderately low and cook until they are just tender but still crisp. Stir in the sugar and peanut butter and simmer for 1 minute longer.

Transfer to a warmed serving bowl and serve at once.

Serves 6
Preparation and cooking time: 30 minutes

BAKED BANANAS

(Malaysia)

Metric/Imperial	American
50g./2oz. butter	4 Tbs. butter
50g./2oz. soft brown sugar	⅓ cup soft brown sugar
¼ tsp. ground cloves	¼ tsp. ground cloves
2 Tbs. orange juice	2 Tbs. orange juice
1 tsp. lemon juice	1 tsp. lemon juice
2½cm./1in. piece of fresh root ginger, peeled and finely diced	1in. piece of fresh green ginger, peeled and finely diced
6 bananas, sliced in half lengthways	6 bananas, sliced in half lengthways

Preheat the oven to fairly hot 190°C (Gas Mark 5, 375°F).

Cream the butter and sugar together until they are pale and soft. Beat in the cloves, orange and lemon juice and ginger.

Lay the bananas on a well-greased medium baking dish and spread the butter mixture over them. Put the dish into the oven and bake for 10 to 15 minutes, or until the top is bubbling and the bananas are cooked through and tender.

Remove from the oven and serve at once.

Serves 6
Preparation and cooking time: 30 minutes

One of the very best of the traditional rijsttafel accompaniments, Baked Bananas have the refreshing tang of oranges and lemons to counteract the slightly dense taste of the bananas.

GLOSSARY

Ajar

An Indian-style pickle, very popular throughout Malaysia and Indonesia. It is closely related to the Indian *achar*.

Annatto

Small red seeds used for flavouring throughout Latin America and in the Philippines. Obtainable from Latin American stores or better supermarkets. If unobtainable use a blend of paprika with a dash of turmeric for the same colouring effect. No flavouring substitute.

Blachan

A form of dried shrimp paste used extensively as a flavouring all over South-East Asia. It has a variety of names depending on its origin – in Malaysia, for instance, it is called *trasi* and in Thailand *kapi*. For ease of reference in this book it is always referred to as blachan (dried shrimp paste). Sold in plastic bags, in dry cakes or slabs, or even in cans. When opened always store in a covered container – as much to keep in the very strong taste as to keep it fresh! Keeps indefinitely. Available in oriental, especially Indonesian, stores.

Candle nuts

A hard, oily nut used extensively in Malay and Indonesian cooking, especially in curries. Virtually unobtainable in the West, so substitute brazil nuts, or even unsalted peanuts if necessary.

Coconut milk

The milk of the coconut fruit is a popular cooking gravy throughout the Orient. If fresh coconut milk is unavailable, make your own using 75g./3oz. creamed coconut slice and about 450ml./15fl.oz. (2 cups) of boiling water. Stir or blend until the liquid is white and has thickened. Increase the amount of coconut to make thick coconut milk, decrease slightly to make thin. If creamed coconut is not available, desiccated (shredded) coconut in the same quantities can be used instead.

Coriander

Many parts of the coriander plant are used in oriental cooking – the seeds and a ground version of the seeds are used in curries, and the leaves are used extensively as a garnish in all types of dishes; in Thailand and Burma coriander leaves are sprinkled over practically everything! Since it is a member of the parsley plant, chopped parsley can be used as a substitute, although the taste will not be nearly so pungent. Available from Indian, Greek and Mexican stores.

Daun pandan

Long, green leaves which are used as a flavouring all over Malaysia and Indonesia. The leaves are crushed and boiled before using. Virtually unobtainable in the West and no substitute. Omit if unavailable.

Fish sauce

A thin, brownish liquid made from fermented dried shrimp paste and used with great enthusiasm in many parts of South-East Asia. Thailand, Vietnam, Burma and Cambodia all have their versions – the Vietnamese, in fact, use it as a garnish in much the same way as the Chinese use soy sauce and Westerners would use salt and pepper. When used in cooking, it should be measured straight from the bottle; when used as a dipping sauce or condiment, it is usually diluted with water to which lemon juice and flesh has been added – and perhaps garlic too (see recipe for *nuoc cham*). Available from most Chinese stores, or other oriental stores and from any shop stocking Vietnamese specialities. If unavailable, an acceptable substitute can be provided by mixing equal portions of anchovy paste and light soy sauce together.

Jaggery

The raw sugar of the palm tree, used in curried dishes throughout the Orient. Available from Indian or other oriental stores. If unobtainable, substitute the unrefined dark sugar available in health food stores, or refined dark brown sugar.

Kapi

See under blachan

Kha

See under laos

Laos

A fragrant spice made from the tuberous galingal plant, which is somewhat similar in flavour to ginger, although more delicate. Found throughout South-East Asia but known by different names in each country. Laos is the Indonesian name; in Malaysia it is called *lengkuas*, in Thailand *kha*. For ease of reference, in this book, it is always referred to as laos powder. Obtainable from Indonesian stores and some better spice chains.

419

Lemon grass	A citron-smelling, bulbous plant somewhat similar in appearance to a small spring onion (scallion). A popular seasoning in South-East Asia, lemon grass is known as *serai* in Malaysia, *sereh* in Indonesia and is also found in Thai and Burmese cooking. For ease of reference, in this book it is always referred to as lemon grass. Sold fresh and in powdered form from Indonesian or oriental stores, but if unavailable in any form, then grated lemon rind can be substituted.
Lengkuas	See under laos
Lotus seeds	Small, fresh-tasting seeds used both in cooking and as a digestive in South-East Asia. Virtually unavailable in the West. No substitute.
Peanuts	Widely used as a garnish in Indonesian cooking and forms the basis of the famous *sate* sauce, used as an accompaniment to pork or chicken kebabs or *sate*. In this latter case, usually roasted then ground and mixed with the other sauce ingredients. To cut out some of the work, an acceptable short-cut is to use crunchy peanut butter for *sate* sauces.
Rambutan	An exotic oriental fruit, often eaten as a dessert. Available throughout Indonesia, Malaysia and Thailand. Virtually unobtainable in the West, though lychees make a near substitute.
Rijsttafel	Literally, rice table in Dutch, and in reality a series of contrasting and complementary dishes served together to make a complete Indonesian meal. The centre is always rice but the other dishes can range from six or eight up to thirty or forty, depending on the grandness of the occasion (and the quantity of the servings). Usually contains at least one *sate* dish with sauce, several different meat dishes (at least one curried), a fish dish, some pickle or sambal dishes and of course the garnish dishes of peanuts and *serundeng*, a mixture of ground peanuts and grated coconut (see recipe). A fuller description of rijsttafel is given in the introduction.
Serai or serah	See under lemon grass
Sambal ulek	A pungent mixture of ground red chillis and salt used both in cooking and as a condiment in Indonesian cooking. Available in jars or cans from better oriental or any Indonesian store. If unavailable commercially, substitute dried red chillis or make your own paste by grinding red chillis and salt to taste, then adding water until it forms a thick purée.
Tamarind	Acid-tasting seeded fruit. Tamarind is sold in thick slabs, usually dried, in Indian and other oriental stores. The juice from the pulp is used more often in recipes than the dried flesh itself. To make tamarind juice, put the tamarind into a bowl and pour over boiling water. Set aside until cool. Pour the contents of the bowl through a strainer and press through as much pulp as possible. It is now ready to use.
Trasi	See under blachan

RECIPE INDEX

Ethnic Index